ROYAL HORTICULTURAL SOCIETY
GARDENING
through the YEAR

ROYAL HORTICULTURAL SOCIETY
GARDENING
through the YEAR

IAN SPENCE

CONTENTS

INTRODUCTION

Gardeners are born optimists, always looking forward to the year ahead, convinced that they will achieve much more than in the previous year. But to get better results, gardeners need to plan ahead and have a good sense of timing and an awareness of the demands of each passing season. In essence, that's what this book is all about.

Gardening essentials include getting sowing and planting times right so the young plants we have nurtured in a warm environment are not put outside and then promptly killed by frost. And if a shrub is pruned at the wrong time, we may discover too late that we have cut off all this year's flowers. Mistakes like this can happen to any one of us, no matter how expert we like to think we are, especially in the mad spring rush when our enthusiasm is fired by the cheering sight of the first snowdrops and daffodils, or the first seedlings germinating in a seed tray. One of my aims is to help you avoid some of the pitfalls.

Climatic conditions can vary widely – there can be a difference of up to four weeks from a plant flowering in the south of the country compared to in the north so there can be no hard and fast rules on the timing of operations in the garden. Another consideration to take into account is the weather conditions at the time a particular job has to be done. If there is a foot of snow on the ground in late April then you cannot sow seeds outside! This actually happened in my native Scotland in the mid-1980s. So the timing of operations in the garden will vary from month to month and from year to year.

In recent years there has been a notable change in our weather patterns, often with one season seeming to merge into the next. This may be the result of global warming, caused by excessive emissions of greenhouse gases such as carbon dioxide. Owing to milder conditions, plants tend to come into flower much earlier than in previous years. And plants that

are considered tender are surviving our increasingly mild winters, while pests and diseases once killed off by snow and frost are now on the increase. We also seem to be experiencing extremes of weather, with parts of the country receiving considerable rainfall in short periods of time. This has led to widespread flooding – in recent years some of the worst floods for centuries. Patterns of work in the garden are changing, and we must adapt when planning which plants to grow and where to plant them.

It is often recommended that you keep a notebook handy and write down jobs as you do them, so you can refer to your notes at a later date. But if your memory is anything like mine, this will be an incomplete record as you'll often forget to note down the jobs you have already done. I hope this book will make it easier to plan your time, not by dictating exactly what should be done when, but by giving general guidelines and realistic advice.

As well as offering a guide to your gardening year, I've also included practical suggestions for improving your plot, in the form of straightforward projects, such as creating a new flower bed or planting a hanging basket, which will take no more than a day or, at most, a weekend. I always get satisfaction from making things myself rather than buying them (perhaps it's in my Scottish blood!).

Despite what I have said about climate changes, try not to worry too much about the timing of jobs in the garden. Nature always seems to have a way of balancing things out, and even if you think you're very late sowing those hardy annuals or planting out the summer bedding plants, they can still surprise you by growing and flowering beautifully, just at the right time. Enjoy your plot and don't let it become a chore. Indeed, gardening may become a passion that lasts a lifetime, as it has for me. Happy gardening!

Ian Spence

FLOWERING PERENNIALS THROUGH THE YEAR

With a little planning you can enjoy flowers all year in your garden, and perennials offer a huge variety. In summer it's relatively simple to create drifts of colour.

JANUARY

Eranthis hyemalis ♀

Winter aconite

A low-growing tuberous perennial, this has bright yellow flowers and striking leaves.

(*see p.294*)

FEBRUARY

Helleborus orientalis

Lenten Rose

A beautiful and long-lasting late winter and early spring flower, this evergreen likes dappled shade.

(*see p.301*)

MAY

Aquilegia vulgaris **'Nora Barlow'** ♀

Granny's bonnet

Pretty and slightly old-fashioned, the flowers of this robust plant are green, white, and pink.

(*see p.277*)

JUNE

Geum **'Borisii'**

Avens

This herbaceous perennial has striking clusters of orange-red flowers with a contrasting yellow centre.

(*see p.299*)

SEPTEMBER

Rudbeckia laciniata **'Herbstsonne'** ♀

Coneflower

The cheerful flowers of this herbaceous perennial are visited by all sorts of pollinators.

(*see p.327*)

OCTOBER

Schizostylis coccinea **'Sunrise'** ♀

Kaffir lily

The delicate salmon-pink spikes of this rhizomatous plant flourish in borders or in containers.

(*see p.329*)

Through the winter there are fewer to choose from, but they reward the closer attention you can give them at a time when the garden is not so demanding.

MARCH

***Doronicum* x *excelsum* 'Harpur Crewe'**

Leopard's bane

The daisy-like flowers of this herbaceous perennial are at their best in partial shade.

(*see p.293*)

APRIL

***Dicentra spectabilis*, syn. *Lamprocapnos spectabilis* ♀**

Bleeding heart, Dutchman's breeches

This unusual perennial produces arches of heart-shaped flowers.

(*see p.293*)

JULY

***Phlox paniculata* 'Eva Cullum'**

Border phlox

Strongly secented, vivid pink flowers appear on this vigorous summer favourite.

(*see p.317*)

AUGUST

***Geranium psilostemon* ♀**

Armenian cranesbill

Forming large clumps with deep pink flowers, this blooms for a long time if deadheaded.

(*see p.299*)

NOVEMBER

***Cimicifuga simplex* 'White Pearl'**

Bugbane

Spires of white flowers cover this plant in autumn.

(*see p.284*)

DECEMBER

***Viola* x *wittrockiana* Floral Dance Series**

Pansy

This winter-flowering pansy comes in a huge mix of colours and is perfect for bedding or in a container.

(*see p.332*)

FOLIAGE THROUGH THE YEAR

Often viewed as a background feature, foliage can in fact be the backbone to a garden, providing structure and a huge range of texture as well as some splashes

JANUARY

***Griselinia littoralis* 'Dixons Cream'**

Broadleaf

Popular for hedging, this vigorous, upright, evergreen shrub has beautifully marked oval leaves.

(see p.280)

FEBRUARY

***Euonymus fortunei* 'Silver Queen'**

Euonymus

This evergreen shrub is useful as ground cover. Its tiny summer flowers are followed in autumn by pink fruits.

(see p.296)

MAY

***Hakonechloa macra* 'Aureola'** ♀

Hakonechloa

Changing through the year, the blades of this deciduous grass are yellow-green in spring, then slowly turn red.

(see p.300)

JUNE

Hosta sieboldiana

Hosta

The blue-green colour and distinctive veins make the foliage of this hosta stand out. It has white flowers in summer.

(see p.299)

SEPTEMBER

***Acer* 'Bloodgood'** ♀

Japanese maples

Deep red-purple leaves on this deciduous shrub start to turn red in autumn.

(see p.274)

OCTOBER

***Cotinus* 'Grace'**

Smoke bush

The purple leaves of this deciduous shrub turn a vibrant red in late autumn.

(see p.290)

of colour, and even taking centre stage from time to time. When selecting plants, consider the contribution of their foliage at different times of the year.

MARCH

Bergenia 'Ballawley' ♀

Elephant's ears

In addition to its bronze, shiny winter leaves, this perennial has crimson flowers in spring.

(see p.280)

APRIL

Elaeagnus angustifolia 'Quicksilver'

Elaeagnus

A deciduous shrub, this elaeagnus has silvery shoots and leaves and yellow summer flowers.

(see p.288)

JULY

Gunnera manicata ♀

Gunnera

Its huge, strikingly shaped, bright green leaves are the main feature of this herbaceous perennial.

(see p.299)

AUGUST

Solenostemon 'Brightness'

Coleus

Often grown as an annual bedding plant for its red and green leaves, this is a tender perennial.

(see p.330)

NOVEMBER

Berberis thunbergii 'Rose glow'

Japanese barberry

Unusual pink, white, and purple marbled foliage makes this deciduous shrub particularly eye catching.

(see p.297)

DECEMBER

Pittosporum tenuifolium 'Irene Paterson' ♀

Pittosporum

The leaves of this evergreen shrub open white, then become green speckled with white, often tinged pink.

(see p.290)

STEMS AND BARK THROUGH THE YEAR

Less obvious than flowers, stems and bark can nevertheless shine out at certain times of year, particularly in winter, and at other times can unobtrusively contribute

JANUARY

Cornus alba **'Sibirica'** ♀

Dogwood

Early spring pruning of this deciduous shrub will ensure a good supply of bright red stems through the following winter.

(see p.288)

FEBRUARY

Cornus mas

Cornelian cherry

A deciduous shrub or small tree, this has a mass of tiny yellow flowers on its bare branches in late winter.

(see p.288)

MAY

Euphorbia* x *martinii ♀

Spurge

One of the many attractive spurges, this herbaceous perennial has red stems that contrast with its lime-green flowers.

(see p.296)

JUNE

Prunus serrula ♀

Tibetan cherry

With beautiful, glowing bark all year, this deciduous tree makes a striking feature. It also has late spring blossom and yellow autumn foliage.

(see p.320)

SEPTEMBER

Eryngium* x *tripartitum ♀

Sea holly

This herbaceous perennial has branching violet-blue stems bearing purple flowers with silvery bracts.

(see p.295)

OCTOBER

Rhus typhina ♀

Stag's horn sumach

In addition to its autumn colour and red winter fruits, this small deciduous tree has downy stems.

(see p.323)

beautiful colour, texture, structure, and interest in a border or as part of a hedge or boundary planting.

MARCH

Corylus avellana 'Contorta'

Corkscrew hazel

This deciduous shrub has twisted branches that look striking all year, but especially when bare or covered with catkins.

(see p.289)

APRIL

Corylopsis glabrescens

Corylopsis

A useful, shade-tolerant, deciduous shrub, this bears aromatic yellow flowers that form a contrast to its bare branches.

(see p.289)

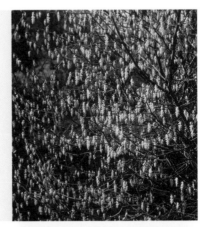

JULY

Artemisia alba 'Canescens' ♀

White sage

This dense, semi-evergreen perennial has silver stems and masses of lacy silver foliage.

(see p.278)

AUGUST

Perovskia 'Blue Spire' ♀

Russian sage

The pale grey stems and leaves of this sub-shrub are eye-catching for much of the year. It has purple-blue flowers in late summer.

(see p.317)

NOVEMBER

Betula papyrifera

Paper birch, Canoe birch

This deciduous tree is fairly fast growing and has white bark that peels to expose orange-brown bark beneath.

(see p.280)

DECEMBER

Salix x rubens 'Basfordiana'

Willow

Unpruned, this is a deciduous tree, but with annual pruning in early spring it becomes a shrub with orange-yellow stems.

(see p.328)

BULBS THROUGH THE YEAR

Bulbs are usually associated with an abundance of spring flowers, but in fact there are bulbs (and corms and tubers) that produce a huge variety of blooms all

JANUARY

Galanthus plicatus* subsp. *byzantinus

Snowdrop

This snowdrop has honey-scented flowers, white on the outside with green on the inner petals.

(see p.298)

FEBRUARY

***Narcissus cyclamineus* ♀**

Wild narcissus

The striking flowers of this vigorous narcisssus look particularly good when planted in drifts.

(see p.311)

MAY

***Tulipa* 'Queen of Night'**

Tulip

At home in a border or massed in a container, this tulip has intensely dark maroon flowers.

(see p.332)

JUNE

***Allium hollandicum* ♀**

Ornamental onion

Holding its round, starry purple flower heads high, this bulb is best grown in a mixed border.

(see p.276)

SEPTEMBER

***Dahlia* 'Bishop of Llandaff' ♀**

Dahlia

Vivid red flowers and deep red leaves make this tuberous perennial stand out. It needs frost-free conditions and rich soil to thrive.

(see p.292)

OCTOBER

***Nerine bowdenii* ♀**

Nerine

The leaves of this bulb appear after the delicate pink flowers. It loves warm, dry conditions.

(see p.312)

year round. They are a low-maintenance addition to a border or pot as they flower and then die down naturally, returning again the following year.

MARCH

Muscari armeniacum ♀

Grape hyacinth

Vivid spikes of blue flowers appear in spring from these reliable bulbous perennials.

(*see p.311*)

APRIL

Fritillaria meleagris

Snake's head fritillary

The flowers of this elegant bulb look spectacular when naturalized in grass.

(*see p.298*)

JULY

Lillium 'Sun Ray'

Lily

This is a vigorous, cheerful lily that works well in a border or in a container.

(*see p.307*)

AUGUST

Crocosmia x crocosmiiflora 'Jackanapes'

Montbretia

Arching orange and red flowers rise up from the clump of attractive narrow, bright green leaves.

(*see p.291*)

NOVEMBER

Cyclamen hederifolium ♀

Hardy cyclamen

Delicately patterned with silver, the leaves of this cyclamen appear with or after the pink or white flowers.

(*see p.291*)

DECEMBER

Hippeastrum 'Apple Blossom'

Amaryllis

This tall, exotic flower flourishes outside in temperate climates, and will flower in winter under cover in cooler climates.

(*see p.302*)

SCENT THROUGH THE YEAR

An intrinsic part of any garden, large or small, scent can be a reason to choose a plant, or simply a wonderful bonus. In winter when colour may be scarce, scent

JANUARY

***Hamamelis* x *intermedia* 'Arnold Promise'** ♀

Witch hazel

Starry, straggly flowers with a wonderful fragrance appear in winter on bare stems.

(see p300)

FEBRUARY

***Viburnum* x *bodnantense* 'Dawn'** ♀

Viburnum

A delicate scent comes from these clusters of small flowers in late winter and early spring.

(see p.334)

MAY

***Wisteria floribunda* 'Multijuga'** ♀

Japanese wisteria

This large, woody climber produces a spectacular display of fragrant hanging flowers in early summer.

(see p.335)

JUNE

***Dianthus* 'Little Jock'**

Alpine pink

This evergreen perennial's small, pretty flowers are clove-scented.

(see p.292)

SEPTEMBER

***Caryopteris* x *clandonensis* 'Kew Blue'**

Blue autumn flowers adorn this deciduous shrub, but the lavender-scented leaves provide the fragrance.

(see p.282)

OCTOBER

***Chrysanthemum* 'Glowing Lynn'**

Chrysanthemum

This tender herbaceous perennial has masses of bronze flowers, and dark green aromatic foliage.

(see p.284)

can bring you out into the garden. Fragrant plants work well when planted next to a door or bench so that they are easy to enjoy.

MARCH

Daphne mezereum

Mezereon

The vivid pink flowers of this deciduous shrub are highly fragrant.

(see p.292)

APRIL

Convallaria majalis ♀

Lily-of-the-valley

At home in the shade, this woodland perennial can also be potted up so the scent of the flowers can be more easily enjoyed.

(see p.287)

JULY

Rosa 'Chinatown' ♀

Modern shrub rose

A very fragrant rose, 'Chinatown' has double yellow flowers and bright green foliage.

(see p.325)

AUGUST

Heliotropium 'Marine'

Heliotrope, Cherry pie

A frost-tender evergreen, this is usually grown as an annual for its sweetly scented flowers.

(see p.301)

NOVEMBER

Lonicera fragrantissima

Winter honeysuckle

The exquisite and very fragrant flowers of this semi-evergreen shrub appear in winter and early spring.

(see p.308)

DECEMBER

Mahonia x media 'Charity'

Mahonia

The prominent, scented flowers are valuable in winter, but this large evergreen shrub is handsome all year.

(see p.309)

ATTRACTING WILDLIFE THROUGH THE YEAR

Wildlife brings a garden to life and helps to create a balance that will benefit your plants. Birds and some insects will eat garden pests, while bees, butterflies, and

JANUARY

Lonicera x *purpusii*

Purpus honeysuckle

This shrubby honeysuckle has fragrant white flowers that provide valuable nectar for early bumblebees.

(*see p.308*)

FEBRUARY

Viburnum tinus

Laurustinus

An evergreen shrub with winter flowers, this provides nectar and pollen for both early and late pollinating insects.

(*see p.335*)

MAY

Camassia cusickii 'Zwanenburg'

Camassia

A popular plant with pollinators, camassia is a bulbous perennial with graceful spires of deep blue flowers.

(*see p.281*)

JUNE

Cistus x *cyprius* ♀

Rock rose, Sun rose

The flowers of this evergreen shrub attract both bees and butterflies over several months.

(*see p.284*)

SEPTEMBER

Sedum spectabile 'Brilliant' ♀

Ice plant

This long-flowering herbaceous perennial is irresistible to butterflies and bumblebees.

(*see p.329*)

OCTOBER

Sorbus commixta

Rowan

This deciduous tree bears white flowers that develop into bright red berries loved by birds.

(*see p.330*)

other pollinators enable plants to set seed or develop fruits. Choose your plants carefully to encourage more wild visitors to your garden all year round.

MARCH

Anemone blanda 'Violet Star'

Mountain windflower

The purple-blue flowers of this tuberous perennial are a magnet for bees of all kinds.

(see p.277)

APRIL

Pulsatilla vulgaris ♀

Pasque flower

Bees and butterflies visit this small herbacous perennial, which has flowers in shades of pink and purple, and sometimes white.

(see p.321)

JULY

Borago officinalis

Borage

This hairy-leaved and blue-flowered annual is very popular with bees.

(see p.280)

AUGUST

Echinacea purpurea 'White Swan'

Coneflower

An herbaceous perennial providing late summer colour, echinacea attracts a variety of butterflies.

(see p.294)

NOVEMBER

Pyracantha 'Golden Charmer' ♀

Firethorn

An evergreen shrub, this has white spring flowers popular with bees, then orange autumn berries, excellent for birds.

(see p.321)

DECEMBER

Ilex aquifolium 'Handsworth New Silver' ♀

English holly

This evergreen shrub produces masses of berries for birds on the female plant if it is planted near a male holly.

(see p.303)

THE JANUARY GARDEN

If you're under the impression that there is nothing to do and that the garden looks boring at this time of the year, then think again! However harsh the weather may be, there are still plenty of plants that you can enjoy, and lots of jobs to be getting on with. And don't forget to look after any visiting wildlife in your garden – it's a tough month for them too.

THINGS TO DO

Protect vulnerable plants from severe weather.

Hoe any germinating weeds.

Continue with winter digging as soil conditions allow.

Brush snow off trees, shrubs, and hedges.

Prune wisteria and other vigorous climbers.

Take hardwood cuttings of trees and shrubs.

Plant deciduous hedging.

Sow some summer bedding under cover, as well as sowing sweet peas.

Look through catalogues for seeds and summer-flowering bulbs.

Check bulbs being forced.

Take root cuttings from perennials.

Start sowing early vegetable crops under cover.

Chit early potatoes.

Continue to plant and winter-prune fruit trees and bushes.

Force rhubarb.

LAST CHANCE

Prune grape vines before the sap starts rising.

Protect container plants from freezing spells and insulate all outside taps against the cold.

GET AHEAD

Warm up some soil with cloches for early seed-sowing outdoors.

Clean all your pots and seed trays for spring sowing.

Send the lawnmower off for servicing so that it's ready when you need it later on.

Honesty Seedheads of *Lunaria annua*, amid fern foliage rimed with frost, catch the sun on a winter's day.

WINTER BEAUTY

The month of January may find the garden asleep to the world, but there is more going on than you think. Evergreens provide satisfying and reassuring silhouettes in a spartan landscape, while a covering of snow can bring true magic, and it may even do your garden some good too.

Cold winds, frost, and heavy rains can often make it seem as if nothing much can be done in the garden now. But even though it is usually the coldest time of the year, January can be regarded as the most optimistic month. Those few plants that do dare to flower really are to be marvelled at and without the distraction of a riot of colourful blooms it's a time to admire the beautiful silhouettes of bare branches, the intriguing colours and textures of bark, and the reassuring solid forms of the evergreens. And a garden covered in snow, if we get any, is always good to look at too.

Watch the weather forecasts

A blanket of snow can actually be good for the garden, killing off unwanted pests and protecting plants from severe frost. Do, however, keep an eye on the weather forecasts and look out for warnings of heavy falls of snow and sharp frosts, as action will have to be taken to prevent damage to some plants in the garden. Conifers, in particular, are prone to being damaged by heavy snowfalls, as the weight of the snow can bring branches down. Fruit cages can also suffer badly and be damaged by the weight of heavy snow.

A delightful sight Pearly snowdrops and golden winter aconites make perfect partners in the garden during the month of January.

A mixed winter border This gorgeous display of colour includes *Prunus davidiana* 'Alba', *Erica carnea*, *Cornus alba* 'Sibirica', *Cornus sericea* 'Flaviramea', *Salix alba* 'Chermesina', *Erica erigena* 'Brightness', and *Carex montana*.

Strong winds are a regular January feature and this is why it is important to make sure young trees and shrubs are well staked, especially in exposed areas. It's also why newly planted shrubs, especially evergreens, need some form of wind barrier. Cold winds can cause severe damage, particularly to evergreen leaves. These biting winds will scorch young foliage and it rarely recovers, so temporary shelter will certainly help preserve the investment you have made in new plants.

You may find that some parts of your garden seem to get much more heavily frosted than others, especially if the garden includes a slope or other change in level. Cold air is heavier than warm air and always finds the lowest level. This is an important point to bear in mind when you are planning where to position slightly tender plants in the garden. You should also beware of planting fruit trees in low parts of the garden where there is a frost pocket, as the flowers may be damaged in the spring.

Time for some exercise

With the days just beginning to lengthen even shortly after New Year celebrations, it's a good time to work off the excesses of the holiday period. If you want to get warmed up on a cold winter's day, continue with winter-digging of borders and in the vegetable garden, as long as the soil is not waterlogged or frozen. If the ground is frozen, it is still a good time to barrow out manure or garden compost and spread it on the ground.

Lawns will also benefit from some attention, even though it's still the middle of winter. Work done at this time of year will pay handsome dividends in creating a smooth green sward in the summer. But do keep off the grass when it is frosted over.

This is also a good month to go around the garden and catch up with repairs to fences and trellises and other tidying jobs, which may not be very exciting but will make all the difference to the appearance of the garden in the summer months. Keep a notebook handy and take this with you when you are pottering around the garden in winter. This is a great help if you're planning any changes to the garden, especially to remind you of all the plants you want to acquire later!

Weather watch

Winter temperatures in the United Kingdom are largely governed by the temperature of the sea, with January and February being the coldest months. Coastal areas are colder in February. The coldest nights occur when there is no wind, the skies are clear, and there is snow on the ground. The coldest air will be found on low ground. Our lowest-ever temperature was -26°C, recorded in a Shropshire valley on January 10th 1982. Average daily temperatures in January will be 6–8°C in the south and 2–4°C in the north.

Windy weather

January is a month of gale-force winds associated with deep depressions crossing near or over the British Isles, with high ground experiencing the worst of all. The number of days with gales and their strength varies considerably between north and south. Northern parts of the country, especially those on exposed western coasts, experience the strongest winds, with on average 7.5 days of gales, whereas the south has on average 0.2 days.

Sunshine in places

Southern regions get the most sunshine, mainly because they are flatter. In the north, eastern parts get more sun for the same reason. Southern regions receive on average 57.2 hours of bright sunshine whereas, say, in Shetland they will get only 22 hours.

Rainfall here and there

Amounts of rain falling on different parts varies according to topography, southern and eastern regions being the driest. In parts of the north-west Highlands 236mm (9¼in) of rain may fall this month; on the south coast of England, 81mm (3in).

Snowy hills

Snow is rare in coastal areas, more frequent over high ground. The amount varies from little in many areas to heavy falls lasting all winter. North-east Scotland fares worst, averaging 16 days of snow, with the south coast of England having on average 0.8 days.

Winter treats Most winter-blooming shrubs, like this *Hamamelis*, or witch hazel, have the most intensely sweet-scented flowers.

Plants to admire

Less strenuously, a walk around the garden on a January day can reveal surprises, with snowdrops and also carpets of the yellow winter aconite coming into flower. Another must for January is the Christmas rose, *Helleborus niger*, which despite its familiar name usually hangs back until this month – but the stunning white flowers are well worth waiting for. To achieve the purest flowers, protect the plants as the buds begin to open, to prevent rain and snow spoiling the blooms.

We mustn't forget the tremendous amount of interest that can be created in the winter garden by using plants with attractive bark and colourful stems. Plants such as dogwoods (*Cornus*) can be pruned back in spring to create eye-catching bright winter stems in shades of red, green, yellow, and even black. Evergreen shrubs and conifers in all shades from dark green to golden yellow also add life and lustre to the winter scene. Scent is another bonus of many winter-flowering plants – wintersweet (*Chimonanthus*), *Viburnum* x *bodnantense* and *Sarcococca*, another shrub which, despite its festive common name, Christmas box, will continue to pour out its stunning fragrance into the air through the New Year.

If the weather is just too cold and wet to venture outside, then there is plenty to be getting on with indoors. It's a good month for planning the rest of the gardening year. One job to do at this time, if you haven't already done so, is to put your feet up by the fireside with a glass of something to keep out the cold and browse through the seed catalogues. Or, you can go down to the local garden centre and pick the seeds you require. And although the first spring bulbs may have yet to open in the garden, it's time to choose summer-flowering bulbs.

Raising plants

It's not too soon to start thinking about sowing some early crops, always the most welcome, and of course the ones which will save you most money. Summer bedding plants that need an especially long growing season, such as pelargoniums and snapdragons (*Antirrhinum*), can also be started off towards the end of the month. If you have a greenhouse or conservatory that can be heated sufficiently to keep out the frost, then you're off to a flying start, but even without a glasshouse there is still plenty that can be done raising plants on a windowsill.

Plants from seed

Raising your own plants from seed is a thrill that never leaves you, no matter how long you have been gardening. It's very easy to do, but there are a few items you will need, especially at this time of year, to provide a little extra heat. To heat a whole greenhouse is very expensive these days and many plants can be started off instead in a propagator. Plants such as tomatoes and the tender summer bedding plants all need that bit more heat, preferably from below the soil, to get the seeds to germinate, and this is where a propagator is so very useful, gently warming the compost from the base. There is quite a selection on the market; your choice will be based on cost, the space you have available, and the amount of seed you want to raise. You'll find even the cheapest and simplest do a great job.

Always be careful with electrical appliances, especially where they will come into contact with moisture, and follow the manufacturer's instructions to the letter. If you have any doubts, be sure to contact the manufacturer or a qualified electrician.

So there you have it – almost as busy a month as in the summer. Bet you can't wait to get going now!

Early starters If you enjoy raising bedding plants from seed you can begin sowing them in January. Keep the young plants in a frost-free environment – a sunny windowsill inside the house or conservatory is ideal.

Bold shapes Even under a dusting of frost, strong outlines and textures, such as silver fir (*Abies amabilis* 'Spreading Star'), as shown in the foreground, enhance the winter garden.

Erica carnea 'Springwood White' ♀
One of the many winter-flowering heathers (*see p.294*)

Garrya elliptica
Evergreen shrub that makes a good hedge in sheltered areas (*see p.298*)

Hamamelis x intermedia 'Arnold Promise' ♀
Scented flowers on bare branches (*see p.300*)

Galanthus plicatus subsp. **byzantinus** ♀
Classic snowdrop with nodding, green-marked flowers (*see p.298*)

Betula papyrifera
The paper birch, with brilliant white peeling bark (*see p.280*)

Lonicera x purpusii
Shrubby honeysuckle with intensely fragrant flowers (*see p.308*)

Skimmia japonica
Tough evergreen shrub that does best in shade (*see p.329*)

Helleborus niger 'Potter's Wheel' ♀
Small perennial for dappled shade (*see p.301*)

Sarcococca hookeriana* var. *humilis ♀
Small but powerfully scented evergreen shrub (*see p.328*)

Cornus alba 'Sibirica' ♀
This shrub has glossy, bright-red stems in winter (*see p.288*)

Prunus x subhirtella 'Autumnalis Rosea' ♀
Winter-flowering cherry tree (*see p.321*)

Eranthis hyemalis ♀
Woodland perennial forming mats of yellow stars (*see p.294*)

WHAT TO DO IN JANUARY

AROUND THE GARDEN

It's amazing how weed seedlings germinate during mild spells, even in the depths of winter. On any winter rambles around the garden, take a hoe with you so that these weed seedlings can be knocked out before they get too big. Collect up annual weeds and put them on the compost heap. Any perennial weeds can be left on the ground to dry and then put on the compost heap.

There are few pests and diseases around at this time of year, but many are lurking in nooks and crannies, just waiting for the warmer spring weather to come along. So it is worth practising good garden hygiene and clearing up any rubbish that has been left lying around. Weeding also helps to keep pests and diseases at bay.

Any decaying leaves should be collected and put on the compost or leafmould heap. Pay particular attention to clearing the crowns of herbaceous perennials and alpines, as these are vulnerable, especially the latter, to rot in prolonged damp conditions under fallen leaves. Leaves are

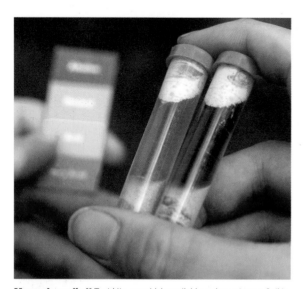

Measuring soil pH Test kits are widely available and easy to use. Soil is rarely uniform, so it's worth testing samples from different parts of the garden. Keep a record of where each sample comes from so that you can exploit any variation when it comes to choosing your plants; an acid patch, for example, could be a prime site for camellias or heathers.

best composted, not burned, as they can then contribute to the goodness of the soil. Be careful when you are disturbing large piles of leaves as there may be a hedgehog hibernating there.

Get to know your soil better. It can be disheartening to see plants struggle because the soil does not suit them. If you're not sure which plants and seeds to choose, testing your soil for its type and pH – its acidity or alkalinity – is always a good idea. Rub some soil between your fingers to get to know its structure: whether it contains a high proportion of clay, making it heavy and wet, or sand, making it light and dry – or something in between, the perfect balance being known as "loam".

The pH of soil can be tested with ordinary kits stocked by garden centres; there are plenty available and costs vary. Knowing more about your soil will help you to choose plants that will really do well in your garden. Regularly adding bulky organic matter to your soil – for example, digging-in compost or well-rotted manure, or mulching with leafmould – can do wonders to improve extreme soil types, stopping plants drowning in heavy clay or drying out in free-draining sand. But it's better and easier not to try to change the pH of your soil in beds and borders, and just to choose plants that like it instead – you can always grow other plants in containers filled with tailor-made soil mixes.

Barrow organic matter onto frozen ground. There isn't much to do outside when the soil is rock-hard, but an ideal job that will save you time later is spreading out well-rotted manure or garden compost. It's quite alright to walk on the soil if it is frozen hard. Barrowing muck or compost about can be a messy job, but in these conditions the barrow can be wheeled over the ground with little effort. Don't, however, take the barrow over a frozen lawn; if you can't avoid going over the lawn put down planks. Spread the load evenly over the surface and the ground will soon thaw out when the weather improves.

TREES AND SHRUBS

■ **Move deciduous shrubs or trees** that have been put in the wrong position. No matter how expert we like to think we are, it is all too easy to make mistakes when we are placing plants.

Now there is still time to move deciduous trees and shrubs if they are wrongly positioned or have outgrown their allotted space. You may need to enlist the help of a friend or relative when you are moving larger ones. Never underestimate the effort that may be needed to move large plants, because you want to take as much of the root system, and the heavy soil around it, as you can. This is important for the plant to survive and grow well.

■ **Check tree ties and stakes.** Young trees and bushes that are being blown about by strong winds will never last long. It is therefore very important to check all the ties and stakes at regular intervals. When trees and bushes are planted too loosely a sunken area may develop around the base of the main stem. This is caused by the continual rocking back and forth as the plant is blown around by the wind and it is all too easy for puddles of excess water to collect in a pool. It is here that the plant will begin to rot and die off, so ties should be secure. However, they should not be so tight that they actually restrict the growth of the plant.

■ **To protect newly planted trees and shrubs,** especially evergreens, from wind damage erect a windbreak to shelter the plant. The windbreak can be in the form of hessian, horticultural fleece, bubble plastic, or strong polythene, tied securely to a framework around the plants.

To increase the level of protection, some straw can be placed inside the windbreak framework, but make sure that the air can circulate and that light can get in, particularly for evergreens.

Planting

■ **Plant bare-root trees and shrubs,** but only if soil conditions allow. If the soil is frozen or very wet, heel in the plants temporarily in a corner of the garden until conditions are suitable. Take out a trench big enough to hold the root system and cover the roots with soil, firming gently. The plants will survive like this for quite some time.

If the soil is too frozen even to heel in the plants, then provided that their roots are wrapped in hessian or sacking, they can be kept in a porch, shed, or garage with some light. For evergreens, unwrap the top growth if it is packed in straw so that some light can get in and never let the roots dry out, so keep the wrapping around the roots moist. If you look after them, plants can last like this for a few weeks.

Pruning and training

■ **This is a good time of year to prune** trees to shape. Young trees often grow out in all directions into other plants in the border, throwing out shoots along the whole length of the trunk. You can prune out misplaced stems this month, always making sure that you cut to a junction or the main stem.

If you want to make a standard tree with a length of bare trunk, then cut back some of the side growths now too. Avoid doing this all at once, but do it instead over two or three seasons, shortening some branches this year and removing them completely next year.

The extra leaves that are left on the main stem over the summer will help to encourage the vigour of the tree; cutting side branches off all at once could severely affect the tree's growth.

Seeds from berries

1 Separate the seeds by washing them in a fine mesh sieve. Or wrap the berries in a teatowel first and crush the pulp under running water.

2 Tap out the remains onto kitchen paper, pick out the seeds, and rinse them again.

3 Sow the seeds in trays or pots of peat-free compost and cover them lightly with coarse grit.

4 Place in a cold frame or by a sheltered wall, covering to keep off rain and protect from mice. Some seeds may take some time to germinate.

Propagation

■ **Sow seeds of berrying shrubs** and trees such as *Cotoneaster*, *Pernettya*, and *Sorbus*. Like alpines, seeds of these shrubs need a period of cold to break dormancy.

■ **There is still plenty of time** to take hardwood cuttings from deciduous shrubs such as dogwoods (*Cornus*), willows, roses, forsythia, flowering currant (*Ribes*), and chaenomeles. Even if your garden is well stocked, it costs nothing to grow on a few of your favourites just in case some of the plants are lost in the future. And if you do end up with a surplus, young rooted shrubs are always a welcome contribution to plant stalls at summer fairs and fêtes.

Hedges

■ **Brush snow off evergreen hedges** before the weight of it splays out branches.

■ **Deciduous hedging plants** such as beech, hawthorn, and hornbeam can be planted now in well-prepared ground, if the weather conditions permit. The cheapest way to buy hedging is in the form of young, bare-root plants known as "whips", which are sold in bundles. If the soil is frozen or waterlogged, heel in the plants temporarily.

To prepare the ground, mark out a strip at least two spade-blades wide along the length of the proposed hedge. Start taking out a trench to one spade's depth at one end and barrow the first load of soil to the other end. If the soil in the bottom of the trench is heavy, compacted clay you may be able to loosen it up by using a garden fork, but be careful not to bring the poorer subsoil to the surface.

Incorporate as much organic matter as you can get into the soil at the bottom of the trench and then cover this with soil by digging the next section of the trench, repeating the process until you reach the end of the line, when the last part can be filled with the soil in your barrow.

Space the young plants out along the length of the trench, fill in, and firm with your boot. In sites that are more exposed, a windbreak of, for example, plastic mesh stapled between posts, on the windward side of the hedge, will help the plants to get established.

Preparing to plant a hedge

Even if the plants are small and slender, digging a trench for them is better than individual holes.

Well-rotted farmyard manure worked into the bottom of the trench will give plants a good start.

CLIMBERS

■ **Brush snow off** dense evergreen climbers and wall shrubs; when snow accumulates on these it can break stems and put strain on ties and supports.

■ **Climbers to prune now** include wisteria (see below), ornamental vines, ivies, Virginia creeper and Boston ivy, and climbing hydrangea. These plants have a habit of working their way into window frames and doors, so cut them back as needed to prevent any expensive damage being done. And don't forget to prune them away from all gutters on house walls.

■ **Wisterias require pruning** twice during the year. In summer they need all the long new shoots cut back to five or six buds from the main stems. Now these same shoots should be shortened even more, to two or three buds from the main stems. You can do the same to any new sideshoots that have grown since summer. The advantage of doing this pruning now is that, with no leaves on the plant, you can see exactly what you are doing. It encourages the formation of flower buds to give a terrific show of colour during the late spring and early summer.

Pruning wisteria In winter, shorten all of the sideshoots from the main framework of stems.

PERENNIALS

■ **Hellebores** have delightful flowers in many colours and by choosing different species you can have blooms from late winter until spring. They are excellent woodland plants and look particularly good growing at the base of trees. Deciduous species actually retain their leaves over winter, but they tend to look rather tatty. Cut these off now, as the first flower buds begin to appear, and you will see the flowers at their best.

■ **Continue to clear weeds** from around plants and cut down any dead stems left for winter interest that are by now looking tatty or diseased.

■ **Order herbaceous perennials** from nursery catalogues now for delivery and planting in the spring. Now is the time to look through bits of paper to find all those notes you made of "must-have" plants that you saw at shows and gardens last year. There is a bewildering array of plants to choose from these days and you can have plants in flower, if you choose them carefully, almost all the year round.

For interest all season and a foil for the flowering plants, choose from some of the beautiful foliage plants that are on offer, especially the increasingly popular grasses, sedges, and ferns.

■ **Continue to lift and divide** overgrown clumps of herbaceous perennials when soil conditions allow – in other words, when the soil is not frozen or so wet that it sticks to your boots.

■ **Inspect dahlia tubers** that you are keeping in store. Take a close look from time to time to see if there is any disease present. Any that are showing signs of rotting off need to be carefully removed from the rest, or the disease may spread through the whole lot. Any individual tubers that seem to be infected can be cut from the main crown of the plant, retaining the rest. Early stages of rotting can be controlled by cutting out the infected area and dusting with flowers of sulphur.

■ **Taking root cuttings** from perennials is an easy way of increasing your plants and it doesn't require a lot of special equipment.

Plants that are ideal for this method of propagation are those with long, fleshy roots, such as Japanese anemones, Oriental poppies, verbascums, and acanthus. Dig up the plant and wash off as much soil as you can to expose the roots. When taking cuttings, make a diagonal cut across the "bottom" (the end that was the farthest from the plant) so you remember which way up to plant them (see below).

Plants with finer roots can also be used, for example phlox, nepeta, and primulas.

Prepare the cuttings in the same way, but lay them flat on a tray of the same "cuttings compost" mixture and cover lightly with compost. Provided that you haven't denuded it of roots, the parent should grow away again if it is carefully replanted and fed.

Alpines

■ **Alpine plants need protection** not from the cold, but from winter rains. If you haven't already done so, make them a shelter to keep off the worst of the wet. A piece of glass or clear plastic placed on four sturdy sticks and held down with a large stone is perfect.

■ **Sow alpine seeds** this month. By sowing now you can give the seeds the period of cold that they experience in the wild, which is essential for germination in spring.

Taking root cuttings

1 Cut off roots the thickness of a pencil and then cut these into sections about 5cm (2in) long, trimming off small fibrous roots. Make a slanting cut at the base.

2 Insert the cuttings, upright, in compost mixed with vermiculite. Cover with grit and water well.

3 Put in a frost-free cold frame. You can use a heated propagator for faster rooting, but it is not essential.

4 New growth should appear in the spring, when you can separate the cuttings and put each in its own small pot of compost.

5 Grow on the young plants over the spring and summer, until they are large enough to plant out.

BULBS

■ **Order summer-flowering bulbs** now in good time for planting in spring. Lilies are the most popular, but why not try some of the more unusual bulbs, such as *Galtonia candicans* (wood hyacinth) and *Ornithogalum* (star of Bethlehem)? Even the frost-tender bulbs such as tigridias, which, like dahlias and gladioli, need lifting and storing in a dry, frost-free place over winter, are easy to grow.

■ **Force bulbs.** Bring bulbs planted in pots and bowls last autumn into the house in batches to give a prolonged flowering display. The time to bring them inside is when they have made about an inch of growth, so watch them carefully. It's best to bring them into a cool room for a week or two first of all; if it is too warm too quickly, they will grow fast, becoming leggy, and produce poor flowers. Water bulbs in bowls without drainage holes carefully or you may overwater them.

■ **Find a sheltered spot outdoors,** out of sight, but in the light, where you can put pots of bulbs as they finish flowering for you indoors. Remove the spent flowerheads to prevent the plants' energy being focused on producing seeds. Feed them with a high-potash fertilizer to build

Galtonia candicans

up flower buds for next year. Continue feeding them regularly until the foliage dies back and then in spring the bulbs can be planted in the garden. It is not a good idea to force the same bulbs year after year. Forcing takes a lot of energy out of the plants and they rarely flower well if forced more than once.

■ **Regularly check bulbs** being stored over the winter to see if there is any disease present. If any bulbs have rotted, remove them immediately, otherwise the disease will spread to other bulbs.

Ornithogalum umbellatum

Tigridia pavonia

ANNUALS AND BEDDING

■ **Sow summer-flowering bedding plants** that need a long season to grow: begonias (tuberous, fibrous-rooted, and semperflorens kinds), snapdragons, lobelias, pelargoniums, and gazanias. To raise bedding in any quantity you will need a greenhouse or conservatory – especially when, like these, the young plants will be taking up space for months.

■ **Sow sweet peas now** unless you got ahead by sowing them in the autumn. They like a good root run, so it is best to sow them in long, sweet-pea tubes. Or, make your own with newspaper rolled into tubes and held together with sticky tape – or keep the cardboard centres from rolls of toilet or kitchen paper. Place the tubes side by side in a seed tray and fill with peat-free compost. Some seeds, depending on the variety (check the packet), need soaking overnight to soften the seed coat. Another method is to "chit" the seed – to remove a sliver of the seed coat carefully with a garden or craft knife at the opposite end from the "eye", where the root will start growing. This allows water to penetrate the seeds more easily, hastening germination. Sweet peas don't need very high temperatures to germinate, so there is no need for a propagator – a cool, light room or sheltered cold frame is sufficient.

■ **Autumn-sown sweet peas** sown several to a pot need potting on to make strong, healthy plants for putting out in May. Soak the compost and gently knock the plants out of the pot, and separate them carefully. Put each into a 9cm (3½in) pot of peat-free compost and gently firm in. Water in gently to settle the compost and put in a light place. A high shelf in a greenhouse or conservatory is ideal; failing that, the sunniest windowsill you've got. You should also pinch out the tip of the young shoots, either now or next month.

CONTAINERS

■ **Deadhead pots** of winter-flowering pansies so that you can keep the display going into spring and check whether they need water.

■ **Even in winter**, container plants may need watering, especially those that are growing at the base of house walls. Here they can be sheltered from rain by the overhang of the eaves of the house. It is surprising how dry plants can get when they are in this position.

■ **All pot-grown shrubs** may need some protection as we enter the coldest part of the winter. It is not the hardiness of the plant that is the point here; during very frosty weather plants in pots are more vulnerable to damage from freezing because the roots in the pots are above ground. If you haven't already protected them, there are several ways to do it. The pots can be wrapped in bubble plastic, or use hessian sacking if you can get it. Extra protection can be given by wrapping straw or bracken around the pot and holding this in place with bubble polythene, hessian, or old compost sacks. Grouping the pots together will also give them some mutual protection.

Alternatively, if you've got the space, take the plants indoors during bad weather. Even a cold greenhouse, or a shed with windows, will provide enough protection from all but the severest frost. You can wrap the pots, too, to be on the safe side.

Remember that empty pots used for ornament in the garden, especially glazed pots and old terracotta, are also vulnerable to cracking by frost and may need protection too.

LAWNS

■ **Keep off icy grass.** Don't walk or work on the grass at all when it is frozen or frosted, otherwise when it thaws out, your footprints will show up as yellow patches.

■ **Improve drainage.** Improve the drainage of the lawn by using a fork. Parts that are badly drained will be easily recognizable as lower patches, where the water tends to collect. Wait until the surface dries out and then push a garden fork 15cm (6in) into the ground and wiggle it about to open up the holes, at about 15cm (6in) intervals over the affected area. Immediately after aerating spread sharp or horticultural sand (not builder's), or a sand and soil mixture, over the area and work this into the holes with a stiff broom. This prevents the holes closing up too quickly and further improves drainage.

■ **Repair hollows and bumps.** Even out bumpy lawns this month if the weather is mild and dry. Hollow areas where water collects can be raised level with the rest of the lawn quite easily. First make H-shaped cuts in the lawn with a spade or lawn-edging iron, and then carefully push a spade under the turf and roll each half back. Add soil to the exposed area, firm it well, and carefully roll back the turf. You may have to add more soil to get the turf

Spike lawns Use a garden fork to aerate grass. You can hire mechanical spikers for large lawns.

slightly higher than the surrounding lawn to allow for settling. After rolling back the turf, tamp down with the back of a rake. To repair bumps do exactly as for hollows, but when the turf is rolled back, scrape some soil from underneath to lower the level of the turf.

■ **Disperse worm casts.** Worms are quite active in lawns now and are most noticeable by their casts. These should be brushed off regularly; if they are left, they will be trodden into the surface of the lawn, looking unsightly and encouraging weed seeds to grow. However, worms do a lot of good in other parts of the garden. Use a flexible cane and swish it back and forth to scatter the casts. On small lawns use a stiff broom. Do this when the surface is dry and the casts will spread easily.

New lawns

■ **Lay turf.** Turf can be laid on prepared ground only if the soil is not frozen or wet. Work from planks so that you do not make compacted dents in the levelled soil. While seed is economical, making a lawn from turf is more or less instant; you will have to keep off it for only a few weeks until it settles in. Turf costs more than seed, but if you can, buy the best-quality turf, guaranteed weed-free.

Bumps and hollows Lift a flap of turf and scoop out or fill in with soil to even them out.

VEGETABLES AND HERBS

■ **Complete winter-digging** of empty beds and new vegetable plots as soon as the weather allows. The sooner cultivation is completed the better, to allow the winter weather to play its part in breaking down large clods of earth, improving the soil structure, and making it easier to work in the spring.

If you cannot dig at all this month, you can at least, if the ground is frozen hard, barrow out manure or compost and spread it on top of the soil. When the soil is very wet it is best to keep off it completely, or it will compact down and become a sea of mud that dries to a hard crust, and you will have great difficulty working it later on when you are trying to make seed beds.

One way of avoiding having to walk on the soil is to use the deep-bed method of growing vegetables. With this, beds only 1.2m (4ft) wide can be tended by reaching over from paths each side. Initially double-dig the beds, incorporating plenty of organic matter. Once this is done, you need never dig them again. Every winter, you simply add organic matter as a surface layer and the healthy worm population that should exist will take it down into the soil for you. It will be possible to grow crops much closer together, the soil is not compacted in any way, and you'll get higher yields than on a conventional arrangement of rows.

■ **Plan your crop rotation.** In order to avoid the buildup of certain pests and diseases, and to make the best use of manures and fertilizers, it is best to practise crop rotation.

Vegetable crops can be divided into three main groups that share some vulnerability to the same plant problems, and also prefer different soil treatments before they are planted or sown. Vegetables within these groups should never be grown in the same place again until at least two years have gone by. The table set out below shows a simple crop

Maintaining deep beds Each year spread organic matter over the beds rather than digging it in. The level will fall over the season.

rotation and it is meant to be a guide only. You may grow all the crops listed, or more, but the principles remain the same.

There are some vegetables that do not lend themselves to crop rotation and don't need it – the perennial crops, such as asparagus, globe artichokes, and sea kale. Asparagus needs its own bed, as it will be in place for many years, but the others are beautiful plants in their own right that make handsome additions to ornamental plantings. Sweetcorn is an annual crop that does not fall into any particular group, so it can move around from year to year and be treated as a gap-filler.

■ **Cover ground with polythene.** When you have dug over an area, cover it with black polythene, anchored around the edges or tucked firmly into the soil, or with cloches. This will keep off the worst of the weather so that the soil can easily be raked down into seedbeds next month. It also helps to warm the soil for early setting out of young plants sown now indoors, and also for earlier sowing outdoors. This way you'll get early vegetables.

Harvesting

■ **Continue to harvest** Brussels sprouts, leeks, parsnips, swedes, and turnips. If you haven't grown any winter greens,

Three-year crop rotation

YEAR ONE

Group one		Group two		Group three	
Add compost over winter and fertilizer before sowing.		Rotted manure in winter and fertilizer before sowing.		Add compost, lime, and fertilizer.	
Grow:		Grow:		Grow:	
Beetroot	Carrots	Beans	Peas	Brussels sprouts	
Kohl rabi	Potatoes	Leeks	Lettuces	Cabbage	Cauliflower
Turnips	Swedes	Onions	Shallots	Broccoli	Kale
Celeriac		Radish		Savoy	Spinach

YEAR TWO	Group two	Group three	Group one
YEAR THREE	Group three	Group one	Group two
YEAR FOUR	Group one	Group two	Group three

remember that turnip tops can be cooked and eaten as a green vegetable.

Sowing outdoors

■ **In sheltered southern parts** seeds may be sown under cloches on land which has already been covered for a few weeks. However, it is usually better to wait until February to sow under cloches, or March to sow direct. Seeds to sow include lettuce, salad onions, radishes, peas, broad beans, and spinach. Sow small amounts at 10- to 14-day intervals, and these crops will follow on from any sown under glass.

Sowing indoors

■ **Sow a few early crops,** either in seed trays or in modules. The advantage of growing in modules is that you need not disturb these young plants until it is time to plant them out, when the little rootballs can be transplanted intact, so the plants get off to a flying start. The plants will be ready to be put out under cloches or blankets of horticultural fleece from late February onwards.

Sow small quantities of lettuce, summer cabbages and cauliflowers, radishes, carrots (choose round varieties for module sowing), spinach, salad onions, turnips,

Baby crops Thin out seedlings sown in trays under cover to ensure that the strongest plants have enough space to develop.

peas, and broad beans. None of these seeds requires high temperatures to germinate – about 13°C (55°F) is adequate, so a windowsill in a warm room will do, or, for faster results, use a propagator. Then grow them on in good light. If you sow in seed trays rather than modules you will need to prick them out once the seedlings are large enough to handle safely.

■ **Sow onion seed this month.** To get the best onions they need a fairly long growing season. The easiest way to start off is to sow them in clusters in modules. Fill the modules with peat-free compost and water to settle it. Sow five or six seeds per cell and cover them with vermiculite. Put in a heated propagator or on a warm windowsill until the seeds germinate.

The onions will be ready to plant out in late March. There's no need to thin, just plant out the whole cluster.

Looking after crops

■ **Bend leaves over cauliflowers** to protect the developing curds, the plants' undeveloped flowerheads. When exposed to a prolonged period of light the curds tend to turn green and flower buds develop, making them inedible. By bending a few leaves over the curd this process is slowed down, making the crops last a bit longer. Just snap leaves near the base of the midrib and tuck them in around the curd. You can tie the leaves up to keep the curds covered in windy weather.

Planning ahead

■ **Start early potatoes.** Freshly dug potatoes are in a class of their own when it comes to flavour. It's time to look out for seed potatoes as they need to be chitted (started into growth) before planting in March. As well as advancing the date on which the potatoes will be harvested,

Sprouting seed potatoes An egg tray is ideal for this purpose, but the potatoes can rest against each other in a shallow box.

chitting will also increase the overall yield. To start them off, lay the tubers in a tray with the "rose" end uppermost. Put them in a light, cool, frost-free place and after two or three weeks, shoots will begin to sprout. To get the best crop thin the shoots to two or three per tuber. Plant out from March.

Beat the seasons

■ **Chicory** forced for tightly packed, blanched leaves is a good alternative when other salad crops are scarce in winter, but it can be eaten cooked as well. You need to have sown the seeds and raised plants outside over the summer. Now, lift the large tap roots and pot them up. A 20cm (8in) pot will take about five roots. Any potting compost will do for forcing. Once you have potted the roots, covering them with the compost, invert another pot over the planted-up one, covering drainage holes to keep out the light. Keep in a temperature of 10–13°C (50–55°F). Keep the roots moist, but not wet. If the compost was well watered to begin with, then little or no watering should be needed, provided that the pot is not sitting in too warm a place. The chicory should be ready three or four weeks after potting up.

FRUIT

■ **Protect fruit cages** from damage by heavy snowfalls. Either roll the roof netting to the centre supports and tie it in, or remove the roof netting entirely and drape it over trees and bushes that may be vulnerable to bird damage.

Picking and storing

■ **Inspect all fruits that are in store** and remove any that are showing signs of rotting off. Disease can spread rapidly, so the sooner it is detected, the better. A place that is cool and dark is ideal for storage. Fruits that have been wrapped in paper are less likely to spread rots.

Looking after crops

■ **Protect fruit trees and gooseberries** with netting. Birds can cause a lot of damage, even in winter. Bullfinches, in particular, love to eat plump, developing fruit buds. Larger free-standing trees can be difficult to protect, so you may have to accept some loss, but restricted forms of trees such as cordons and fans grown against a wall or fence are easily protected with netting. Make sure this is well secured so birds don't get trapped. Plastic mesh or fleecy web are safer.

■ **Towards the end of the month** is a good time to apply an organic fertilizer to all fruit. Even in late January things are beginning to stir and sap is beginning to rise. An organic fertilizer such as blood, fish and bone, or seaweed meal is ideal, because organic fertilizers release their nutrients slowly over a long period; the plants don't get the sudden boost to growth as they would get with inorganic, or chemical, fertilizers. Too much soft growth early in the season is more susceptible to damage from frosts, pests, and diseases. Pull away any mulch around tree bases and bushes before feeding; water the ground and renew the mulch.

Inspect ties Look at all stakes and ties, especially on the growing stems of young trees.

■ **Check all fruit tree ties** and stakes are sound. Older ties can break, so it is as well to check them regularly. Also, do bear in mind that as a tree grows the stem expands, so check that ties are not too tight on young trees.

■ **Examine apple trees** for signs of canker. The symptoms to look for are flattened areas of bark that show signs of splitting, causing the bark to flake off. The branch may also become swollen. During the winter, red fungal fruiting bodies can also be seen. Canker is caused by a fungus called *Neonectria galligena*; it is spread by wind-borne spores and attacks the tree through open wounds or pruning cuts. To control canker you may have to cut out whole branches or fruiting spurs. Make sure you remove all damaged bark and wood back to healthy tissue. Cut to a healthy-looking bud, a branch junction, or the main trunk. Look at the pruning cut: if the wood is white, you have pruned back to healthy wood and the cut should heal well. If it still shows brown staining, you should prune further back.

■ **Spray fruit trees and bushes** with a plant oil winter wash, unless you did so last month. Many pests like to hibernate in little cracks and crevices in the bark. It is important to spray really thoroughly with the wash to make sure any pests lurking there are killed. Be careful when using winter wash because it can damage evergreen plants, including grass. If fruit trees are growing in grass, put polythene down to protect it. Protect other plants nearby by covering them with polythene. Black bin bags are ideal for small plants. Do any spraying on a frost-free, calm day, so that spray does not drift on the breeze onto other plants.

■ **Spray peaches** against peach leaf curl. This disease is quite noticeable in spring and summer. The foliage of the tree becomes puckered and turns red and purple, dropping off prematurely. It is not fatal for the tree; leaves produced later in the season usually remain healthy. But year on year it will weaken it, and it is certainly unsightly and distressing.

Trees grown under glass are usually unaffected as the disease is spread by spores carried by wind and rain. Dwarf varieties are now available and these are easily grown in large pots for the patio; they can be taken inside for the winter if you have the space.

A way of protecting outdoor fan-trained trees is to erect a temporary open-ended polythene shelter. Put the shelter in position from midwinter until mid-spring.

Peach leaf curl This is a fungus spread by wind and rain. Affected leaves pucker and blister.

This keeps the tree dry and prevents the fungus from infecting the emerging leaves. Spray with a fungicide at intervals from mid- to late winter, following the instructions carefully. Stop spraying as flower buds begin to open.

Pruning and training

■ **Continue to winter-prune apples,** pears, red- and whitecurrants, gooseberries, and blackcurrants.

■ **Winter pruning of apples and pears** consists mainly of pruning back the leaders of trained fruit trees, whether they be fan-trained, espaliers, cordons, or bush trees. The leading shoots of main branches should be cut back by about one-third to a half, depending on the vigour of the tree. The one basic rule to remember about pruning is that the harder you prune, the stronger will be the subsequent growth from the point of pruning. Also, thin out overcrowded fruiting spurs on trained trees. This allows better air circulation, reducing the risk of disease.

■ **Pruning of red- and whitecurrants** and gooseberries is similar. If fruiting shoots were summer-pruned, they can now be pruned further to a couple of buds from the main branches.

■ **Blackcurrants are pruned** in a slightly different way. Some people prune blackcurrants just after the fruit has been picked, but in winter you can see better what you are doing without a lot of foliage on the plants. Blackcurrants fruit on new and old wood and they are grown as a stool plant (that is, branches grow in a clump from, or just under, ground level). Pruning is all about maintaining a balance between old and new wood. Around one-third of the bush should be removed each year to maintain the vigour of the

Long branches Shorten by a half or a third any branches that have grown too long. Cut them back to a side branch (lateral).

plant. Wherever possible cut out older stems to the ground, leaving younger wood to fruit in the summer. When finished, you should have a balance between old and new branches on a fairly open bush. Mulch after pruning. Do not let it touch the stems.

■ **Prune and train** summer-fruiting raspberries if this was not done in the autumn. This is quite a good time of year to do the job, as it's easier to see what you are doing. The old canes that bore the fruit last year need to be cut from the wires to which they were tied last year, and cut to ground level. Tie in the new canes that grew last year, but did not fruit, about 10cm (4in) apart. Any stems that are taller than the support wires can be cut back to the top wire, or the tip of the shoot can be brought down and tied to the top wire. Whichever way you decide on, this will encourage the formation of fruit-bearing sideshoots in the summer.

■ **Prune outdoor grape vines.** Finish this task if you haven't already, as the sap will

soon begin to rise, and if vines are pruned any later it will cause "bleeding": the sap will seep badly out of the pruning cuts. All laterals should be pruned back to two or three buds and leading shoots pruned back to within the allotted space.

Planting

■ **Continue to plant** fruit trees and bushes, but only when the soil conditions are right. If trees are planted when the soil is too wet, firstly the soil will get compacted with walking on it. Secondly, even if only the surface of the soil is frozen, it is not good practice to put frozen lumps of soil around plant roots. The ideal condition for soil to be in for planting is moist, but not sticking to your boots. If conditions are not right for planting, heel in the plants in a sheltered corner or put them in the shed for a day or two. They will be fine if you keep the roots moist.

Beat the seasons

■ **Begin to force strawberries** which were potted up last August, taking them under cover.

■ **Force rhubarb** for delicious, tender young stems in the spring. Clear away all the dead foliage from the crown. If the winter has been mild, you may see fresh growth already starting at ground level; be careful not to damage it. Cover the plant with an old dustbin or a large pot. Alternatively you can buy special terracotta rhubarb forcers. These are upturned clay pots, sometimes decorative, with a lid to check on the forced rhubarb. Place one of these over the crown of the plant and surround the forcer with fresh horse manure, leaving the lid uncovered. The heat generated by the decaying manure forces the rhubarb on even quicker.

UNDER COVER

■ **Check greenhouse heaters** are working properly. Electric heaters that are not functioning efficiently will waste electricity, costing more to run. With paraffin heaters make sure the wick is trimmed regularly; if the flame does not burn properly, toxic fumes will be given off and these will harm the plants. Gas heaters should also be checked regularly by a qualified engineer. Don't tinker with any appliance if you're not sure about what you are doing; call in a professional to do the job safely.

■ **Clean the greenhouse** or conservatory inside and out. Now is a good time to do it, before seed-sowing begins. You may have to move plants about or put them outside if the weather is not too cold. Cleaning the glass, inside and out, is the most important job, as plants need all the light they can get when the days are short. The inside should be scrubbed down with a garden disinfectant – floors, walls, and benches. Pay particular attention to corners where glass meets frame and the roof meets the sides; these are the places where pests lurk and hibernate through winter.

■ **Ventilate on mild days.** Even in January, on the occasional sunny day, temperatures inside can rise dramatically. Open the ventilators for a few hours on such days, but close them well before sundown.

■ **Keep an eye out for fungal diseases** like *Botrytis*, commonly called "grey mould" after its appearance on stems and leaves. It is difficult to control as the spores are air-borne. It attacks plants through wounds and decaying stems, leaves, and flowers. The best way to control it when cold weather makes ventilation difficult is by practising good hygiene. Remove any yellowing leaves or stems from plants before the fungus gets a chance to invade.

Clear any fallen leaves away promptly and put them in the bin, not on the compost heap, where the spores may survive. There are no fungicides available to amateur gardeners for the control of botrytis.

■ **Watch out for vine weevil** in heated greenhouses and conservatories, where the larvae of this pest may be active all year. Symptoms are a general lack of vigour or wilting, caused by damage to the roots by the grubs of the weevil: legless, creamy-white larvae, up to 10mm (⅜in) long, with curved bodies and a brown head. A wide variety of plants grown in pots can be affected. In a heated house, you can use a biological control to combat vine weevil, even at this time of year.

■ **Clean pots and seed trays,** ready for seed sowing. Using clean containers, especially for seed sowing and rooting cuttings, will help cut down the incidence of pests and diseases, reducing the need for chemicals. Use a garden disinfectant and rinse thoroughly. Make sure children cannot get near these solutions.

■ **Inspect any bulbs, corms and tubers** stored in the greenhouse and throw away any that show signs of rot.

■ **Watering at this time of year** needs to be done with some care. Only water plants when they absolutely need it. The best way to gauge whether a plant needs water is to regularly lift the pot and feel the weight; the lighter the pot the more water it will need, and the heavier it is the less water it will need. Plants that are almost dormant this month, such as overwintering fuchsias and pelargoniums resting in frost-free greenhouses, should be watered very sparingly; just enough to keep them alive. Too much water and they will put on too much growth. Actively growing plants like

winter-flowering azaleas, poinsettias, and bulbs will need more watering. It's best to do any watering early in the day in winter. This gives the greenhouse or conservatory time to dry out before the cold night.

■ **Prune established fuchsias** in heated greenhouses and conservatories. Fuchsias can be started into growth now by watering more often and moving them into the lightest position; indeed, they may already have started, with buds beginning to burst. To keep the plants bushy and healthy prune them quite hard, pruning all the sideshoots back to one or two buds from the main framework of stems. The plants also need repotting at this time. Remove the plants from the pots and tease out as much of the old compost as you can. Then repot into the same-sized pot with fresh peat-free potting compost and water in well to settle the compost around the roots. Spray the plants occasionally with a fine mist of clear water to encourage buds to swell.

Raising plants for outdoors

■ **Sow seed** of those summer-flowering bedding plants that need a long growing season to produce flowers in time for summer – all kinds of begonias and antirrhinums, pelargoniums, lobelias, and gazanias. To germinate successfully these seeds need to be grown in a propagator that can be maintained at a constant temperature of 21–22°C (68–70°F). Most propagators give a lift of about 10°C (20°F) above the ambient temperature, so on very cold nights some extra heating may be needed. At this time of year light is at a premium, so place the propagator on a south-facing bench.

The fine seeds of antirrhinums and begonias do not need covering. Even the lightest covering of compost is likely to be too deep for these very fine seeds. More

Sowing tender perennials

1 Fill a pot with peat-free compost and tap on the bench to settle it. Strike off the surplus and press lightly.

2 Water the compost thoroughly before sowing the seeds thinly over the surface.

3 Larger seeds like those of pelargoniums can be covered with sieved compost or vermiculite – just enough to cover the seeds.

4 Place a sheet of glass over the pot and place in a propagator until germination.

information about this can be found on the back of seed packets. When the seeds are large enough they can be pricked out into trays or potted up separately. Seeds sown in the warm, moist conditions in a propagator are prone to "damping off". Avoid this by sowing the seeds thinly, to avoid overcrowding, and use clean trays and pots. Cheshunt compound is recommended to prevent damping off.

■ **Sow sweet peas** if you didn't get this done in the autumn and pot on and pinch out the tips of any sown in autumn.

■ **Start off vegetables** and sow onions.

Glasshouse and house plants

■ **Keep winter-flowering pot plants,** such as azaleas and poinsettias, in a cool place in good light. If the room or conservatory is too warm the flowers will go over much more quickly. A light windowsill facing south, if you haven't got a greenhouse or conservatory, is the ideal place. The plants will have to be turned every two or three days to prevent them growing one-sided.

■ **Forced bulbs** Bring in pots of spring bulbs that were plunged outside in autumn. A greenhouse or conservatory makes a good staging post on their way into the house, to get them used to warmer temperatures. Pots of bulbs that have finished flowering can be put outside now.

■ **Pot up some lily bulbs** for early flowers indoors. Lily bulbs are available in the garden centres now and will be spectacular grown in containers indoors. Not only do you get the beautiful flowers, but the scent is terrific too. Put three or four bulbs into a 17cm (7in) pot containing peat-free multi-purpose compost. Cover the bulbs with 7–10cm (3–4in) of compost and put in a light place. After a few weeks

Lilium martagon

the bulbs will come through and in late spring, the flowers will fill your home with colour and with many wonderful scents. The bulbs can be planted in the garden when the flowers are over.

Crops under glass

■ **Prune vines under glass** as soon as possible, because even in winter the temperature under glass can rise considerably and the vines will start into growth very quickly. If they are pruned when the sap is rising they will "bleed": sap will ooze out from the pruning cuts, weakening the plant.

To prune them, untie the fruited stems from the supports and cut back to one or two buds from the main stem, or rod, as it is called. Prune back the rod if it is growing beyond its allotted space. Check for pests by gently removing any flaking bark and spray with a plant oil winter wash, as used on fruit trees. Don't spray if you see green buds starting to swell or they will be damaged; wait until next winter.

■ **Bring in strawberries** that were potted up last August to be forced. If you have enough plants, bring in half now and the rest next month, then the fruiting season will be extended. Remove old, dead, and diseased foliage and place the pot in as much light as possible.

THE FEBRUARY GARDEN

This month sees the sap beginning to rise, not only in plants but in the gardener too. It can actually be a colder month than January, but a few days of watery sunshine is all that it takes to tempt us outside. Check over your tools, make sure your pots and seed trays are clean, and that you have enough potting compost and labels. It's time to get growing!

THINGS TO DO

Feed garden birds in severe weather.

Apply organic-based fertilizers towards the end of the month.

Check that plant supports are sound and not too tight before they are hidden by new growth.

Continue planting bare-root trees, shrubs, fruit trees, and bushes.

Firm any newly planted trees and shrubs that have been lifted by frost.

Repot or top-dress shrubs in containers.

Prune winter-flowering shrubs – including winter heathers – when the flowers have faded.

Remove the old stems of herbaceous perennials.

Start tender perennials into growth under cover.

Divide and replant snowdrops.

Start dahlia tubers into growth indoors.

Prepare seedbed for vegetables seed sowing outdoors.

Prick out or pot up seedlings already growing.

Protect gooseberry bushes from bird damage.

LAST CHANCE

Cut back overgrown shrubs and hedges before the nesting season starts.

GET AHEAD

Prune roses if not already done.

Prepare the ground for sowing a new lawn or laying turf.

Sow annuals under cover.

A winter border Christmas roses, winter aconites, crocuses, and snowdrops make a delightful seasonal display.

NEW SEASON APPROACHING

This is a month of anticipation: spring is on the doorstep, and new green shoots are readying themselves to burst into bloom. On the mildest days you can get on with winter-pruning jobs, and cultivate the soil, but if you're huddled up indoors, why not fill the time with a spot of garden planning?

There is now a noticeable difference in the length of daylight and a feeling of anticipation, too, as a new season is just around the corner. It's a lovely month to just wander around the garden and look at the buds beginning to swell. Many buds are attractively coloured at this time and they're packed with youthful energy, ready to burst forth. Towards the end of the month, early spring-flowering bulbs such as *Narcissus* 'February Gold' are in flower and the earliest primroses are also appearing. And in many parts of the country, early-flowering shrubs such as chaenomeles and daphnes will start to bloom.

Winter wet

Weatherwise, however, February can be very cold, with heavy snow, severe frosts, and a lot of rain. Try to keep off the soil when it is excessively wet as you will do more harm than good. Tramping over very wet soil compacts it, pushing out all the air and damaging the structure. Once this has happened, raking the soil down into a fine, crumbly tilth that will give seeds a good start becomes much more difficult. If you really must tread on soil in these conditions, work from a plank that will spread your weight evenly over the soil and reduce compaction.

Promise of spring Daffodils such as *Narcissus* 'February Gold' burst into flower this month and mark the transition between winter and spring.

Winter rations Well-stocked feeders attract birds into the garden, especially on wintry days when natural food sources are scarce.

Towards the end of the month, a fairly mild spell may often delude us into thinking that spring has sprung already. But beware; winter can often return with a vengeance. Always be guided by your local weather conditions when considering planting, sowing, or doing any other work in the garden. You will find that from year to year the timings of sowing and planting will vary quite considerably, depending on the weather conditions at the time. Don't get too frustrated if you are stuck indoors – take the opportunity to do some garden planning instead. A little bit of thought now about where plants should go in the garden will save you a lot of time in the busy spring season ahead.

Beat the blues

But it's not all doom and gloom outdoors and February can often be a good month for working off the winter blues. There is plenty to do as the garden begins to come to life. Check on any newly planted trees and shrubs to see if they have been loosened by frost and refirm gently where necessary, but don't tread too heavily when doing this, because if the soil is very wet you will drive out all the air from around the roots.

It's also an ideal time for planting bare-root deciduous trees and shrubs. The conventional wisdom on planting bare-root stock is that it can be planted at any time in the dormant season, from November until March. This still holds true, but current thinking now leans towards planting on a mild day in February rather than in the autumn. The reasoning for this is that often with autumn planting, the trees and shrubs will just sit through winter in the cold, wet soil doing nothing, and they may be killed off in very cold spells. But if they are planted in February, then with spring just around the corner, they will get off to a much better start.

Another way to bring some cheer into the garden in late winter is to encourage the birds to visit. Keep your bird feeders well stocked and provide fresh water for them to drink and bathe in. This is also an ideal time to buy or build nesting boxes in preparation for spring, when birds will be looking for homes for their new families. A simple wooden box that you can make or buy is sure to attract some feathered visitors to your garden this spring.

Weather watch

As far as temperatures are concerned, January and February are very similar, with February being, on average, colder. Temperature over land is largely governed by the temperature of the sea, which is at its lowest in February. Average daily temperatures in the south will be around 6–8°C, and in the north 4–6°C. Hard frosts are still common, so continue to protect vulnerable plants outdoors.

Windy days

February can still be windy, but less so than January. Northern areas will have on average 3–4 days of gales this month, the south only 0.1 day on average. These figures vary according to height above sea level and topography. Coastal areas are always windier.

More sunshine

Generally there is more sunshine in February compared to January, with southern parts of the country getting around 7.6 days, and northern parts around 5.2 days of bright sun. The days are getting longer, but there can still be bad weather to come.

Varying rainfall

Rainfall varies from one part of the country to another, south-eastern parts generally getting the least rain, with on average 35–38mm (1–1½in). In Scotland this month, the north-east coast is driest, but the south-west is one of the wettest parts of the country, with on average 110mm (4⅓in) of rain.

Persistent snow

Thick snow can persist in high areas for most of the winter, but on lower ground amounts vary. Western coastal areas have very little snow and mild temperatures – there are gardens on the west coasts of Scotland and Ireland growing plants usually found in warmer regions. In the north, on high ground above 100m (300ft) there will be on average 2–3 days of snow, increasing to around 15 days over 300m (984ft). In southern parts 1–2 days is the average snowfall for the month.

Winter landscape Sumach trees are dramatic in snow,
with chunky, felted, rust-coloured seedheads.

Prunings and fertilizers

This is a month for pruning woody plants. Hardy shrubs that flower on new wood later in the summer, such as the butterfly bush (*Buddleja davidii*), can be cut right down, generating piles of twiggy prunings. You can recycle the sturdiest of these to make plant supports, but the rest of the debris is still too useful to burn. If you shred it, it can be added to the compost heap or used as a mulch. There are many types of shredder available to buy or hire.

Shredded prunings make a good home-grown mulch, but wait until next month, when the soil has warmed up a little, then you will lock some of that warmth in under the mulch blanket. What you can do now is give the soil a dressing of an organic-based fertilizer, so that the nutrients it contains will be available to plants as they start into growth. Although this book is not specifically about organic gardening, organic fertilizers, such as blood, fish and bone, hoof and horn, fish and seaweed meals and pelleted chicken manure, deserve a few words. The synthetic or chemical fertilizers available today normally act as a quick tonic or quick fix to get plants off to a good start. But with these fertilizers plants often produce soft, sappy growth, which is much more susceptible to attack from pests and diseases. The nutrients are used up more quickly and so they have to be applied more often. They also do little to improve the soil, whereas some organic fertilizers, especially those based on seaweed meal, do have soil-conditioning properties.

With organic fertilizers, the nutrients are released more slowly and are available to plants over a longer period. So instead of a rapid boost to growth, the plants grow more steadily and sturdily. They are also easier to use because quantities don't need to be as precise as when using artificial fertilizers. Because the nutrients of organic fertilizers are released slowly they are best applied two or three weeks before sowing or planting, so they are available to the plants right away.

If you have a greenhouse or a conservatory it will be a busy time, but don't be in too much of a hurry to sow a lot of summer bedding plants yet. Better to start them off next month to reduce heating costs. If sowings are made too early, the plants will become leggy due to poorer light, and they also risk becoming starved from being in seed trays or pots for too long. Later sowings will produce much better-quality plants for planting out at the end of May and beginning of June. For now, be sure you have a good supply of seed-sowing compost, pots, and seed trays on hand for the busy sowing season ahead.

Sowing for early crops

This is a good time to sow some early vegetables for planting out under cloches next month: lettuce, radish, beetroot, salad onions, peas, and broad beans. The easiest way of doing this is to sow the seeds in plastic modules. These seeds don't need heat, but they do need the lightest spot you can find for them. Once you've sown seeds inside, cover the piece of ground outdoors where the young vegetable plants are to be put out, using a cloche or a sheet of polythene to protect the soil from further rain and snow and to warm it up. Then you will have the tastiest, freshest, and most welcome, vegetables in the neighbourhood.

Changing crops The tight florets of sprouting broccoli make a welcome change from leafy winter greens.

Helleborus orientalis
Evergreen perennial with variably coloured flowers (*see p.301*)

Iris 'Harmony'
Dwarf bulb ideal for an alpine trough or raised bed (*see p.304*)

Narcissus cyclamineus ♥
Short-stemmed, flowering earlier than larger daffodils (*see p.311*)

***Cyclamen coum* Pewter Group** ♥
Low, clump-forming perennial with marbled leaves (*see p.291*)

***Euonymus fortunei* 'Silver Queen'**
Brightly variegated evergreen shrub (*see p.296*)

***Erica* x *darleyensis* 'Arthur Johnson'** ♥
Low-growing heather ideal for ground cover (*see p.295*)

Clematis cirrhosa 'Freckles' ♀
Small-flowered evergreen climber for very early spring (*see p.286*)

Viburnum tinus
Bushy evergreen shrub with perfumed flowers and black berries (*see p.335*)

Chaenomeles speciosa 'Phylis Moore'
One of the first flowering quinces to come into bloom (*see p.283*)

Cornus mas ♀
Deciduous shrub or small tree; the leaves colour well in autumn (*see p.288*)

Crocus tommasinianus ♀
Carpeting bulb that naturalizes well in grass (*see p.291*)

Camellia x williamsii 'Anticipation' ♀
Evergreen, glossy-leaved shrub for acid soil (*see p.281*)

WHAT TO DO IN FEBRUARY

AROUND THE GARDEN

If you use chemicals in the garden, even "organic" kinds, it is a good idea to go through them and see which have been lying around for a long time and can be discarded. There may be bags that have split open and the contents spilt on the floor or shelves, or bottles with only a few drops left in them, or others that have been left in the shed unused for years. Don't be tempted to pour them down the drain or scatter old fertilizer over the garden as you may cause a lot of harm. Take this sort of stuff to your local authority waste site and let them deal with it properly. Numbers will be in your local phone book or you can find them online.

Make sure garden birds have plenty of food and water. February is a very hungry month for wildlife and putting food out may distract birds and small mammals from taking your buds and bulbs instead.

Put up bird boxes. Birds need a little time to get used to new boxes before they will select them to nest in.

Check all tools and machines are in working order. Once the busy gardening season really gets under way, it is maddening to go to the shed and only then remember that your favourite spade has a broken handle – just when you need to get on with digging or planting a newly bought plant. Wiring of all electrical appliances should be checked for cuts, too, and if you are not sure what to do, contact a qualified electrician, or take the tool and flex to your nearest stockist for advice.

Apply organic-based fertilizer to all borders. It is a good time of year to do this; organic fertilizers release their nutrients more slowly than inorganic ones, which means the nutrients will be available to your plants just as they start into growth in the spring. A sprinkling of organic fertilizer like seaweed meal, blood, fish and bone, or pelleted chicken manure around the plants will do them the world of good after the long winter.

Tool care Clean your tools after use: they last longer and it reduces the risk of spreading diseases to other plants. Brush off dirt and sap and give carbon steel blades a wipe with an oily rag to protect them against rust.

Spread the fertilizer according to the maker's instructions and lightly stir it into the surface of the soil with a hoe or garden fork.

Order plenty of compost, pots, and seed trays for the busy season ahead. Having a good supply on hand saves a lot of unnecessary trips to the garden centre – time that you could spend gardening. Buying in bulk in partnership with your neighbours or as part of a local gardening society could save you a lot of money. The use of coir compost (which comes from coconut husks and is a renewable resource) and other peat substitutes is becoming more popular as we all become more environmentally aware. The less peat we use, the more we help to conserve the fast-disappearing peat bogs, where precious native flora and fauna exist.

TREES AND SHRUBS
Planting
■ **Bare-root trees and shrubs,** including roses, can be planted at any time during the dormant season from November to March, but recent research has shown that February can be the ideal time.

Provided that the soil is not actually frozen, or so wet that it sticks to your boots, plants that you put in this month will get off to a really good start. The main reason for this is that the plants are not stuck in cold, wet soil all winter, when new roots will not grow much at all, especially so soon after they have been lifted from the nursery. But by planting during this month it is not long before the soil begins to warm up and those new roots will get growing, quickly establishing the plant. Remember to look after new plants well and water them thoroughly during any dry spells, especially as they are getting established in their first year.

■ **Deciduous shrubs** in the wrong place can be moved.

Pruning and training
■ **There may be quite a lot of pruning** to be done this month, especially if you haven't been able to brave the winter weather so far. Birds will soon be looking for nesting sites, so you should get pruning out of the way this month to avoid disturbing them later. Any overgrown or misshapen deciduous trees and shrubs can all be pruned to improve their health and shape. You can probably also start pruning roses this month in sheltered parts of the country. Many people start pruning roses in November, but in colder parts of the country, as in my native Scotland, the winters can sometimes be harsh, causing dieback, and if the roses have already been pruned this means you will have to go over them again in spring. For details of how to prune *see March*, the traditional

time to tackle roses and the safest in the north and cold regions.

■ **Evergreens** that have become overgrown can be pruned now, provided that they are completely hardy plants like *Prunus laurocerasus*; more tender shrubs such as *Choisya ternata* (Mexican orange blossom) should be left until later in the year. Shoots that have become overcrowded or grown out awkwardly can be pruned back, to the main stems if necessary, to maintain the shape of the plant. Cutting back to ground level may be an option if the plant is one that tolerates drastic pruning – for example, *Prunus laurocerasus*, spotted laurel (*Aucuba japonica*) and *Viburnum tinus*. This will encourage strong growth from the base of the shrub. Feed after pruning, preferably with an organic fertilizer, and mulch with organic matter.

■ **Trim winter-flowering heathers** as they finish flowering. This job has to be done, otherwise the plants will become straggly and the centre of the plant will become bare. The easiest way is to go over the

plants with a pair of garden shears. Trim back to the base of the flower stalks: this will encourage sideshoots to grow, keeping the plant bushy and compact. Mulching the plants with a peat substitute and feeding in a few weeks' time will do a lot to encourage strong growth.

■ **Larger winter-flowering shrubs** such as witch hazel (*Hamamelis*) don't as a rule need regular pruning, but at this time of year, once the flowers are over, you can remove any stems that are rubbing or spoiling the shape of the plant.

■ **Late-flowering shrubs** can be pruned this month. These include *Buddleja davidii* (the butterfly bush), *Caryopteris* x *clandonensis*, *Ceanothus* 'Burkwoodii' (the deciduous ceanothus), hardy fuchsias, *Santolina, Ceratostigma, Lavatera*, and *Leycesteria* (the nutmeg bush). These shrubs flower best on growth made since the spring. It's a terrific job if you've had a bad day, as you can be quite brutal with them! Cut them back almost to the ground (see below), leaving one or two buds or shoots on each stem. You may feel you're

Pruning summer shrubs
Pruning *Buddleja davidii* Use loppers to cut the thick stems back to a stubby framework.

Pruning *caryopteris* Cut back all of the whippy stems and a new crop will grow and flower.

cutting off far too much, but it is the right thing to do to get the best show of flowers. Where you want to increase the size of the shrubs, leave a few stems on and prune these lightly. After pruning, give a feed of organic fertilizer and mulch with garden compost or farmyard manure to get them off to a flying start.

Hedges

■ **Brush snow off evergreen hedges** before the weight splays out branches.

■ **Overgrown or misshapen hedges** can be pruned now to improve their health and shape. Most deciduous hedges may be pruned back hard, as can broadleaved evergreens such as *Prunus laurocerasus* and laurel, but you must never cut conifers back into the bare wood, with the exception of yew. Yew is thought of as being slow-growing, but it is surprising how quickly it does grow, and even if it is regularly trimmed, it can gradually creep outwards if it is not trimmed hard enough. Unlike other conifers such as Leyland cypress, yew will take very hard pruning: cut it back as much as you like and it will grow away again from the stumps. Other conifers must be lightly but regularly trimmed from the word go to keep them compact; never let them become overgrown.

■ **Conifers may need some attention.** If you didn't tie them in as a precaution, wind or snow may have bent branches down, spoiling the shape. If these are then pruned off it can leave an unsightly gap. So the thing to do is to tie them up again. Plastic-coated wire is fine as long as it is cushioned against the trunk with a piece of hessian or similar – an old rag cut into strips and folded, for example – otherwise the wire will cut into the trunk, eventually killing the tree.

CLIMBERS

■ **Brush any snow** off dense evergreen climbers and wall shrubs; when snow accumulates on these it can not only break stems but also puts strain on all the ties and supports.

■ **Prune late-flowering clematis.** Towards the end of the month, you can prune *Clematis orientalis, C. texensis, C. viticella* and its many cultivars, such as 'Madame Julia Correvon' and 'Gravetye Beauty', and also the late large-flowered hybrids such as 'Ville de Lyon' and 'Jackmanii'. In some books these are all classed together as the "Group 3" clematis.

In sheltered parts of the country they may already be starting to produce shoots. These can be rather brittle, so you need to be careful when you are pruning and pulling away the old growth from last year. Apart from this, they are the easiest of all clematis to prune.

All you have to do is cut down all of the growth to 23–45cm (9–18in) from the ground, cutting each stem back to just above a healthy bud. These clematis are ideal for growing through other shrubs, because as they start afresh each year, they never become so overgrown that they swamp their host.

After pruning, feed with an organic fertilizer and mulch with organic matter, or put a large stone at the base of the plant. Clematis like their heads in the sun but their roots shaded and cool.

■ **Winter-flowering jasmine** can be pruned now that the flowers have gone over. This lanky plant needs some attention to prevent it from becoming very untidy. First prune out any dead or damaged wood. Then tie in any stems that you need to extend the framework or coverage of the plant, and then shorten all the side growths from this main framework to 5cm (2in) from the main stems. This will

encourage plenty of new shoots for flowering next winter. Feed and mulch in the same way as for clematis.

■ **Summer-flowering jasmines** can also be pruned, but you must tackle these by taking out an entire main stem or two to the ground. If you prune back all the side growths as with winter jasmine, they produce a mass of tangled leafy growth that is no good to anyone.

■ **Plant new climbers** exactly as you would trees and shrubs (although they are more likely to be container-grown rather than bare-root), digging holes at least 9in (22cm) away from walls and fences so that the plant is not in a dry "rain shadow". Take care to encourage the plants to grow into the support.

Planting new climbers To train a new climber along a fence, put the wires in place beforehand. Plant the climber well away from the fence, and then guide the young stems up to the permanent framework using temporary supports.

PERENNIALS

■ **Finish weeding and digging over** the borders and new planting areas, incorporating organic matter if you can. Cut down any old, dead growth from plants such as sedums and acanthus that was left on for effect over the winter. The sooner this is done the better, as new shoots will already be emerging from some plants towards the end of the month and they are all too easily damaged.

■ **Towards the end of the month** herbaceous perennials will be starting into growth; now is a good time to feed them with an organic-based fertilizer.

■ **Continue taking root cuttings** from perennials.

■ **Check all the stakes and supports** that you removed in autumn and stock up if you don't think you'll have enough for your plants later on in the spring. One economical way of doing this is to keep the best of the prunings from shrubs pruned this and next month.

■ **Pot up dahlia tubers** stored during the winter and they will produce shoots that make good cuttings. The tubers can be potted up singly, or several can be put into large trays. Place the tubers in good light and spray them occasionally with water to encourage the buds to grow.

New tubers bought from the garden centre can be treated in exactly the same way. There are many different dahlias available from the smallest pompon blooms to blowsy, decorative ones like the large cactus-flowered types. But the best ones for attracting bees and butterflies to the garden are single-flowered cultivars.

BULBS

■ **Plant and divide snowdrops** and winter aconites after flowering, but while the foliage is still green. Both of these bulbs should be bought "in the green", as it is known. They often do not grow well when they are planted as dry bulbs in the autumn. Look through the gardening press now and you will see plenty advertised by specialist nurseries, who will supply them in the green by mail order. Many garden centres also sell them in pots. It's as well to buy snowdrops, in particular, from a reputable supplier, then you can be sure that they haven't been uprooted from the wild; an illegal practice which is causing great conservation worries.

Work in some compost or leafmould to enrich the soil before planting; a little bonemeal won't go amiss either. Put the plants in a little deeper than they were previously and water them in if the soil is dry. Overcrowded clumps in the garden can be also be lifted carefully with a fork after flowering and separated out. Replant them singly in informal drifts at the same depth as they were growing.

■ **Pot lilies for planting later.** Lilies are normally planted in autumn in borders and

Planting snowdrops Unlike most other bulbs, snowdrops are planted while in leaf.

Iris reticulata

patio tubs, but if you didn't manage to do it then, you can still have lilies in flower this summer. Even if the soil is too wet for planting outside you can pot up some lily bulbs and either move them or plant them out later in the spring. There should be plenty of lily bulbs in the garden centres to choose from now. Look for good, plump bulbs, avoiding those which have become shrivelled and dry in the sun.

Plant the bulbs three or four to an 18cm (7in) pot and keep them in a cool greenhouse or cold frame. Grow on inside, watering whenever the compost feels dry, to plant out later.

■ **Protect emerging bulbs** in the rock garden. Delightful dwarf bulbs like *Iris reticulata*, *I. histrioides* and *I. danfordiae* will all be coming into flower this month. If they are growing outside they will benefit from some overhead protection. Use a sheet of glass or perspex on bricks or a cloche to prevent the flowers being spoiled by rain and snow. Covering with a cloche brings them into flower a bit earlier too.

An ideal way of growing these wonderful bulbs is in pots or shallow pans. The containers can then be stood on a table or on a low wall and the flowers can be appreciated without having to get down on your knees.

ANNUALS AND BEDDING

■ **Keep a watchful eye** on germinating seedlings sown last month to ensure they get enough light.

■ **Sow hardy annuals in modules.** These cheerful plants are ideal to give a splash of colour. And they are the perfect way to get children interested in gardening. It's very easy to sow hardy annuals outside next month, but if you want to get a head start and have earlier flowers, or if you want young plants to fill containers, then sow them in modular trays. Their advantage is that the plants can be planted out without disturbing the root systems and so they get off to a flying start. Fill the trays with compost, give a sharp tap on the bench to settle the compost, strike off surplus and gently firm with the bottom of another tray. Water the trays and then sow the seeds. Sow a small pinch of seed in each cell and cover with vermiculite. Place in a cold frame or sheltered area and they will germinate in a few days. Plant out when they are big enough to handle.

■ **Continue deadheading winter pansies.** The display will be prolonged. Although they are called "winter-flowering", they will continue to flower into early summer if you are assiduous about deadheading.

■ **Sweet peas can be sown outside** in sheltered southern parts of the country. Sow the seeds 1cm (½in) deep, and to speed up germination and protect the seedlings, cover each one with an improvised cloche, using the cut-off top half of a discarded plastic bottle. Pot up sweet peas sown in autumn under cover if you didn't get around to doing it last month. These plants will be growing well by now and if you want plenty of flowers, pinch out the growing tip to encourage sideshoots. If left unpinched the leading shoot often grows "blind".

CONTAINERS

■ **Check tubs, troughs, and pots** outside for water. Evergreen shrubs are particularly at risk of drying out, as their foliage stops rain from getting into the pot.

■ **Plan now for summer planting** schemes in containers. Time spent now planning what plants and how many to grow in containers is well spent. It's fun browsing through seed catalogues, dreaming up plant and colour combinations. It's all a matter of personal choice and deciding which plants will suit a particular situation, for example sunny or shady positions. If you have space, grow the plants from seed or if you haven't the time for this, all the seed firms sell young plants now, and if you can bring these on under cover you get a much wider choice by buying early.

■ **Top-dress pot-grown shrubs.** Shrubs that have been growing in large pots for many years benefit from top-dressing with fresh compost each year. Scrape away as much of the old compost from the surface as you can – about 2.5cm (1in) is ideal. Then add fresh potting compost with some slow-release fertilizer added. This will feed the plants over a period of several months, doing away with the chore of feeding them every week or month through the spring and summer.

Top-dressing Refreshing the compost makes more nutrients available to pot-grown plants.

LAWNS

■ **Keep off the grass** when it is frozen or frosted, otherwise later, when it thaws out, your footprints will show up as yellow patches on the lawn where the grass has been damaged.

■ **In milder areas**, start mowing. It may seem early, but in warm areas and mild spells, even in winter, the grass will continue to grow, albeit not a great deal. So it does no harm at all to give the lawn an occasional light trim, setting the blades of the mower at their highest setting. Don't do this if the lawn is soaking wet or frozen, or you'll do more harm than good. In more exposed, colder parts of the country, don't mow until next month.

■ **Disperse worm casts.** Brush away worm casts on the lawn regularly. There are no chemicals currently available to amateur gardeners that can be watered onto the lawn to kill worms, but in any case, it is far better to preserve these creatures, which do so much good in the soil by breaking down organic matter and aerating the earth as they move through it.

   Though unappealing, a few worm casts are a small price to pay for having a healthy population of worms in your garden. Brushing the casts to disperse them is the best option.

Worm casts Exposed soil invites opportunistic weeds, so remove worm casts regularly.

A clean sweep Remove worm casts with a stiff broom; brush the exposed earth into the border.

■ **Dig out lawn weeds.** If you have only a few weeds in the lawn, then the ideal way of removing them is individually. Weeds with fibrous root systems such as daisies and plantains are quite easy to deal with; dandelions, which have long tap roots, are trickier. You have to make sure all of the root is removed as any portion left in the soil will grow again. If dandelions are too big to remove with a knife, or weeds are too extensive, use a selective lawn weedkiller or a spot-weeding treatment in the spring.

Making new lawns

■ **Lay turf.** Turf can be laid during this month on ground prepared earlier, provided that the soil is not frozen or so wet that it sticks to your boots.

■ **Prepare ground** for sowing grass seed. If you haven't dug over the ground, now is about the latest time to get the work done for making a new lawn in the spring. By the end of March the soil will have warmed up enough to give grass seed a flying start. The ground should be dug over, incorporating organic matter to help retain moisture and removing all perennial weeds. Remove large stones as you see them. Now leave the ground to settle for a few weeks.

VEGETABLES AND HERBS

■ **Start preparing seedbeds** and cover them with cloches. Soil that has already been covered with polythene for a while should now be dry enough to make a start on preparing seedbeds ready for sowing next month. Rake down the soil until it is reasonably level, removing all the large stones. Apply an organic fertilizer now, about two weeks before sowing, and its nutrients will be available for the young seedlings as they germinate.

Put cloches or polythene over the prepared soil. This will keep off the worst of the winter rain and snow and also help to warm up the soil, enabling earlier sowing and planting outdoors. By making use of cloches you can probably gain about three weeks.

Kits to build cloches and, of course, ready-made cloches are available from garden centres. There are many types to choose from; the more decorative ones usually tending to be the more expensive. I think it's more satisfying to make them yourself if you have the time.

The easiest way to do this is to put wire hoops into the soil at regular intervals and stretch a long sheet of clear polythene between them, burying or pegging the ends of the polythene in the ground at each end to anchor it firmly in place.

■ **Finish preparing deep beds.** Digging of new, deep beds and top-dressing of established ones should be finished now, before the busy seed-sowing time gets under way.

■ **Lime if necessary.** If you follow the crop rotation plan shown in January, about one-third of the vegetable plot probably needs to be limed every year, generally where the brassicas – Brussels sprouts, cabbages, and cauliflowers – are to be grown, as these all like alkaline soil. Lime should be added at least two months before planting, so if you do it now, the beds will be ready when you move transplants into them. But before applying any lime always first check the existing pH (its acidity or alkalinity) of the soil with a soil-testing kit, as this will determine the amount of lime you put on. It may be that if you naturally have a very alkaline soil, you do not need to add lime at all.

The pH of the soil is measured on a scale of 1–14, by which the alkalinity or acidity of the soil is assessed. Around 7 is neutral; values less than 7 are acid, and higher than 7, alkaline. Soil-testing kits are remarkably easy to use; most come with a numbered chart to which you match the colour of your soil sample, after mixing it with the solutions provided.

Once you know your soil's pH, the instructions on the packet will help you add the correct quantity of lime. Wear gloves, goggles, and a face mask, and choose a still day. It's safest to use ordinary garden lime, calcium carbonate – or the organic alternative, dolomitic limestone – rather than quicklime or slaked lime; although more effective, these are highly caustic.

Warm up seedbeds Make simple tunnel cloches with plastic sheeting and wire hoops.

Harvesting

■ **Continue to harvest winter crops** and make checks on any chicory being forced.

Sowing indoors

■ **Keep on sowing early crops** and take care of those sown earlier.

■ **Sow peas in guttering.** An ideal way of sowing peas is to sow them in a piece of plastic guttering, choosing an early variety such as 'Douce Provence'. You will have to drill drainage holes in the bottom of the guttering, then fill with a peat-free seed compost. Sow the seeds evenly in two rows 2.5–5cm (1–2in) apart and about 2.5cm (1in) deep, and water thoroughly. Keep them on a windowsill or in a greenhouse; it does not need to be heated, although bottom heat will speed up germination. When the seedlings have sprouted a few leaves they can be planted out under a cloche by carefully sliding them out of the guttering into a shallow trench already made in the soil.

Sowing and planting outdoors

■ **Sow seeds under cloches** – towards the end of the month in colder areas – provided that the soil has been covered for a few weeks to warm it up. Seeds to sow include lettuce, radish, salad onions, peas, broad beans, beetroot, summer cabbage, and spinach.

To sow the seeds, rake the soil to a fine tilth, which should be easy if the soil has dried out under cover. Then make shallow drills with a cane to the depth required and space the drills at the distance given on the seed packet. Water along the drills first, before you start sowing. If you water after sowing the seeds may be washed deeper into the soil, making germination more difficult or even impossible. After watering, sow the seeds as thinly as possible and cover over carefully with

Sowing peas in guttering

Space out all the peas before pushing them in, so you don't lose track of where you've got to.

Once the seedlings have a few pairs of leaves, the whole lot can simply be "shunted" into a trench.

dry soil. Firm down with your hand and the job's done. Put a cloche on top and wait for the seeds to germinate. Thin out the seedlings when they are large enough to handle; the spacing to thin to will be given on the back of the seed packets, too, so don't throw them away, but keep them somewhere safe.

■ **Plant shallots.** It may seem too early to be doing this, but now is the time. Prepare the ground thoroughly, if you have not done this earlier, incorporating plenty of organic matter. Add an organic fertilizer and rake the soil to a fine tilth. Plant the shallots 15–18cm (6–7in) apart, in rows the same distance apart. Don't just push them into the soil, or the new roots, as they form, will push the bulbs up and out again. Birds love to pull them out, too, if they see them. The best way to plant the shallots is with a trowel, with the bulb tips just beneath the surface of the soil.

■ **Plant Jerusalem artichokes.** These are difficult to site within a traditional

vegetable plot because they grow enormously tall and cast a lot of shade. But they are ideal plants if you want a productive summer screen for a garden shed or the compost heap. Do be aware, though, that they will spread rapidly, so keep an eye on them before they take over the garden. The tubers, which look like long knobbly potatoes, should be planted in a single row 15cm (6in) deep and 30cm (1ft) apart. They will grow quite tall in their first year, perhaps to 2m (6ft), and may need some staking, as the tall stems can be battered to the ground in wet weather. One way of supporting them is to drive four stakes into the ground, two at each end of the row and run string or thin wire around them. The tubers are harvested from autumn through winter.

Planning ahead

■ **Prepare a bed for planting asparagus.** This delicious vegetable is quite easy to grow in the garden, but it is a long-term crop and will occupy a place of its own for several years, so you need to plan for this.

This month, prepare the soil by digging thoroughly, removing perennial weeds completely and incorporating plenty of organic matter.

■ **Prepare trenches for runner beans.** If you want a delicious and heavy crop of runner beans, now is the time to prepare a bean trench. The better the preparation is now, the better the crop will be later on. Take out a trench, to the depth of a spade and 45cm (18in) wide, and heap the soil up on either side. It need not be a straight trench – it could be a ring shape if you are planning to grow the beans up wigwams. These are often easier to site than rows in a small garden, because they only cast a slim pointer of shade that moves around with the sun. Put as much organic matter as you can into the bottom of the trench and fork it in well. If you are short of organic matter, old newspapers torn into strips will do fine. After digging in the organic matter leave the trench open, just as it is, to allow the weather to break down the soil, improving its structure right up until it's time to sow or plant.

■ **Sprout early seed potatoes** if this was not done last month.

Looking after crops

■ **Feed spring cabbages.** Cabbages that have been standing all winter will benefit from a feed now. Use a general organic fertilizer to help boost the growth. As you harvest, cut every alternate plant in the row, leaving the others to grow on and form a heart in late spring.

It is possible to get a second crop from cabbages that have already been cut. Leave the stem and root in the soil and make a cross-cut on the top of the stump. Feed the plant and in a few weeks "mini-cabbages" will grow from the cuts.

Preparing a runner bean trench

Because they grow so large, runner beans are notoriously hungry plants. A specially dug bean trench filled with compost or manure is the traditional way to create a super-rich bed to supply all the nutrients they need.

1 Mark out the position of your row and dig a trench about 60cm (2ft) wide. Loosen the soil in the base with a fork.

2 Tip manure plus kitchen or garden waste into the trench, replace the soil, and scatter over pelleted poultry manure. Leave it all to rot down thoroughly.

Herbs

■ **Cover parsley** and other overwintering herbs with horticultural fleece or cloches. This will help to protect the plants from pests and bring them into growth a little bit earlier.

■ **Mint is an excellent herb** to have with the first of the early potatoes dug fresh from the garden. A few roots dug and potted up now will provide sprigs in the kitchen ready for the first vegetables of the new season. This is quite a good way to grow mint outside, as it tends to be very invasive, easily taking over parts of the garden. Grow it in a large pot and stand this on the terrace, or plunge the pot into the ground, leaving the top 5–10cm (2–4in) of the pot proud of the soil surface. This will usually prevent the mint from creeping over the rim into the soil, but it's best to keep an eye on it anyway.

■ **Top-dress shrubby herbs in pots,** such as bay and rosemary, with fertilizer.

Propagating mint suckers Cut above a leaf node into sections 8cm (3in) long and insert four or five into a pot so that at least one pair of young leaves is just above the surface.

FRUIT
Picking and storing
■ **Continue to check all fruit** you have in store. Any that are showing signs of rotting should be removed immediately. If left, rot will quickly spread through the rest of the fruits. Put not-too-rotten fruits out for the birds to feed on.

Looking after crops
■ **Feed all fruit,** unless you did so towards the end of last month.

■ **Sprinkle sulphate of potash** around fruit trees – or use rock potash. To get good-quality crops, fruit trees need a high-potash fertilizer. Normal organic fertilizer is not especially high in any one nutrient, so supplementing it with a little extra potash will go a long way to helping you produce good-quality fruit. Spread it below the trees or bushes in an area equal to the spread of the branches. Use fertilizers strictly according to the manufacturer's instructions.

■ **Mulch all fruit** with well-rotted manure or garden compost. It is well worth doing this after pruning and feeding has been done. Not only will a mulch help to keep down weeds, it will also hold in moisture. This cuts down watering in the warm summer months and will give you better-quality fruit. If the soil is dry, soak the ground first before applying the mulch. Mulch is as good at keeping water out as retaining it in the soil. You can lay seep- or tricklehose beneath the mulch to make watering in the summer simple.

■ **Complete spraying** with plant oil winter wash. Winter washes can help to prevent pests and diseases later in the year, but they must only be used on trees and bushes that are fully dormant – which means this month is your last opportunity to use them until next winter.

■ **Check that newly planted fruit** is not lifted by frost. February can often bring the most severe weather of the winter, with hard, penetrating frosts.

When soil freezes, the water in the soil expands and this can ease newly planted trees and shrubs slightly out of the soil. This loosens the plant's grip on the soil, and if left, it will be rocked about in windy conditions, eventually killing it. So it is a good idea to check newly planted fruit when the frost has thawed and firm in any plants affected.

■ **Check tree ties and stakes.** Loosen any ties that are too tight or they will strangle the tree.

■ **Check fruit trees** for signs of canker.

■ **Continue to protect fruit trees** and bushes from birds using netting, mesh, or webbing. Bullfinches, in particular, are especially fond of gooseberry buds. If you didn't net the plants last month, do it now. Make sure coverings are supported off the plants, yet taut and held down firmly on the ground, otherwise the birds may get caught up in and be injured. An ideal way of growing gooseberries is to train them as cordons (one single stem) or as fans against a wall or fence. This way netting them against birds is a much easier task. If you have a lot of gooseberries and other fruits it may be worth investing in a proper fruit cage.

■ **Protect peaches and nectarines** against peach leaf curl if this was not done last month. This disease's symptoms show up as puckering and blistering of the leaves later in the year. The disease develops when spores lodged in the buds infect emerging leaves under wet conditions. The ideal way to prevent it is by covering the plants through the winter or by taking pot-grown trees under cover. You will need to hand-pollinate the flowers using a soft brush; brush pollen from flower to flower all over the plant, at least twice while the flowers are open.

Pruning and training
■ **Finish winter-pruning fruit trees,** which will be starting into growth any time now. If pruning is done as the trees come into growth, the rising sap will ooze out from any large cuts, weakening the tree. This may also encourage disease to invade the wound.

■ **Prune autumn-fruiting raspberries.** Make sure you know the distinction between the pruning times and methods for summer- and autumn-fruiting raspberries. If you get it wrong then you lose a crop for the year. Autumn-fruiting raspberries, which are pruned now, produce their fruit from August or September onwards on long stems – canes – that grew during that summer. The best variety is called 'September'. Summer-fruiting raspberries will fruit on the canes that grew the previous year.

Prune autumn raspberries Canes left over winter should be pruned right down to ground level now. New canes will soon grow.

Autumn-fruiting raspberries should now have all their growth pruned to the ground. Sprinkle a high-potash organic fertilizer around the plants, and you should get strong canes growing that will produce a good crop of fruit. The stems of autumn-fruiting raspberries are quite sturdy and they don't need tying in and training. You can wind twine along the rows and around posts at each end to keep them neat, but don't restrict them too much, to allow sun to reach all of the ripening fruits.

■ **Summer-fruiting raspberry canes** that have grown taller than their support frame can have the tips of the canes pruned back to one or two buds from the top wire. Alternatively, they can be arched over and tied down to the top wire. Both options encourage the formation of sideshoots along the length of the cane, which means you will be rewarded with a heavier crop of fruit.

Planting

■ **Plant bare-root fruit trees and bushes** this month. If the soil was not prepared during the winter, be sure to incorporate plenty of organic matter before planting. The best way to do this is to dig in muck to the entire planting, but only use well-rotted farmyard manure. Fresh stuff will scorch the roots. A feed of general fertilizer will also help your trees get off to a good start. When planting out bare-root stock, always match the depth at which they were planted in the nursery: look for the darker mark on the main stem. Insert a stake for trees, tying the tree to it with a proper tree tie, before refilling the hole and you won't cut through any roots. Mulch with organic matter after planting and keep the young trees or bushes well watered in their first year until they get established.

■ **Plant raspberries and blackberries, and hybrid berry canes.** Towards the end of the month is the latest time for planting bare-root cane fruits. Have the soil thoroughly prepared by digging a trench all along the proposed row and working in plenty of organic matter, if not done during the winter. All except the autumn-fruiting raspberries will need support for the fruiting canes. This is usually given by posts at either end of the row with at least three horizontal wires strained between the posts. Freestanding rows should be at least 1.5m (5ft) apart. If you are using a wall or fence for blackberries and hybrid berries, then you may be able to attach the wires to vine eyes in the wall. Plant raspberries about 45cm (18in) apart in the row. Blackberries and hybrid berries need to be at least 1.5m (5ft) apart, and some vigorous cultivars may need even more space: ask the nursery for advice. Prune the newly planted canes to about 22cm (9in) from the ground. This is essential to encourage the good, strong-fruiting canes from the base of the plant. Later in the summer you can cut it right out. Tie the canes to the wires as they grow through the season, but don't take a crop this year.

Planting raspberries Plant new canes in trenches with plenty of organic matter and provide support such as three wires stretched between posts at each end of the row.

The odd fruit is alright, but remove flowers if there are a lot of them. At this time you are trying to get the plants established. They will then give a good crop next year.

Beat the seasons

■ **Continue to force rhubarb.** If you didn't cover rhubarb last month, do it now, because it will soon be starting to grow.

■ **Cover strawberries with cloches** for an early crop. As well as forcing strawberries in pots in the greenhouse, a succession of fruits can be obtained by covering some plants outside with cloches. Any cloche will do, but once the strawberries are in flower, open the sides during the day to allow pollinating insects to go in. Keep an eye out for pests, especially greenfly. Use an insecticide if you do not garden organically, or an organic spray. Alternatively, be vigilant, and squash any greenfly you see.

UNDER COVER

■ **Clean out greenhouse** and conservatory gutters, as these may be full of leaves.

■ **Ventilate on good days.** With the lengthening days in February we often get warmish sunny spells that can send temperatures under glass soaring rapidly. Open ventilators, when you can, to maintain more even temperatures, but not so much that you let in cold draughts, which can affect growth. Remember to close the ventilators well before sundown.

The aim is to keep the temperature even. The less difference between day and night, the better for plants, otherwise they may produce spindly growth because of the warmth and the relative lack of light during the short days of winter. Keeping air circulating will also cut down diseases.

■ **Fuchsias in heated greenhouses and conservatories** can be sprayed with water to encourage growth. Those fuchsias that were started into growth and repotted last month will be showing signs of growing. Spraying with clear water occasionally helps buds to break and also keeps a humid atmosphere around the plants, which is ideal. Plants pruned early last month should now be producing new shoots and some can be used for making cuttings to increase your stock. Taking tip cuttings from a stock plant will also encourage more sideshoots, and therefore more flowers.

■ **Prune tender perennials** such as pelargoniums (geraniums), fuchsias, argyranthemums, lantanas, and salvias that have been overwintering, dormant, in cool greenhouses. These older plants can now be taken out of their pots or boxes. If they are not pruned now, they become very tall, with all the flowers at the top of the plant. Prune all the main stems back to two or three buds, or 5–8cm (2–3in) from their point of origin. Prune sideshoots quite hard to one or two buds from the main stems. Any prunings about 8cm (3in) long can be made into cuttings, increasing your stock. At the same time prune out dead or diseased material and any shoots crossing each other, to open up the centre of the plant. Repot the plants into pots of fresh compost, gently firming around the roots, and water them in. After a few weeks new shoots will grow to give a stunning display over summer, inside or out.

■ **Make sure seedlings** get enough light, otherwise they will grow tall and leggy trying to reach the light – and then, being weak, they will be more susceptible to attack from diseases such as botrytis and damping off. Once germinated, move them to a high shelf, to get maximum light. If they are growing on a windowsill, turn them at least once a day.

■ **Watch for damping off** in seedlings. Warm, moist conditions encourage damping-off disease, causing rotting off and collapse. The best way to control damping off is to practise good greenhouse hygiene and not to sow seeds too thickly. Don't allow seedlings to get too wet either.

■ **Prick out seedlings.** If you sowed seed in small pots or trays in order to fit more into your propagator, then once they have developed two leaves move them into more spacious surroundings to give them room to develop and reduce the risk of damping off. This is called "pricking out".

Replant the seedlings either 2.5cm (1in) apart in larger trays, or into the individual cells of a module tray to grow on. Gently hold them by the leaves, but do not pull them; rather lever them out from below. Drop them into holes dibbled in the compost and just nudge some compost into the hole to fill. Don't be tempted to firm or press the surface. Water them in.

Cuttings from fuchsias

1 **The tips of shoots** at least 2.5cm (1in) long can be rooted successfully. Remove the cutting just above a bud. Trim just below it and remove the lower leaves, making sure that there are at least two leaves left at the tip.

2 **Slice the leaves** in half to reduce transpiration of water from the leaves.

3 **Dip the base** of each cutting in hormone rooting solution and put each in a module cell containing a mixture of equal parts peat-free compost and vermiculite.

4 **Water the cuttings** and put in a propagator at 18–21°C (65–70°F). The cuttings will root in three to four weeks and can then be moved onto a bench or windowsill.

Prick out seedlings Carefully hold the seedling by its leaves and use a dibber or pencil to gently ease it out of the pot from below.

Raising plants for outdoors

■ **Order plug plants.** With a greenhouse, you have the first choice of young bedding plants to raise under glass, so place your orders now.

■ **Sow hardy annuals in modules.**

■ **Sow seeds of *Impatiens*** (busy Lizzies). This is a difficult plant to grow from seed, so if you're a beginner, it's probably not worth trying yet. But if you have a knack for raising seedlings, it will save you some money. The seed can be difficult because it needs light to germinate, so it can't be covered and it also needs a constant warm temperature with a humid atmosphere.

The easiest way to get them to germinate is to draw shallow drills with a label across the compost in a seed tray, sow the seeds in these little drills, and lightly cover them with vermiculite. The vermiculite holds moisture and still lets light through. Place the tray in a propagator, put a sheet of glass over the tray to hold in the moisture and keep at a temperature of 21°C (70°F). The seeds should germinate in two to three weeks.

■ **Sow sweet peas** if not done last month, and pot up those sown in autumn.

■ **Sow early crops** in succession to those sown in January: for example, peas in guttering and broad beans in modules.

Glasshouse and house plants

■ **Freesias and lachenalias** that have finished flowering can be rested. Bulbs planted last August will be coming to the end of their flowering period and will have to be fed to build up their reserves before resting for the summer. Feed them every week now for three or four weeks with a high-potash liquid feed to build up the bulbs for next year and then gradually reduce watering until foliage dies back. The best way of resting the bulbs is to lay the pots on their sides under a bench, to be restarted into growth next autumn.

■ **Start off *Begonia*, *Gloxinia*, and *Achimenes* tubers.** All can be started into growth this month and through to March. *Begonia* and *Gloxinia* tubers can be placed several to a seed tray, or potted individually into small pots and then potted into larger pots as they grow. The tubers of both are slightly hollow on one side and this should be uppermost when the tubers are planted. Plant them so that they are just covered with compost, as they form roots all over the surface of the tuber. *Achimenes* have small tubers about 2.5cm (1in) long, and these can be laid on their sides several to a pot and potted on as necessary. Normal room temperature is quite sufficient. It is an easy way of growing these plants if you cannot maintain high enough temperatures to germinate their seed.

■ **Prune indoor climbers** such as plumbago and passion flowers. These popular climbers for heated greenhouses and conservatories are pruned in similar ways. The passion flower is a vigorous climbing plant and can be trained against a wall. Prune all the shoots to within two or three buds from where the previous year's growth started. Plumbago is best tied to a support. To prune it, shorten all sideshoots to one to two buds of the previous year's growth.

■ **Repot or top-dress citrus trees.** These will be putting on new growth, so they will need either potting on into larger pots – or, larger, more mature, plants can be top-dressed with fresh potting compost. To top-dress, scrape away as much of the old compost as you can without exposing and damaging roots, and replace it with fresh loam-based compost such as John Innes No 3.

■ **Plant out lily-of-the-valley** that was lifted and potted in the autumn for indoor display. Now plant in fertile, humus-rich soil outside in sun or partial shade.

Crops under glass

■ **Continue to force strawberries.** The first batch brought in in January will be starting to grow, so a second batch brought in now will provide a succession of succulent fruits much earlier than outside. If you cover a few plants outdoors with cloches this will continue the succession from those in the greenhouse, until uncovered plants fruit naturally.

Water and feed the indoor plants with a high-potash fertilizer to ensure good-quality fruits. Once they begin to grow, watch for aphids, which can become quite active. Once any flowers appear, they will need hand-pollination in the sheltered conditions under glass.

THE MARCH GARDEN

The first month of spring has arrived at last and the garden really begins to come alive after the long dreary winter. But this can be a tricky month as far as the weather goes; it's possible to get mild sunshine one day, only to be followed by a hard frost the next, so be sure to make the most of bright spells. You can mulch and prune, take cuttings, reseed lawns, and sow half-hardy annuals.

THINGS TO DO

Start mowing lawns regularly, and reseed any bare patches.

Mulch bare soil in borders.

Put pond pumps back into the pond, making sure they're safe.

Water your indoor plants regularly.

Propagate shrubs by layering.

Prune shrubs with colourful winter stems.

Prune bush and shrub roses.

Move evergreen shrubs.

Increase stocks of herbaceous perennials by taking basal stem cuttings, and take cuttings from dahlia tubers.

Split polyanthus after flowering.

Sow sweet peas outdoors, or plant out young plants raised under cover.

Sow hardy annuals where they are to flower, and sow vegetables outside.

Harden off young vegetable plants to put outside.

Plant early potatoes and asparagus.

Protect fruit blossom against late frosts.

LAST CHANCE

Finish planting bare-root trees and shrubs.

Plant snowdrops and winter aconites.

GET AHEAD

Take growing bags into the greenhouse to warm up before planting.

Put stakes in to support perennials later in the year.

Willow talk The buds breaking on bare willow stems (*Salix*) reveal silky, silver-grey catkins: a sure sign that spring is on the way.

COMING ALIVE

The clocks going forward gives gardeners much-needed extra time for getting everything done – and there's quite a list. But the riot of spring colours in flowering shrubs and blossoms will give plenty of encouragement. March can be cold, but you'll get plenty of bright days, too.

A profusion of spring flowers should now be brightening up the garden. Spring-flowering bulbs are coming into their own and towards the end of the month, those stalwart flowering shrubs, the forsythias, bring forth their stunning show of bright yellow flowers. Some early-flowering cherry trees herald the spectacular display of blossom to come next month.

Later in the month the clocks go forward, lengthening daylight hours. Even at this time of year you'll find there aren't enough hours in the day for all the gardening you want to do.

Take it easy at first

If you've been slumbering in an armchair all winter and have a sudden urge to get out and put the garden to rights now that it's spring, then do take it gently at first. But don't let me put you off! Gardening is great exercise and there is nothing better for clearing out the cobwebs than working in the garden on a clear, warm spring day. Just take it easy to begin with. Before starting any strenuous jobs such as digging, do some warm-up stretching exercises to ease yourself into the work. And jobs such as digging are best done in short spells – a

Deep-red new shoots *Paeonia lactiflora* 'Sante Fe' emerges against a blue background of *Chionodoxa forbesii*, creating a striking contrast.

whole day doing one job with repetitive movements may harm your back. So do about half an hour's digging at first, before switching to another job that does not involve too much bending.

Changeable weather

The weather can be fickle at this time of year, with one day having clear, blue skies and the next wintry showers. Make the best of good weather and crack on with tasks such as making seed beds for sowing hardy annuals outside and in the vegetable garden, on the soil which was covered with polythene sheets or cloches earlier in the year. Do always bear in mind that we can still get sharp frosts, so don't be tempted to buy bedding plants starting to appear at garden centres – unless you have a greenhouse or frost-free place in which to keep them until all danger of frost has passed. And don't be in a hurry to remove protection from those frost-tender plants which were covered or wrapped up over winter. Plants can be uncovered during the day, but keep the protective material to hand in case frost is forecast at night.

Deciding when to sow outside

Sowing seeds of hardy vegetables and annual flowers outside can begin in earnest this month in most parts of the country, but in northerly parts wait until the end of the month or until early April before making a start. And if you have a heavy clay soil, then you, too, may have to delay sowing, unless you've had the ground covered during part of the winter. Remember that while books such as this one can give general advice about when to do certain jobs, you should always be guided by local weather conditions before deciding to sow seeds or plant out young plants.

This year, try planting vegetables among flowers if your garden is small. Most modern gardens are too small to accommodate a separate kitchen garden, but fruit, vegetables, herbs, and ornamentals can be grown together very successfully. Many vegetables are attractive plants in their own right and they can make wonderful contrasts to other ornamental plants in the borders. The fine, feathery foliage of carrots contrasts well, for instance, with the bold leaves of hostas.

Weather watch

Although March can be a cold month, on the whole temperatures are rising. However, sharp frosts may descend on the land on clear nights, turning the ground hard, so don't put out tender plants yet. Cloud cover and wind will also have a direct effect on temperatures throughout each day.

Cold winds

March winds can be bitterly cold, but they do help to dry out the soil after winter rains and snow. High ground above 100m (328ft) and exposed coastal areas, especially the west coast, can still be subject to gales for 0.6 to 4.3 days. In the south gales will occur on an average of 0.2–1.5 days in the month. All coastal areas, whichever way they face, are windier than inland, and the winds carry salt spray, which can damage plants.

More sunshine

The longer days of spring bring more chance of increased hours of bright sunshine each day. The north will still have less, on average, than the south. Clouds will, however, cut down the amount of direct sunshine everywhere on most days.

Rainfall

The amount of rain falling depends on how hilly or flat it is. Areas like the Lake District and the Western Highlands of Scotland have similar amounts of rain. But in the south-east of England the average is 41mm. Low-lying areas may be prone to floods as snow on hills begins to thaw.

Late spring snow

Heavy snowfalls are rare this month, but in north-eastern areas, especially, snow can still be thick on the ground, making spring later than in other parts. At Braemar in north-east Scotland, one of the coldest places in the country, even in March there will be 10 or more days of snow. In the south of England 0.9 to 1.4 days of snowfall is an average figure. It's rare that snow lies on the ground at sea level.

New shoots Salad leaves sown under cover will be ready to be transplanted outside in the vegetable patch.

Prevent weeds You can reduce weeding by planting through a permeable membrane. Clear perennial weeds, cultivate and level the soil, then lay the fabric. Cut small holes to plant into, and cover with a decorative mulch.

Bright-coloured bedding plants can be set against the rich foliage of beetroot and ruby chard. Globe artichokes and cardoons are striking architectural plants and stand out in any border. You can have great fun mixing and matching plants and as well as the garden looking attractive it will be productive, too. Sow or plant the vegetables in groups rather than the conventional rows, and they will blend in perfectly.

Watch out for weeds

Remember that many little jobs contributing to help keep the garden looking good can be done at the gentlest of paces. While having constitutional walks around the garden, keep a watch out for germinating weed seedlings and have them out with a hoe. The best time to do this is on a dry, sunny day, so that the weeds can be left on the surface of the soil to dry off and shrivel up in the warmth of the sun. Dig out any perennial weeds while they too are small, and they will be easier to control.

Weeding can become a bit of a chore, so to cut down on the time spent doing it, it is a good idea to mulch borders with a thick layer of organic matter after beds and borders have been tidied. An effective way to prevent weeds growing, mulching is also the perfect way to help conserve soil moisture, cutting down on the need to water as frequently during dry summer spells. Although it may seem hard to believe, water is becoming a scarce commodity, owing to adverse changes in weather patterns worldwide caused by global warming and we must all do our best to conserve it.

The best time for applying a mulch is early in spring while the soil is still moist; this way the moisture will not evaporate from the soil surface so rapidly. Water first if the weather has been dry. If a layer of mulch is applied to dry soil then it will make it difficult for water to penetrate the soil at all.

Rose pruning

This is the traditional time for pruning bush and shrub roses, although it can be done at any time over winter. Firstly, the more growth in general you can leave intact in the garden over winter, the more shelter you give to hibernating wildlife. Secondly, if your roses have taken a

A decorative willow fence This has been created by pushing live willow wands into the soil. Bluebells emerge from the grass behind it.

battering over winter – and pruned roses are not immune to this – then you can tailor your pruning to leave you with the best-shaped plants after removing the damage. Don't be shy about pruning bush roses hard. Modern bush roses tend to be grafted onto the roots of more vigorous species and are strong growers – they rise to the challenge of hard pruning by producing really good growth and flowers.

Pest patrol

Pests and diseases begin to make their presence felt in earnest from this month onwards, particularly in the greenhouse, conservatory or the home – on house

plants, not the family! Consider using biological controls this year, such as predators or tiny nematode worms that kill specific pests. These are regularly advertised in the gardening press and you can order them by mail. Most are for use in the greenhouse, but there is one that can be watered onto open ground to control slugs. The sooner you can get on top of a slug or snail problem the better – at this time of year, they're just as eager as we are to see all that tender new growth emerging from the soil!

***Doronicum* x *excelsum* 'Harpur Crewe'**
One of the earliest-flowering perennials (*see p.293*)

Fritillaria imperialis
Striking plant with clusters of bellflowers on tall stems (*see p.297*)

Muscari armeniacum ♀
The grape hyacinth, with small but intensely coloured flowers (*see p.311*)

***Salix caprea* 'Kilmarnock'**
Small tree with drooping branches festooned with catkins (*see p.327*)

Iris danfordiae
Dwarf bulb ideal for an alpine trough or raised bed (*see p.303*)

***Pulmonaria angustifolia* 'Azurea'** ♀
Herbaceous ground-cover perennial for sun or shade (*see p.321*)

***Narcissus* 'Dutch Master'** ♀
Classic golden-yellow daffodil with trumpet flowers (*see p.311*)

***Chionodoxa forbesii* 'Pink Giant'**
Small bulb, lovely planted under deciduous shrubs (*see p.283*)

Daphne mezereum
Exquisitely perfumed pink flowers clustered on bare branches (*see p.292*)

***Hyacinthus orientalis* 'City of Haarlem'** ♀
Bulb for indoor forcing or spring bedding (*see p.302*)

***Corylus avellana* 'Contorta'** ♀
Hazel bearing long catkins on contorted branches (*see p.289*)

***Anemone blanda* 'Violet Star'**
Plant tubers in autumn for a starry spring display (*see p.277*)

Lysichiton americanus ♀
Perennial for damp ground or shallow water (*see p.309*)

Iris 'Katharine Hodgkin' ♀
Dwarf bulb, ideal for an alpine trough or raised bed (*see p.304*)

Primula 'Miss Indigo'
Small but showy perennial for early spring display (*see p.319*)

Caltha palustris ♀
Water-loving perennial for pond margins and boggy ground (*see p.281*)

Prunus sargentii ♀
Flowering cherry tree with young leaves, to 20m (60ft) tall (*see p.320*)

Narcissus 'Cheerfulness' ♀
Double-flowered narcissus with a powerful scent (*see p.311*)

***Chaenomeles* x *superba* 'Knap Hill Scarlet'** ♀
Stiff-branched shrub perfect for wall-training (*see p.283*)

***Scilla siberica* 'Spring Beauty'**
Bulb, similar to but less invasive than bluebells (*see p.329*)

Forsythia* x *intermedia
Cheerful shrub tolerant of most soils and positions (*see p.297*)

***Primula* Gold-laced Group**
Showy, unusual polyanthus-type primula (*see p.319*)

***Crocus vernus* 'Pickwick'**
A spring favourite with attractively striped petals (*see p.291*)

***Tulipa tarda* ♀**
Small species tulip, short-stemmed, pretty in a rock garden (*see p.333*)

WHAT TO DO IN MARCH

AROUND THE GARDEN

With warmer weather, pests are now on the increase, so keep an eye open for signs of infestation. If you pick or rub pests off as soon as they appear (or prune out badly infested shoots) you can stop them multiplying and causing more trouble later on.

Mulch bare soil, having weeded and tidied it first, with organic matter like well-rotted farmyard manure, cocoa shells, garden compost, chipped bark or spent mushroom compost (avoid using the latter around acid-loving plants like rhododendrons, because it contains lime). Soil in borders left bare will very quickly lose water in dry spells. Covering with a thick layer of organic matter will cut down the rate at which water evaporates from the soil, reducing the need to water. This is especially important for young trees, shrubs, and perennials that have been recently planted. After spending hard-earned cash on plants, never let them go short of water in their first year. A mulch will also suppress weeds and it looks good too. Never put a mulch on top of dry soil. If the soil is dry, water it first. A layer of compost is just as good at keeping water out as sealing it in.

Mulching Use a spade to spread a generous layer of organic matter over the soil; it should be at least 5cm (2in) deep.

TREES AND SHRUBS

■ **Move any evergreen shrubs.** Evergreens moved in winter are unable to replace water lost from their leaves through the action of frost and strong cold winds. Plants generally do not take up water from the soil until the temperature rises above 4–5°C (around 40°F). Now the soil is beginning to warm up and the shrubs will shortly begin to grow; they will therefore lose less water, helping them re-establish. When moving shrubs, take as large a rootball as you can manage. Provide protection from cold winds with a screen of hessian and if you keep the shrub well-watered it should grow away well.

■ **Feed winter-flowering heathers** pruned in February with a high-nitrogen feed. For an organic option choose dried blood, fishmeal, or pelleted poultry manure.

Planting

■ **Finish planting bare-root trees** and shrubs. This really is the last month, until autumn, to get these plants in. With the leaves opening up they find it much more difficult to establish, because they are losing water rapidly from the foliage. Plants grown in containers can be planted year-round, although spring and autumn, the traditional times, are best.

■ **Prune roses now** unless you got a head start last month. Prune bush and shrub roses now. Climbers are usually pruned in the autumn, so that they can be tidied up and tied in before winter winds blow them about. Never prune ramblers in the spring unless you need to drastically renovate them, as you will lose this year's flowers. Prune them after flowering. The main reason for pruning roses is to build a healthy framework of shoots that will produce a good display of flowers. Thinning overcrowded growth allows in light and air, so there will be less chance of problems with pests and diseases, and also

Transplanting a shrub

1 Mark out a circle around the outer edge of the roots using a spade. The rootzone is usually a similar area to the spread of the branches.

2 Dig a trench around the circle and use a fork to loosen the soil around the roots. With a spade, dig under the rootball so that it can be lifted.

3 Tilt the plant to one side and feed a piece of hessian or ground sheet under it. It usually helps to have a second pair of hands.

4 Carry the shrub to its new location in the garden. Two or more people may be needed if the rootball is large and heavy.

5 Dig a hole that is twice as wide and the same depth as the rootball at the new site. Carefully lower the shrub into the new hole and fill in with soil.

6 Firm the soil with your foot and water in very well before and after you refill the hole with soil. Ensure there are no air gaps and apply mulch.

encourages strong healthy growth. Cuts must be clean, not ragged or bruised, so use a good pair of sharp secateurs. You may also need loppers for thicker shoots.

The first thing to do on any type of rose is to remove any dead or unhealthy wood. Leaving this on the plant can encourage diseases to invade. The next is to cut out any shoots that are crossing and rubbing against another.

Now the flowering wood can be pruned and here the method varies depending on the rose type. Always prune to outward-facing buds. The main rule to remember is that the harder you prune, the more vigorous the subsequent growth will be.

Clear up rose prunings carefully or they will ambush you later. It's best to dispose of or burn them, rather than shredding them for composting, as they can harbour disease. Then mulch around the roses, with well-rotted farmyard manure, or a bagged product such as shredded bark.

■ **Prune shrubby eucalyptus.** Not all of us have room to grow eucalyptus as a tree, but it responds well to hard pruning, making a lovely foliage shrub. Just prune all last year's growth to 15cm (6in) from the ground and you will be rewarded with the attractive, round juvenile leaves on a small bushy plant.

■ **Prune dogwoods** and shrubby willows grown for their ornamental coloured stems. The best stem colour from *Cornus* and *Salix* is produced by one-year-old shoots and this is the reason for pruning them in spring. Ornamental *Rubus,* with their white stems, should be pruned now too. Prune all these shrubs hard, to about one or two buds of last year's growth, to leave a stubby framework.

■ **Finish pruning late-flowering shrubs** such as *Buddleja davidii.*

Planning ahead
■ **Prepare for moving** large, deciduous shrubs. You can still move them, but it's better to start preparing them for moving after the summer. Trees and shrubs often transplant more successfully when they have a good fibrous root system. Many shrubs and trees don't make very fibrous root systems, but rooting can be encouraged. Dig a narrow trench around the plant to be moved, to at least a spade's depth. This will cut through some of the roots and encourage the formation of new, fine roots within the circle. The trench can either be refilled with the soil taken out or with a compost mixture. Old potting compost is quite good, or fine, well-rotted garden compost mixed with the soil. In autumn, when you dig around the shrub to move it, you will find that finer roots have formed and the shrub will have a much better chance of re-establishing well.

Propagation
■ **Layer shrubs to make new plants.** This is a good month to increase shrubs by layering. Many shrubs, like hydrangeas and philadelphus, will layer themselves, forming roots on shoots touching the ground.

■ **Layering** is quite easy. Usually, wounding the stem is enough to stimulate root growth, but if you want to encourage the process, you can also dust the wound with hormone rooting powder before pegging it down. The layered shoot will have formed roots by the following spring, when it can be cut from the parent plant and planted elsewhere.

Hedges
■ **Buy and plant** bare-root hedging plants. This is your last chance; from now until the autumn only container-grown plants will generally be available, which can make buying in bulk for hedges expensive.

CLIMBERS
■ **Plant new climbers**. Make sure supports such as wires and trellis are fixed up before you buy and plant. Wires may stand out at first, but are soon hidden by the plants.

■ **Finish pruning** late-flowering clematis.

■ **Prune climbing roses now** if you didn't do so in autumn.

■ **Renovate climbers.** Tackle overgrown climbers. Wait for the buds to break before you start so that you can see which stems are dead. Climbers to cut back hard include honeysuckles, rambling roses, and winter jasmine.

Training up a pergola
1 Twist in four metal screw eyes at the top of each support and repeat this at the bottoms. Thread plastic-coated wire, secure, and pull taut.

2 Secure the climber to individual wires with soft garden twine. Twirling the plant around the support and tying it in ensures maximum coverage.

PERENNIALS

■ **Cut down all growth left over winter.**
Even if seedheads and stems are still managing to look good, you need to get rid of them now to make way for new growth.

After a good tidy up, if you didn't feed plants last month, you can dress the soil with a fertilizer now so that it is ready for a layer of mulch.

■ **In the south and in mild areas,** remove any cloches or protective blankets from plants susceptible to frost, or new shoots may be damaged. In colder regions it may be safer to wait until April. Give the plants a feed to get them going. You can also divide overgrown clumps.

■ **New shoots** should now be growing strongly from the crowns and it is an ideal time to increase plants such as achilleas, anthemis, delphiniums, gypsophilas, and lupins by a type of cutting called a "basal stem cutting". They are very easy to take, when the shoots are about 8–10cm (3–4in) high. Remove the shoots from as close to the plant as possible using a sharp knife. It's very like taking dahlia cuttings, except that the parent plant is in the ground. Insert the cuttings into a pot containing a mix of equal parts peat-free compost and perlite or vermiculite, cover with a polythene bag, and put on a shady windowsill or in a cold frame until they root in a few weeks' time.

Sometimes, you can take root cuttings with a small piece of shoot attached – especially from asters, and also campanulas, lupins, chrysanthemums, and sedums. These are known as "Irishman's cuttings" and hardly ever fail.

■ **Take cuttings from dahlia tubers.**
Cuttings should be taken when the shoots have reached 8–10cm (3–4in) long, but before the stems become hollow (this is normal for dahlias as the stems mature).

Trim the cuttings below a leaf joint and remove the lower leaves. Dip the cuttings into fungicide (wear gloves for this) and then dip the bases into hormone rooting solution. Dibble the cuttings into pots containing equal parts peat-free compost and perlite or vermiculite. Put the pots in a propagator set at 10–13°C (50–55°F), with a polythene bag over them, to encourage a good root system. More shoots will grow from where the cuttings were taken, so you can take more later.

■ **Plant new plants.** Hardy perennials will grow away quickly if they are planted now. Feed and mulch them after planting and keep well watered until they establish.

■ **Towards the end of the month** split up polyanthus-type primulas as the flowers go over. To divide them, dig up each clump with a fork. With very large clumps you will have to push two forks back to back into the centre of the clump and push the fork handles apart. The sections can then be divided by hand. Trim off most of the old foliage, leaving about 5cm (2in). Apart from making the plants tidier, this reduces loss of water from the leaves: the plants establish more quickly and new leaves soon grow. Either plant the divisions back *in situ*, after revitalizing the soil with garden compost or manure, or plant them in rows in a corner of the vegetable garden to grow through the summer and plant out again in the borders in the autumn. The plants will then give a terrific splash of colour next spring.

■ **Lift and divide overgrown** clumps of summer-flowering herbaceous perennials. Most can be lifted and divided in spring, just as growth gets under way and if the divisions are reasonably sized they should flower later in the year. Plants that need dividing are usually quite easy to see. As

perennials age the clumps push outwards, with fresh, young growth to the edge of the clump, and the centre dies out. This is the stage at which they should be divided. Lift each clump with a fork and insert two forks back to back and prise them apart; smaller pieces can then be pulled apart by hand. Add organic matter and fertilizer to revitalize the soil and plant the young divisions in groups of three, five or more, depending on the space you have. Water them in well if the soil is dry.

■ **Protect the young, tender shoots** of delphiniums and hostas from slug damage. Slugs and snails can do a lot of damage to young buds before they've barely emerged from the soil, and you may not be aware of the damage until the leaves begin to open up. The tiny holes, at this stage perhaps the size of pinheads, expand with the leaves and by the summer there may be a great hole, or series of holes, ruining the foliage. There are general measures you can take to combat slugs and snails, but it's worth taking extra precautions to protect individual plants. One way to prevent slugs getting to your (and their!) favourites is to use a physical barrier that

Slug prevention A physical barrier such as copper tape can help prevent slugs getting at the juicy young shoots of pot-grown hostas.

the pests will not want to negotiate to get to the plants. The easiest barrier of all is a thick layer of coarse grit; slugs and snails really dislike moving over its rough surface. Slug controls containing metaldehyde are very effective.

■ **Support herbaceous perennials.**
Towards the end of the month many herbaceous perennials will be making plenty of growth and at the first sign of rain or a strong breeze the shoots will be flattened. There is a wide variety of supports available today, and what you choose depends on the depth of your pocket. The easiest and cheapest are twiggy sticks ("peasticks") pushed in around each clump, provided that they are straight and strong enough. Supports you can buy include canes, plastic-coated stakes that link together and around mesh supports, which the plants grow through, some of which can be raised as the plant grows. The most important point about staking is to get it done early on in the year and the plants will then look natural as they grow. Don't leave the job until the plants flop or are blown about; trying to stake stems that are growing in all directions can be problematic. Plant

Plant supports Push in twiggy sticks early so the plant can grow up around them.

Gritty barriers Surround new plants with a thick layer of crushed eggshells or coarse grit to protect them from hungry slugs and snails.

supports can look rather unsightly to begin with, but the plants soon grow and hide them completely.

Alpines

■ **In the rock garden** weed seedlings will be growing in grit or gravel between the plants. Although a covering of gravel is fairly good at suppressing weeds, seeds of annual weeds like groundsel and annual grasses can germinate in the moist soil beneath and push through. They are easy to control by pulling them out or digging them up. Never use a sprayer in the rock garden to apply weedkiller; the plants are too close together for this and might be damaged. The best way to deal with perennial weeds is either to pull them by hand or by spot-treating them with a weedkiller painted onto the foliage, usually built into the lid of the product. If the weed is growing up through the centre of a plant, place a piece of wood or cardboard under the foliage of the weed to protect the plant, then paint on the weedkiller.

After weeding, top up any bare patches where the gravel may have been washed away. This will give the rock garden a neat and tidy finish as the alpines come into their main flowering period in spring.

BULBS

■ **Deadhead daffodils** as the flowers fade, but leave the foliage alone. If the old flowers are left on, the plant's energy will be used for seed production. At this time the important thing is to build up the bulb's reserves so that a new flower bud forms inside it for flowering next spring.

■ **Plant snowdrops in the green** if this was not done last month. Snowdrops very rarely grow well from dry bulbs, so the best time to divide them or buy new ones is now, while they are still green. Overgrown clumps can be lifted and divided now or new plants can be bought from specialist mail-order nurseries.

■ **Plant summer-flowering bulbs** this month and next month for a succession of flowers. They all enjoy a sunny position in well-drained soil. All summer-flowering bulbs, if planted at intervals over a period of a few weeks, will give a succession of flowers throughout the summer and into autumn. However, in northern parts of the country wait until next month before planting the frost-tender bulbs such as gladioli, eucomis, and tigridias.

Gladioli can be grown in several different ways: in rows for cutting, in tubs, and in groups in borders. For the best effect in ornamental borders plant gladiolus bulbs (or, more correctly, corms) in groups of five or more. Plant the corms 10–15cm (4–6in) apart and 7–10cm (3–4in) deep. The deeper the corms are planted the less likely will be the need to stake the plants. On heavy clay, dig the hole a little deeper and place the corms on a layer of coarse grit. Plant tigridias 5–8cm (2–3in) deep and 10–15cm (4–6in) apart. Plant galtonias 10–15cm (4–6in) deep and 22–30cm (9–12in) apart, and eucomis 15cm (6in) deep and 15–22cm (6–9in) apart.

Other bulbs to consider planting over the next few weeks include lilies and de Caen anemones. Lilies can be planted outside in well-prepared soil in groups in any mixed border. Plant the bulbs to three times their own depth and 7–10cm (3–4in) apart. On heavy clay soils, plant the bulbs on a layer of coarse grit to aid drainage. Lilies don't like to sit in damp soil. Plant de Caen anemones about 2.5cm (1in) deep and 10–15cm (4–6in) apart.

■ **Cannas for setting out** in June can be started into growth now.

■ **Bulbs that were forced** into flower inside can be planted out when the flowers are over, if this was not done earlier. Bulbs like narcissus, hyacinths, and dwarf irises will have finished flowering by now, so the best place for them is in the garden. Remove them from their containers and plant them just as they are, without disturbing the roots. This will help the bulbs to get well established. Feed them with a fertilizer high in potash to encourage the formation of next year's flower bud within the bulb. Don't try to force the same bulbs for a second year as they rarely flower as well again. It's best to buy new ones in the autumn.

Deadheading daffodils Pinch off the head below the bulbous part, leaving the stem intact.

ANNUALS AND BEDDING

■ **Sow and plant sweet peas** outside in southern parts. The easiest way to grow sweet peas is to sow them where they are to flower. There are many different ways of growing sweet peas and they have many uses in the garden. The scented varieties are the best to grow. Erect a support, if necessary, first. You can making wigwams from canes or let them scramble up through shrubs.

Germination will be improved by soaking the seeds overnight to soften the seed coat. Then plant two seeds at 30cm (1ft) intervals and 1cm (½in) deep. When the seeds have germinated, the weaker of the two can be removed or moved to fill in any gaps. The young plants may need to be attached to the support with sweet pea rings initially, just to get them started. Soon the tendrils will twine themselves around the support. In sheltered parts, you can also plant out sweet peas sown last autumn, in well-prepared soil.

■ **Sow hardy annuals outside** (*see October*). Now it is safe to begin sowing hardy annuals outside in most areas. In northern parts you may have to wait until the end of the month or into early April.

■ **Hardy annuals look best** grown in informal drifts. If the soil has not been prepared lightly fork it over, but don't add any manure or garden compost. If the soil is too rich, the plants will produce a lot of soft growth and very few flowers. All that needs to be done after forking over the soil is to apply a light dressing of a general fertilizer and rake the soil to a fine tilth. Now comes the fun part: marking out the informal drifts and sowing. The only rule to remember when planning an annual planting is that the taller plants such as larkspur (*Consolida*) and *Cosmos*, go to the back and the shortest, such as *Nemophila* (or baby-blue-eyes), *Lobularia*, and the

poached egg flower (*Limnanthes douglasii*) at the front. You can spend time making elaborate colour schemes or theme borders. But from these plants all we really want is a good splash of colour.

By sowing in drills rather than broadcasting the seed over each drift area, the young seedlings will be easier to tell apart from weeds. Once they grow together, you won't be able to tell that they are in rows. Varying the direction in which the drills cross neighbouring drifts also helps avoid a regimented look. When the seedlings are large enough to handle, they will have to be thinned out.

■ **Any hardy annuals** sown under cover can be hardened off now to acclimatize them to outdoor conditions. Put the plants in a cold frame, top closed, for a few days. Then, gradually increase ventilation until the lid can be left off or up. This is usually done over a week or ten days. Keep some insulation like horticultural fleece to put over at night if a sharp frost is forecast.

■ **Sow seed under cover** of half-hardy annuals and tender perennials for summer bedding.

Hardening off Acclimatize seedlings by moving them outside during the day and back in at night.

CONTAINERS

■ **Plant up roses in pots.** Roses, particularly the "flowering carpet" varieties, miniature roses, and elegant standards, look excellent on the patio, in containers filled with a soil-based compost such as John Innes No 3. Soil-based composts are far better for shrubs in containers; they hold a supply of nutrients more easily than soilless ones and also retain moisture better, cutting down the need for watering. After planting, prune the roses hard to encourage plenty of new growth. After a couple of months, feed regularly with a high-potash feed to encourage a profusion of flowers and you will be rewarded with a smashing display for weeks on end. Remember, though, that in dry weather watering may have to be done once, if not twice, a day. The roses may fare better if they are moved into the shade in fiercely sunny weather.

■ **Many other plants** can be grown in containers: small trees, shrubs and climbers, herbaceous perennials, annuals, alpines, and ground-cover plants. Let your imagination run riot. The only real rule is to look after the plants well; watering, feeding, and deadheading regularly. Using slow-release fertilizers and the water-retentive crystals now available can save you some work through the year.

Water storage Gel granules added at planting time expand and hold moisture, creating a built-in reservoir for container plants in dry spells.

LAWNS

■ **Get the mower serviced** if you haven't already done so. This is usually a busy time of year for servicing agents. There is nothing worse than trying to mow a lawn with a blunt mower. The grass, rather than being cut cleanly, is more likely to be torn with a blunt machine. It doesn't look good and it harms the grass too.

■ **Start mowing regularly.** By this time in most parts of the country grass will be growing steadily now and needs to be cut regularly to keep it in good condition. A lawn will be much healthier and stay greener the less grass you remove every time it is cut. Now, for the first few cuts, set the blades at the highest setting. Even if you tend to leave clippings on the lawn in summer, keep the box on the mower in spring, so that air, rain, and fertilizer can penetrate the turf.

■ **Feed the lawn** towards the end of the month in southern parts. In the north or in cold springs, wait until next month: the grass needs to be actively growing in order to make the best use of the fertilizer.

■ **Remove thatch.** If you did not scarify the lawn last autumn, rake out the moss and dead grass, which inevitably accumulates in the grass over the course of a season. If moss is a problem in your lawn, then scarify it after applying any moss killer later on in the month. Don't be tempted to rake out the moss before you have applied a moss killer, as you will just spread the moss all over the lawn.

Moss in a lawn is a sign that all is not well. The application of a moss killer is a short-term answer, but to eradicate moss permanently you have to tackle the underlying likely causes; these could be compaction, poor drainage, shade, the grass being cut too short, or a combination of any of these. Raking out the thatch can

Scarifying Vigorously pull a spring-tined rake across the lawn to remove thatch and dead moss; it also allows air to penetrate the surface.

be a backbreaking job if you're using the traditional tool; a spring-tined rake. On a small lawn it will be fine, but on a larger area it may be best to use an electric scarifier; these can be bought from most garden centres or you can hire one from a local hire shop. Petrol-driven scarifiers are available if you have a very large lawn and these, too, can be hired very easily.

It's amazing how much material you will be able to remove from the lawn and you may find that it looks worse than it did before for a time; you might wonder what you've done. But take heart: it will soon recover and look vastly improved.

■ **Repair damage to lawn edges.** Over the summer lawn edges can easily be damaged and often, especially with light, sandy soils, edges can crumble away in places. To repair a broken edge, cut out the entire damaged portion of turf and turn it around so that the good side now becomes the edge. Fill in the hollow edge with soil and sow grass seed onto this. Water and peg polythene over the top to encourage the grass seed to grow and then you will have a perfect repair. You can reseed any other bare patches in the middle of the lawn in exactly the same way all through

Neat edges Take the opportunity to tidy lawn edges and make repairs before perennials and bedding plants spill over their borders.

the summer – by scarifying the bare patch first to roughen the surface and then spreading on a mix of potting compost and grass seed combined in equal proportions.

New lawns

■ **Finish preparations for sowing** a new lawn or laying turf. Soil that was dug over during the winter can now be levelled off and raked down to a fine tilth (a fine crumbly surface for sowing seeds).

Seed-sowing can be done at any time from the end of this month through until the autumn, although sowing during the hot, dry summer months is not as effective as in spring or autumn.

Although turf can be laid any time, it is better to carry out this task between autumn and this month, so that it can benefit from the seasonal rain. When you are laying turf, always work outwards from the laid turf, using boards to spread your weight. You will need to lay turf with the joints staggered – in a similar pattern to that of house bricks. The joints must never be in line. It is absolutely crucial to keep newly laid turves well watered. If they dry out at this stage, even slightly, they will shrink and leave persistent unsightly gaps in the lawn.

VEGETABLES AND HERBS

■ **Prepare seedbeds** for direct sowing. Even if it's been left exposed, soil should be beginning to dry out now and will be in a better state for the making of good seedbeds for sowing. Getting the timing of this job right can be tricky sometimes. The soil doesn't need to be so wet that it sticks to your boots, nor so dry that it takes a lot of effort to break it up, but hopefully nature has given a helping hand and broken down the worst of the clods. If the soil is rather too moist for treading on, then use planks to stand on. These will distribute your weight and prevent localized areas becoming too compacted.

Break larger lumps of soil down by bashing them with a fork, then use a rake to smooth out smaller lumps and create a fine tilth, pushing and pulling the rake back and forth to a depth of about 2.5cm (1in). Tread the soil to firm it, and apply an organic fertilizer, such as one based on seaweed, about two weeks before sowing. Rake that in and the seedbed is ready for the seed.

Sowing indoors

■ **Harden off early sowings** of vegetables. Those vegetables sown under cover in late January or February can be hardened off (put in a cooler environment) to acclimatize to cooler conditions. A week or ten days should be enough to acclimatize them before planting them out. Ideally, put them under cloches that have already been in place for a few weeks to warm up the soil.

■ **Lettuce, cabbage, and cauliflowers** can still be sown indoors to give a succession of crops from those sown earlier. The plants will get off to a better start if they are grown in modules. With no disturbance to the plants' roots when they are transplanted, there is less chance of growth being checked and there will therefore be less risk of the crops bolting,

Sowing cabbages

1 Fill a seed tray with potting compost and firm down, either using a similar tray or a board. Water the compost – a fine rose is best – and then allow to drain.

2 Scatter the seeds over the compost, distributing them evenly and sparingly so the emerging seedlings won't become overcrowded.

3 Cover the seeds with a fine layer of compost, using a garden sieve so you don't introduce any lumps, then lightly firm the compost over the seeds.

Globe artichokes Sow these statuesque perennials now – they are among the most beautiful productive plants.

or running to seed prematurely. Cauliflowers are particularly prone to bolting, or the heads not forming properly, if they receive the slightest check.

■ **Sow globe artichokes** for planting out in May. These are quite large seeds and can be spaced out easily. Sow two seeds each in small pots, watering the compost first and cover with sieved compost. Place in a propagator at a temperature of around 18°C (65°F). When they germinate, move to a sunny bench or windowsill. Remove the weaker of the two young plants or transplant it to its own pot.

Sowing and planting outdoors

■ **Plant out young vegetable plants,** hardening off in cold frames. Prepare the ground by raking it down to a tilth and spreading on an organic fertilizer before planting. Plant at the distances recommended for final spacing after thinning on the seed packets. Water in well after planting, and ideally, cover with a cloche. A good tip is to plant up one half of a cloche with young plants and sow seeds in the other – this way you get a succession

of crops. On deep beds, the plants can go in much closer than would normally be the case. Because the soil is never compacted by being trodden on, plant roots tend to grow downward into the soil, rather than spreading out, so crops can be grown more closely together.

■ **Start sowing outside regularly.** This month seed-sowing outside can get under way in earnest. In northern parts, wait until late in the month or early next month before sowing outside. Sowings of lettuce, other salads such as endive, radish, salad onions, peas, broad beans, spinach, cabbage, turnips, and beetroot can all be made now. Sow short rows at a time, at weekly or ten-day intervals; this way a succession of vegetables will become ready throughout the summer and autumn. Many seeds are now sold in small vacuum-packed foil sachets within the main packet. When the foil pack is opened the vacuum is broken and air gets in, so it's important to store the seeds between sowings in a cool, dry place – the fridge is ideal. Seeds not packed in foil sachets are also better kept in the fridge. These cool conditions ensure the seeds remain viable (capable of germinating) for longer periods.

■ **To sow all of the fine-seeded vegetables,** take out shallow drills with a cane. Water the drills before sowing if the soil is dry. Sow the seeds thinly along the drill and cover lightly with dry soil. Once the seedlings are large enough to handle it is important to thin them.

With peas and broad beans the technique is a little different. Take out a trench about 2.5cm (1in) deep with a spade and sow the seeds of peas about 2.5cm (1in) apart in the bottom of the trench and cover over. With broad beans, space the seeds about 15cm (6in) apart in rows and cover over with soil. Peas and

broad beans will have to be protected with netting or horticultural fleece to prevent mice and wood pigeons digging them up.

■ **Sow parsnips outside.** Sowing parsnips requires yet another, slightly different, technique, because parsnips are notoriously erratic at germinating. Take out a narrow drill as described above, but instead of sowing the seeds thinly along the drill, sow them in clusters of three or four seeds at 15cm (6in) intervals along the drill. This way, if some of the seeds don't germinate, there won't be any gaps in the row. Because germination can be slow and erratic, it's a good idea to sow a quick-maturing crop like radishes along the drill between the parsnip seeds; this way the row can be easily identified.

■ **Plant early potatoes.** There are several ways to do this. In 1.2m (4ft) wide deep beds, potatoes are easily planted with a trowel. Plant about 30cm (1ft) apart and about 10–15cm (4–6in) deep. Another way to get a really good crop is to mound up the soil into ridges about 60cm (2ft) apart across the beds. Plant the tubers on the ridges at the same depth with a trowel, spacing tubers about 30cm (12in) apart in the rows. After planting, cover the ridges with clear polythene, holding it in place between the ridges with planks of wood. After a few weeks, watch to see the shoots growing and when you see them through the polythene cut slits in the sheets to let them grow through. Keep fleece handy in case frost is forecast, as the young shoots are very prone to frost damage. The polythene helps to retain heat in the soil so the potatoes can be harvested early.

The traditional way of planting on allotment-style beds is to take out planting trenches about a spade's depth and 60cm (2ft) apart. Scatter an organic fertilizer along the bottom of the trench and then

Planting seed potatoes Make a shallow drill about 15cm (6in) deep, and plant seed potatoes, shoots upward, at intervals of 30cm (12in).

add the organic matter. Plant the tubers in the trench about 30cm (12in) apart and cover with the soil taken out.

■ **Plant onion sets** from now onward. Prepare the ground as for preparing seedbeds – although the soil doesn't have to be as fine for onion sets – and apply an organic fertilizer. Plant the sets about 10–15cm (4–6in) apart in rows the same distance apart. Plant each set with a trowel: don't just push them into the soil, because as the roots form they will push the set up and out again. It is also worth trimming off the dry skin at the tip of the onion set, cutting straight across with a sharp knife, as birds use this to get a hold on the sets and pull them out of the soil.

If growing onion sets on deep beds plant them about 8cm (3in) apart. The eventual onions may be smaller, but you will achieve a higher overall yield.

■ **Plant asparagus crowns.** This is a good time to plant asparagus. If you haven't already prepared a bed, dig the soil deeply now, incorporating plenty of organic matter. If your soil is a heavy clay, add pea shingle to improve the drainage. The beds should be about 1.2m (4ft) wide and as

long as you like. Make the bed slightly higher than the surrounding soil to improve drainage. This should automatically happen if you are adding plenty of organic matter. Many firms sell asparagus crowns by post. All male varieties of asparagus, such as 'Franklim', 'Lucullus', and 'Dariana', produce the heaviest crops. When the crowns arrive they may have to be soaked for a couple of hours. To plant them, dig out shallow trenches about 15cm (6in) deep and 45cm (18in) apart, mounding up the bottom of each trench to make a slight ridge. Place the crowns on top of the ridges 45cm (18in) apart, with the roots spread down each side of the ridge, and replace the soil. Keep well watered. Don't cut any asparagus the first two years to allow the plants to get established.

Looking after crops

■ **Feed winter lettuces.** Plants sown to overwinter will benefit from an application of a general organic fertilizer after the long, dark days. Sprinkle it between the plants according to the manufacturer's instructions. Water it in well if the soil is dry. Cut every other lettuce when required and leave the others alone to grow on and heart up.

■ **Watch out for pests and diseases.** Always try to prevent pests and diseases becoming serious by taking preventive measures. If you want to use chemical sprays, do so in the evenings, when bees have gone for the day.

Even some so-called safe organic sprays contain substances that are harmful to a wide range of predators that do a lot of good controlling pests. It has been shown that by building up a diversity of plants and flowers in the garden and making beneficial predators, such as ladybirds, welcome, the need for most spraying against pests is eliminated.

■ **Keep the hoe going** to keep weeds down. Now that spring is here, weeds seem to grow more vigorously than anything else. This is why it is important to hoe between rows of vegetables. Not only do weeds take valuable moisture and nutrients, they also act as host plants to pests and diseases. The more you can keep on top of them, the better for the garden.

Hoeing is best done on a dry day when the weeds can be left on the soil surface to dry out in the sun. A Dutch hoe is the tool to use for this job, walking backwards with a pushing and pulling motion, slicing off the tops of the weeds. Perennial weeds will have to be dug out, because if any piece of root is left in the soil it will grow again.

Harvesting

■ **Harvest the last of the winter crops.** Put all the resulting debris on the compost heap, if it is not diseased. Spring greens should be cropping now.

■ **Sow new chicory plants** and completely pull out all the remains of any existing crop once it has all been harvested. Put the remains on the compost heap.

Planning ahead

■ **Make a seedbed** for sowing winter crops. Towards the end of the month prepare an area, perhaps a corner of the vegetable garden, for sowing crops such as Brussels sprouts, winter cauliflower, winter cabbage, broccoli, and kale. Prepare the soil in the usual way, raking it to a fine tilth, and apply a general fertilizer. Again, sowing the crops at intervals over a few weeks will ensure that they mature at different times, giving a succession of vegetables over winter when they are at their most scarce.

■ **Take out shallow drills** with a cane about 15cm (6in) apart and sow each vegetable variety thinly in each row, watering beforehand if soil is dry. Cover the seeds with dry soil and label each row. Cover the seedbed with fleece to prevent damage from flea beetle. These tiny insects eat holes in the leaves. When the seedlings have made two or three true leaves they can be transplanted.

■ **Make runner bean trenches.** If this was not done at the end of winter do it now. Take out a trench to a spade's depth, about 90cm (3ft) wide and the length of the proposed row. Break up the bottom of the trench with a fork, but don't bring poorer subsoil to the surface. Put plenty of organic matter in the trench. Even shredded newspapers in a layer in the bottom are good at holding moisture, and they will have rotted down by the end of the summer. Just before planting the beans in early June, replace the soil taken out after mixing with general fertilizer.

■ **Add manure to celery trenches.** Celery requires plenty of water through the growing season and to grow it well good soil preparation is essential. Take out a trench to a spade's depth, about 60cm (2ft) wide, and the length of the row. Put plenty of well-rotted manure in the trench and lightly fork it into the soil, being careful not to bring the poorer subsoil to the surface. Then partly fill the trench with some of the soil taken out. Celery plants are not planted until early June, but the sooner preparation is done the better.

Herbs

■ **Sow herbs outside** and buy young plants. Herbs that are hardy can be sown outside now. These include chervil, chives, dill, fennel, marjoram, coriander, and parsley. Sow the seeds in exactly the same way as for vegetables, in drills, and plant them out when they are large enough to

handle without damaging. Young plants of herbs that are more difficult to raise from seed can be bought now. These include mint, tarragon, and shrubby herbs such as thymes and rosemary. Choose French tarragon rather than the Russian kind, which has a coarser taste and is very invasive. So is mint in nearly all its forms: plant it in a pot and partially sink the pot in the ground to discourage it from taking over your entire garden.

A dedicated herb garden is one of the most attractive ways to grow these plants, but they also look wonderful growing in borders with other plants, so if your garden is too small for a separate herb feature, grow them in with other plants, or in pots on the patio.

■ **Divide chives now** they are starting to grow. Lift each clump with a fork and divide them up. You can afford to be quite ruthless with them. Small clumps can be replanted in soil that has been revitalized with organic matter. Make sure you water them well after replanting. They make pretty edging for beds.

Fresh herbs Chives germinate quickly; you can start them under cover, or sow direct outside.

FRUIT
Looking after crops

■ **Check that fruits have water** in dry seasons as fruits of all description need plenty of water to develop properly. Those growing in containers and trained against walls and fences should be checked from time to time, should we happen to have a dry spring. Trees trained against house walls are especially vulnerable, as the eaves often keep off a lot of rain.

■ **Protect open flowers** from frost damage. The buds and flowers of peaches, nectarines, and cherries open up early and are more prone to frost damage. Wall-trained trees can easily be protected using polythene sheets or horticultural fleece. The sheet can be fixed to two poles leaned against the trees at night and then taken off during the day. Free-standing trees are a bit trickier to protect, but draping horticultural fleece over small trees or bushes will give protection from all but the most severe frosts. Large trees just have to take their chances.

■ **Continue to protect peaches, nectarines, and almonds** against peach leaf curl. The symptoms of this disease show as puckering of the leaves during summer. Copper or mancozeb fungicides can be effective if applied the previous autumn and again in January and February, but by March it is too late. Protecting the trees with a physical barrier from early January, as described above, is the best option. If you are plagued by this disease, grow dwarf varieties of peach and nectarine in large pots and keep them indoors until late spring or early summer.

■ **Hand-pollinate peach and nectarine trees.** During cooler spells in spring there are few pollinating insects around, and if you cover your trees, or have pot-grown trees under cover at the moment, you also

Frost protection Cover young peach, nectarine and cherry tree blossoms to reduce risk of peach leaf curl, encouraged by winter rain and frost.

reduce the chances of insects getting at them, so it is advisable to pollinate these trees by hand. Use a small, soft artist's paint brush and transfer the pollen from one flower to another, going over the whole tree. Do it two or three times over the course of a few days to ensure that all the flowers are pollinated. The best time of day to pollinate flowers is around midday, as the pollen is running freely at this time.

■ **Feed all fruit with potash** if you didn't do so last month. Most general fertilizers contain some potash, but it is a good idea to give a little extra to get really luscious fruits. Always follow manufacturers' application rates. Draw back any mulch before applying the potash and water it in. Water in really well if the weather is dry at the moment. If the fertilizer is not watered in properly, it will not go into solution in the soil and therefore will not be available for the plants. Renew the mulch.

■ **Spray apples and pears** to prevent scab. If you use chemicals, then this is the time to start using a preventative spray against scab. Most garden centres supply a range of chemical controls. Look at the labels and follow the instructions carefully.

Spray firstly while the flower buds are tightly closed and again when they begin to burst and show colour.

■ **Pears** that have been attacked by pear midge can be sprayed with a preventative spray containing bifenthrin. Spray when the buds are white, but closed. Don't use sprays when flowers are open or you will kill off pollinating insects. Do any spraying in the evening when they are not around.

Pruning and training

■ **Tie in briar fruits** such as blackberries and loganberries. These plants grow at a terrific rate from early spring and if you don't tie them in at regular intervals you will end up in a mess. Briars produce fruit on the stems that grew the previous year and the easiest way to train them is to tie in last year's canes on the supporting wires to one side of the plant and the new growth made this year, which will produce next year's fruit, to the other side. This makes pruning them later on very straightforward and less painful.

■ **Prune autumn-fruiting raspberries** if you have not already done so. All of the old fruited canes from last year should be cut down to ground level. Be careful now not to damage any emerging new shoot tips.

■ **Prune gooseberries** now if they were left unpruned over winter. If birds are a problem eating the gooseberry buds you can sometimes gain some protection by leaving the bushes unpruned until spring. This makes it more difficult for the birds to get at the buds. But now is the latest time to prune gooseberries for the best fruit. All the sideshoots can be pruned to two or three buds from the main stems and the leading shoots pruned by one-third to half, depending on the vigour of the shoot (prune weaker shoots harder). Treat the

head of a trained standard gooseberry exactly as if it were a bush. Gooseberry cordons are also pruned similarly, shortening all of last year's shoots to only 1–2 buds. Occasionally, when a really knobbly "spur system" has got very crowded, you can remove a portion of it completely. After pruning the gooseberries, feed with a general fertilizer and mulch with organic matter.

Planting

■ **Complete planting of bare-root fruit trees and bushes** this month. This is the last month when these plants will be in a near-dormant state and the sooner they are planted the better. If you have missed out on bare-root stock there will be container-grown fruit on offer at garden centres that can be planted through the spring. Older plants may be in flower at this time and you may get a small crop of fruits this year. But if you plant young trees and bushes, it's best to pinch any flowers out this year, so that the plants' energies go into establishing a good root system over the summer.

Beat the seasons

■ **Cover some more strawberries** with a cloche, to give a succession of early fruits.

Protect strawberry plants Use clear plastic cloches to encourage early cropping.

UNDER COVER

■ **Keep the windows of greenhouses and conservatories clean** to give seedlings maximum light. Long, thin, straggly seedlings rarely make good plants and the cleaner the glass the sturdier they grow. It is surprising how much dust and dirt accumulates on glass even in dry weather.

■ **Ventilate** whenever the weather is good. It is surprising how quickly the temperature rises even when the sun is out for a short time. Plants grow best when they are protected from extremes of hot and cold and ventilation is important in regulating the temperature inside. It can be a nuisance if you leave for work on a fine, sunny morning and later on it cools down, or vice versa, but there are many different types of automatic vent openers on the market. These can be set to open when the temperature reaches a certain level, closing again when it falls.

■ **Watch for pest damage.** Now the temperatures are rising all sorts of pests are on the move, enjoying the warm, still, humid atmosphere in the greenhouse and conservatory. By far the best way to control pests under glass is by using biological controls, very small living creatures that destroy pests. Most of the firms producing them advertise in the gardening press, giving details of which are appropriate for which pests. These tiny organisms need a warm atmosphere to thrive. If you have a heated glasshouse, you can introduce them now. If your greenhouse is unheated, then order controls now for delivery next month, when temperatures have risen. If you are not sure which pests you have, or want an early-warning system for pest attacks, hang yellow sticky traps in the greenhouse. You will be able to examine what you catch and identify it more easily, and be alerted early to any problems.

Clean greenhouse windows The more light plants receive, the more strongly they will grow, so wash down the glass, inside and out.

■ **Feed plants and water them regularly.** By this time of year most plants are growing actively and we all have to keep up with the watering and feeding. On warm, sunny days watering may have to be done several times as the temperature inside rises. Plants that have been growing in their pots for a few months will need regular feeding as most of the food reservoir in the compost will have been used up.

■ **Continue to take cuttings** from fuchsias.

■ **Prune and repot pelargoniums** and other tender perennials kept over winter if you didn't do so last month.

■ **Take cuttings** from overwintered tender perennials that started into growth last month. Take cuttings about 8cm (3in) long, making a clean cut above a leaf joint with a sharp knife. Remove the lower leaves and trim the cutting just below a leaf joint and dip the base of the cutting into hormone

rooting solution. There is no need to use hormone rooting solution on fuchsias, heliotrope, and pelargoniums as they all root very easily.

Put into a pot containing cuttings compost (most multi-purpose composts, or any peat-free compost mixed with perlite, will do) and water in. Put a polythene bag or propagator, cover over the pot and leave in a shaded area until the cuttings root in three or four weeks.

■ **Prick out and pot on cuttings,** seedlings and young plants. Seeds sown last month will need pricking out now, unless you used module trays. Seedlings pricked out last month may be being planted out now, but those that have to stay indoors until all danger of frost has passed will be needing some more room, as will growing cuttings, and these can be potted up into their own small pots of multi-purpose compost.

Watch out for damping-off on your seedlings. This disease causes seedlings to rot off and die. It is caused by several fungi, but can be largely prevented by sowing seeds thinly and not over-watering them. If it does become a problem water the seedlings with a solution containing Cheshunt compound. It is difficult to control once it gets going, so prevention is the best course of action.

■ **Shade young seedlings** and cuttings on bright days. Plants lose water in the form of water vapour from their leaves and on sunny, warm days this transpiration, as it is called, increases. Young seedlings and cuttings are less able to cope with this and so it is important to shade them on sunny days. There are several ways of providing shading, one being roller blinds fitted in the greenhouse or conservatory. But these can be rather expensive; the cheapest way to shade is to put newpaper over the windows to create more shade.

Raising plants for outdoors

■ **Sow half-hardy annuals.** Most half-hardy annuals can be sown now and with even a modest greenhouse you may have enough space to raise all the bedding and container plants you need. Sown too early the plants will become leggy and no good for planting out when June comes.

Seeds to sow now include *Ageratum*, *Alyssum*, stocks, *Nicotiana*, and marigolds. Don't forget to include "everlasting" flowers such as statice and strawflowers for dried arrangements – botanical names to look for include *Rhodanthe*, *Limonium*, and *Xerochrysum*. Keep in a propagator at 16–18°C (61–65°F), at least until the seedlings have two true leaves, then you can move them to a bench, covered with a clear seed tray cover for extra warmth. Plants needing a minimum of 18°C (65°F) include lobelia, nemesia, phlox, and zinnias.

■ **Sow seeds of tender bedding** like salvias and gazanias. Sow the seeds thinly and cover lightly with vermiculite as some of them need light to germinate. They need a minimum temperature of around 18°C (65°F). These plants can also be bought in as mini-plants or plugs for potting on. This is an easy way to grow them as it cuts down the costs of heating to germinate the seeds. They will need at least frost-free conditions to grow on until threat of frost is past, around the beginning of June.

Plants that need longer growing times as well as high germinating temperatures, like *Begonia* Semperflorens Cultorum Group and busy Lizzies, are from now also better bought as young plug plants, as there isn't time for them to grow. You can, however, still sow seed of pelargoniums and have plants in flower this year provided that you buy specially "primed" seed. It has been pre-treated to germinate rapidly so that the seedlings will catch up with plants sown earlier.

■ **Lettuce, cabbage, and cauliflowers** can still be sown indoors to give a succession of crops from those sown earlier.

■ **Start cannas into growth.** The fat rhizomes of these showy plants can now be brought out of store and started into growth, for planting out in June. Split them up into short sections, each with a bud. Pot these up each to its own small container of peat-free compost and keep in a light place at 16°C (61°F). Water them sparingly at first. Once the roots fill the small pot, move each into a bigger pot and grow on in good light, watering more regularly.

Glasshouse and house plants

■ **Feed and water hippeastrums** (amaryllis) as the flowers go over. As the flowers fade it is important to feed the bulb to build up next year's flower bud. Continue watering and feeding with a high-potash liquid fertilizer until the foliage begins to go yellow and dies down. Then watering can be stopped and the plants allowed to rest for the summer.

■ **Sow seed** *of Solanum capsicastrum* (winter cherry) exactly as for tomatoes. These plants with their bright, ornamental fruits are a cheerful sight in winter.

Crops under glass

■ **Sow aubergines,** peppers, and tomatoes for the greenhouse. There is no point in sowing these too early: towards the end of the month is quite soon enough. Sow seed in small pots or trays of seed compost. Water the compost before sowing, sow the seeds thinly on the surface and lightly cover with a thin layer of vermiculite or sieved compost. Cover with a sheet of glass and paper to exclude the light and place in a propagator at 21°C (70°F). Germination takes two or three weeks. When you see the first signs of them

Planning summer crops Sow aubergines, tomatoes, and peppers this month to germinate under glass.

coming through, remove the paper and glass. When the seedlings are large enough to handle (usually when the seed leaves, or cotyledons, are fully expanded and you can just see the first leaves developing in the centre), they need transplanting into pots.

■ **Lay out growing bags** to warm up before planting. Plants can sometimes receive a check to their growth if planted into a cold growing medium. Think how you'd feel plunging your feet into a bucket of cold water at this time of year!

■ **When forced strawberry plants** start coming into flower you will have to pollinate the flowers for the fruits to set if they are under cloches. This is easily done using a small paintbrush, such as those used for painting model aeroplanes – or a piece of cotton wool on the end of a cane. Dab pollen from one flower to the next, doing this a couple of times at intervals of a couple of days to ensure pollination. Water and feed with a high-potash fertilizer and wait for the fruits to grow.

THE APRIL GARDEN

Now we are well and truly into spring, April is perhaps the most exciting month of the year. The garden suddenly begins to look green and vibrant and the warmer days and lighter evenings help to gladden the heart of every gardener. You can begin to prune early-flowering shrubs now and start dividing perennials. Regular weeding and deadheading will keep your garden in trim.

THINGS TO DO

Provide protection for newly planted trees and shrubs in cold, exposed positions.

Continue watering newly planted trees and shrubs.

Plant evergreen trees and shrubs.

Tie in the new shoots of climbers.

Prune early-flowering shrubs as well as those grown for large or colourful foliage.

Give grey-leaved shrubs a trim to keep them bushy.

Spray roses against black spot.

Divide perennials, and stake tall-growing ones.

Pot up or transplant self-sown seedlings.

Sow annual climbers and grasses.

Deadhead your daffodils.

Keep hoeing to suppress weeds, but always dig perennial weeds right out.

Sow or lay turf for new lawns, and feed established lawns.

Sow greenhouse crops such as tomatoes and continue sowing and planting vegetables outdoors.

Prick out or pot up seedlings before they get congested and grow leggy.

LAST CHANCE

Cut down any dead growth of perennials if you have not already.

Plant summer-flowering bulbs and sow sweet peas.

GET AHEAD

Prepare trenches for runner beans.

Plant up hanging baskets if you have space under cover to shelter them for a few more weeks.

The days are lengthening The soil is warming up and apple blossom (Braeburn is shown here) is now at its very best.

THE EXCITING MONTH

Typical April showers, which can sometimes be quite dramatic, are interspersed with warm and cold snaps, so frost protection may still be needed. You'll feel inspired by colour from flowers as well as foliage and a variety of delicious scents. Now's the time to start mowing the lawn regularly.

Gardens are now awash with a bright spring display of flowers. All the plants seem to start growing really fast this month, with April showers and warmer soil providing ideal growing conditions. Colour and interest come not only from bright flowers but also from the unfolding foliage on trees and shrubs, as the plants fully wake from their winter rest. These opening buds come in all shades, from the palest green to deepest coppery bronze. The garden seems transformed into a place for all to enjoy – birds are building their nests and creatures such as hedgehogs are coming out of hibernation, looking to eat up those pests that are also emerging, eager to set upon your precious plants.

Walking around the garden on a warm April day, taking in the sights and smells of spring, will really lift your spirits. But don't get too complacent; with all this exuberant growth around us there is a tremendous amount of work to be done. So take this book out into the garden, if you must, but do get out there – there's no time to sit indoors reading!

Sudden cold snaps

The month of April may often seem more like a month of deluges, with long spells of heavy rain. In fact, the weather can still be quite variable in all parts of the country, with fairly cold periods in northern parts. It is not unusual to get snow in April, but it rarely lasts for very long. Nights can still feel a bit nippy wherever you are, so keep an eye on the weather forecasts and protect any tender plants on frosty nights with cloches or fleece – even a few sheets of newspaper can make all the difference, giving several degrees of frost protection. Or, if you have the space in your home, bring the plants inside for the night, but remember to put them out again during the day so that they don't grow tall and straggly due to lack of light.

Scented spring flowers

Scented plants are an absolute must in the garden at any time of the year, but particularly so in springtime. Many of the spring bulbs and shrubs, such as *Viburnum carlesii*,

Spring perennials The bright pinks and yellows of early spring are now joined by the cooler tones of perennials such as pulsatillas and muscari.

Trays of vegetable seedlings Make sure these are acclimatized before you plant them out.

produce wonderful scent. One point to bear in mind with these plants is that they are best grown close to the house or in pots so that they can be positioned near doors, windows, and pathways to get the maximum benefit of the fragrance. Hyacinths and lily-of-the-valley are easily grown in pots. Bring them into the house, where their sweet scent will fill the air in no time at all.

The short and the tall

Some of the most exquisite spring flowers are borne by those tiny jewels of the garden: the alpine plants. Carpets of pink and purple aubrieta and furry-petalled pulsatillas will brighten up a free-draining spring border or alpine trough in April. It's also time to plant out hardy annuals, including climbers, such as sweet peas. A mainstay of cottage gardens, these sweetly scented plants would combine well with the rustic willow obelisk, which is a practical project (*see p.97*) featured this month. The obelisk is easy to construct and makes a decorative feature in itself, adding height and interest to a border before it disappears beneath a veil of flowers.

Get the mower out

The job which heralds the start of spring for many gardeners, mowing the lawn, will be a weekly task from now on. For some people it's just a chore to get over and

Weather watch

On the whole, days are warming up, but do beware of very cold nights with sharp frosts. These can damage fruit-tree blossom. Clear, warm, balmy weather makes it very tempting to put young plants out now, but slightly tender plants still need daytime protection with cloches. Some garden centres will have bedding plants for sale; don't buy yet unless you have a frost-free greenhouse.

Some strong winds

Winds are generally much calmer now, but some parts, especially coastal areas in the north-west, will still have 1–2 days, on average, of gale-force winds. In southern parts winds can still be strong at times, especially on high ground, so give newly planted plants some protection.

Even sunshine

The amount of sunshine over the country as a whole is fairly even: Argyll, in Scotland, gets around 170 hours on average this month, and Plymouth, on the south coast of England, 180 hours. Cloud cover on a day-to-day basis will have a dramatic effect on the amount of direct sunshine brightening up each area.

Showers

April showers may well bring forth May flowers, but we all hope the showers ease off soon. High ground in the north-west of the country can still experience high rainfall. Fort William in the north-west Highlands gets an average of 100mm of rainfall in April, while in the Home Counties and East Anglia the average is much lower: 42–47mm. There is, therefore, more need to conserve water in the south-east, by collecting rain and only watering when necessary.

Rare snowfall

Heavy snowfalls are rare now, but there can be exceptions. One April in the mid-1980s, 15cm (6in) of snow fell in Ayrshire on the south-west coast of Scotland. This area is usually quite mild and rarely gets any snow.

done with. For others, though, it's a deeply satisfying job, because once trimmed, the lawn sets off the rest of the garden so beautifully. A well-cared-for lawn, recently mown, with alternate light and dark stripes and the edges neatly trimmed, will really enhance the rest of your garden. Well-tended green lawns are admired by everyone – so why not get the mower out?

Vegetables to be sown

The vegetable garden is a hectic place to be just now. There is plenty of seed-sowing to be done outside – all kinds of salad leaves, radishes, salad onions, peas, broad beans, and many more can be put in now. The point to bear in mind here is to sow little and often so you don't get a glut of produce reaching maturity all at once. Short rows of each type of vegetable sown at, say, seven- to ten-day intervals will give you a succession of crops that will keep your kitchen well supplied without being overwhelmed.

Plants under cover

Under cover, greenhouses and conservatories will be bulging at the seams with plants now. With such an increasing number of plants you will have to keep up with the watering: plants soon dry out as temperatures soar inside on sunny days. On warm spring days, open ventilators or windows and doors to keep the maximum amount of air circulating and splash water on the greenhouse floor and under staging to increase the humidity levels. This not only helps to cool the atmosphere as the water evaporates, but will also reduce the likelihood of pests, such as red spider mite, getting a hold, because they do not like humid conditions, preferring to be warm and dry.

Shade young seedlings and cuttings with newspaper on warm days to prevent them being scorched by the sun, especially when they have just been watered. Droplets of water on the leaves act like miniature magnifying glasses and will burn the leaves in bright sun.

Catching problems early

Pests are also on the move outdoors now, with the warmer weather. As the saying goes, prevention is always

better than cure. By keeping the garden clean and tidy and ensuring plants are healthy, there is less chance of pests and diseases causing much harm. A watchful eye can also alert you to problems early, so inspect plants regularly. Even though it's not a busy month in the fruit garden, don't forget to make regular checks on fruit trees and bushes and you may be able to take preventive action before your crops are affected. However, no matter how careful we try to be it is inevitable that some problems will occur through the growing season. If you

Blossom time Spring-flowering magnolias (*Magnolia stellata*) make beautifully shaped and manageably sized trees for small-to-medium gardens.

do not garden organically and feel that you must use a commercial spray, please do follow the instructions on the packaging of the chemical – to the letter. It's important to always try and spray when the weather is still and to do it in the evenings when there are fewer bees and hoverflies around. If, like me, you prefer to garden organically, then no spraying should be done at all. It is possible to rely on building up a wide diversity of plants in the garden, especially those that will encourage wildlife. Leave the odd corner here and there undisturbed, where beneficial

creatures such as hedgehogs and toads can take shelter. It can take a few years to build up the natural balance between pests and predators, which keeps problems under control, but be patient – it is a much healthier way of gardening.

So, life gets busier in the garden with each day that passes. Perfect!

Amelanchier lamarckii ♀
Shrubby tree with pinky-bronze young leaves (*see p.277*)

Dicentra spectabilis ♀
Tall, arching perennial with pretty foliage (*see p.293*)

***Erythronium* 'Pagoda'** ♀
Low-growing, clump-forming perennial for shade (*see p.295*)

Vinca minor
Creeping stems, studded with flowers in spring and summer (*see p.335*)

***Bergenia* 'Sunningdale'**
Tough, leathery-leaved perennial; good ground cover (*see p.280*)

Corylopsis glabrescens
Large deciduous shrub that prefers acid soil (*see p.289*)

Magnolia stellata ♀
Compact, to 3m (9ft) tall, an ideal magnolia for a small garden (*see p.309*)

Epimedium x warleyense
Clump-forming perennial making good ground cover (*see p.294*)

Fritillaria meleagris
The snakeshead fritillary; a small bulbous perennial (*see p.298*)

Euphorbia polychroma ♀
Neat mound-forming perennial, very bright even in part shade (*see p.296*)

Prunus 'Kanzan' ♀
Double, deep-pink flowers, profusely borne in clusters (*see p.320*)

Clematis alpina 'Frances Rivis' ♀
Bell-flowered climber needing little pruning (*see p.285*)

Pieris 'Flamingo'
Large but rounded, compact evergreen shrub for acid soil (*see p.318*)

Cytisus x praecox 'Warminster' ♀
Drought-tolerant shrub with arching branches (*see p.292*)

Pulsatilla vulgaris ♀
Small perennial ideal for a rock garden, raised bed, or paving (*see p.321*)

Convallaria majalis ♀
Lily-of-the-valley; a sweet-smelling perennial that can be invasive (*see p.287*)

Erysimum cheiri **Bedder Series**
Plant wallflowers in autumn for bright spring bedding (*see p.295*)

Ribes sanguineum
Pinky-white flowering currant; a rounded upright shrub (*see p.324*)

Pyrus salicifolia 'Pendula' ♀
Weeping ornamental pear tree with willow-like leaves (*see p.321*)

Malus x _moerlandsii_ 'Liset'
Rounded tree with bronze-green leaves and dark purple-red fruit (*see p.310*)

Viburnum x _juddii_ ♀
Bushy deciduous shrub that often has good autumn leaf colour (*see p.334*)

Aubrieta 'J. S. Baker'
Creeping perennial, perfect tumbling over rocks or low walls (*see p.279*)

Jasminum mesnyi ♀
Primrose jasmine; a twining climber with sweet-scented flowers (*see p.305*)

Rhododendron yakushimanum
Small mound-forming azalea covered in flowers (*see p.323*)

WHAT TO DO IN APRIL

AROUND THE GARDEN

Pests are on the move now, with the warmer weather. Get on top of any problems as soon as you spot them and nine times out of ten you can stop them getting a hold.

Protect plants. The warmth and spring rains now will see huge increases in the populations of slugs and snails, which can cause enormous damage to plants. If you're not gardening organically, spread slug pellets in among the plants affected. There are several organic ways to control slugs, including a biological control, a tiny nematode that attacks them that can be watered onto the soil. Traps are also effective. One of the oldest and best known is the beer trap: a jar sunk into the ground with the lip just proud of the surface, filled with beer. Hedgehogs, frogs, toads, and thrushes all prey on these pests, so encourage them. Lay a flat stone in a border and you will soon notice whether a thrush is using it as a handy "anvil" on which to smash snail shells.

Give borders a tidy up. Set aside a morning or afternoon to go around the garden doing those small jobs that make all the difference to its appearance. Lightly fork

Thorough weeding Clear the ground before planting up a border.

over the soil, pulling out any weeds. Any plants taking up too much space and growing across other plants can be lightly pruned into shape to keep them looking tidy. Don't be too hard with the pruning or you may cut off all this year's flowers. Put in plant supports as you go.

Watch out for self-sown seedlings when working on the borders. It is amazing just how many plants seed themselves freely around the garden. A lot of hardy annuals seed quite prolifically and many shrubs and herbaceous perennials can, at times, almost become weeds. One group of plants particularly good at self-seeding are foxgloves (see p.98). They are quite happy to be moved at this time of year and will flower later, so it's a good time to "edit" their population. Sadly, seedlings from white foxgloves often turn out purple in flower – but they are beautiful nevertheless. Remember to water any seedlings you move.

Apply synthetic fertilizers now. If you didn't give plants an organic fertilizer earlier in the spring, a chemical fertilizer will give them an instant boost now, just when they need it. Pull back any mulch, lightly fluff up the soil with a rake, and apply according to the maker's instructions. Replace the mulch.

All plants need nutrients to survive, but there is no need to feed absolutely everything every year. Trees and shrubs, for example, will grow quite happily for years, provided that the initial preparation before planting has been done thoroughly. With these, all that may be necessary is to apply some fertilizer in the first two or three years after planting. After that, unless there is any obvious deficiency, they will cope well on their own. But do remember to water them well in dry weather in the early stages of getting established. The areas of the garden most in need of fertilizers every year are the vegetable and fruit garden, annual borders, and plants in containers, where the plants are taking more out of the soil. With all fertilizers, wash your hands well after use.

TREES AND SHRUBS

■ **Remove frost-damaged shoots** from any slightly tender evergreen shrubs like *Choisya ternata* (Mexican orange blossom). At the same time you can, if necessary, prune back any misplaced stems. In colder parts pruning these shrubs is best left until next month, in case a late, hard frost causes more damage. Stems should always be cut back to a healthy leaf lower down the shoot, or to a stem junction.

■ **Spray roses** with a recommended fungicide to control black spot, which looks exactly as you might expect – black spots, or blotches, on the leaves. This will have to be done at regular intervals, as black spot is difficult to control. Follow the manufacturer's instructions for dosages and intervals between spraying.

Better still, try to grow only those varieties of roses that are resistant to black spot, such as 'Graham Thomas', 'François Juranville' or *Rosa mundi* – more correctly called *Rosa gallica* var. *officinalis* 'Versicolor'. Catalogues will highlight many more that are available. Rose breeders are constantly bringing out new varieties of roses that are more resistant to disease, therefore cutting down on the need to spray. A visit to a rose nursery in summer is not only a pleasant day out, but well worth the trip just to see which roses are more disease-resistant, but be aware that they may be sprayed for disease control.

■ **Check roses for aphids.** Rub or hose greenfly off to avoid using sprays, or use one of the hand-held sprays to direct the pesticide accurately. By doing this as soon as you spot them, you can help prevent colonies building up.

Planting
■ **Plant container-grown trees and shrubs.** Bare-root deciduous stock will no longer be available, but all plants are now

A good watering Give all plants grown in containers a good soak after planting.

sold as container-grown specimens to plant at any time of the year, although spring and autumn are best for the plants. Water the plant well in its pot an hour or two beforehand, then ease the rootball out of the pot. Set it firmly in a generously sized hole so that the top of the compost is level with the ground around it. Work soil down around the sides of the root ball with your fingers, water well again, and mulch

around the plant to lock in that precious moisture. For advice on sheltering evergreens in exposed sites, *see p.96*.

Pruning and training
■ **Trim winter-flowering heathers** with shears if you didn't do it earlier in the year. The spent flowering stems will now be looking quite tatty, so remove them completely in order to show off the more attractive new growth.

■ **Prune shrubs** grown for their colourful foliage, such as elder (*Sambucus*) and cotinus (smoke bush). The best-coloured foliage is produced by new stems, hence the reason for pruning hard now. If you want to increase the size of the plants it is worthwhile leaving two or three shoots unpruned and these can grow on, making the plant larger without compromising on the colourful foliage. As always after pruning feed with a general fertilizer and water it in if the weather is dry.

■ **Prune forsythias** and chaenomeles after flowering. These two shrubs put on a terrific show of colour in the spring, on

Pruning early flowers

Pruning forsythias Cut the flowered stems back to strong, new leafy sideshoots, pointing upwards and outwards.

Pruning chaenomeles Cutting sideshoots back to one or two buds encourages flowers. The shoot on the left was left unpruned.

wood made the previous summer and now is the time to prune them for flowers next spring. Pruning for both shrubs is the same procedure. When the flowers have gone over cut back the flowered shoots to two or three buds from their base. On more established shrubs cut out about a third of the older growth to the base of the plant. This will encourage new shoots to grow from the base.

These shrubs can also be trained to grow against walls or fences and very attractive they look too. Pruning in this situation is a slightly different procedure. After you have tied in any stems you need to fill gaps, prune all flowered shoots to one or two buds from their point of growing. You can do the same in summer to keep chaenomeles, and also pyracanthas, flat where space is limited. Leading shoots can be pruned to keep the shrubs within their allocated place.

■ **Cut back lavender** once the plants approach the size you want them to grow to. If lavender plants are left unpruned the centre of the shrub grows sparse, they look unattractive and they don't like being pruned into older wood. So it is a good idea to prune them every spring to keep them bushy and compact.

Other silver-leaved shrubs to prune in the same way are *Helichrysum serotinum* (curry plant) and santolina (cotton lavender). Go over the whole plant, trimming off 2.5–5cm (1–2in) of growth. Use shears to speed things up if you have a lot of lavender, for example a low hedge. It may seem a bit harsh, but the plants stay compact and the centre does not open up.

Propagation

■ **Increase conifers by taking cuttings.** This is a good time of year to propagate your favourite conifers.

Trim lavender In spring, prune the tips of all the shoots with secateurs or shears.

Hedges

■ **Plant evergreen hedging plants.** This is a good time to plant evergreens; not only conifers but the many broad-leaved plants that make excellent hedging. Most can be clipped to shape or grown informally, only being trimmed when they become overgrown.

By planting evergreens at this time of year there is less chance of them being damaged by cold winter winds, but they may still need some protection. It's not just winter winds that cause problems. Even in spring and summer, high winds can be just as damaging. The speed of the wind going over the surface of the leaf draws water from it more quickly than the plant can replace it from the soil, especially in summer if the ground is dry, and this causes withering.

If your plants are regularly scorched in this way, consider erecting more screens and windbreaks to shelter your garden – or research some more wind- and drought-tolerant shrubs to replace casualties.

CLIMBERS

■ **Climbing and rambling roses** need to be tied in, training the shoots as near to horizontal as possible. By doing this the flow of sap is restricted; this causes more sideshoots to develop along the whole length of the main stems and therefore more flowers are produced. If left to grow vertically, all the flowers are produced at the tips of the stems, where they are difficult to see. If you are growing roses on a stout post, wind the stems around the post in a spiral fashion and tie in, and this will have the same effect of restricting the flow of sap.

■ **Tie in shoots of twiners,** such as clematis, as they are growing fast now. With clematis, once they get hold of their support they can usually be left to get on with it, especially if growing through other shrubs, but they may need some guidance if encroaching too much on other plants.

■ **Plant container-grown climbers** as for trees and shrubs.

■ **Prune wall-trained forsythias and chaenomeles.**

Training climbing roses Tie in shoots horizontally for more flowering sideshoots.

Make a willow obelisk

An obelisk is an attractive, rustic willow-wand structure that can be used for lightweight climbers such as sweet peas, late-flowering clematis, or runner and climbing French beans.

You will need
- Nine lengths of two-year-old (or older) willow, seven of roughly equal length for the uprights, and two for the main ribs of the horizontal bands
- six lengths of year-old willow for weaving
- a bundle of thin willow, less than one year old, or twine, for tying
- a half-barrel or large tub
- secateurs

1 You can make the obelisk *in situ*, but I find it convenient to use a tub as a guide. Insert the seven stoutest of the two-year-old wands, evenly spaced so that they form a circle of uprights.

2 Make the lower band by twisting one of the remaining two-year-old wands around itself. Drop it over the uprights and adjust its size until they are slightly pulled together.

3 Using thin pieces of willow or twine, tie the band to each upright, about 30cm (12in) from the base.

4 Starting at one of the uprights, weave one of the year-old wands in and out and around the band and the uprights.

5 Finish the weave by pulling the tip of the wand sharply upwards at one of the uprights to secure it.

6 Starting at different uprights, weave two more of the year-old wands around the band in exactly the same way (see Steps 4–5).

7 Bind each of the joints with the thin willow or twine, winding each roughly around and threading it in between the willow joint until you have a stout, knobbly "knot".

8 Trim off any protruding wand tips with secateurs for a neat finish.

9 Make the upper band in exactly the same way as the lower one, but slightly smaller so that it draws the uprights together a little more.

10 Finish off the top by holding the uprights together and binding and tying them very firmly with your longest, most flexible, piece of thin willow. As with the bands, if you finish with a sharp pull upwards between uprights, the pressure of the structure trying to spring apart should hold the end securely in place.

11 The finished obelisk lets me use more vertical space for climbers, such as a clematis, in my border.

PERENNIALS

■ **Continue planting new plants.** Getting plants in by the end of the month will give them time to establish while the weather is mild and wet. They'll have a better chance of putting on good growth in the season.

■ **Continue taking basal cuttings.**

■ **Remove winter protection** from borderline hardy plants.

■ **Top up grit and gravel** around plants growing in a Mediterranean or scree-bed setting if it has been lost or shifted by winter weather. This will really smarten the area up before plants get going, to set them off perfectly when at their best.

■ **Finish dividing** and replanting summer-flowering perennials. This is the latest month for lifting and dividing if you want these to flower in the summer and autumn. Whenever possible, always revitalize the soil with well-rotted farmyard manure or garden compost before replanting perennials. Water in well after planting if the weather is dry.

Dividing clumps Carefully part congested clumps of herbaceous perennials.

Thinning shoots Some perennials flower better if you reduce the shoots at the base.

■ **Thin shoots on perennials.** To get top-quality flowers from border plants it is sometimes necessary to thin out overcrowded shoots. Plants most likely to need thinning include delphiniums and lupins, especially if you are growing these for showing at your local flower show. Phlox will also put on a bolder show if it is thinned. Remove about one in three or four of the shoots, depending on crowding.

■ **Dahlia tubers** can be planted in milder parts of the country. In other areas, wait until next month. Make sure the ground has been prepared well as dahlias are gross, or greedy, feeders. Add plenty of organic matter and a good dressing of organic fertilizer before planting, and also, insert a stake into the ground to support the plants before you plant – then you will not damage the tubers. The tubers should be planted so that the crown of the tuber is at least 7.5cm (3in) deep.

Alpines

■ **Remove all winter protection** from alpine plants and beds.

■ **Plant new alpines** now. The cold rains they dislike so much should be tailing off.

Self-sown seedlings

1 **Foxglove seedlings** form a flat rosette of slightly coarse leaves, oval in shape, coming to a point.

2 **Water the soil** first if it is dry, then lift the seedlings gently with a trowel, taking a good ball of soil up around the fragile roots.

3 **Plant the seedling** in its new position, firming gently with your fingertips – do not press too hard. Water the young plant in very gently.

BULBS

■ **Deadhead the last of the daffodils** now that the flowers are going over. Snap the flowerhead off behind the swollen part; you can leave the stalk intact. If the spent flowers are left on, the plant's energy will be diverted into the production of seeds. By removing the old flowers, the plant's energy is instead diverted into the formation of next year's flower bud within the bulb. For this to happen, the foliage must be left on the plant. For many years the practice was to allow the foliage of the bulbs to die back completely, to give the plants the longest time to build up that flower bud for next year. But recent research has shown that the foliage can be cut down six weeks after the flowers are over. You can choose which method you prefer. The old foliage of daffodils can look messy, but do not tie it up with raffia or elastic bands. The best way to hide it is to grow daffodils in among other plants such as hostas, which have large, bold leaves.

■ **Plant out all summer-flowering bulbs.** They should all be planted by the end of the month, in time to flower during the summer. Tender bulbs, such as gladioli, can

Carpets of gold Daffodils look superb naturalized in grass.

go out now, wherever you happen to live. These prefer a sunny spot in well-drained soil, so if you garden on heavy clay, put a layer of coarse grit in the hole and plant the corms on top to improve drainage.

■ **Divide nerines.** Overcrowded clumps of these beautiful autumn-flowering bulbs can be split and replanted now. Put the spade or fork in the ground a little way out from the clump or you risk slicing through, or spearing, the bulbs. Do not replant any damaged bulbs, as they attract rots that may spread through the rest.

ANNUALS AND BEDDING

■ **Continue sowing hardy annuals outside.** In colder parts of the country it is perhaps best to wait until this month before sowing outside, to give the soil a chance to warm up. Heavy clay soils, in particular, take longer to warm up than light sandy soils.

■ **Plant out hardy annuals** raised in modules. Prepare the soil in the same way as for direct sowing and mark out drifts in the same way. Plant the young plants in the drifts and that's it. There is no need to thin out the plants and they will flower a little earlier than those sown outside.

■ **Sow half-hardy summer bedding plants.**

■ **Pot up cuttings** of tender perennials that you took last year. Keep them under cover until next month, when you can start hardening them off for planting out.

■ **Buy plug plants** of bedding if you have the room to grow them on in frost-free surroundings. Keep them inside until it is safe to plant them out.

Dividing nerines

1 Lift the clumps carefully and shake off as much soil as possible, then separate out individual bulbs. Retain as much root on each as you can.

2 Clean the bulbs up before replanting singly at the same depth as before, about 5cm (2in) apart. Peel off brown, flaky debris, but leave a layer of white, papery skin, or tunic, intact.

Lobelia plug plant Tiny plug plants are ideal if you are fortunate enough to have indoor space.

Ipomoea tricolor

Asarina procumbens

Tropaeolum peregrinum

■ **By the end of the month** spring bedding may start to look past its best, but summer bedding cannot be planted out safely for a few weeks yet. So do what you can to keep plants neat, rather than pulling them out too early to leave bare ground that weeds will colonize.

■ **Sweet peas** should really have been sown earlier, but a late sowing now will still produce some flowers in late summer and autumn.

■ **Plant out sweet peas** sown in autumn. In cold areas, it's safe to do this towards the end of the month and into the next as long as they have been hardened off first for one or two weeks. Prepare the ground and sprinkle a little general fertilizer before planting – not too much or you will get a lot of growth and few flowers.

■ **Sow more unusual annual climbers.** Climbing plants have many practical uses: adding height to a border or hiding ugly buildings or other unsightly places like the compost heap. To use permanent perennial climbing plants such as roses and clematis can be a little expensive and many do take some time to get established and cover a given area.

For a cheap and quick way to cover an eyesore such as a compost heap, old shed, or unattractive wall, or to add height to a planting, annual climbers are really the ideal choice.

Another way to make use of annual climbers is to let them scramble through evergreen shrubs or through trees, extending their period of interest.

Like sweet peas, nasturtiums (*Tropaeolum majus*), in all shades from brilliant reds to yellows, can both be sown directly into the soil now, but other more unusual climbers can be raised in pots and planted out in June. Many are tender perennials grown in our climate as annuals. Lovely plants to try include *Ipomoea* (morning glory), with large blue or pink flowers; *Cobaea scandens*, with violet and purple flowers; *Canarina canariensis*, the Canary bellflower, with almost courgette-like orangey flowers; *Eccremocarpus scaber*, or Chilean glory vine, with funnel-shaped red and yellow flowers; purple rhodochitons; black-eyed Susan, or *Thunbergia alata*; *Tropaeolum peregrinum*, and in small spaces, *Asarina procumbens*, which makes an effective trailing plant in a raised rock garden. Sow the seeds thinly and cover lightly with vermiculite as some of them need light to germinate. They will all need a temperature of around 18°C (65°F).

These plants can also be bought in as mini-plants or plugs for potting on. This is an easy way to grow them, as it cuts down on the cost of providing heating to germinate the seeds. They will need at least frost-free conditions to grow on until the threat of frost is passed, generally not until around the beginning of June.

■ **Sow annual grasses.** Their delicate foliage and attractive seedheads contrast well with broad-leaved plants in the

Hordeum jubatum

Briza maxima

CONTAINERS

■ **Clean containers and pots** that are to be used for summer bedding displays. All pots should be cleaned thoroughly using a weak solution of ordinary household bleach. This is well worth doing as it will reduce trouble from pests and diseases.

You could also spruce up older, scruffy containers with some of the multi-surface garden paints that are now on offer, perhaps even experimenting with some more unusual shades to enhance summer colour schemes.

■ **Plant up alpine troughs.** Whether you buy a trough or sink, or make your own, this is an ideal month for doing this job as many alpines are coming into flower now and you can get an instant effect when the job's done. The most important point to bear in mind when growing alpines is that they like good drainage, so make sure any container used for growing these plants has plenty of drainage holes in the bottom. Before filling the container with compost put a 5cm (2in) layer of broken pots or coarse gravel in the bottom to help with drainage.

The compost used for filling the container should be what is called an "alpine mix", consisting of equal parts garden soil, garden compost or coir compost, and coarse grit.

After planting spread a layer of coarse grit over the surface of the compost between the plants. This not only sets off the plants well, but also keeps down weeds and prevents the plants being splashed with soil in rainy weather.

borders. It's an excellent, inexpensive way to try out the new way of growing perennials among grasses for a more "naturalistic" border look and all of the seedheads can be dried and used in indoor flower arrangements.

Annual grasses to look out for on the seed packet shelves include *Briza maxima*, the quaking grass; *Lagurus ovatus*, hare's tail grass, and *Hordeum jubatum* or squirrel tail grass. They can be sown outside from now on.

You can sow them *in situ* in drifts as with annual flowers – in drills, so you can tell them from weed grasses when they germinate – or in drills on a spare piece of ground, to transplant in among plants in the border when they are big enough.

Sow the seeds in shallow drills that you have scratched out with a stick and water the drills if the soil seems dry. Cover the seeds lightly and label them. Thin out the young seedlings and transplant them, if necessary, when they have grown large enough to handle.

Alpine display This planter makes a natural-looking home for alpines. Use a range of plants that flower in different seasons for a long-lasting display.

LAWNS

■ **Mow your lawn regularly.** If grass is left to grow long and then cut short it will turn yellow and be weakened, so regular mowing – by summer once a week, or if you're really fussy twice a week – is the order of the day. Blades should be at their highest setting when you start mowing in spring – by the end of this month, start gradually lowering them each time.

■ **Continue to repair** and renovate established lawns. It is especially important to level off lumps and bumps, as these cause the mower to scalp the grass, weakening it and encouraging weeds and moss to grow. Continue to remove weeds individually. Coarse grasses, which are extremely vigorous and somewhat out of place on a finer lawn, can be removed by criss-crossing the clump with an old knife, then pulling out the tufts of grass. After this regular mowing will discourage coarser grasses from taking root.

■ **Feed established lawns,** unless you did so late last month. Always use fertilizers according to the manufacturer's instructions. There is no point in putting on a little extra to "speed things up". Plants will only take up a certain amount and the excess leaches into the water table and then into streams and rivers.

There are several methods of applying lawn fertilizer. One is to mark out the lawn into square metres or yards with string and canes and measure out and scatter the fertilizer by hand, wearing gloves, in measured doses, the same as when you are sowing seed. This can be laborious if you have a large lawn, so use a fertilizer spreader, which gives a more even effect. There are many types available.

■ **You can treat moss** with a mosskiller now, but do bear in mind that this only treats the symptoms rather than the actual cause. The main causes of moss in lawns are usually poor drainage, weak grass, and compacted soil. The best way to remedy these faults is to aerate the lawn each year using a machine or fork to spike the lawn and to rake out "thatch": the moss and dead grass that accumulates. By doing this and feeding the lawn regularly the grass will be much healthier and moss and weeds will be far less able to establish themselves in it.

New lawns

■ **Sow new lawns on prepared ground,** if this was not done last month. With the weather warming up grass seed will germinate quickly now. The area for a new lawn should have been dug over during the winter, incorporating organic matter to retain moisture. You can still get away with this preparation now if you have a light sandy soil. After digging, the ground will have to be levelled off and the soil raked down to a fine tilth. Firm the soil well by treading it with your weight on your heels, rake the soil again, tread it at right angles to the previous direction, and finally rake it level. To sow the seed, first mark out the area in metre squares, as when spreading fertilizer, using canes and string. Weigh out the quantity of seed required per square metre, as recommended by the manufacturer on the packet, once on kitchen scales, and then put it into a cup and mark its level on the side.

Now you can either use the cup to measure out all the subsequent "doses" of seed, or tip a measure into your hand, see how it feels, and then take up similar-sized handfuls each time. This saves a lot of weighing. Scatter the seed evenly over each area; rake in and water with a fine spray or sprinkler. A quick alternative for a large area is to use a fertilizer spreader set at the seed-sowing setting.

Most grass seed these days is treated with a bird repellent, so there is no need to protect it. This may not be the most "organic" option, but it is certainly kinder than risking birds becoming entangled in netting or thread.

■ **Finish making new lawns** from turf (keep well watered) before the weather becomes too dry. Newly turfed lawns should grow away quite quickly now, and you may find that those laid earlier in the year are already in need of a trim.

Sowing grass seed

1 Broadcast the seed evenly over measured square metres. Scatter half one way and the rest the other, until you become more confident.

2 Rake very gently to just cover the seed, using short strokes, so that you do not redistribute it unevenly.

VEGETABLES AND HERBS

Sowing under cover

■ **Sow tomatoes** for planting outdoors in early June. Although you may have sown tomatoes for the greenhouse during the previous month, there is no point in sowing tomatoes to grow outdoors much more than six to eight weeks before you can plant them out.

Sow the seeds in trays or small pots containing seed compost. Overfill the container, give a sharp tap on the bench to settle the compost, strike off the surplus, and firm gently with the base of a pot to level off. Water before sowing. Sow the seeds thinly and cover with vermiculite until the seeds just disappear.

Place in a propagator at a temperature of 22°C (70°F). Cover with a sheet of glass and paper, removing this when the seeds germinate in a couple of weeks. When the seedlings are large enough to handle them, either prick out into trays or pot up into small pots.

There are many tomato varieties to choose from and which you grow is a matter of taste, from the small cherry tomatoes to the large, beefy, slicing types. However, they do grow in different ways. Cordon varieties of tomatoes are the tall kind with a single, central stem needing support, but there are bush varieties, many of which are relatively hardy, which do not need training and look very decorative, especially in containers on the patio. There are even trailing tomatoes that can be grown in hanging baskets.

Cordons are the traditional choice for glasshouse-growing because you can use the full height of the greenhouse to ripen a good crop, but the bush and trailing varieties look equally good on greenhouse benches and conservatories.

■ **Sow celery and celeriac** for planting outdoors in early June, exactly as you would tomatoes.

■ **Sow sweetcorn,** marrows and courgettes, and pumpkins and squashes towards the end of the month. If they are sown any earlier, they will get drawn and starved before it is safe to plant them out, at the beginning of June. Sow these crops two seeds per 8cm (3in) pot, pushing them into the compost on their edge. They don't need quite as high a temperature as tomatoes to germinate: 16°C (61°F) is sufficient. When the seeds have germinated, remove the weaker one and grow on the other. Pot up into larger pots if necessary before planting out in June.

■ **Sow leeks in modules.** You can sow leeks outside this month, but if you're growing vegetables on deep beds the ideal way of growing leeks is to multi-sow them in modules. Fill a modular tray with seed compost and firm gently. Put some leek seeds onto a piece of card or paper and with the point of a knife, sow five or six seeds per cell. Cover the seeds with compost or vermiculite. When the seedlings are about 10cm (4in) high they can be planted out in their clusters, 30cm (1ft) apart each way. Although each leek will be smaller you get more crop per square metre than when growing in conventional rows.

Sowing and planting outdoors

■ **Continue to plant asparagus crowns.**

■ **Carrots** sown late this month may need carrot fly protection.

■ **Plant maincrop potatoes.** This is the latest month for maincrops if you want to get a decent crop. To plant them, take out trenches 60cm (2ft) apart to the depth of the spade, heaping the soil to one side. If no organic matter was dug in earlier in the year, put some well-rotted manure or garden compost in the trench and set the

Young lettuces Protect your plants against night frosts with cone-shaped plastic cloches.

tubers on this. Space the tubers about 38cm (15in) apart. Sprinkle fertilizer in the gaps along the row before filling in. Cover the tubers with soil, leaving it slightly mounded up.

■ **Keep up with successional sowings** of vegetables like lettuce, radish, beetroot, peas, broad beans, salad onions, and turnips. By sowing little and often you will avoid having a glut of produce all at one time, which may be difficult to manage. Sow in shallow drills made with a stick, watering them before sowing if the soil is dry. Sow the seeds thinly, cover with soil, and label them. Thin out when the seedlings are large enough to handle.

■ **Plant out onions** sown earlier in the year. Rake in a general fertilizer before planting and don't grow on soil that had onions on it the previous year. Onions being grown as single plants can be planted 22cm (9in) apart, in rows 30cm (12in) apart. Those that were sown in modules and grown as multiple plants can be planted out in their clusters on deep beds, 15cm (6in) apart each way. As these onions grow they push each other apart.

The individual onions may be smaller than when plants are grown singly, but the overall crop yield per square metre is greater because there are more plants.

■ **Sow dwarf French beans** under cloches in milder parts of the country. Take out a wide drill about 2.5cm (1in) deep and space the seeds 15cm (6in) apart in an arrangement of staggered rows. Water if the soil is dry and put cloches over the rows to protect them from the frost. They should be up in a few days.

■ **Sow leeks.** It is now safe to sow leeks outside in a nursery bed (a spare piece of ground used to raise plants before transplanting them to their final cropping positions). Sow them in short rows by taking out narrow drills in the usual manner. Water the drills if the weather is dry and sow the seeds thinly along the drill. Cover with dry soil and label the row. When they are 10cm (4in) high they can be transplanted. The easiest way to do this is to make a hole with a large dibber. You can make one from an old spade handle or you can buy one. Drop one plant into each hole. Water in and some soil will be carried into the hole, anchoring the plant.

■ **Plant seakale.** This unusual vegetable is normally blanched for harvesting stems in winter and spring. It can be grown from seed, but for crops within the year it is far better to buy it as roots or "crowns". Plant them about 30cm (12in) apart, with the top of the root just below the surface of the soil. When the young shoots begin to grow, remove the weakest ones, leaving just one shoot on each root. By the autumn the plants will have formed good crowns for forcing.

■ **Sow kohlrabi** at intervals from now until August. It is the swollen part of the

Kohlrabi Harvest the curious, swollen stem bases when they are small and tender and leave the central shoots on the plant.

stem that is eaten; it has a turnip-like flavour. Sow the seeds in narrow drills in the usual way and thin the resulting seedlings, leaving them 22cm (9in) apart each way.

■ **Sow Florence fennel** in drills 60cm (2ft) apart and thin the seedlings to 38cm (15in), when they are large enough to handle. These are quite decorative plants with feathery foliage and they grow to a height of around 1.25–2m (4–6ft). It's the swollen stem bases, which have an aniseed flavour, that are eaten.

■ **Sow seeds of salsify and scorzonera.** These are two unusual root vegetables, little grown in the UK because they are fiddly to prepare, the roots being very long and thin. In countries such as France, where food preparation is taken very seriously, they are very popular. Salsify tastes rather like oysters and scorzonera has a nutty flavour, which, though difficult to describe, is delicious. Grow both in soil that has been manured for a previous crop, applying a general fertilizer before sowing. Rake the soil level and to a fine tilth and sow the seeds in narrow drills 30cm (1ft) apart, watering the drills before sowing if

the weather is dry. Thin the seedlings to 30cm (12in) apart. You can use the roots in the autumn or store them in boxes over the winter.

■ **Winter brassicas** – broccoli, cabbages, cauliflowers, and Brussels sprouts – can all be sown outside on a prepared seedbed early in the month, if this wasn't done last month. Those sown last month and ready for transplanting should be moved to their permanent bed before the plants get too large, the ideal time being when the plants have made two or three true leaves. Spacing varies tremendously with the type and variety of crop, but will be given on the seed packets. Water well after transplanting and place brassica collars around the young plants to ward off cabbage root fly. Adult flies lay their eggs at the base of the plant and the resulting white larvae eat the plant's roots. Collars that fit snugly around the base of the stem prevent the adult flies laying the eggs in the soil and they fail to hatch. There are no chemical controls available, so prevention is the only and, of course, the organic, way. Planting through mulching sheets and membranes also does the same job. You can even use old carpet, cut into 15cm (6in) squares.

Looking after crops

■ **Water regularly in dry weather.** All young vegetable plants need plenty of water to develop well.

■ **Thin out rows of seedlings** sown earlier. If seedlings are not thinned out the plants will become straggly and not crop well at all. The distances to thin each type of vegetable will vary and it is best to check the back of the seed packet for details of individual plants. The thinnings of most vegetables, except root vegetables such as carrots, beetroots, and turnips, can be

Thinning seedlings Be careful not to damage the remaining plants as you thin along the row.

transplanted. The advantage of this is that these thinnings, having been disturbed, will mature that little bit later than the seedlings left in the row, therefore extending the succession of cropping. Water seedlings before and after thinning in dry weather. Seedlings being transplanted should also be watered gently, but well after planting.

■ **If any shoots** of early potatoes are starting to show through, keep a sheet of horticultural fleece handy and cover them if any sharp frosts are forecast. They are vulnerable to cold damage. If you have planted the potatoes under sheets of clear polythene, cut slits in it as soon as you see the shoots, to allow them to grow through.

■ **Watch out for flea beetle.** These small insects attack brassicas, turnips, and radishes, nibbling small holes in the foliage. They are so-called because when they are disturbed, they jump. You can spray with an insecticide to control them, but one way you could try to keep the numbers down, or indeed if you want to confirm that flea beetles are the problem, is to make use of the fact that they do hop up when disturbed. Get a small, square piece of wood or cardboard and smear one side of

it with grease or petroleum jelly. Run this over the tops of the leaves and the beetles will jump up and stick to the card.

■ **Support peas sown earlier.** Peas have rather straggly growth and if they are not supported some of the crop will be lost, because it will become spoiled lying on the soil. There are several ways to support peas. Plastic green support mesh, specially made for the purpose, can be bought from the garden centre, or use twiggy sticks. One method that is useful is to use the prunings from other shrubs in the garden, provided they are strong enough and are reasonably straight. An ideal shrub for this is buddleja (the butterfly bush). It produces large purple or white flowers on long shoots made through the summer and these shoots make ideal supports for peas, but any other shrubs with reasonably straight stems will do. Keep them to one side after you have pruned them from the shrub in spring. The tips with the old flower heads may have to be removed to make them look more presentable.

Prunings These are the most economical option for supporting young pea plants.

Growing herbs Make sure that you keep young plants watered regularly – even the easy-to-grow types such as mint.

Herbs

■ **Divide chives,** if this was not done last month. With larger clumps, you may have to use two forks back to back to prise the clump apart, but otherwise they can be pulled apart by hand. Water well after replanting in soil that has been revitalized with garden compost.

■ **Propagate thyme by layering.** This method is very similar to that used on strawberry runners. Fill small pots with a mixture of equal parts of peat-free compost and sharp sand, and sink the pots into the soil beneath the vigorous outer stems to be layered. Peg the stems into the pots and in a few weeks roots will have formed. The new plants can be cut from the parent and planted out into their permanent positions. Thymes require a well-drained soil in a sunny spot.

■ **Continue sowing** and planting herbs. By now most herbs can be sown outside and any sown earlier inside can be planted out from the end of the month, after hardening off in a cold frame. Many varieties of young herb plants are available and it's a real treat to make a trip to a herb nursery, to see, and most enjoyably, to smell all the different herbs on offer.

FRUIT

Harvesting

■ **Check under rhubarb forcers** regularly until the crop of young, pale stems is ready. When you have cut them all, leave the forcer off and feed the plants. Do not take a crop from the regrowth.

Looking after crops

■ **Feed blackcurrants, blackberries, and hybrid berries** with a high-nitrogen feed. These plants make a lot of growth during the season and an extra dose of a high-nitrogen feed will give them a welcome boost. Don't use too much – follow the directions on the package. Too much nitrogen will result in very soft growth, which is more susceptible to attack from pests and diseases.

■ **Control weeds around cane fruit.** Weeds take valuable moisture and nutrients from the soil and also act as hosts to pests and diseases. The easiest way to keep down weeds around fruit is to mulch with a thick layer of farmyard manure, garden compost, or straw.

■ **Keep frost protection** on early-flowering fruits; however mild the weather appears to be now compared to the earlier months of the year, night frosts are still common. Remember that this will also involve hand-pollinating flowers.

■ **Keep an eye out for pests and diseases** by inspecting fruits regularly. If you feel you must use chemical sprays then spray in the evenings when there are few pollinating insects around. Don't spray during the period when the flowers of any fruits are fully open – not even in the evenings – as you will harm pollinating insects. We have to do all we can to encourage a wide range of insects and mammals into the garden as their habitats in the countryside in general gradually

disappear. Even so-called "safe" organic sprays kill a wide variety of insects and will harm the beneficial ones.

By building up a diversity of plants in the garden you will attract beneficial insects, birds, and mammals and these will keep the pest problem to a minimum. You never know, you may not have to spray at all. Sow or plant some annual flowers in the fruit garden, such as phacelia, as these will attract friendly pest predators such as hoverflies that will do the work of pest control for you.

■ **Watch out for American gooseberry mildew** on gooseberries. This shows as a white powdery coating on the leaves. If you want to spray, use a fungicide recommended for the purpose, bought from the garden centre. Read the instructions carefully. But it's better to grow varieties like 'Invicta', which are resistant to mildew, removing the need to spray at all. Winter-pruning, watering, and feeding well also help plants to grow strong and more resistant to attack.

■ **Blackcurrants are often** affected by a mite that spreads a virus on its mouthparts: watch out for swollen buds in late winter and be aware of virus symptoms now. If the bush is affected by virus, the flowers will be red instead of pinkish grey. There is no choice but to dig it up and burn it. There is no effective cure. Replace lost bushes with the mite-resistant cultivar 'Ben Hope'.

Pruning and training

■ **Prune fan-trained stone fruits** such as cherries, plums, and nectarines. First prune out any shoots that are growing either into the wall and directly away from the tree. Then thin out any overcrowded and crossing shoots, while at the same time removing any dead, diseased, or damaged

Pick blackcurrants Do this in sequence, selecting ripe berries individually from strings.

shoots. The remaining shoots can be tied to the training wires.

The reason for pruning these trees now rather than during the winter months is that they are prone to the fungal diseases silver leaf and bacterial canker. These enter the plant through open wounds; by pruning now, when the plant is in growth, the pruning cuts heal over quickly, reducing the risk of disease getting in.

■ **Tie in vines.** Outdoor vines will be growing fast soon and the shoots will need tying in if they are not to get completely out of control. Vines grow extremely fast and can put on more than 3m (10ft) of growth in a season. So tying in, thinning, and stopping the shoots are important to encourage a good crop of grapes instead of a mass of leafy growth.

The easiest way to train grapes is to use a central, vertical main stem, or rod, that is kept pruned back to the height of the supporting system of wires. Each year, train selected sideshoots out sideways, to form an espalier shape. These shoots will carry the fruits, then in winter you can cut them back to within two or three buds of the main rod.

Planting

■ **Plant container-grown trained fruit trees.** By this month it is too late to plant bare-root fruit trees and bushes, but there are many different kinds, trained in attractive ways, available in containers. The advantage of container-grown plants is that they can be planted at any time of the year because the root system is not disturbed. You can even buy them in flower and may get some fruit from them in the first year after planting, but don't take a lot of fruit in the first year. It's better to let the plants get established now and they'll fruit all the better in subsequent years. Lay a seephose when you plant new fruit and mulch on top of it to water efficiently and conserve soil moisture.

Apples, pears, plums, red and white currants, and gooseberries can all be trained in several different ways: espaliers (tiers of horizontal branches), cordons (single-stemmed trees grown at an angle to save space), and fans (branches trained to resemble the spokes of a fan). These are all both attractive and productive, and with modern dwarfing rootstocks they can be fitted into the smallest of spaces, so no garden need be without some fruit.

Planting a blackcurrant bush Ensure that the bush is planted deeper than it was in its pot.

UNDER COVER

■ **Ventilate well on sunny days.** It may be necessary to leave vents and doors open all day in warm weather, as the temperature can climb dramatically in a short time when the sun is out.

■ **Damp down on warm days.** On hot days the atmosphere indoors can become very dry – not the best conditions for plants. Damping down simply means splashing water onto the floor to increase the humidity of the atmosphere as this is much more conducive to plant growth.

Another advantage is that it reduces the incidence of red spider mite. This pest attacks the leaves of plants, causing them to become mottled and then to die off. It thrives in warm, dry conditions, so damping down can reduce the problem without having to use sprays.

■ **Shade young plants** during sunny weather. As with newly pricked-out seedlings, cuttings will need to be shaded from strong sunlight too. Until new roots develop, the cuttings are continually losing water from their leaves, but in the meantime they have no roots to replace the water that has been lost. Shading them will reduce water loss from the leaves in hot weather. Temporary shading for young plants is easily provided by using sheets of newspaper.

■ **Watch out for vine weevil.** This pest has become a serious problem in recent years, especially on pot plants. The little creamy-white grubs live in the compost and eat roots, easily going unnoticed until you see the plants wilting.

There is a biological predator available to control them: a microscopic nematode worm that attacks the grubs. It can be bought by mail order and watered into the pots. Alternatively, water plants with a proprietary insecticide.

■ **Introduce other biological controls** if this was not done earlier. In fact this is perhaps a better time to introduce them, especially in unheated greenhouses, as they do not work in temperatures below 10°C (50°F). These controls are usually in the form of nematodes or small predatory insects or mites, and there are specific ones for specific pests – for example, the tiny wasp *Encarsia formosa*, which kills young whitefly. Under cover, they do the job of friendly garden insects such as hoverflies and ladybirds, which are encouraged by all good gardeners.

■ **Whitefly can be a problem,** especially if you are growing tomatoes, which seem to attract every specimen in the neighbourhood.

Put up yellow sticky cards to catch them. Hang the cards on string near the tops of plants and raise them higher as the plants grow. It's amazing just how many will be caught on these traps. Whitefly seem to be strongly attracted to the colour yellow. Before an infestation becomes really severe, use a biological control as well. Growing some French marigolds in the greenhouse or conservatory is also believed to deter whitefly.

Whitefly These pests lay their eggs on leaves and feed on the sap.

Raising plants for outdoors

■ **Buy bedding plants as plugs;** in the south and in sheltered areas they will grow on happily in an unheated greenhouse now. Buying bedding this way is growing in popularity among those who have space under glass to bring on the young plants. Many people don't have the time to sow seeds early on, then look after them until it's time for them to be planted out. So buying young plants also cuts out the time when seeds require the most heat to germinate. It's also easier than sowing tricky seed such as busy Lizzie (*Impatiens*).

Most bedding plants are now available in this way. They come in small modular trays, one plant per cell. The advantage of this system is that the plants can be potted up with no disturbance to the root system, so that they grow away better. When the young plants arrive, pot them up into 9cm (3½in) pots containing peat-free compost and grow them on in a cool greenhouse or conservatory. Don't give too much heat as the plants will grow too fast and become drawn. Harden off for a week or two before planting out.

Towards the end of the month, plant up hanging baskets. Although these cannot be hung outside until the threat of frost has passed, in early June, now, or early next month is a good time. This will allow the plants to fill out before being put outside.

■ **Complete sowing** of half-hardy annuals by the end of the month. Fast-growing, half-hardy annuals like French marigolds can be sown as late as this, but others requiring a longer growing season to flower should have been sown by now.

■ **Continue pricking out** seedlings of half-hardy annuals sown earlier. Pricking out means spacing the seedlings about 2.5cm (1in) apart in trays, so that they have more space to develop. Water

seedlings in well after pricking them out. On warm, sunny days they will benefit from shading from strong sunshine until they get established in the trays.

■ **Give young plants** more growing space. Continue to pot on growing young plants and cuttings. The ideal time to put plants into larger pots is just as the roots have filled the available compost, without becoming pot-bound. Generally pot on to pots one or two sizes larger than the one the plant is already growing in.

■ **In mild areas,** begin to harden off bedding plants towards the end of the month.

■ **Sow winter-flowering pansies.** These can be sown outside, but you will get better plants by sowing them in gentle heat now. Sow the seeds thinly in trays or in small pots, cover with a thin layer of compost, and put a sheet of glass and paper over the tray. Prick out the seedlings when they are large enough to handle, then pot up into module trays with large cells or in small pots. They can sit outside in a sheltered, shady spot throughout the summer, provided you remember to water them regularly. Planted in autumn, they will produce a terrific display right through the winter.

■ **Sow tomatoes, celery, and celeriac** for planting outdoors in early June.

■ **Sow sweetcorn, marrows, and courgettes** towards the end of the month.

■ **Continue to take cuttings** from tender perennials like fuchsias and pelargoniums. Those which were taken earlier and have rooted can be potted up if you have not done this already. To encourage the plants to bush out pinch out the growing tips.

Fuchsias and pelargoniums being trained as standards should not have the growing tips removed. Instead, let the main stem grow to the height you want, tying it to a cane as it grows to keep the stem straight. Pinch out any sideshoots that form. When the stem reaches the required height, pinch

Pot hydrangea cuttings

1 Take stem-tip cuttings by removing the top 8–10cm (3–4in) of young, healthy, non-flowering shoots.

2 Remove leaves at the base and tip, and cut the remaining leaves cleanly across in half.

3 Dibble the cuttings into a mixture of peat-free compost and perlite or vermiculite, at the edges of the pot.

out the tip and then the sideshoots will grow to form the head. Pinch out the sideshoots to make a dense, bushy head full of flowers.

Glasshouse and house plants

■ **Take hydrangea cuttings** from pot-grown plants. Mophead hydrangeas are increasingly popular as pot plants, but they are difficult to keep going year after year. Remove stem-tip cuttings about 8–10cm (3–4in) long. Cut off the lower leaves and trim the base of the cutting. There is no need to trim immediately below a leaf joint, as is normal practice with cuttings, as hydrangeas root perfectly well without. To reduce water loss from the large leaves, however, cut them in half. It may seem rather brutal, but it works. Put the cuttings into pots of cuttings compost and place on a shady windowsill or on the greenhouse bench. No extra heat is needed. Pot up when they have rooted.

■ **Rest amaryllis after flowering.** Give the bulbs several feeds of high-potash fertilizer to build up the flower bud inside the bulb for flowering next time. When the foliage begins to turn yellow reduce the watering and dry off. Put the pots on their sides under a bench.

■ **Take leaf cuttings** of streptocarpus (Cape primrose). Remove a mature leaf from the plant, and cut it into 2.5cm (1in) sections. Bury the base of each section in a pot, or put several in a tray of equal parts peat-free compost and perlite or vermiculite. The part of the leaf that was nearest the plant should always face downwards. Put in a warm, shady place and after a few months new plantlets will emerge from the base of each leaf section. These can be potted up individually. Another method is to take a mature leaf and cut it along the length of the midrib.

Rest cyclamen Laying cyclamen on their sides prevents overwatering as they go dormant.

Put in a tray with the midrib in the compost and plantlets will develop along the length of the midrib.

■ **Rest cyclamen** that have flowered in pots over the winter. This is done by gradually reducing the amount of watering until the foliage begins to die down. Place the pots on their sides under the greenhouse bench or in a cold frame until they are started into growth again.

■ **Pot up begonia** and gloxinia tubers that were started off last month, into 12.5cm (5in) pots. Water them after potting on.

Crops under glass

■ **Tie in vine rods.** Vines growing inside will be galloping away now and it is essential to keep up with tying in and pinching out growths, otherwise the vine will get out of hand. Fruiting stems should be pinched back to one or two buds beyond each flower truss and all sideshoots from these stems removed.

■ **Pot up tomato seedlings** sown last month. Tomato seedlings should be transplanted when you can see the first true leaves beginning to emerge from

between the two first, or seed, leaves (the cotyledons). Watering the seedlings an hour or two beforehand makes it easier to ease them out of the tray or pot. Pot up into 9cm (3½in) pots, with the seed leaves almost level with the compost. Water in well and stand on the greenhouse bench or on a warm windowsill. If they are on a windowsill, turn them around every day, otherwise they will grow towards the light and bend over.

■ **Remove sideshoots** from older tomato plants. Those sown earlier will be growing strongly now and cordon varieties (those grown as a single stem) need to have any sideshoots growing from the leaf axils removed. If these are not removed you will end up with a mass of growth and poor-quality fruits. The best time to remove sideshoots is when they are small; just large enough to handle. Take the shoot between your thumb and forefinger, push or pull the shoot to one side and it should snap off cleanly. If the shoots have been left on and grown quite large, use a knife or secateurs.

■ **Plant tomatoes in growing bags.** When earlier-sown tomatoes are potted up they grow away quickly and towards the end of the month they can go into growing bags or be potted into 20cm (8in) pots for cropping. Place the growing bags in the greenhouse for a few days to warm up the compost before planting. Similarly, if you're potting them up, warm up the bag of compost in the greenhouse. You can plant either two or three plants per growing bag. Tie cordon plants to canes or support wires attached to the framework of the glasshouse. There are also support frames made specially for growing bags and these can be purchased from garden centres.

THE MAY GARDEN

Many gardeners regard May as one of the best months in the garden, with spring's freshness and the promise of summer. It's also the month of the most famous flower show of all, the Chelsea Flower Show. May's warmer weather makes gardening particularly engrossing, so you can enjoy getting your plot ready for summer and planning for the months ahead.

THINGS TO DO

Protect tender plants from late frosts.

Prune spring-flowering shrubs and prune *Clematis montana* after it has flowered.

Trim box and other formal hedging lightly.

Continue taking cuttings from herbaceous perennials.

Plant out dahlias at the end of the month.

Protect young plants from slugs and snails.

Clear out spring bedding for planting summer bedding plants.

Thin out annuals and vegetables sown earlier.

Mow lawns once a week from now on.

Sow and plant out tender vegetables, and continue successional sowing of vegetables.

Remove all frost protection from plants at the end of the month.

Ventilate any greenhouses or conservatories in warmer weather.

Move tender plants outside now for the summer.

LAST CHANCE

Sow or turf new lawns before the conditions become too dry.

Finish planting evergreen shrubs.

GET AHEAD

Sow biennials for next year's spring bedding plants.

Inspect plants regularly for signs of pests and diseases and nip potential problems in the bud.

A mass of tall, pinky-mauve flowers Alliums, with blue Jacob's ladder in the foreground, stand out beautifully against fresh, green foliage.

THE BEST MONTH OF ALL

Make the most of May's warmer weather to start getting ready for summer. Your garden should be looking its best at this time, with bright spring bedding in flower and trees in full leaf, and the flower-show season will give you even more ideas and inspiration for the coming months.

There are signs of summer everywhere, yet many spring-flowering bulbs, especially the tulips, are still at their best. Trees are in full leaf and shrubs like rhododendrons are in full flower in most parts of the country during this month. There is a huge range of rhododendrons available, from dwarf shrubs only a few inches tall, which can be grown in pots and tubs, to great tree-like shrubs usually covered in large clusters of flowers. They are well worth growing if you have an acid soil. If your soil is alkaline then grow the smaller-growing rhododendrons in pots or raised beds filled with ericaceous compost. With quite mature, container-grown shrubs now widely available year-round, you could buy a rhododendron that is already in flower and have it installed in a tub on the patio the same afternoon.

Spring border Try a mixed planting of primroses, tulips, saxifrages, hyacinths, and grape hyacinths.

Change your bedding

While many plants are gearing themselves up for their summer display, the spring bedding plants will soon be over and it's time to think about their replacements. A wide selection of summer bedding plants will be on show at nurseries and garden centres, but as in April, resist the temptation to buy these too early in the month unless you have a frost-free greenhouse, conservatory, or cold frame to keep them in. The majority of these plants are still quite tender and in northern parts of the country it may not be safe to plant them out until the end of the month or into June. In more southern, sheltered parts of the country you may get away with planting summer bedding around the middle of the month, but do keep an eye on weather forecasts.

If you are new to an area, then a visit to a local park or just a stroll around the area having a look at some local gardens will tell you a lot about when to plant out summer bedding safely in your area. Talk to local gardeners – there may be a gardening club you can join too – and find out as much as you can about the weather conditions. You'll most likely find that they are quite a friendly bunch and will be glad to give out hints and tips on how to grow all manner of plants – and they often swap plants between themselves, so you might get a few plants for nothing as well as good advice!

Plants to protect

The weather in May is usually quite settled, but it can be changeable and there may still be the occasional sharp frost. So any tender plants being hardened off should be watched carefully and given protection with fleece or sheets of polythene, or put into a cold frame whenever required. The signs of a night frost coming are a clear blue sky at the end of a warm, sunny day.

Start of the shows

This is also the month when the flower-show season starts, with the greatest flower show of them all, Chelsea. Held in the grounds of the Royal Hospital, Chelsea, London, under the auspices of the Royal Horticultural Society, it is without doubt the highlight of the gardening year. Here you will see millions of blooms and hundreds of

Weather watch

The days are really warming up now, but be aware that the nights can be cold and we can still get sudden sharp frosts at any time this month. Late frosts are the scourge of fruit growers. Most varieties of fruit trees will be in flower now and it only takes one sharp frost to destroy a year's potential crop.

Windy days

It's not a month for frequent gales, but there may be windy days. Exposed north-western coastal areas still get 0.5–0.7 days of gale-force winds, but it's rare for sheltered south-eastern parts to get high winds.

Sunshine and cloud

The amount of direct sunshine will depend on the cloud cover, but generally southern parts of the country get the lion's share of sunshine, although some north-eastern parts compare favourably with the south-east. The western half of the country is more prone to cloud because weather fronts are driven over the Atlantic ocean and because of the topography of that part of the country.

Rainfall levels

Although, in general, rainfall decreases in all parts by now, some parts are inevitably wetter than others. The north-west Highland region of Scotland averages 107mm of rain this month and the south-west Borders region and the Lake District in England are not far behind with 95mm. It's not until you get to East Anglia that there is a considerable drop in rainfall: this region will only get around 44mm over the month.

Rare snowfall

The only places you are likely to find snow this month are in the hills above 100m, as at Cape Wrath in the northern Highlands of Scotland. Here snow can persist for most of the year. It is very rare indeed for snow to fall on other parts of the country, but there can still be hail storms from time to time, which can be quite destructive.

Intersowing lettuces and sweetcorn This is good practice. Lettuces are fast-growing and will be ready to harvest before the sweetcorn grows up and shades the ground.

innovative ideas for your own garden. There are, of course, many other flower shows throughout the summer, from large-scale national events down to small, local shows, and all of them are worth visiting. Here you will meet like-minded people who are fascinated by plants, and lifelong friendships can be forged at these events.

Spring is also a good time of year to visit other gardens opening to the public for the season and to plan trips to those that are open for charity for a few days each summer. Here again there are many ideas to be gleaned, which can be adapted to suit your own garden. Look out for the "Yellow Book" (*Gardens of England and Wales Open For Charity*, published by the National Gardens Scheme), listing gardens open to the public in aid of good causes. This is a mine of information on many small, delightful gardens, where you will find treasures of plants, often with cuttings or seedlings for sale – not to mention, in many cases, a welcome cup of tea.

Back to work

However, there is plenty to do in your own garden in between visiting flower shows and other people's gardens. In the vegetable plot you should now be harvesting delicious early vegetables planted out under cloches earlier in the year. To guarantee a succession of young vegetables throughout the summer, continue with regular sowing of all vegetables at seven- or ten-day intervals. Hoeing also becomes a very regular chore among vegetables now, as weeds burgeon in the milder conditions. With the warmer, drier weather watering may now become necessary, but don't use water indiscriminately, especially at this early stage in the season. Water only those plants that really need it – your precious young vegetables, developing fruits, and newly planted trees, shrubs, and perennials.

The pace hots up

Under glass, temperatures can get very high and it's vital from now on to shade young plants, open ventilators, windows, and doors whenever possible and damp down to prevent the air becoming too dry. Towards the end of the month it should be safe in all but the coldest regions to move pots containing tender shrubs and succulents such as agaves outdoors for the summer. Reducing crowding in the greenhouse will also help to increase good air circulation in the hot months to come.

Outside, ornamental borders will be brimming with colourful displays of late spring flowers and fresh foliage, the sound of birdsong will fill the garden, and beneficial insects will be pollinating flowers. Herbaceous perennials are now growing fast and need to be staked, if this has not already been done. This is a job that often gets forgotten until it is too late and the plants begin to flop all over the place and look unsightly. By this stage trying to tie up the stems is a hopeless task and it is often better to cut the plants back hard and let them grow away again. The flowers may be later, but the plant will look much better for cutting back.

A word about water

One aspect of the Chelsea Flower Show that never fails to inspire most visitors is the wealth of water

Waterside perennials Plants such as ferns, hostas, and the lovely candelabra primulas thrive in moist soil on the banks of streams and ponds. At this time of year burgeoning new foliage still retains all the freshness of spring.

features on show. Water not only cools and refreshes the air around it, but it's also a real treat for wildlife, including frogs and dragonflies, which will be drawn to even the smallest pool. Small features, such as half-barrel ponds, also provide space for pretty aquatics, and they are quick and easy to make. Simply buy a half barrel from an aquatic specialist, ensuring it has not been pre-treated against rot. Fill it with water and leave it to stand – the barrel will leak for a while until the wood swells and seals it. Then fill the barrel with water plants. Use aquatic compost and plant in baskets, setting marginal plants on bricks to raise their stems out of the water.

***Laburnum x watereri* 'Vossii'** ♀
Good small-to-medium tree with cascading yellow flowers (*see p.305*)

Clematis montana* f. *grandiflora ♀
A vigorous climber for quick cover (*see p.287*)

***Papaver orientale* 'Cedric Morris'** ♀
Showy perennial poppy with dark-centred flowers (*see p.315*)

***Aquilegia vulgaris* 'Nora Barlow'** ♀
Cottagey perennial that will self-seed (*see p.277*)

***Exochorda x macrantha* 'The Bride'** ♀
Notably free-flowering deciduous shrub (*see p.297*)

***Rhododendron* 'Golden Torch'** ♀
Compact, upright evergreen shrub with salmon-pink blooms (*see p.322*)

Digitalis* x *mertonensis ♀
Perennial foxglove that readily self-seeds (*see p.293*)

***Trollius* x *cultorum* 'Earliest of All'**
A lovely poolside perennial (*see p.332*)

***Wisteria floribunda* 'Multijuga'** ♀
Woody-stemmed climber that needs twice-yearly pruning (*see p.335*)

***Tulipa* 'Spring Green'** ♀
One of the green-flecked viridiflora tulips (*see p.332*)

***Choisya* 'Aztec Pearl'** ♀
Evergreen shrub with sweet-scented flowers (*see p.284*)

***Camassia cusickii* 'Zwanenburg'**
Bulb with tall conical spires of vivid flowers (*see p.281*)

Allium hollandicum ♀
Drumstick seedheads look good long after the flowers fade (*see p.276*)

Euphorbia x martini ♀
Bushy clump-forming perennial for a sunny site (*see p.296*)

Prunus padus 'Watereri' ♀
Flowering cherry popular with garden birds (*see p.319*)

Crataegus laevigata 'Rosea Flore Pleno' ♀
Plant hawthorn as a tree or informal hedging (*see p.290*)

Kerria japonica 'Picta'
Clump-forming shrub with variegated foliage (*see p.305*)

Syringa vulgaris 'Madame Lemoine' ♀
Bears large, double white flowers from creamy buds (*see p.331*)

Corydalis flexuosa ♀
Low-growing perennial with ferny leaves (*see p.289*)

***Viburnum sargentii* 'Onondaga'** ♀
Deciduous shrub with lacecap clusters of flowers (*see p.334*)

Paeonia mlokosewitschii ♀
Herbaceous peony with lemon-yellow flowers (*see p.315*)

Hyacinthoides non-scripta
The English bluebell; spreads vigorously once established (*see p.302*)

***Prunus* 'Amanogawa'** ♀
Very slender flowering cherry tree for small gardens (*see p.320*)

***Clematis macropetala* 'Markham's Pink'** ♀
Looks good climbing through trees and large shrubs (*see p.286*)

WHAT TO DO IN MAY

AROUND THE GARDEN

Now the weather is warming up, you will have to watch for pests and diseases on a regular basis. It may be necessary to use chemical controls in severe cases, but be aware that long-term use of synthetic chemicals can actually cause problems to build up. These chemicals kill off not only the pests, but also the beneficial insects that prey on them, such as ladybird and hoverfly larvae. If you feel it necessary to spray, carry out the task on a still day, as late in the evening as possible, when there are fewer beneficial insects around.

Water new plants Give newly installed plants a good soak regularly to help them establish.

Keep plants in the garden growing strongly and they will be less susceptible to attack. Prepare the ground well to get them off to a good start. Keep new plants well watered during dry spells, so that they don't suffer stress. Mulch newly planted plants to retain valuable moisture in the soil. The mulch will slow the evaporation rate from the surface of the ground.

Keep the garden tidy, especially now that it's time to clear spring bedding away and keep weeds, which often act as hosts to pests and diseases, under control. The most organic way of all to control pests is by using your fingers to squash them, but you have to be vigilant and persistent to keep on top of them. The memory of two days spent squashing cabbage white butterfly caterpillars on brassicas in a large garden remains with me. It might have been more sensible to have excluded the pests with some kind of barrier, such as netting or fleece.

Hoe bare ground to keep down weeds as they germinate. Weeds are more easily killed off at this stage, rather than leaving them until they get bigger. Then there is also no chance that they will be left too long and set seeds that will be spread around the garden. Hoe on dry, sunny days and the weed seedlings can be left on the surface of the ground to dry out and shrivel up in the sun. A mulch with organic matter will help to prevent the growth of further weeds. Water the soil first if it is dry, before applying the mulch. Alternatively, put some plants in the gap to add colour to the border.

Night frosts Even though daytime temperatures should now be mild, night frosts are not uncommon this month, especially after clear, bright days. Keep a sheet of horticultural fleece or even some old newspapers handy to cover any plants that are vulnerable to frost if night temperatures are forecast to fall.

TREES AND SHRUBS

■ **Water newly planted trees and shrubs** regularly if the weather is dry. A few days of sunny weather accompanied by drying winds now will dry out the soil surprisingly quickly. You may need to water on a daily basis. It is important to water new woody plants well until they get established and their roots develop enough to be able to seek out moisture deep down. Any organic matter, such as rotted manure or garden compost, either dug into the soil or applied as a mulch, has good water-holding potential, which will help new, growing roots. Even grass clippings spread in a layer about 5–8cm (2–3in) thick around the plant (not touching the stems) will help to retain moisture.

Try to water in the evenings, when there is far less chance of the water evaporating from the soil, as it is certain to do in the heat of the day.

■ **Keep checking roses** for aphids.

■ **In milder regions,** tender shrubs in pots can be moved outside for the summer.

Pruning and training

■ **Prune evergreens** to remove any frost damage and tidy wayward shoots, unless you did so last month.

■ **Prune pyracanthas** trained against a wall or fence. Prune out shoots growing directly into the wall and any growing directly away from it too. Shorten the others to about 8cm (3in). This encourages formation of short spurs, which bear the flower buds and then the beautiful berries in autumn.

■ **Prune early-flowering shrubs** like *Kerria japonica* and *Spiraea* 'Arguta', which will finish flowering about now on wood produced the previous year. For kerria, prune all the shoots that have produced

flowers back to young sideshoots lower down. This shrub tends to spread out by underground suckers and these can also be removed if the plant seems to be encroaching on other plants. *Spiraea* 'Arguta' should similarly have its flowered shoots pruned back to buds or shoots lower down on the shrub and on older plants. In addition, cut out about one in three of the older stems completely to the ground. This will encourage new, young growth from the base of the plant, keeping it vigorous and healthy.

■ **Take softwood cuttings** from shrubs. Most shrubs in the garden will now be producing plenty of young, fresh shoots and these are excellent for making softwood cuttings through until July, when the wood begins to ripen. Take a few shoots from any part of the shrub where their absence will not show. About half a dozen should ensure that you get at least one new shrub. It's always best to take more than you need as an insurance policy. Have a polythene bag to hand when you take the cuttings. Cut shoots about 8–10cm (3–4in) long from the plant, cutting just above a bud or leaf. Pop the cuttings into the bag straightaway and keep it out of the sun. This prevents the cuttings from wilting.

Trim the cuttings below a leaf joint with a sharp knife and remove the lower leaves, leaving them about 5–8cm (2–3in) long. Immerse the cuttings in a fungicide solution, wearing gloves, and then dip the cut ends into hormone rooting solution. Five or six cuttings per 12cm (5in) pot, containing a 50:50 mix of peat-free compost and vermiculite, will be sufficient. Cover with polythene, making sure it is held off the foliage of the cuttings (you can use short sticks to support it) and secure in place with a rubber band. Place the pots in a shady part of the greenhouse or in a cold

Hedge cutting You can make this task much easier if you use a guide (a length of taut garden twine or a cane) to keep lines straight.

frame and the cuttings should root within six to eight weeks. They can then be potted up to be grown on.

Hedges

■ **Lightly trim formal evergreen hedging** such as box (*Buxus sempervirens*), even if it has not yet grown to the desired size. Box hedging does not take to being cut back hard, so the sooner it starts being trimmed to keep it in shape the better. This is best done with hand shears rather than with a mechanical hedge trimmer, which can bruise rather than cut the leaves cleanly, making them turn brown and unsightly. It may take more time using the shears, but the overall appearance of the hedge will be much better.

You can make cuttings from any shoots about 7.5cm (3in) long. Trim each cutting below a leaf joint, put into pots containing cuttings compost, cover with a polythene bag and stand the pot in a shady part of the garden and in a few weeks the cuttings will root. You can then pot them into their own pots or space them out on a spare piece of ground until autumn or next spring, when they can be placed in their final positions.

CLIMBERS

■ Prune *Clematis montana* after it has flowered. The amount of pruning will depend on where it is growing. This is a very vigorous climber so it's best to allow it to scramble through trees and large shrubs or up a fence or wall. In these situations, little pruning will be needed unless it is outgrowing its space. However, in more confined spaces some pruning will be necessary to prevent it taking over the whole garden. Pruning is easy, although the untangling can be tricky; all you have to do is prune out any dead or diseased wood and prune the remaining stems back as far as you need to. This encourages young growth to take place and flowers to come next spring.

■ Prune wall-trained pyracantha.

■ Tie in climbers regularly. Vigorous climbers such as clematis, roses, and vines need their shoots tied in at regular intervals, otherwise they may smother other plants in the border. Trying to untangle climbers from other plants is a tedious job, to be avoided if at all possible. Fixing wide-mesh wire netting to walls and fences is the easiest way to provide support for vigorous climbers. Trellis is more decorative, so choose lighter climbers for this so that the plants' growth does not hide it from view.

Tying in Make figures-of-eight with twine so that stems do not rub directly on supports.

PERENNIALS

■ Continue staking and tying in perennials, particularly tall-stemmed kinds such as delphiniums. These will need several bamboo canes placed around each plant, with string tied around the canes. Alternatively, you can tie each stem to an individual cane.

■ Cut back and divide clump-forming, spring-flowering perennials such as doronicums and pulmonarias. Doronicum just needs the old flower spikes cut off to neaten up the plant. But pulmonarias should have all the old foliage cut to the ground, as it will usually be covered in mildew by now and look dreadfully shabby. It may seem a drastic thing to do, but new, fresh foliage soon grows, transforming the appearance of the plants. At the same time, lift, divide, and replant overgrown clumps. After pruning and dividing, feed with an organic fertilizer, watering it in if the soil is dry.

■ Cut back alyssum, arabis, and aubrieta. These spreading and trailing plants all tend to become bare and tatty, especially in the centre of the plant, when the flowers have gone over. Trim them back hard, almost to the ground and fresh new growth will soon appear, producing a mass of flowers on a neat, compact plant next year. If you don't do this every year, then as the plant ages it will be more reluctant to grow from the base when cut back hard. After pruning, feed with an organic fertilizer. Mulch with fresh gravel or grit if the plants are growing in an alpine setting.

■ Divide early primulas after flowering. With larger clumps you may have to use two forks back to back to prise them apart initially, but after that the clumps can generally be pulled apart by hand. Cut off most of the old foliage, leaving about 5cm (2in) on each division and replant in the

Staking delphiniums Tall plants need tall stakes. It is best to top them with corks or some other type of protector to prevent accidental eye injury when working in borders.

original position after revitalizing the soil with garden compost or manure. Water in well if the soil is dry. Alternatively, line out the small divisions in a corner of the vegetable garden and replant them in the border in the autumn.

■ Sow seed of perennials outside. There is no cheaper and more satisfying way to grow perennials than from seed, especially collected from plants growing in the garden rather than from a packet. Most perennials can be grown this way: achilleas, alstroemerias, and hardy geraniums are especially easy examples. Take out shallow drills in the soil after raking it to a fine tilth. Water the drills if the soil is dry, allowing it to soak away before sowing the seeds as thinly as possible, then cover them lightly with dry soil. Label each row. After a few weeks, when the seedlings are large enough to handle, they can be transplanted to a nursery area to grow on and bulk up. You can also sow the seed in pots ready to plant out in autumn, just as for ornamental cabbages (*see p.124*).

BULBS

■ **Continue deadheading** spring-flowering bulbs that are still going. Snap off tulip heads and leave the stalks. You must leave the foliage intact for at least six weeks after the last flower. If you must move them before this (for example, if they have been grown in among wallflowers and forget-me-nots for a spring display), you can move them temporarily, heeling them in in a corner of a border or in the vegetable garden. Lift the bulbs carefully with a fork. Dig a shallow trench where they are to be heeled in and place the bulbs in the trench with the foliage above ground. Cover the bulbs with some soil and lift them when the foliage has died down. Don't forget to label the row or if you have a memory like mine you'll forget where they are.

■ **Feed spring-flowering bulbs now,** whether they are still in place or heeled in, to encourage the development of the new flower bud in the bulb for next spring. A general organic fertilizer sprinkled around the bulbs according to the manufacturer's instructions is ideal. Water it in if the weather is dry.

Lifting bulbs These tulips can be uprooted carefully and heeled in in a corner to die down.

ANNUALS AND BEDDING

■ **Clear spring-flowering bedding plants** and prepare the ground for summer bedding. Now that spring-flowering plants such as wallflowers, forget-me-nots, and winter-flowering pansies are coming to the end of their flowering time they need to be cleared away and the ground prepared for summer bedding to go in. The old spring-flowering plants can be consigned to the compost heap to ensure a supply of valuable organic matter next year.

After the old plants have been removed, lightly fork over the soil, removing any weeds. At this time you can add a little organic fertilizer, as it breaks down slowly in the soil and will therefore be available to the plants when they are planted out. But don't apply too much or you will get a lot of soft growth at the expense of flowers. A light sprinkling is sufficient. Also, don't dig in organic matter at this time for the same reason. The time for digging in organic matter is in the autumn.

■ **Most of the tender summer bedding** plants we grow originate in warmer parts of the world such as South Africa, where the soil is baked and very poor as far as the availability of nutrients is concerned, and this is why they don't require a lot of fertilizer to grow well.

■ **Harden off summer bedding plants.** Plants like petunias and French and African marigolds – whether bought now or raised from seed – need to be acclimatized to outdoor conditions before planting out at the end of the month and into early June. Do this by putting them into a cold frame and gradually opening the tops of the frames more each day until they can be left off altogether. Close the frame at night and keep something like fleece handy to throw over the frames, just in case a sharp frost is forecast. If you are bringing a lot of plants out in batches, then in mild areas

Frost protection If you can't resist buying frost-tender bedding, make sure you shelter it until the end of May.

the plants can be moved under a plastic cloche after a few days – but still be ready to give them extra protection at night.

■ **Take cuttings from tender perennials** like argyranthemums, pelargoniums, and fuchsias. You may have overwintered such plants from last year especially for the purpose of taking cuttings. Or, you may have some that have miraculously survived in sheltered spots and taking cuttings from these will produce stronger, fresher plants that will flower better than the parent (as well as increasing your stock). Alternatively, you can now buy quite good-sized plants from garden centres, from which you can harvest several young shoots for cuttings without harming the parent unduly. Cuttings taken now will provide plants for flowering well into autumn, but you must have somewhere frost-free to raise them until all danger of frost has passed. Shoots from all these plants can be removed when they are about 7.5–10cm (3–4in) long. Trim the cutting immediately below a leaf joint and dip the end in hormone rooting solution. Put the cuttings into pots containing cuttings compost and water in well. Place a polythene bag over the pot and put it on a shady windowsill if you have not got a

Support for annuals Twiggy sticks make informal supports for cottage-style annuals.

greenhouse. They will root in about three to four weeks, when they can be potted up ready to plant out in June.

■ **Thin out hardy annuals sown earlier.** If they are not thinned, the plants will become leggy and will not flower well. Thin out to leave one seedling at least every 15cm (6in). The taller the plants, the more space required. Check packets for details.

The easiest way to thin out seedlings is to choose the one you want to keep and pinch out the others. Measure the gap to the next one and do the same until the job's done. Most hardy annuals don't transplant well when they grow taller, so if you thin out as soon as the seedlings can be handled, they can be transplanted to fill gaps, or put them in other parts of the garden. Some of the very tall annuals need some support with twiggy sticks to prevent them flopping over.

■ **Train sweet peas.** Sweet peas planted out earlier will be growing vigorously towards the end of the month and they may need a little steering in the right direction. If the plants are being grown for general display in the garden, tying them to the support initially will be all the help they need as the tendrils will then twine themselves around whatever they touch.

■ **Sow spring-flowering biennials.** These are the wallflowers, *Bellis perennis*, forget-me-nots, sweet Williams, and winter-flowering pansies that have just been cleared to make way for the summer bedding. The easiest way to remember the time for sowing these to flower next spring is to do it when the old ones are beginning to fade. Find a corner to sow the seeds. Try not to grow wallflowers in the same piece of ground year after year. They belong to the same family as cabbages and cauliflowers (brassicas) and are subject to the same diseases such as clubroot, which is incurable and persists in the soil for many years. The preparation for sowing is the same for other seeds. Rake the soil to a fine tilth and level it off. Take out shallow drills with a stick or cane about 15cm (6in) apart and water them before sowing, if the soil is dry. Sow the seeds thinly along the row and cover lightly with dry soil and firm gently. Label each row. In a few weeks the seedlings will need to be thinned or transplanted to grow on with more space between them, before being planted in their final positions in autumn.

■ **Sow ornamental cabbages and kales.** These handsome ornamental plants are grown for winter bedding displays. Their coloured foliage comes in shades of red, green, and white. The colours are more intense when temperatures drop during autumn. Sow the seeds in 8cm (3in) pots of seed compost at a temperature of 18°C (65°F). Pot on when the plants are large enough to handle. They can be kept outside until planting time in autumn.

CONTAINERS

■ **Clear out spring bedding** from containers to make way for summer bedding plants. It is worth removing some of the old compost if it has been in the container since last year. Some new compost will give the plants a fresh start. For containers, John Innes potting compost is best as it contains soil and does not dry out as quickly as soilless composts.

■ **In mild areas plant up containers** with frost-tender plants towards the end of the month. But bear in mind not to plant out tender plants until at least the end of the month or early next month in more northerly parts. Keep fleece handy to drape over at night if frosts are forecast.

■ **If you buy ready-planted hanging baskets** this month, harden them off to get them used to outdoor conditions. Leave them out for increasingly long periods until they can be left out at night.

■ **Water and feed all containers** regularly. As the weather warms up, watering containers can become a daily or twice-daily task. Hanging baskets, in

A beautiful display Blue and pink cultivars of *Nemesia* Karoo Series are shown to advantage.

particular, are prone to drying out quickly. Mixing up a feed solution every time plants need feeding can be very time-consuming; the easiest way to feed lots of plants in containers is to make up a feed solution in bulk. Fill a large tank with water, mixing in plant food according to the manufacturer's instructions. This solution can be fed at every watering. A high-potash feed is best for the production of flowers and a prolonged display. High-nitrogen fertilizers will result in a lot of leafy growth at the expense of flowers.

■ **Watch out for vine weevils** and make sure you don't introduce them into containers along with new plants. They can wreak havoc when they multiply within the closed confines of a tub or windowbox. Knock new plants out of their pots and look for the small white grubs, which eat at the roots. The adult weevils are rarely seen as they only come out at night; notched foliage is a giveaway sign. However, it is the grubs that do the most damage. There are several proprietary products available on the market for controlling vine weevil. The most effective organic control is a biological nematode, which can be bought by mail order.

■ **Tender perennials in pots** and tender shrubs can be put out towards the end of the month in most parts. In northern areas wait until early June. The sooner these plants can be put outside the better. The fresh air and rain after their prolonged period indoors will do them the world of good. Larger-leaved shrubs, such as bay, can have their leaves wiped with a damp cloth. This will remove dust and dirt accumulated indoors. Be sure to keep up with watering and feeding because during warm weather pots can dry out very quickly. During hot spells you may have to water once or twice a day.

Plant a hardy annual border

Hardy annuals are terrific plants to have in the garden; they flower for weeks and are the easiest of plants to look after. They are also great for getting children interested in sowing and growing plants. Generally, the taller plants should be positioned nearer the back of the border, with shorter ones at the front. However, slight variations here and there, with taller, more open, plants nearer the front or middle of the border will make the display more interesting. The four plants suggested need no special treatment and prefer poorer soil to flower well. Too rich a soil produces more foliage than flowers. All prefer to be grown in full sun. Some will seed themselves about at the end of the season. For a minimal amount of care, hardy annuals will reward you with a splendid show all summer long.

Eschscholzia **'Single Mixed'** A low-growing annual for the front of the border, especially as the ferny foliage is also very attractive.

Limnanthes **'Scrambled Eggs'** A good variety of what is commonly called the poached egg plant, excellent for attracting bees. They are suitable for the front of the border.

Nigella **'Allsorts'** Love-in-a-mist in a variety of soft pastel colours; both the flowers and the seedheads are good for cutting. They are suitable for the middle of the border.

Tropaeolum **'Peach Melba'** This nasturtium is more compact than some of the scrambling varieties, with an unusual flower coloration. It is suitable for the front of the border.

LAWNS

■ **Mow established lawns** once a week now that the grass is growing well. Each time you mow, lower the blades of the mower slightly, cutting the grass a little closer each time. Try not to lower the blades too much or the lawn will be "scalped". This will make the grass turn yellow and it will cause bare patches to develop, allowing weeds and moss to get established – and it looks unsightly too.

■ **Feed established lawns** if you haven't already done so. Follow the manufacturer's instructions carefully. Some modern fertilizers have anti-scorch properties, so it doesn't matter if you are a little heavy-handed – within reason, of course. But it is also wasteful to apply too much.

■ **Treat weeds in the lawn** with a selective weedkiller, but remember to check that the weeds you want to kill can be dealt with this way, before you buy. This is a good month to do this, as weeds are now growing vigorously and the weedkiller will act more effectively. It is important always to use a selective lawn weedkiller on a lawn. This only affects the broad-leaved weeds in the lawn. Any other sort of weedkiller will kill off the grass too. Follow instructions to the letter. Don't put on a bit extra for luck, as this may harm the grass. If your lawn has only a few weeds, then you could use one of the "spot-treatment" weedkillers. These are painted or dabbed onto the leaves of individual weeds.

   Grass clippings taken from the lawn just after applying weedkiller should not be put on the compost heap, as traces of the herbicide will be in the clippings and could harm other plants in the garden. If you haven't the time to apply fertilizer and selective weedkiller separately, there are several products on the market that combine a fertilizer, weedkiller, and mosskiller all in one.

■ **Renovate damaged edges** and bare patches all through the summer until autumn, as needed.

New lawns

■ **Finish sowing new lawns** before the weather becomes too warm. The best times to sow grass seed are spring and autumn, when the soil is warm and generally moist.

■ **Roll newly sown lawns,** if you can, when the seed has germinated and the new grass is about 2.5cm (1in) high. The roller on the back of a cylinder mower is perfect for the job. Rolling encourages the grass shoots to grow from the base of the plant, ensuring a close-knit sward.

■ **Newly sown lawns** can have their first cut when the grass is about 5cm (2in) high. Set mower blades at their highest setting. Gradually reduce the height of cut each time you mow, but don't cut new lawns from seed too close in their first year.

New grass Newly sown or turved lawns may need their first cut this month, but don't cut too close in the lawn's first year.

VEGETABLES AND HERBS
Harvesting

■ **Harvest early crops,** such as radishes and salad leaves, as they mature.

Sowing indoors

■ **Vegetables can still be sown indoors** to shorten the growing period. Crops to sow now include courgettes, marrows, runner beans, French beans, squashes, and sweetcorn. This month, sow indoors and outside at the same time. The plants sown indoors will grow a little quicker than those outside, giving a continuity of crops rather than an unwelcome glut all at once.

■ **Sow cardoons.** These are often grown for ornamental value alone, mainly for their blanched stems rather than the flower buds, as with globe artichokes. It's rare to grow them for eating these days. Sow two seeds to each small pot and cover lightly with compost. They don't need high temperatures to germinate: putting the pots on a warm windowsill is sufficient, but placing them in a heated propagator will hasten germination. Pull out the weakest seedlings when they are large enough to handle and plant out the one left in the pot in early to mid-June.

■ **Sow ridge cucumbers.** These can be sown early in the month for planting out at the beginning of June. Sow them in small pots containing a compost suitable for seed-sowing, placing two seeds in each pot. Push the seeds down into the compost to about 2cm (1in) deep and cover lightly with compost. To achieve quick germination, use a propagator.

Sowing and planting outdoors

■ **Continue successional sowing** of beetroot, cabbage, carrots, salad onions, lettuce, peas, broad beans, radishes, and turnips. Sow in short rows to prevent a glut. Take out shallow drills and water before sowing the seeds if the soil is dry. Sow the seeds thinly and cover with dry soil. When the seedlings are large enough, thin them out.

■ **Leeks sown earlier** can be planted out if not done last month. The method of planting will depend on the way the young plants were raised, but with all planting, apply a general organic fertilizer a few days beforehand. If the seeds were sown in seed trays and the plants left to grow on in the trays until 10–12cm (4–5in) high, they can be planted in individual holes. Make a hole about 15cm (6in) deep with a dibber and put one plant in each hole. Complete the row and water in. The plants should be about 30cm (1ft) apart each way. Do not firm: watering them in will automatically wash some soil down the hole to cover the roots. If seeds were multiple-sown in modular trays for deep beds, the small clumps of five or six plants can be planted in their clusters, 15–22cm (6–9in) apart each way. This way you get more weight of crop per square metre than if they are grown in conventional straight rows.

■ **Plant out self-blanching celery** towards the end of the month. Make sure the ground has been prepared thoroughly, incorporating plenty of organic matter to retain moisture. Unlike blanching celery,

Planting out celery Arranged in blocks, the plants will shade each other, aiding blanching.

there is no need to grow this type in a trench to blanch the stems. It is best, though, to grow it in blocks rather than in straight rows.

■ **Globe artichokes sown earlier under cover** can be planted out towards the end of the month. Traditionally globe artichokes are grown as perennials and planted at a distance of 90cm (3ft). You can grow them as biennials and plant them much closer together: 45cm (18in) apart. This year, pinch out flower buds from every other plant. After taking crops from the others this summer, remove them. The pinched-out plants will provide good crops next year, when you can also plant new plants between them, setting up a year-on-year cycle. Growing young plants each year also gives a continuity of crop throughout each season.

■ **Plant out marrows and courgettes** at the end of the month. These plants are tender and prone to damage from frosts. Plant into soil that has been enriched with plenty of organic matter, as marrows and courgettes require a lot of water during the growing season. They do take up quite a bit of room, so space them at 90cm (3ft) each way. Keep the plants well watered through the summer. If you do not have room on the vegetable garden to grow these plants, why not grow one or two in ornamental borders? The large leaves are bold and attractive and will provide a good contrast to other foliage plants in the garden – and the edible parts are a bonus. Trailing varieties can be grown up strong canes, bean poles, or other forms of support to make an attractive feature, which also saves space at ground level.

■ **Direct-sow runner beans, French beans, and sweetcorn.** Although these are all tender, by sowing outside this month

the seeds will germinate when the threat of frost has passed in most areas. Seeds of runner beans can be sown two to the base of each bean pole or bamboo cane. The weaker seedling can be removed when the seeds have germinated. Sowing two seeds per "station" is an insurance policy should a seed fail to germinate.

Sow sweetcorn in blocks, 60cm (1ft) apart each way, again with two seeds in each hole. French beans can be sown in rows 60cm (1ft) apart with the seeds 15–22cm (6–9in) apart in the rows. However, this method is less reliable than sowing beforehand in containers – and the seed may be eaten.

Seedlings of all of these plants can be damaged by slugs as they germinate. To avoid this problem, after sowing the seeds cover them with plastic lemonade or water bottles that have had the bottom cut out, pushing them into the ground.

■ **Transplant Brussels sprouts** and other winter brassicas sown earlier. These plants can now be transplanted to their cropping positions. They do take up a fair amount of space over a long period of time. But other short-term crops such as lettuce, radishes, and turnips can be grown between the brassicas to use the space efficiently. All the brassicas to be planted out should be well watered beforehand, as they wilt very quickly. One point to bear in mind is that cauliflowers will not produce a proper curd if they receive even the slightest check to their growth. So watering before planting out and afterwards is very important. The ideal stage at which to transplant the seedlings is when they have made two or three true leaves. The plants should be set out at a minimum of 60cm (2ft) each way.

■ **Sow chard and leaf beet.** Swiss chard has large leaves and pure-white stems, both of which can be eaten, the leaves being used in a similar way to spinach. There are also ruby and "rainbow" chards, with deep-red and multicoloured midribs respectively. Leaf beet, or perpetual spinach, is also a good substitute for spinach as it, like chard, is less susceptible to bolting (running to seed) than spinach is. Often spinach will start bolting just a few weeks after the seeds germinate. Sow the seeds in drills, watering first if the soil seems dry. Thin out the seedlings when they are large enough to handle and keep them well watered during the summer.

■ It's now too late to sow tomato seeds, but garden centres will have a choice of plants. Try bush varieties 'Red Alert' and 'Tornado', and you won't have to stake them or pinch out sideshoots. Plant about 60cm (2ft) apart and mulch with straw to prevent the fruits rotting on the soil.

Looking after crops

■ **Pinch out the tops of broad beans** when they flower to discourage blackfly, which love the young, succulent tips of the plants.

Pinching out broad beans Remove the tender tip, which is the part blackfly like best.

By removing the young tips when several trusses of flowers have developed, there should be less need to spray to control these aphids. Provide some support for broad beans with string stretched between canes at either end of the row. The plants tend to flop over when the pods develop.

■ **Protect carrots from carrot fly.** The female of this pest flies around just above soil level seeking out juicy carrots by their smell and laying her eggs at the base of the foliage. The small larvae of the fly burrow into the root of the carrot, making holes in it, causing rot to set in. The carrots are then unappealing to eat and certainly useless for storing over winter. This pest also attacks parsnips and parsley. The easiest way to protect the plants is to cover them with horticultural fleece, leaving it over the crop permanently as there is another generation of carrot fly later in August. Or, erect a barrier at least 45cm (18in) high from horticultural fleece, fine mesh or polythene supported on a wooden framework, preventing the carrot fly from getting to the crops.

To minimize the threat of carrot fly, sow seeds as thinly as possible to reduce the need for thinning the seedlings. Don't leave thinnings lying around, as the smell will attract any carrot fly that are around. You could also try growing alternate rows of onions and carrots, the theory being that the strong, pungent aroma from the onions will mask the smell of the carrots, so confusing the carrot fly. Some varieties of carrots, 'Flyaway' and 'Resistafly', are less susceptible to attack.

■ **Hoe regularly to keep down weeds.** This job is well worth doing regularly, as it will save a lot of back-breaking work if the weeds are left to grow. Catch weed seedlings when they are small and they can be left on the surface to dry out.

Carrot fly barrier Fence carrots with fine mesh around canes to keep this pest away.

■ **Earth up early potatoes,** drawing a little soil up over the emerging shoots. This not only protects them from any late frost, but also encourages the development of roots further up the stems, therefore increasing the yield. Keep earthing up potatoes at intervals as it covers any developing potatoes that are exposed, preventing them from turning green in the light. This is because when potatoes turn green they become poisonous.

■ **Tomatoes sown last month** need potting on now. Those being grown as cordons should have sideshoots, which form at the leaf axils, removed. Do this when they are quite small, by rubbing them out with your forefinger and thumb and it won't be such a shock to the plant. Once the first truss of flowers has faded and fruits are setting, feed weekly with a high-potash fertilizer.

Herbs

■ **Lift and divide mint.** It can become invasive so lift and divide it before it takes over the garden. Be sure to remove as much of the roots spreading out from the plant as possible, because if these are left in they will continue to grow. New, small divisions can be replanted in the same place. To prevent mint becoming too invasive, grow it in pots.

FRUIT
Looking after crops

■ **Control pests by putting up pheromone traps.** Many pests are very difficult to control these days because they are becoming immune to the chemicals we use to control them. An alternative way to control some pests is by using traps. Codling moth is a good example, which responds well to this method. During May and June the moths mate and lay eggs on apples and the eggs hatch into maggots, which tunnel into the fruits. Male codling moths are attracted to the females by a pheromone, or hormonal scent, which the females give off to attract the male when they are ready to mate. This pheromone is now produced artificially and can be purchased in a small container that is placed in a small plastic housing, rather like a bird house. In the house is a piece of sticky paper impregnated with this substance to capture males attracted by the scent. This reduces the mating success of the moths and so fewer viable eggs are laid. You will need one trap for every three to five trees.

■ **Tuck straw under strawberries** to protect the fruits from rotting. This also prevents the fruits being spoiled by rain-splashed soil and slugs. Garden centres stock special strawberry mats as an alternative to straw. As the fruits develop, cover the plants with netting to keep the birds from getting them. Make sure the netting is properly secured to prevent birds getting tangled up in it. If you are concerned about birds being caught in netting, use horticultural fleece to cover the plants instead.

■ **Remove runners from strawberries** if they are not required for propagating new plants. If runners are allowed to develop then a great deal of the plants' energy will go into producing them. The crop of fruit will be poorer and the strawberry bed will end up as a mass of tangled plants, which will be difficult to weed. Putting straw or strawberry mats down to protect the fruits from being splashed with soil will also be next to impossible. If you want to let a few plants develop runners for new plants, pick the flowers off and sacrifice their crop so that you get really strong young plantlets.

■ **Take off all covers** and protection from peach, nectarine, and cherry trees. But continue to protect late blossoms on fruit trees and bushes from late frosts. Sharp frosts can still occur at any time this month, especially in northern parts of the country. The easiest way to give protection in a hurry is to use horticultural fleece. This can be thrown over small trees or draped over trees trained against walls and fences and will help keep off a few degrees of frost. You might get fed up with hearing gardeners going on about late frosts at this time of year, when it seems so mild, but they do happen often, so it is always better to be aware of them and not allow them to ruin your crop of hard-earned fruit later in the summer.

■ **Keep newly planted fruit plants** well watered. Young plants need tender loving care to help them get established in their first year after planting. If they suffer stress due to lack of water at any time, it makes them more vulnerable to attack from pests and diseases and reduces the amount of growth and subsequently the quantity of fruit produced. It is far better to give them a good soaking once a week rather than give smaller amounts on a daily basis during dry spells. Scant watering encourages the roots to come nearer to the surface of the soil in search of moisture, making them even more vulnerable in drought conditions. And they will be more easily damaged when weeding among the plants.

■ **Mulch all fruit,** if you have not done so before, to retain moisture in the soil. Use well-rotted farmyard manure, garden compost, spent mushroom compost, or any other organic matter you can get hold of. If the soil is dry, make sure it is watered well before applying a mulch, as mulches are just as good at keeping moisture out of the soil as keeping it in. If you have the luxury of a sprinkler, leave it on one area at a time

Protecting strawberries

Tuck straw under strawberries and the fruits will not be damaged by splashes of mud.

Strawberry mats are an alternative to straw. They should be stocked by any garden centre selling fruit plants.

for at least two hours to give the area a good soaking and then mulch. There is no point in giving small amounts of water every day. Instead, concentrate on watering small areas really well in turn, otherwise the water is just wasted. Be sure to check there are no hose restrictions in your area before using a sprinkler.

Pruning and training

■ **Prune out unwanted shoots on all raspberries.** If too many new canes are allowed to develop, as with strawberry runners, more energy will be put into developing these new canes than into fruit production. Thick, crowded rows are difficult to care for and the fruits will receive less ripening sunshine. Another important point is that the more congested the shoots are, the less air will be circulating through the plants, making them more susceptible to fungal diseases such as botrytis. This fungal disease will attack the fruits, causing them to turn brown and rot off. The more air that can circulate around the plants, the less likelihood there is of them being attacked by disease. The canes that are left will also be all the more sturdy, because they have more light and room to develop.

Delicious plums 'Warwickshire Drooper' plums.

■ **Prune plums and cherries** trained against walls and fences. The pruning of these trees is done in spring and summer because they are vulnerable to silver leaf disease, the spores of which enter through wounds. By pruning at this time wounds heal more quickly and the period of heaviest spore production is avoided. When this year's young shoots have made six leaves, pinch out the growing tip. Once the fruit has been picked, prune back these shoots to about half their length, taking out any overcrowded and unhealthy-looking stems at the same time.

Trained acid cherries such as 'Morello' are pruned slightly differently. These produce fruit on two-year-old wood and so you have to think about this when pruning. To start what is an ongoing process, tie in one shoot made last year to fruit this year and tie in a new one alongside it for fruiting the following year. Don't prune these shoots, but remove any surplus ones. When the fruit has been picked, prune out the fruited shoot altogether and the other one tied in alongside will be its fruiting replacement next year, when it, in turn, will have a new shoot tied in alongside it.

Propagation

■ **If strawberry runners are required** to make new strawberry plants, reduce runners to five or six per plant and peg them into small pots of peat-free compost sunk into the ground around the parent.

Beat the seasons

■ **Strawberry plants** that were covered with cloches to hasten fruiting should have them opened up for part of the day now, to allow pollinating insects in – otherwise, no fruits will develop. It may be worth going over a few plants with a small, soft paintbrush, transferring pollen from one flower to another to ensure pollination has taken place.

UNDER COVER

■ **Damp down regularly** in the greenhouse and conservatory, splashing water on the floor and under staging to increase the humidity levels, ideally two to three times a day by midsummer. This is beneficial to plant growth and it also helps in the control of red spider mite. This microscopic pest can be detected by the mottled appearance it gives the foliage of affected plants. It can also be controlled chemically; alternatively, there is a tiny predatory mite that can be used as a biological control.

■ **Shade the greenhouse or conservatory.** It is best to try to avoid great fluctuations of temperatures under glass and the best way to reduce the temperature is by using shading. The cheapest form of shading is a wash for the glass; it comes as a powder (available at most garden centres), which is mixed with water and painted or sprayed on. It can be wiped off with a duster at the end of the summer.

The one problem with this type of shading is that it is there even on dull days, reducing light inside. The alternative is to fit roller blinds. Ideally they should be fitted to the outside. A compromise is to use fine mesh netting, which can be thrown over the structure on sunny days and taken off on dull days.

■ **Continue to prick out** and pot on seedlings, cuttings, and young plants as they need it.

■ **Check all plants regularly** for signs of pests and diseases, which become more prevalent as the weather becomes warmer; be vigilant, to stop them building up into serious problems. Look on the undersides of leaves for whitefly and the tips of shoots for greenfly. Small infestations of pests can be picked off or may be caught on yellow sticky cards. Don't use these traps if you have plenty of predatory insects around, as these will be caught too. Another way to keep pests at bay is with biological controls.

Raising plants for outdoors

■ **Plant up hanging baskets** and other containers, provided that you can keep them frost-free in the greenhouse or conservatory to grow on, giving them a head start before putting them outside early next month.

■ **Harden off hanging baskets** that were planted up last month so that they can get used to the outdoor conditions. Leave them out for increasingly long periods until they can be left out at night – so long as frost is not forecast.

■ **Harden off bedding plants** for planting out at the end of the month and early next month. This means getting the plants used to growing in cooler conditions, without checking their growth. The usual way of doing this is to put the plants in cold frames and keep the lids closed for a few days. Then gradually open them, increasing ventilation over about a week until the lids can be left off – except on nights when frost is forecast. Or stand the plants outside for short periods, increasing the time they are left out.

Don't be in too much of a hurry to plant out, even though space in the greenhouse and cold frame will be at a premium. If the plants have been in pots or trays longer than they should have been and are consequently looking starved, give them a feed with a liquid fertilizer.

■ **Sow half-hardy and hardy annuals** now for autumn colour. Some half-hardy annuals such as clarkia, calendula, and candytuft (*Iberis*) can still be sown early in the month to produce flowers in late summer and autumn.

Cold frame Gradually extend the time you leave a cold frame open, to harden off your plants.

■ **Sow ornamental cabbages and kales.**

■ **Vegetables can still be sown indoors** to shorten the growing period.

Glasshouse and house plants

■ **Pot on begonias and gloxinias** that were potted into small pots earlier. Be sure to water the plants well beforehand, otherwise the root ball will remain dry and the roots will not grow into the new compost very well. 12–15cm (5 or 6in) pots are a perfectly adequate size for normal pot plants. If you are growing them for exhibiting they will have to be potted on again into larger pots later in the summer. Leave a gap of about 2.5cm (1in) between the surface of the compost and the rim of the pot to allow room for watering. Water them in after potting to settle the compost around the roots.

■ **Sow half-hardy and hardy annuals** now for winter-flowering pot plants. Some half-hardy annuals make excellent pot plants in the winter – for example, browallia, calceolarias, cinerarias, and schizanthus. Sow them thinly in small pots or trays in a temperature of 18°C (65°F).

Prick out the seedlings into small pots when they are large enough. Pot on into larger pots when the roots have filled the smaller pots and you will have a glorious mix of colour through winter and spring.

Crops under glass

■ **As forced strawberries in pots** finish cropping, discard the plants. They will not be capable of cropping well a second time. Pot up some runners from plants in the garden for next year.

■ **Plant up tomatoes, peppers, and aubergines** sown earlier. Young plants can be potted on into large pots to crop, or put into growing bags, or planted in the soil in the greenhouse border. Don't overcrowd them, as they will become drawn and leggy if they are planted too close together. Cordon tomatoes have weak stems and they will need supporting all season. An alternative to canes or frames is to run baler twine under the plant's rootball when planting, tying the other end of the twine to wire supports strung across the greenhouse roof. The plants are wound around the string as they grow.

■ **Continue to remove sideshoots** from cordon tomatoes. The smaller the shoots when this is done the better. The best way to do it is to bend them to one side with your thumb and forefinger; they should snap off cleanly. If the shoots have grown too large to snap off, use a sharp knife, but have a weak solution of a garden disinfectant in a container with you and dip the knife into it each time a shoot is cut off. This sterilizes the knife and prevents the spread of virus diseases.

■ **Feed all tomatoes, peppers, and aubergines** with a high-potash fertilizer every week from now on through the season to achieve good crops.

THE JUNE GARDEN

Summer is really here. There is still plenty to keep you occupied, such as cutting back and mowing, but this is a time of year when you can really begin to enjoy the fruits of your labours. So above all else, do take the time to sit and savour the sensory delights of your garden and reward yourself for all the hard work you have put into it. Gardening shouldn't become a chore.

THINGS TO DO

Continue weeding and deadheading.

Water new and young plants as necessary.

Look out for pests and suckers on roses.

Finish pruning spring-flowering shrubs.

Propagate climbers by layering them.

Cut back and tidy up perennials if not already done.

Take cuttings from pinks.

Sow seeds of perennials.

Lift and divide overgrown clumps of bulbs.

Plant out summer bedding plants.

Mow the lawn and trim edges regularly.

Give tired lawns a boost with a liquid feed and water new lawns made in the spring.

Harvest vegetables as they come to maturity.

Plant winter brassicas, protecting them from pests.

Keep fruit and vegetables well watered during dry spells.

Shade and ventilate the greenhouse.

LAST CHANCE

Plant new plants before the summer really starts to heat up.

Continue to sow hardy annuals outside to flower this year.

Plant out tender vegetables such as tomatoes.

GET AHEAD

Sow chicory to force in winter.

Peg down strawberry runners to make new plants.

Annual colours Poppies create a wonderful summer display, offset against their marvellous blue-green leaves.

TIME TO RELAX AND ENJOY

Think of this month as the moment when things hit their peak – borders look perfect and summer vegetables and soft fruit are flourishing. You need to take time to admire the results of your hard work, but don't forget to keep an eye on pests and be alert to drier spells, when you will need to do plenty of watering.

Ornamental borders will soon be at the peak of perfection and there are plenty of early summer vegetables to be savoured now. Towards the end of the month soft fruit will also be ripening, to provide a mouthwatering selection of currants and berries during the rest of the summer. Again towards the end of the month, roses begin to flower in earnest. With most the scent is wonderful and there is a terrific selection of flower colours and shapes available. Climbing and rambler roses look particularly good around doors and scrambling up through trees and large shrubs. At your local garden centre there will be wonderful displays of roses in bloom; take some home and plant them out for instant colour in the garden or in containers on the patio.

Most of the sowing, pricking out, and potting on will have been done, so you can now spend a little time relaxing in the garden. The long summer evenings are pure joy and there is nothing better to do in the cool at the end of a long day than to sit quietly in the garden with a glass of something refreshing. Listen to the birds and insects and take in the scents (which are often stronger in the evening) and enjoy the sights and sounds of your own private piece of paradise. Pure bliss!

The start of dry spells

The weather in June is usually quite warm, with few days of rain. There are often occasional thunderstorms followed by hot, dry spells, so keep a watchful eye on all newly planted plants and water them as and when required. With the sun now quite strong it is time to shade greenhouses and conservatories throughout the day to prevent plants being scorched in oven-like

Meadow mood Grasses and wildflowers will attract bees and butterflies, but are also rich food resources for many other less conspicuous creatures.

A water butt is a great asset for gardeners. The stored water is suitable for all plants, except for young plants and seedlings.

temperatures. Good ventilation is also vital and the ventilators can usually be left open day and night through the summer. Thankfully, all tender plants can now be put outside as there should be little fear of night frosts. Now is the time to plant up all those container, basket, and bedding schemes you have been dreaming about. Cluttered greenhouse benches, conservatories, and windowsills can be cleared of all the young and tender plants sheltering indoors. If you haven't been growing on your own summer bedding, then get down to your garden centre or nursery as soon as possible, before all the best plants are snapped up. Even if you don't think you're a "bedding person", just take a look. You're bound to be tempted by some of the lovely new selections that have appeared in the last few years. Don't be afraid to plant up closely, leaving much less space than when setting out hardy garden plants. After all, the plants only have to last a season. It's no bad idea to overestimate your needs when raising or buying bedding plants, as you will always be able to find gaps for any spares.

Pests on the march

Pests and diseases are now on the attack in full force in the warm conditions, both inside and outside. Biological controls are the way forward, especially in the greenhouse. Conditions indoors are more favourable to biological controls because most need warm temperatures to be effective.

Wherever possible, try to use organic means to control pests and diseases, rather than resorting instinctively to an arsenal of chemicals. Most problems with pests and diseases can be controlled by good garden hygiene and by good growing and gardening practices: not allowing plants to grow too closely together and feeding them to encourage strong growth – but not lush, soft growth, which is more susceptible to attack. By following these simple steps the plants will not only be healthier but also more able to shrug off attacks from pests and diseases, thereby reducing the need for chemical controls.

The way ahead for the weather

There is considerable debate these days about climate change and how this will affect us in the future, but it is

Weather watch

At last we can look forward to warm, sunny days: very warm at times, with temperatures reaching 20–22°C in places. In northern areas, average temperatures will be slightly cooler, but still a respectable 16–18°C. Don't let young plants suffer through lack of water during hot spells. Getting them well established in their first year is the most important consideration.

Winds higher up

June is usually calm, with the exception of the south-western approaches, other coastal areas, and north-western coasts. As the height above sea level increases, so does the strength of the winds; this is often why wind farms, with their huge windmills, are seen on high ground and near coasts.

Sunny days

Thankfully there are usually more sunny days than dull, overcast ones this month. Northern parts get less sunshine, with the higher areas averaging 157 hours this month and southern parts around 204 hours.

Varying rainfall

This is usually one of the driest months. There are occasional thunderstorms, but they tend to pass quickly and do little to replenish water in the soil. But the weather does vary from year to year and sometimes June can be quite wet in northern and north-western parts. Average rainfall for the month falls sharply from 114mm in north-west Scotland down to 50mm in the north of England and 47mm in the south-east. On average it will rain on one day in every three in England, so you can never be guaranteed several dry days in succession.

Sudden snow falls

Although it has been known for freak weather conditions to produce a sudden fall of snow in June, this is an extremely rare occurrence. Certainly no snow will lie on the ground anywhere except on the very highest peaks.

Herb plantings Aromatic herbs, such as marjoram, chives, and mint will flourish in a sunny spot, yet survive really cold winters. A hanging basket is ideal, as it can be moved about according to conditions.

plants. There is a very wide choice of plants available from garden centres and nurseries that form a very effective green cover over the soil.

If you haven't already got one, install a water butt outside the greenhouse or conservatory to catch valuable rain water. Plants grow much better when watered with rainwater than with tap water, especially if you live in an area with hard water, which is alkaline. You can tell if you've got hard water if you see lime deposits on the inside of your kettle. Plants like rhododendrons and azaleas in pots need acid conditions and hard water doesn't do them much good. Keeping a water butt for rain water for these plants is very worthwhile.

Keeping the garden looking good

There are plenty of opportunities to enjoy the garden on warm, sunny June days yet there are plenty of jobs to be getting on with too. Spring-flowering plants may need attention now that their main season of display is over. Pruning shrubs and trimming and dividing perennials will ensure that they give a good show next year and their neat appearance will set off your summer-flowering plants, rather than being a tatty, overgrown distraction.

One task that is important but is often regarded as being rather tedious is deadheading – removing fading flowers to encourage a fresh crop of blooms. Some plants, such as pansies, may have a very short flowering period if they are not deadheaded. All of the repeat-flowering roses also benefit from being deadheaded as the flowers fade; it is the best way to encourage a further flush of blooms throughout the summer and into the autumn.

Pack in more plants

Gardens are ablaze with colour in June, but if yours is looking a little lacklustre, now is the time to liven it up. One way is to fill a few containers with summer bedding, providing an instant, if temporary, lift. Alternatively, make new flower beds, and plant them up with colourful perennials. An underused patch of lawn can be transformed into a blooming border in just a day or two, the instructions for which are given on page 143. Select plants that will suit your site and soil and leave gaps between them to allow for growth – many perennials will

difficult to predict what may happen in the longer term. The consensus of opinion seems to be that the south and east will become drier and warmer, while the north will become wetter and cooler. There will also be a tendency towards more extreme weather such as excessive rainfall and high winds, and we have already witnessed severe droughts and dramatic floods in some countries.

Conserving water

With the effects of climate change becoming more apparent, we must do our best to conserve the natural resources of the planet. If you have not already done so earlier in the year, spread a mulch of organic matter over any bare soil after rain or watering to conserve as much moisture as possible. Another way to do this and to keep weeds at bay at the same time is to use ground-cover

Clearing the greenhouse By now, the greenhouse may be full to bursting point, but thankfully June nights should be reliably warm and all the plants here can be put outside.

spread rapidly once they are fully established. If you want to keep some structure to the plants throughout the winter you can also work in a few flowering evergreen shrubs, such as cistus and choisya.

Nepeta x faassenii ♀
Spreading perennial with a pungent scent (*see p.312*)

Cistus x cyprius ♀
Sun-loving shrub that flowers over a long period (*see p.284*)

Achillea 'Fanal'
Perennial with flowers popular with beneficial insects (*see p.275*)

Astilbe 'Bronce Elegans' ♀
Perennial; good for a shady spot that is not too dry (*see p.279*)

Genista aetnensis ♀
The Mount Etna broom; a large, drought-tolerant shrub (*see p.299*)

Iris germanica ♀
Bearded iris, often with several flowers on each stem (*see p.304*)

Geranium himalayense
Perennial that gives its best display in early to midsummer (*see p.299*)

***Potentilla fruticosa* PRINCESS**
Small, bushy shrub that enjoys sun and dry soil (*see p.318*)

***Dianthus* 'Little Jock'**
Small perennial forming flower-covered mounds (*see p.292*)

Crambe cordifolia ♀
Statuesque perennial with huge sprays of flowers (*see p.290*)

***Santolina chamaecyparissus* 'Lemon Queen'**
Low-growing, grey-leaved shrub (*see p.328*)

***Geum* 'Borisii'**
Perennial that flowers over a long period in summer (*see p.299*)

Clematis 'Fireworks'
Large-flowered, deciduous climber with blue-mauve flowers (*see p.285*)

Philadelphus microphyllus
Free-flowering shrub with orange-blossom fragrance (*see p.317*)

Alchemilla mollis ♀
Spreading perennial, good along path edges and as ground cover (*see p.276*)

Polemonium carneum
Jacob's ladder; a clump-forming perennial with pretty leaves (*see p.318*)

Lupinus 'The Page'
Clump-forming perennial with carmine-red flower spikes (*see p.309*)

Tamarix tetrandra ♀
Arching shrub that grows well in coastal districts (*see p.332*)

Lonicera x heckrottii
Vividly coloured honeysuckle for a sunny wall (*see p.308*)

Veronica gentianoides ♀
Perennial with palest blue to white flower spikes (*see p.333*)

***Viburnum plicatum* 'Mariesii'** ♀
Large deciduous shrub with tiered branches (*see p.334*)

Buddleja globosa ♀
Large shrub with honey-scented flowers (*see p.281*)

***Paeonia lactiflora* 'Sarah Bernhardt'** ♀
Herbaceous perennial with large, double rose-pink flowers (*see p.314*)

***Lavandula angustifolia* 'Munstead'**
Compact, bushy lavender, ideal for edging (*see p.306*)

WHAT TO DO IN JUNE

AROUND THE GARDEN

In case night frost is forecast, as it may still be in some northern parts, use horticultural fleece or old newspapers to give protection to bedding and vulnerable young vegetables, including the shoots of late-planted potatoes.

Apply and renew mulches over the soil. This is a good idea at any time of year, but especially now, to reduce water loss from the soil and suppress weeds. The most important point to bear in mind when putting down a mulch is to make sure the soil is moist beforehand. If the soil is dry the mulch is just as good at keeping water out as it is at retaining it in the soil. Don't forget that you can also "mulch" newly planted containers; there is a wide range of decorative chippings now on offer that will complement stone, terracotta, and glazed pots.

Water plants thoroughly during hot spells, concentrating on newly planted plants, young vegetables, and plants in containers, which need it most. If there's a lot to do, it is no good going out every night and splashing a little water everywhere. In drought periods, divide the garden into areas and every evening give a different one a good soaking, which should last for up to a week. This is more beneficial because the roots will go deeper into the soil in search of water. Smaller amounts of water encourage the roots to come to the surface of the soil, causing more harm in the long run; roots near the surface make the plants even more vulnerable in drier conditions.

Hoe or hand-pull annual weeds while they are still small. Choose a dry day and leave the weeds on the surface to wither. Perennial weeds have to be dug out, leaving no trace in the soil. If any roots are left they will start to grow again, effectively propagating the weed.

Any gaps in borders are better filled with bedding plants for the summer now and then more permanent plants can be put in in the autumn. These gap-fillers will give instant colour to what may have been a bare patch of earth. Any annuals will do, whether hardy or half-hardy. If you need height among medium-sized plants, you can even drop in a whole pot of summer-display plants. Hardy annuals sown now will flower in late summer and autumn, so extending the flowering display in the borders.

Deadheading is a regular task in all parts of the garden as some flowers go over. With many plants – perennials, repeat-flowering roses, and hardy and half-hardy annuals – the flowering period can be extended considerably if old flowers are removed as soon as they fade. This will prevent the plant's energy going into seed production and channel it into new growth and flowers later in the summer and autumn. Most deadheading can be done with secateurs, cutting back to just above strong buds lower down the stems. Some plants, like the hardy geraniums, can be quickly trimmed back hard with a pair of garden shears when the flowers fade. It may seem rather drastic action, but new foliage soon appears.

Deadheading This phlox is among many plants that will produce more flowers if deadheaded.

TREES AND SHRUBS

■ **Control greenfly on roses** with a proprietary insecticide available from garden centres. Spray either early in the morning or, preferably, in late evening, when there are fewer beneficial insects around. Also spray susceptible varieties against black spot with an appropriate fungicide. Avoid combination products containing insecticides unless pests are actually present.

■ **Watch out for leaf-rolling sawfly** on roses. The symptoms of this pest are easy to identify because the leaf edges roll tightly downwards and inwards. There is little detrimental effect to the plant other than it looking unsightly. Minor infestations can be treated by picking off affected leaves and putting them in the bin. There are sprays that can be used, but by the time you see rolled-up leaves, it is too late. Much better to be vigilant and remove leaves as soon as the problem is noticed.

■ **Disbud hybrid tea roses** to encourage larger blooms. These roses often produce several buds at the tip of each stem, making perfectly adequate blooms, albeit fairly small in size. If one show-stopping bloom per stem is needed, remove all the smaller buds, leaving the central, larger, bud to open up. This will also give a longer stem, ideal for arrangements.

■ **Remove fading flowers** from rhododendrons, camellias, and lilacs. By removing the fading blooms the plant's energy is diverted from producing seeds into building up buds. Be careful when removing the spent flowers from rhododendrons and camellias, as the new shoots develop immediately below the old flowerheads. With lilacs, cut back the flowered stem to just above a pair of leaves or buds, or even small shoots, lower down the stem.

Removing rhododendron flowers

Remove the faded flowers very carefully between finger and thumb.

With the flower removed, you will see why care is needed: new leaf buds lie just behind it.

■ **Remove suckers from roses.** Most modern bush roses are grafted, or budded, onto a rootstock, which gives the plant the vigour it needs to produce all those beautiful blooms. One slight drawback with budded roses is that every so often the rootstock itself throws out the odd shoot. It is clearly identifiable because the foliage is generally lighter in colour. It is better if suckers can be pulled off the plant at their point of origin on the roots rather than cut off. If they are cut off the sucker is more likely to grow again. If it is pulled off a little of the root is damaged and it is therefore less likely to be able to regrow.

Pruning and training
■ **Prune mature deciduous shrubs** that finish flowering. These include deutzia, kolkwitzia, philadelphus, and weigela. First, look over the whole plant and remove any dead or damaged growth, cutting to a stem joint or leaf. Then take a worm's eye view through the thicket of stems at the base of the plant and cut out one in three quite low down, selecting the oldest and thickest for removal. Larger stems can be cut with loppers. Really tough old wood will need a pruning saw. Prune away any

that does occur. After pruning, feed with a general organic fertilizer and mulch with organic matter. The new growth produced over summer will flower next year.

■ **If lilacs have become overgrown** and leggy, now is the best time for drastic action, just after you have enjoyed the flowers, but early enough to let the shrub make some new growth over the summer. Saw them right down to about 45cm (18in) from the base. A mass of new shoots will regrow and you should thin those growing inwards across the centre of the plant. The result will be a much bushier, better-shaped shrub.

Planting
■ **You may still plant container-grown** plants, but it isn't advisable now the weather has started to heat up. A woody plant needs a lot of care and watering to get established in summer – far better to use a stop-gap, such as tall lilies, and plant something more permanent in autumn.

Propagation
■ **Continue taking softwood cuttings** from shrubs.

CLIMBERS

■ **Keep on top of training climbing and rambler roses.** These produce so much growth, at such a rate, that if you don't tie them in regularly they trail over other plants and catch on clothing. Whenever possible tie in the stems as close to the horizontal as possible.

■ **Propagate climbers by layering.** Growing your own new plants is one of the most fascinating aspects of gardening. An easy way to propagate many climbers, including clematis, *Akebia quinata*, wisteria, and honeysuckle, is by layering. Many plants layer themselves when a branch or shoot touches the ground, forming roots at that point. If you spot any of these shoots with roots already forming, peg them directly into the soil or into a pot full of compost sunk into the ground as you would with strawberry runners. The young plants can be severed from their parent either in autumn, over-wintering in a cold frame, or next spring.

■ **Prune** *Clematis montana* if you didn't do so last month. This is a vigorous clematis, but it only really needs pruning if it is getting out of control and smothering other plants. Thin out the growth and trim back to its allotted space.

Akebia quinata

Layering a climber

Peg down a stem still attached to the plant at intervals along the ground. Roots should grow into the soil below the pegs.

1 In autumn, or next spring, carefully uproot the stem and separate each rooted section.

2 Pot each up individually in a mixture of peat-free compost and vermiculite. Water thoroughly and place in a cold frame.

PERENNIALS

■ **Remove old leaves and flower stems of hellebores.** The old foliage does look very tatty now and is often infected with leaf spot and other diseases. Remove the leaves at ground level and discard them. The new, young foliage can often be seen growing from the centre of the plant. A feed with a general fertilizer and a mulch with organic matter will also do no harm at all.

Hellebore seeds can be collected from the plants and you can sow them straight away. If the seeds are left on the plants to ripen this will inhibit germination. They don't require any special conditions to germinate. Sow the seeds in a tray or a small pot, cover them lightly with compost and stand the container in a shady cold frame or at the base of a sheltered wall. When the seeds germinate, pot them on once they are large enough to handle.

■ **Cut back Oriental poppies** when they have finished flowering. This is good to do, since once the flowers go over these plants tend to look rather a mess. It's one good reason for siting them in the middle or near the back of a border, so that when the flowers are finished other plants will hide them. To make them look better, cut the foliage to near ground level. It may seem a bit drastic, but it is the thing to do. Once cut back, sprinkle a little organic fertilizer around the plants and water it in thoroughly. This will encourage new growth to come and, if you are lucky, a few more flowers later in the summer.

■ *Euphorbia robbiae* and *E. characias* will look a lot tidier if the old flowerheads are removed when they are going over. Always be sure to wear gloves when you are pruning euphorbias, as the milky white sap can irritate sensitive skin. Remove the old growths to ground level. This will encourage new growth from the base of the plant and keep it bushy and healthy.

Hellebore seeds Wear gloves to collect the ripe capsules, which can irritate some skins.

■ **Every year a new crop of seedlings** appears around the hellebore plants and these can be potted up and grown on as new plants. They will never come true to type – that is to say, if the seeds come from a pink flower, you may not necessarily get pink flowers from the new plants. But you never know – you may come across a stunning variation!

■ **Continue to stake tall-growing** perennials. Nothing looks more unsightly than plants that have been battered about by rain and wind lying all over other, smaller, plants in the borders. Try to stake before this happens. The earlier it is done the better, but it is still not too late to continue doing this task. There are many ways of supporting plants and many products readily available from garden centres. The types you use will largely depend on the depth of your pockets. Bamboo canes and string are cheap, but they have to be used carefully if they are not to look too rigid and prominent in the border, and you must remember to fit eye protectors on top of the canes. Twiggy sticks are another easy means of support. The advantage of these is that the plants can grow through and hide them.

■ **Deadhead lupins and delphiniums** as they finish flowering. If this is done as the flowers fade there is a good chance of further blooms being produced later in the summer. Cut the faded flower spires off at ground level or cut them back to strong new shoots.

■ **Take cuttings from pinks.** The cuttings taken from pinks (*Dianthus*) are called "pipings" and they are very easy to root. Look for healthy, young, non-flowering shoots. Hold the stem about four pairs of leaves from the tip and pull the cutting off. The cutting should come away quite cleanly. Put several cuttings around the edge of a 10cm (4in) pot in a mixture of peat-free compost and perlite, water them in, and place in a shady cold frame. The cuttings will start to root in three or four weeks, when they can be potted up individually into 8cm (3in) pots.

■ **Continue to pot up cuttings of** perennials taken earlier in the spring. As soon as the plants have made a good root system, pot them up. Otherwise, if there are several cuttings to a pot, the roots will become entangled and you will damage them as you try to separate them. Water the cuttings before and after you have potted them up. A shady, sheltered corner will be suitable over the summer; they can be planted out in autumn.

■ **Sow seeds of hardy herbaceous** perennials outside. Perennials like lupins, delphiniums, and hollyhocks can be sown in shallow drills now in a corner of the garden. If space is limited, sow perennials in trays or small pots and place them in a cold frame or at the base of a sheltered wall. When the seedlings have become large enough, pot them on into individual pots and grow on during the summer. Plant them out in the autumn.

BULBS

■ **Cut down the foliage of bulbs** that have been naturalized in grass. By now at least six weeks should have elapsed since flowering and the bulb foliage and the grass can be trimmed. If you cut the leaves down too soon, the bulbs will be "blind" next year. Don't be too concerned about the grass turning yellow after it has been cut where the bulbs are planted. It will soon recover with watering and feeding.

■ **Plant out cannas,** and also lily bulbs that were potted up earlier in the year. Cannas started into growth in March and lily bulbs potted up when the weather was too cold outside to plant can be planted out in the borders. Or, simply put the whole pot in a gap in the border, either sinking it into the ground or, if the surrounding plants are tall enough to hide it, just setting it on the soil surface. Left in pots, they will need extra watering, so be sure to watch them carefully.

■ **Lift and divide bulbs** that have finished flowering. Bulbs can be lifted, dried, and stored when the foliage has died down, but if you tend to leave yours *in situ* year after year, lift overcrowded clumps now and divide them so that they can spend the summer re-establishing.

Dividing Clump of bulbs that have become overcrowded can be divided using a fork.

Anemone coronaria '**Lord Lieutenant**'

Anemone coronaria **De Caen Group**

■ **Plant anemones to flower in autumn.**
Anemones generally flower about three months after planting, so timing the flowering can be quite accurate. By planting some now the small tubers will give a delightful show of flowers just when other plants are beginning to go over. Plant some in pots at the same time to enjoy these wonderful flowers on the windowsill. The ones to look for are *Anemone coronaria* and the de Caen types, which make flowers up to 8cm (3in) across in glowing colours. When planting late like this, it is best to soak the tubers overnight, to get them off to a good start. Plant them 5cm (2in) deep and 8–10cm (3–4in) apart. Incorporate organic matter and the plants will repay you with a glorious display.

ANNUALS AND BEDDING

■ **Plant out summer bedding plants.**
By this time of year it is safe to plant out all bedding plants, including tender kinds like begonias, without fear of frost damage. Look out for plants like bidens, felicia, and brachyscome as well as old favourites such as pelargoniums, salvias, and lobelia. Make sure any old spring bedding is removed, if this was not done last month, and lightly fork over the soil. Spread a little general fertilizer before planting, but not too much, otherwise the plants will produce a lot of lush growth at the expense of flowers. Water the plants well an hour or so before planting them out. This is particularly important where young plants are growing together in a seed tray and the roots will be disturbed when they are planted out. And don't forget to give the plants a thorough watering after planting too.

■ **Water bedding plants** regularly after planting. The plants will have to be watered at regular intervals during dry spells and for a few weeks after planting. The best way to do this and conserve water at the same time is by using a seephose. This is a hose which allows water to seep through its walls along its entire length. The advantage is that the water is concentrated at the plants' roots, instead of being sprayed through the air. The seephose can be buried under the surface or snaked between the plants. If you do have to water with a sprinkler, do so in the early morning or in the evening or the plants will get scorched.

■ **Thin out seedlings of hardy annuals** sown earlier. They should be thinned out as soon as they are large enough to handle, otherwise the plants will become too tall and leggy. Some of the taller-growing annuals may also benefit from some firm support from thin, twiggy sticks.

■ **Some hardy annuals** sown directly now will still have time to flower in late summer and autumn, extending the flowering display. Choose fast-growing annuals such as clarkia, godetia, candytuft, and calendula. Sow them in shallow drills and thin them out when they are large enough to handle and they will flower for you later.

■ **Continue to sow seeds of biennials** to flower next spring. Seedlings sown last month can be transplanted to a spare piece of ground to grow on during the summer until planted in their flowering positions in the autumn. If space is limited, then sow biennials in trays or small pots and place in a cold frame or at the base of a sheltered wall. When the seedlings are large enough, pot them on and grow on during the summer. Plant them out into their flowering positions in the autumn.

■ **Sow polyanthus** for flowering next spring. Unlike other biennials such as wallflowers and myosotis, polyanthus primulas need a little heat to germinate; 15°C (60°F) being about right. A sheltered cold frame should keep the temperature at the right level. Sow the seeds in trays on moist compost without covering them. It is all too easy to cover fine seed too deeply, inhibiting germination. Cover the container with clear polythene and place in a light cold frame. When the seedlings are large enough to handle, pot them up and grow on through the summer. Plant out into their flowering positions in the autumn.

■ **Sow winter pansies.** These are sown in a similar way to polyanthus (see above) except that the seeds are covered to exclude the light. After a couple of weeks, check to see if the seeds have germinated and uncover them if they have. Grow on in exactly the same way as for polyanthus.

Make a new flower bed

A passion for plants has one disadvantage – there is never enough room for all those you want to grow. One solution is to sacrifice an underused area of lawn to extend your planting area. A new bed against a background of other plants, wall, or fence, will soon look settled in. Here, I added an area for sun-loving perennials to provide foreground to a dull shrub border and created a semi-circular shape to give the extended bed a natural outline.

You will need

- garden hose - half-moon edging tool
- spade - fork - well-rotted garden compost or manure - trowel
- selection of perennial plants

1 Make a temporary outline using the garden hose, keeping the curve simple. Group the plants that you want to include in your bed within it, at the correct planting distances. Stand back and look from all sides to make sure that you are happy with the effect.

2 Adjust the hose to even up the shape – for example, to line up with existing edges and corners in the garden – while trying not to enlarge the total area too much.

3 Cut along the edge of the hose, pushing a half-moon lawn edger (or a spade) into the soil to create what will become the new edge to the bed.

4 Strip off the turf from the entire area inside the hose, removing about 2.5cm (1in) of topsoil. Stack the turf, grass-side down, in a corner of the garden. Given time it will rot down into a wonderful compost.

5 Dig over the site to break up the soil to at least one, and preferably two, spits' deep (spade's depths), forking over the bottom as you work to aerate farther down. Remove large stones, leaving smaller ones to assist drainage. Pull the soil away from the new lawn edge and check that you're happy with the bed's outline.

6 Once the soil is broken up, add organic matter, such as well-rotted manure or garden compost.

7 Fork the organic matter well into the dug-over soil. This will have been impoverished by the grass growing on it, so needs plenty of nourishing and conditioning.

8 Put in the new plants, planting as many as possible by reaching from the new lawn edge, so that you do not compact the soil. Keep the new plants well and regularly watered.

9 The new border, with late-summer flowering perennials in warm tones. The plants gave instant colour in their first year and by next year will spread and look even better.

CONTAINERS

■ **Water all plants** in containers regularly during dry spells.

■ **Containers and hanging baskets** that were planted up earlier in the season and kept indoors to protect them from the threat of frost can now be placed outside for the summer months.

■ **Plant up half-hardy annuals** and tender perennials in tubs, troughs, and other containers outdoors now that any danger of night frosts has passed. If you have been raising half-hardy annuals and tender perennials indoors, either from seeds or cuttings, you can plant them out in safety from now on. If you haven't raised any plants yourself then most garden centres will have a tempting selection of plants for sale now. Put as many plants as you can get into each container in order to get the best effect. Upright plants will give some height and trailing and semi-trailing plants look most effective tumbling over the sides and softening the hard edges.

■ **Hanging baskets** are an effective way of showing off bedding plants and they are very easy to plant up. Use one of the many types of liner available from garden centres. If you can avoid it, don't buy sphagnum moss, as its excessive collection can endanger rare wildlife habitats. However, if it comes from a sustainable source, such as your own garden, of course this is quite OK. You can put a disc of polythene in the bottom of the basket to help retain the moisture or you could sink a pot into the compost, as shown in Step 4, right. Use taller plants in the centre to give height to the display and tuck in plenty of trailing plants around them and around the outside of the basket. When the plants grow the basket will be completely hidden and you will have a mass of flowers to enjoy all summer long.

Planting up a hanging basket

1 Sit the basket in a pot or bucket to keep it stable throughout the planting process. Put the liner (coir in this case) in position and trim it to fit along the rim. A circle of polythene placed at the bottom will help retain water.

2 Cut slits for trailing plants. Add a 5cm (2in) layer of soilless compost, mixed with controlled-release fertilizer and water-retaining gel.

3 Remove the trailing plants from their pots and thread them through the slits. Use a plastic bag to protect the stems and leaves.

4 Place a pot in the centre to act as a reservoir and plant around it. Use upright plants centrally and trailers around the rim. Add more compost and build up the planting in tiers until the compost is just below the rim.

5 Firm the compost and water thoroughly through the plastic pot.

6 Hang your basket in a sheltered spot where you can easily reach it for watering. Use fittings strong enough to take the weight of saturated compost. Water carefully, using a watering lance if possible, so that the water doesn't puddle in one section.

LAWNS

■ **Mow lawns regularly.** By this time of year the lawn should be cut at least once a week and preferably twice a week, if this is possible. The reason for this is that the less grass taken off at each cut, the healthier it will remain. It is also important to mow in a different direction each time, because if you mow in the same direction several times in a row, the grass begins to grow in that direction and the mower blades, especially those on a cylinder mower, will not cut it as well. By this time the mower blades should be at the lowest setting required; for most lawns, about 1.25cm (½in), or a little higher for a lawn that takes a lot of use. If there are dry spells, when the grass goes a bit brown, reduce the frequency of mowing and raise the blades a little so as not to cut it too close.

Now that grass is generating a lot of clippings, don't dump them in a mass on the compost heap or they will clump together and rot down into a slimy mess rather than good compost. This is because they are too close-textured to admit air. Keep the clippings separate until you have some looser material to mix in with them. Torn and crumpled newspaper will do if the garden is not generating much suitable debris at the moment.

Mowing direction Be sure to mow in a different direction each time so that the mower blades cut as efficiently as possible.

Long-handled shears These make edging the lawn a great deal less backbreaking.

■ **Don't forget edging.** Another job to bear in mind is to trim the lawn edges at the same time as the grass is cut. It makes all the difference to the appearance of the garden if the edges are cut regularly. And it's less work doing the edges once a week as the trimmings are few and don't have to be cleared up.

■ **Feed lawns with a liquid fertilizer.** These fast-acting feeds are the perfect thing to give a tired-looking lawn a quick tonic. Diluted in water, following the instructions on the bottle, they are easily applied with a watering can or sprayer. One advantage they have over dry fertilizers is that they don't have to be watered in if the weather remains dry.

New lawns

■ **Water new lawns** made in spring either from seed or turf. It is vitally important not to let newly laid turf dry out: it shrinks when it dries and it's almost impossible to get it back to how it was. One way to ensure that a sprinkler is watering the ground evenly is to place a number of empty jars around the lawn. You'll soon see, by the level of water collected, whether any areas are going short.

VEGETABLE AND HERBS
Harvesting

■ **Continue to harvest all crops as they mature.** Early peas will be ready to pick now. Cut down the top growth of the plants (known as the "haulm") after harvesting, but leave the roots of the peas in the soil, as these will return valuable nitrogen to it. Nodules on the roots of peas and beans are able to fix and store atmospheric nitrogen in the soil. Follow peas with a leafy crop, such as cabbages, which require a higher nitrogen content in the soil. This is one way, by practising good crop rotation, of reducing the amount of artificial fertilizer we put on the soil.

■ **Japanese onions** that were sown last year will now be ready to harvest. The tops should have begun to fall over and the skins to harden. Lift them to break the roots in the soil and let them dry out in the sun. If it rains, put them in a greenhouse or cold frame to dry out.

■ **You may be able to start harvesting** early potatoes towards the end of the month. There is nothing like digging the first potatoes and taking them straight to the kitchen to be cooked. To harvest them, push a fork into the ground a little way from the base of the plant to reduce the chance of piercing any of the vegetables. Root around a bit to make sure you've got all the potatoes, as any left in the ground will re-grow again next year. They always seem to grow slap bang in the middle of a row of seedlings, making it difficult to get them out.

Sowing and planting outdoors

■ **Plant celery in trenches** prepared during winter or spring. Apply a general fertilizer before planting and put the plants in rows 30cm (1ft) apart. Water the plants well after planting and keep them well watered throughout the growing season.

Celery requires a lot of water to produce a good crop in the autumn. The soil that was heaped up on either side of the trench to be used for blanching the celery in the autumn and winter can be used in the summer to grow fast-maturing salad crops like lettuce, radish, and salad onions.

The technique of growing quick-maturing crops on spare ground like this is known as "catch cropping". Self-blanching celery does not have to be planted in trenches, but is better planted in blocks 23cm (9in) apart, rather than rows, so that each plant blanches its neighbour.

■ **Plants of celeriac raised earlier** can also be planted out now.

■ **Sow radicchio (red chicory)** in rows 23cm (9in) apart. Sow in the usual manner, watering the seed drill if the weather is dry, before sowing the seeds. This is a leafy chicory, unlike the forcing type: the leaves are eaten fresh and it makes a useful vegetable for autumn and winter salads, being able to stand through cold weather in the garden.

Cloches will protect the heads from weather damage. There are several varieties available with attractively coloured foliage. They certainly add a touch of colour to any winter salad.

Pea seedlings When these are nearly ready to start climbing they are liable to attack by pigeons, so cover them up with netting.

Climbing frames These must be sturdy enough to support fully laden runner bean plants.

■ **Continue to sow peas** for maincrops later in the year.

■ **Plant out runner beans.** Now that the threat of frost has passed these plants can go out into ground that was prepared during the winter. Put up whatever supports you require before planting, either making wigwams or parallel avenues of canes with 60cm (2ft) between the rows. Slugs love young runner-bean plants; so you need to protect the seedlings from slugs and snails. To ensure runner-bean flowers set and produce pods, spray them with water regularly and make sure that they don't dry out at the roots.

Dwarf runner beans can also go out now. These don't require much support. It may be worth inserting a few twiggy sticks around the plants, as they do often flop over, even though they are dwarf. This will prevent the pods being splashed with soil when it rains. Dwarf and climbing French beans can be treated in exactly the same way as runner beans.

■ **Keep sowing salad vegetables** in small quantities at regular intervals of two or three weeks. This will provide a continuous supply of fresh salad stuff over a long period, rather than a glut all at one time.

One point to bear in mind now is that lettuce seed will not germinate in high temperatures, so if the weather is hot and dry, sow the seeds in a shady part of the garden, or sow them in seed trays and put these in a shady part of the garden. Transplant the seedlings when they are large enough to handle.

■ **Plant tomatoes outside.** Tomatoes can be planted in the soil at intervals of 45cm (18in), or planted two or three to a growing bag. Tomatoes prefer a sunny spot against a south-facing wall if possible. Cordon plants will need staking with 1.2m (4ft) canes. When planting tomatoes outside, leave a slight depression in the soil. This helps to retain water around the roots of the plants when watering them in. It can be difficult to push canes into growing bags as there is insufficient compost to hold the canes upright. There are frames that hold canes, especially for use in growing bags, which you can buy from the garden centre.

Feed all tomatoes with a high-potash fertilizer every week from now on through the season, to get a good crop. Be careful not to let tomatoes, especially those in growing bags, go short of water. If they are neglected or watered irregularly, going dry in between times, they will be prone to blossom end rot. This appears as a sunken brown area at the end of the fruit farthest from the plant. It is due to calcium deficiency, brought about by a lack of water, even for a very short period. Regular watering is the key to preventing this problem. Another problem that may be caused by irregular watering is splitting of the fruits.

■ **Plant out ridge cucumbers.** Although these are called "ridge" cucumbers, they do not actually have to be grown on ridges of soil. Plant out the young plants in early

Plant ridge cucumbers The young plants will thrive in soil enriched with lots of organic matter.

June, in soil that has been enriched with plenty of organic matter to retain as much moisture as possible. Pinch out the growing tips of the plants when they have made six pairs of leaves, to encourage sideshoots to form and produce the cucumbers. Feed and water regularly with a high-potash fertilizer through the summer and you'll get delicious cucumbers all summer long.

■ **Plant and sow marrows and courgettes,** and pumpkins and squashes, outside. Young plants should be spaced about 60cm (2ft) apart in soil that has been enriched with plenty of organic matter to retain moisture. If plants were not raised earlier under glass, all is not lost. They can be sown directly outside now. Sow two seeds together in the place they are to crop. Pull out the weaker of the seedlings when they germinate, leaving the stronger one to grow on.

■ **Sow turnips for an autumn crop.** Sow the seeds in rows 15cm (6in) apart. Thin the seedlings as soon as you can handle them without damaging the young plants. Thin them to leave one plant every 10cm (4in). The turnips are best harvested when they are young, before they get to the size of a tennis ball. You can leave some roots in for longer, as their leafy tops can be cooked for winter greens.

■ **Sow Witloof chicory** for forcing. Sow the seeds in rich, fertile soil to fatten up the roots for forcing in winter. Give a good dressing of a general fertilizer and sow the seeds in rows 30cm (12in) apart. Thin the seedlings to 15cm (6in) apart when they become large enough to handle. Keep them well watered during dry weather.

■ **Sow Chinese cabbage** and other Oriental vegetables. These vegetables can be sown now at regular intervals until August. One way to get quick results is to sow the seeds under cloches. This way some of them will germinate in two or three days. These leafy vegetables are all excellent for stir-frying, making delicious meals fresh from the garden in a matter of minutes. Some are prone to attack from flea beetle and it may be worth growing them permanently under cloches or covered with horticultural fleece to stop the beetles getting at the plants.

■ **Plant out all winter brassicas** sown earlier. The young plants will need protection against cabbage root fly. These crops generally need plenty of room to grow – at least 60cm (2ft) apart each way. But other, quicker-growing crops can be grown between the brassicas until they reach their maximum size. Salad crops such as lettuce, radish, and spinach can all be grown between the brassicas. This is known as "intercropping" and utilizes the space, fertilizers, and organic matter added to the soil to the best advantage.

Plant out sweetcorn

Plant sweetcorn in blocks, 30cm (1ft) apart each way, rather than in rows. The reason for this is that sweetcorn is pollinated by wind. The male flowers appear as the tassels at the tip of the plant and the pollen falls onto the female parts lower down. By growing the plants in blocks there is more chance of pollination being successful than if the plants are growing in conventional rows.

Use a marked plank to plant in blocks, the same distance each way.

Flowering sweetcorn planted in blocks means that pollen will be blown onto other sweetcorn flowers.

Herbs in containers For a space-saving alternative to a herb garden, plant up a selection of herbs in a container. This example shows a yellow-foliage combination of feverfew, sage, marjoram, and thyme.

Looking after crops

Keep watering young vegetable plants and hoe off weeds regularly.

■ **Protect young brassicas** against birds. Birds love to eat young brassicas as soon as they are planted out. In fact wood pigeons often seem to sit and watch me planting, ready to pounce as soon as my back is turned. There are many bird-scarer products on the market, with varying degrees of effectiveness. Whichever you use, the birds sooner or later come to realize that it poses no actual danger. The only foolproof way of stopping birds eating the plants is to grow them under cover. Support either netting or fine-weave mesh sheeting on stakes with strong twine or wire strung between them, so it is held above the plants like a tent. If it is left resting on the plants, the birds will peck through it. Always make sure netting is well anchored at ground level so that small garden birds do not get tangled in it. It's not a very pleasant job trying to untangle a bird from netting.

■ **Cabbage white butterfly caterpillars** will be hatching out now. A lot of damage can be prevented by going around inspecting the undersides of the leaves on all brassicas. You will usually find small clusters of yellow eggs here. The eggs can be squashed, but if you can't face doing that spray with a proprietary insecticide. This will kill off any young caterpillars. If you don't grow many brassicas, it is worth covering them with fleece as a physical barrier to prevent the butterflies laying their eggs in the first place.

■ **Carrot fly are still around,** so be sure to protect carrots with a barrier that the pest cannot penetrate.

■ **Feed asparagus after flowering.** You won't be cutting spears from young crowns, but once they are established and giving you a crop, stop cutting in late June to allow the crowns to build up strength for next year's crop. Apply a general organic fertilizer to all plants, young and old, and let the foliage grow until it turns brown later in the summer, when it can be cut to the ground. Asparagus doesn't attract many pests, but asparagus beetle can be damaging, so look out for it: it has a red body and black and yellow wings. To control it, spray with pyrethrum at dusk to avoid harming bees, or pick off adults and their greyish-cream grubs by hand.

Herbs

■ **Plant herbs in containers** for the patio or by the back door close to the kitchen. Most herbs are extremely effective grown in containers, but some are not very suitable; tall herbs like angelica and lovage can become top-heavy and also may look out of place in a pot – better to grow these in a border. All other herbs are suitable for containers and with many of them, particularly the sages, having attractively coloured foliage, you can make stunning plant combinations by grouping pots together or planting several different herbs in one large container.

FRUIT

Harvesting

■ **Remove cloches** from strawberries and the fruits should ripen for picking.

■ **Harvest your rhubarb** until the end of the month.

Looking after crops

■ **Put up pheromone traps** for codling moths. One trap will protect up to five apple trees.

■ **Continue pruning and pinching out** shoots on wall-trained fruit. Get all the pruning of peaches, plums, and nectarines done through the summer. Wounds heal more quickly and the silver leaf disease fungus releases few spores in warmer, drier weather. Remove unwanted shoots as soon as possible and tie in those that will be used to replace the current year's fruiting wood. Select two new shoots at the base of the fruiting shoot and retain these for tying in. One is just for insurance purposes in case the other is damaged. Cut out any other new shoots. Any sideshoots from the fruiting shoots can be pinched out to five or six leaves.

■ **Control grey mould on strawberries.** Spells of wet weather encourage the spread of grey mould (*Botrytis*). Inspect fruits regularly and remove all the infected ones. Don't compost these, as they may spread the disease to other plants in the garden. Removing infected fruits early enough should help to keep the problem under control.

There are no fungicides available to home gardeners to control grey mould. However, you can ensure plenty of air circulates around the plants and keep developing fruits off the soil by putting straw or mats under them. This stops soil being splashed on the fruits by rain, which can spread mould.

Gooseberries These are borne on one-year-old wood. Prune sideshoots to encourage fruiting.

■ **Gooseberries can also be thinned** for larger fruits and the thinnings can be cooked. Look out for gooseberry sawfly caterpillars. They can attack right through the summer and a bad infestation can completely defoliate a plant. The caterpillars are up to 2cm (¾in) long, pale green in colour and marked with black spots. They rear up when disturbed. Spray with a proprietary insecticide or inspect the plants regularly from spring onwards, paying particular notice to the undersides of the leaves and squash any eggs and caterpillars you see.

■ **Don't be tempted to thin out apples and pears** until the "June drop" has happened. It is all too easy to plough ahead with thinning out the fruits, only to see that the ones you have left all fall off, leaving you with none at all.

■ **Blackcurrants can often suffer** from a viral disease called "reversion". This distorts the leaves and usually makes them smaller than they should be. Any badly infected plants should be dug up and burned. If you want to replace them, buy only certified stock that is free of the virus.

The virus is spread by the blackcurrant big bud mite, which lives in the buds and gives them an enlarged appearance. Buds like this should always be picked off in winter.

■ **Keep all fruit well watered in dry spells** to ensure a good crop of quality fruits throughout the summer. Mulching with organic matter will help in retaining moisture and reducing the need to keep watering. Mulching will also keep down weeds, which compete for water and nutrients in the soil; many weeds also act as hosts to pests and diseases.

■ **Heavy crops of plums** can be thinned early in the month to prevent the brittle branches of plum trees from breaking. It also discourages biennial bearing. Thin in two stages, removing only any damaged or diseased fruit first. Don't remove too many fruits to begin with as the trees will naturally shed some fruit around now. This is called the "June drop".

Wait until this has happened, then carry out a second thinning if the fruits still appear to be overcrowded. You can also support heavy branches if you are worried that they will be damaged by the weight of fruit, especially if the trees are quite young.

Plentiful plums Heavy crops can break branches, so support them if necessary.

Tie in blackberries The long canes need to be secured at regular intervals or you may find that the thorns become dangerous.

Pruning and training

■ **Continue tying in new canes** of blackberries and hybrid berries. Methods of training are many and varied and some are unnecessarily complicated. The easiest is to train the shoots in the form of a fan, with the current year's fruiting canes spaced out to one side of the plant on the framework of wires and new canes tied in on the other side, completing the fan shape. After fruiting, the old canes are cut out and the process repeated next year.

■ **Prune excess growth on vines.** "Stop" or pinch out the tip of the fruiting shoots at a leaf beyond three or four developing fruit clusters. Pinch back any sideshoots from these stems to one or two leaves. Vines grown outdoors in our climate will only ripen a few decent bunches of grapes on each sideshoot from the main stem or rod, so it is counter-productive to allow any more to develop.

Propagation

■ **Strawberries will now be producing lots of runners.** These can either be removed or pegged down to make new plants, depending on your needs.

UNDER COVER

■ **Damp down regularly** to keep the atmosphere in the greenhouse or the conservatory humid. "Damping down" just means splashing or spraying water around. This will benefit plants enormously, especially if you can close the ventilators and doors for a short time after damping down, to allow the temperature and the humidity to rise and create a wonderful growing atmosphere. It will also help to keep down the incidence of glasshouse red spider mite.

■ **Water and feed all plants regularly** now that they are all growing fast. If soilless or peat-free composts become dry it is almost impossible to re-wet them properly, so never let them dry out completely between waterings. If pot plants have become dry at the roots, give them a good soaking by sitting them in water overnight, before feeding with fertilizer. If the fertilizer is applied to dry compost it may scorch roots. Feeding flowering pot plants and bedding plants with a fertilizer high in potash will ensure a continued display of good-quality flowers through the summer until the first frosts of autumn. Be careful not to splash water on the foliage of plants in bright, sunny weather. The water droplets on the leaves act like small magnifying glasses, scorching the leaves. Watering is best done in the evenings, if possible, when there is less chance of the water evaporating than in the heat of the day.

■ **Shade the greenhouse or conservatory** with paint-on shading or blinds. Ventilate whenever you can by opening windows, doors, and vents. Warm sunshine on a glasshouse can cause the temperatures to rise to dramatic levels. It is best for the plants if temperatures can be kept as even as possible. Big fluctuations in temperature will not encourage good sturdy growth in the plants. There are many different automatic ventilator openers on the market, which take the guesswork out of whether to leave the vents open or shut when you leave for work in the morning. They can be set to open and close at a set temperature and so give you peace of mind. Working in conjunction with shading, these should help to control the temperature on the hottest of days.

■ **Pot on all young plants and seedlings** as necessary. Plants that become pot-bound over a period of time rarely recover and grow well. The ideal time to pot on any plant is when, after you have knocked the plant from its pot, you can see a good tracery of roots around the sides of the root ball, without it looking congested with roots.

Another good indication that plants really need potting on is roots growing out through the drainage holes in the bottom of the pot. Keep young plants well watered, and shade them from the sun if the roots have been disturbed when the plants were potted up (for example, when separating a pot full of cuttings). It takes a few days for the roots to take up water after they have been disturbed.

Potting on Gently tease each plant out of its compartment.

Glasshouse and house plants

■ **House plants** that have been stuck in stuffy rooms can be moved to the greenhouse for a holiday. Even if house plants are sitting on a sunny windowsill, they never really get all the light they need and the dry atmosphere in most houses is far from ideal for plant growth. So a spell in the greenhouse will be like a well-earned holiday for your plants. The foliage of large-leaved plants such as rubber plants will benefit from a sponge-over. The leaves will be shiny again and look a lot better and the plants will be healthier, too. When that layer of dust has been removed, air can pass through the pores in the leaves much more easily.

■ **Sow seeds of** *Primula malacoides, P. sinensis*, cinerarias, and calceolarias for pot plants to flower in the winter and spring. Sow small batches of the seeds in small pots of seed compost and place near a window. They don't need a lot of heat to germinate at this time of year. Pot on the seedlings, holding them by the seed leaves, when they are large enough to handle. Do be aware, though, that people with sensitive skin should handle primulas with gloves, as they can irritate some skins. If you are a sufferer, you may find it almost impossible to grasp the little seed leaves to transplant them without wearing gloves. You either need the thin surgical-type gloves, or a kind friend to do you a favour. Grow the plants on in a cool place – a shady cold frame is ideal – to get good sturdy plants to take into the house in the autumn and winter. Whitefly and greenfly can be a problem, particularly with cinerarias. Inspect the plants at regular intervals and squash the aphids before they get out of control.

■ **Pot on cuttings taken earlier** from potted hydrangeas. Water the cuttings

Solanum capsicastrum

well before potting them on to larger pots. Knock the cuttings out of the pot and carefully tease the roots apart. Pot each cutting into a small 8cm (3in) pot, or for a really dramatic display pot three cuttings into a 12.5cm (5in) pot and pot these together into a larger pot when the roots have filled this one. This way you get three plants bushing out in place of one, making a spectacular show later in the year. Grow the plants on outside and feed them regularly with a high-potash fertilizer to build up the flower buds. Bring the plants inside in the autumn.

■ *Solanum capsicastrum* **plants** sown earlier in the spring will also benefit from being put outside for the summer. The plants will produce fine, sturdy growth, which will ripen over summer. Putting the plants outside also allows pollinating insects to get at the plants easily, ensuring that a good crop of attractive fruits appears in early autumn.

Crops under glass

■ **Fruiting crops** – tomatoes, peppers, and aubergines – need watering regularly and a high-potash feed every week to help the fruits swell and develop.

■ **Check the base of grape vines** to make sure they are not drying out. Traditionally, grape vines are planted outside the glasshouse and their stems trained in through a low hole in the wall. That way, the roots benefit from rainfall. Grape vines are completely hardy – improved ripening of the fruits is why we, with our short summers, grow them under glass. At this time, when the bunches are developing, check around the roots, whether outside or in, and give the plants a regular soak if they need it.

■ **Continue removing sideshoots** from tomatoes. The sooner the sideshoots are removed, the less of a shock it is to the plant. They are easily removed by bending them to one side with your thumb and forefinger. Larger sideshoots can be cut off with secateurs. Dip the secateurs in a weak solution of a garden disinfectant after each cut to avoid spreading virus among the plants. Tomatoes are very prone to picking up viruses – this is one reason why they are often used in plant research work.

Tomato sideshoots Pinching sideshoots needs to be done at regular intervals.

THE JULY GARDEN

Your garden will now be looking its very best and will have reached its peak for the year. All your earlier sowing and planting will be paying dividends in the border and beds and in the vegetable garden too. There is always plenty to be done, but make the most of the long summer evenings after work and enjoy them to the full at weekends, relaxing and entertaining friends.

THINGS TO DO

Make sure that the birds have water in dry spells.

Keep new and young plants well watered, and feed and water plants in containers regularly.

Be on the alert to get rid of any pests and diseases.

Continue deadheading flowers as they fade.

Prune shrubs that flowered in early summer and take semi-ripe cuttings from shrubs.

Trim conifer hedges and take cuttings from them.

Summer-prune wisteria.

Divide bearded irises, and layer and take cuttings of carnations and pinks.

Plant autumn-flowering bulbs.

Transplant seedlings of biennials sown earlier.

Water vegetables regularly. Lift new potatoes, onions, and garlic and pinch out runner beans at the top of their canes.

Pinch out outdoor tomatoes when four trusses have formed, and remove all sideshoots.

Pick raspberries and currants and harvest herbs.

Damp down and ventilate greenhouses.

LAST CHANCE

Fill any gaps in beds and borders with bedding.

Sow the last vegetables for harvesting in autumn and plant out all winter brassicas.

GET AHEAD

Plan to have your plants cared for if you are away.

Order spring-flowering bulbs.

Prepare the ground for new lawns in autumn.

Sow salads under cover for autumn and winter, and prepare new strawberry beds.

Essence of summer It's not surprising that roses are such favourites; there is one to suit most gardens. A fine display of *Rosa* 'Perception' is shown here.

HIGH-SUMMER COLOUR

It's summer time; the garden is full of colour and the scent from flowers such as roses and sweet peas fills the air, especially towards the end of the day. Gardening in hot weather needs to be leisurely, though you'll need to devote energy to keeping everything well watered, either in the morning or evening.

July is the month for taking time to enjoy the garden, having relaxing meals *al fresco*, appreciating the flowers, and watching the abundance of wildlife in residence.

Beat the heat

There is still plenty of routine work to be done, but by this time the work can be done at a slower pace than in the hectic spring period. Care must be taken when working in the sun for long periods, even if you are taking it easy.

Lavender is at its very best This long-stemmed fragrant, blue-purple flower sets off any mixed or herbaceous border.

Take plenty of breaks, wear a broad-brimmed hat, and use sun cream to protect your skin from the harmful effects of sunlight. It's best to try not to work during the hottest part of the day. Wait until evening to do any strenuous work, if you won't be too busy with the barbecue. Hot days are often followed by thunderstorms and it's often a relief to do the gardening in the cool of the evening or in the early morning.

If the weather is very hot you will have to pay careful attention to watering your garden, especially trees and shrubs that were planted during the autumn and winter. The most beneficial times to do your watering are also early morning or in the evenings, when it is cooler. By watering at these times, the precious moisture will not evaporate from the surface of the soil nearly as rapidly as in the heat of the day. Do be aware, however, that in exceptionally dry periods there may be watering restrictions in your area and the use of hosepipes – even the seephose variety – may be banned. Check with your local authority if you are in doubt.

Use water wisely

During hot spells the lawn may begin to look rather brown and worn. At such times it is all too tempting to water the lawn, but it really is not necessary, as grass has a remarkable ability to regenerate itself when the weather gets cooler. Whenever rain does fall, the grass will, as if by magic, be transformed back into a lush green sward again. It's far better to use the water for plants that really need it: newly planted trees and shrubs, thirsty vegetables, and other precious plants in the borders and containers, especially hanging baskets, which need water daily in high summer.

Height of summer So many different crops should be ripening that you could well be harvesting something every day.

Perfect your plantings

During your morning or evening rambles around the garden, take a notebook with you and look at your planting schemes carefully to see which combinations of plants and colours have worked this year and which seem to be a bit of a disappointment. You can then make notes and use them to plan changes in the autumn or during the spring.

Weather watch

July and August are generally the hottest months of the year, with the highest temperatures occurring inland, away from the cooling influence of the sea.

Sea breezes

It's not really a month for gales or high winds, except in parts of the north-west and in coastal areas, where sea breezes can be very welcome on hot, sultry days. North-west areas average 0.2 days of gales this month, rising to 0.3 days in the north of Scotland, especially on the west coast and western islands.

Sun and clouds

The sunniest parts of the United Kingdom are along the south coast: owing to the formation of cumulus clouds over land, the skies over the sea usually remain cloud-free. Northern parts of the country are generally the cloudiest, due to the hillier nature of the terrain and on western coasts the close proximity of low-pressure weather systems over the Atlantic may also bring in plenty of cloud cover. However, some parts of the north-east and south-west areas of Scotland compare favourably with Ireland and north-west England for hours of direct sunshine. The far northern coasts of Britain usually receive around 133 hours of sun in July, while the south of England averages 213 hours this month.

Short rainy spells

July can be a dry month, but we don't escape rain altogether. The trouble is that the sudden but short spells of summer rain do little to add to soil reserves of moisture. So it makes sense to save water when we can, especially in areas more prone to drier weather.

Freak hail

There is no snow on the ground in July except in small isolated pockets on the highest peaks. But there are times when a freak shower of hail can make for a temporary wintry scene, even in July.

Blueberries Harvest your first blueberries now. Look for the plumpest, softest berries, with the darkest blue-black colour.

Vegetables on show Designing colour schemes with differently coloured vegetable, herb, and salad plants can be as satisfying as carpet bedding – and, of course, you can eat the results too.

Earlier-flowering plants will now have to be deadheaded if you don't want to save seed from them. Many perennials will, if deadheaded regularly, produce further blooms through summer and into the autumn. It's quite a pleasant and relaxing job to carry out on a warm summer's evening.

Native flowers and grasses attract a host of birds, bees, and other beneficial insects to the garden. An attractive way to incorporate these plants in your plot is to create a small wildflower garden or "flowery mead". Choose an open, sunny area, where the soil has not been enriched with fertilizers because wildflowers tend to perform best on poor soil.

Summer symptoms

In the warm, moist weather that can be characteristic of this month, pests and diseases may spread rapidly. Keep a careful watch for them as many can be controlled easily if they are caught early enough. Aphids, for instance, can be killed simply by squashing if they are not present in large numbers. If you have a heavy infestation of one particular pest and feel that you must use an insecticide, use one specific to that pest, where possible, so that it does not harm other, beneficial, insects. And spray in the evening, when the bees have gone for the night.

As for diseases, any parts of a plant that are showing signs of disease should be removed and either burned or put in the bin, so that they are not able to infect other plants. Never compost diseased material or leave it lying around, as this increases the risk of spreading the disease to other plants in the garden.

For plants that are grown under glass, scorch and heat stress are the most common problems, so you need to pay particular attention to watering and ventilation. Another way of cooling the atmosphere is to damp down several times during the day, splashing water onto the floor to increase the humidity.

Flavours to savour

You can continue to make regular sowings of salad crops that will see you well into the autumn. Weeds continue to seed themselves too, so you still need to carry out regular hoeing and weeding in the vegetable garden. Crops will also benefit from a mulch of organic matter to retain

the moisture in the soil. This is the month when your vegetable patch will be providing you with plenty of produce for the kitchen, not forgetting the lovely, summery flavours of freshly picked bunches of herbs.

Beat the heat Make the most of shady areas in the garden, which will become welcome refuges in the heat of summer. Areas shaded from full sun will not get so dry, suiting many plants better.

***Papaver rhoeas* Shirley Series**
Papery poppy that self-seeds freely in the garden (*see p.315*)

***Nemesia strumosa* 'KLM'**
Bedding plant with unusual bicoloured flowers (*see p.312*)

***Hebe* 'Gauntlettii'**
Neat, bushy evergreen shrub that needs little pruning (*see p.300*)

***Oenothera fruticosa* 'Fyrverkeri'** ♀
Perennial evening primrose (*see p.314*)

***Nymphaea* 'Marliacea Chromatella'** ♀
Waterlilies with olive-to-bronze leaves and canary flowers (*see p.313*)

***Diascia barberae* 'Blackthorn Apricot'** ♀
Slightly tender perennial that may need winter shelter (*see p.293*)

Verbascum 'Cotswold Queen'
Perennial bearing all flower spires (*see p.333*)

Campanula lactiflora
The milky bellflower; a tall perennial that may need support (*see p.281*)

Phlox paniculata 'Eva Cullum'
Hardy perennial that will flower into autumn (*see p.317*)

Hemerocallis 'Gentle Shepherd'
Perennial: flowers last only a day, but keep on coming (*see p.301*)

Gunnera manicata ♀
Perennial; by high summer the huge leaves are at their best (*see p.299*)

Helianthemum 'Raspberry Ripple'
Sun-loving shrub with greyish leaves (*see p.300*)

Rosa 'Chinatown' ♀
From summer to autumn, scented double, deep-yellow blooms (*see p.325*)

Centaurea hypoleuca 'John Coutts'
Pink cornflower; a nostalgic perennial (*see p.282*)

Solanum crispum 'Glasnevin' ♀
Sprawling shrub, best trained on a warm wall (*see p.330*)

Nicotiana sylvestris ♀
Very tall, elegant perennial tobacco plant, strongly fragrant (*see p.313*)

Clarkia amoena
The satin flower; a hardy annual that thrives in poorer soils (*see p.284*)

Lilium 'Sun Ray'
Summer bulb that makes an elegant container plant (*see p.307*)

Antirrhinum majus 'Trumpet Serenade'
Cheery, cottage-style perennial grown as an annual (*see p.277*)

Borago officinalis
Borage; an annual herb with flowers in steel blue (*see p.280*)

Ipomoea tricolor 'Heavenly Blue'
Aptly named cultivar of the morning glory (*see p.303*)

Nicotiana x sanderae Starship Series
Annual for evening fragrance (*see p.312*)

Artemisia alba 'Canescens' ♀
Foliage plant that makes a lovely foil for summer flowers (*see p.278*)

Fremontodendron 'California Glory' ♀
Lanky shrub to train on a sunny wall (*see p.297*)

Lychnis chalcedonica ♀
Perennial popular with beneficial insects (*see p.309*)

Cleome hassleriana 'Colour Fountain'
Imposing annual, to 1.5m (5ft) tall (*see p.287*)

Alcea rosea Chater's Double Group
Hollyhock with pompon flowers (*see p.275*)

Matthiola Brompton Group
Strongly scented annuals, ideal for cutting (*see p.310*)

Cosmos bipinnatus Sensation Series
Annual with flowers in pink and white (*see p.297*)

Eschscholzia californica ♀
California poppies; annuals that will reappear every year (*see p.295*)

Astrantia major
Cottage-garden style perennial; the flowers dry well (*see p.279*)

Nigella damascena 'Miss Jekyll' ♀
Love-in-a-mist; an old-fashioned hardy annual (*see p.313*)

Tagetes 'Naughty Marietta'
Small but striking plants for summer display (*see p.331*)

Verbena bonariensis ♀
Tall, airy perennial with stiff, slender stems (*see p.333*)

Lobelia Waterfall Series
Half-hardy annual; a container classic (*see p.308*)

Helianthus annuus 'Teddy Bear'
Double sunflower with fluffy blooms (*see p.300*)

WHAT TO DO IN JULY

AROUND THE GARDEN

With warm weather, pests and diseases can multiply rapidly. Greenfly and blackfly breed especially fast and it can be a job to keep on top of the problem. If you can build up diversity in the garden by growing a great variety of plants, you will attract a lot of beneficial insects and other wildlife and a healthy balance should develop between pests and predators. There may be a little bit of damage to some plants, but that is a small price to pay. There are many biological controls available now and these are widely available by mail order.

Irrigation hose Use one of these to make sure your plants have an even supply of water right through the summer. They can be automated, if necessary, which is a great help if you are going away for a couple of weeks.

Plan for holidays July and August are generally the holiday months and it is better to prepare the garden so that you don't come back to a jungle or a sea of dead plants. Ask a neighbour, family member, or a friend to attend to watering and feeding plants and mowing the lawn. Ask them to pick vegetables such as beans and courgettes. If beans and also cutting flowers are picked regularly, they will continue to produce crops and blooms well into autumn. Mow the lawn, but not too close or you'll encourage rapid growth. Most house plants can be moved outside and you can plunge the pots in the soil to lessen water loss. Automatic trickle irrigation systems are inexpensive and easy to install.

Save water It is inevitable that if we have a few weeks of dry weather, water may be in short supply, so it is wise to conserve as much water as we can.

■ Water can be collected from guttering along the roof of the house in a water butt. There are many types available, from plastic to genuine wooden casks; the latter are an attractive addition to the garden.

■ Mulch borders with any organic matter you can get your hands on, making sure the soil is moist before applying the mulch. Even old newspapers will reduce water loss from the surface of the soil.

■ Only water plants that really need it: newly planted trees, shrubs, and other plants. Newly sown or turfed lawns should be kept watered, established lawns will soon recover if they have gone brown.

■ Give plants a good soaking when you do water them. It is better to water a few at a time, giving them a thorough soak, than to give everything a little water each day.

■ The ideal, water-efficient way of watering plants in the border is to use the leaky pipe or seephose system. This lets the water seep out around the roots of the plant, just where it's wanted, so avoiding waste.

TREES AND SHRUBS

■ **Deadhead roses** to prolong the display. Many people, when deadheading roses, just snap the old flowerheads off. But if you want to continue the display into autumn you have to prune back to a bud in a leaf axil lower down the stem, to encourage strong new shoots. Prune to an outward-facing leaf to keep the centre of the rose bush open. Wild roses should not be deadheaded as they produce attractive hips in the autumn.

After deadheading, give the roses a feed to boost growth and encourage more flowers later in the summer. Use a fertilizer specific to roses, or one high in potash to encourage strong shoots. A fertilizer high in nitrogen will result in soft, sappy growth that is more prone to attack from pests and diseases.

■ **Diseases like black spot, rust, and mildew** are more of a problem in summer, the first two especially if the weather has been damp. Mildew tends to appear when the weather is drier. To minimize the spread of diseases, gather up and burn all infected leaves that have fallen to the ground. Never put them on the compost heap as this may spread the spores of the disease around the garden. If you spray for black spot, use a recommended fungicide, but do it early in the season before the disease has got a hold. Once black spot is

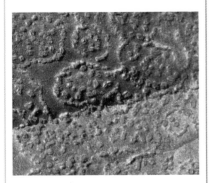

Rust infection A leaf covered in a rust-coloured fungal infection.

Deadheading roses Cut through the stem well below the faded flowers, just above a leaf.

established, spraying is useless. Rust disease, the symptoms of which appear as orange spores on the undersides of the leaves, is more prevalent on plants that are deficient in potash, so feeding with a rose fertilizer, which is high in potash, will help to reduce the problem.

Mildew will attack plants that are under stress due to lack of water. Control mildew by keeping plants well watered and spray with an approved fungicide if it seems to be persistent. Shrubs growing in containers should be watered regularly and fed once a week with a high-potash fertilizer. Watering may have to be done twice a day in very hot weather.

Pruning and training

■ **Cut lavender for drying** just the same as you would everlasting flowers.

■ **Prune early-summer-flowering shrubs** such as philadelphus and weigela if this was not done last month.

■ **Remove any unwanted growth** from the bases or trunks of trees and shrubs. Many trees and shrubs often produce a mass of shoots at the base of the plant. One of the most common groups of plants

with this habit is the *Sorbus* species, such as rowan and mountain ash. These shoots need to be cut away cleanly to prevent them sapping all the strength of the plant. At the same time, remove any shoots that have grown with plain green leaves on variegated plants.

Propagation

■ **Take semi-ripe cuttings** from shrubs. Semi-ripe cuttings are taken from growth made in the current year once the stems have started to become woody at the base. It's a remarkably easy and successful way to take cuttings, increasing your stock of plants quickly.

Remove shoots about 10cm (4in) long with a sliver or heel of older bark from the main stem, or just trim them below a leaf joint. Trim the tail of the heel off, if there is one. Remove the lower leaves. Pinch out the tip of the cutting if growth is very soft. Dip the whole of the cutting in a fungicide solution wearing protective gloves. Then dip the base of the cutting in hormone rooting solution. Put the cuttings around the edge of a pot containing peat-free compost mixed with an equal amount of vermiculite. Put a polythene bag over the pot to create a humid atmosphere and put the pot in a shady part of the garden – in a cold frame or below a sheltered wall. The cuttings will root in about six to eight weeks, when they can be potted up and grown on.

■ **Take cuttings from hydrangeas.** These showy garden shrubs, a delight in late summer, can be propagated easily. Remove non-flowering shoots 8–10cm (3–4in) long, cutting just above a bud. Remove the lower leaves and trim the base of the cutting with a sharp knife. There is no need to trim the cutting immediately below a leaf joint, as the cuttings will root perfectly well if cut between buds.

Hydrangeas have quite large leaves, so to reduce water loss from them, cut the leaves across in half. Put into a pot of cuttings compost, cover with a polythene bag and stand in a shady corner. The cuttings will root in about four weeks, when they can be potted up.

■ **Take conifer cuttings.** After trimming your conifer hedge, make cuttings if you want to increase the number of plants to make another hedge. Pick out healthy shoots with sideshoots 5–8cm (2–3in) long and becoming woody at their base. Tear the sideshoots off with a heel of older wood and treat them in exactly the same way as for semi-ripe shrub cuttings.

■ **Pot up or plant out softwood cuttings** taken earlier that have now rooted, watering them well before and after. If you have space, line them out in a corner of the vegetable garden, where they can grow on during the summer, forming excellent plants by autumn. Otherwise pot them into individual pots, but don't let them dry out.

Hedges

■ **Trim conifer hedges** to keep them under control. Conifer hedges have received quite bad press in recent years, due mainly to the notoriety of x *Cuprocyparis leylandii*. This is an excellent hedging plant, but it can grow very tall very quickly. It is too vigorous for small gardens as it grows fast, putting on 60–90cm (2–3ft) in a year. As with all conifer hedges, it needs trimming at least once a year, preferably twice, to keep it in order, but don't cut into old wood as it will not regrow and the plants will need replacing. If you start trimming when the conifers are small, long before they reach the height and width you eventually require, you will build up a good, thick layer of leafy growth over the entire surface of the hedge.

CLIMBERS

■ **It is very easy to propagate** from clematis cuttings at this time of year. Try this easy method by taking "internodal" cuttings. Take a strong main stem and cut it into sections, midway between leaf joints, or nodes. Trim the stem below the node so that 2–5cm (1–2in) remains and trim the stem above the node to 1cm (½in) long. Dip the base in hormone rooting solution and put in pots containing cuttings compost. Cover cuttings with thin polythene held off the foliage and tucked under the pot. Put in a shady frame and they will root in six to eight weeks. Pot them up and grow on.

■ **Try air-layering climbing plants** like clematis and akebia. Select a main shoot and make a cut at a sharp angle into the stem, without cutting it completely. Wrap sphagnum moss around the cut and hold it in place with clear polythene, tied top and bottom. When a good root system has formed in a few weeks, remove the young plant from the parent and pot up.

■ **Prune wisteria by cutting back** the whippy growths made during the summer so that they are within five or six buds of the main stems.

Wisteria pruning This encourages the formation of flower buds for next year.

PERENNIALS

■ **Divide bearded and other rhizomatous irises** after the flowers are over. After several years these irises tend to lose vigour and need to be divided up. It's also a good opportunity to clear weeds from within iris clumps, as these are otherwise difficult to get out – a spot weedkiller is usually the only answer.

Once the flowers are over, lift the clump carefully with a fork and then separate out the younger pieces from around the outside of the clump. Cut off the younger pieces with a sharp knife. The older pieces can be thrown away. Cut off faded leaves and cut across the remaining foliage about 15cm (6in) from the root, leaving a fan shape of trimmed leaves. This helps reduce water loss from the leaves and stops the wind catching the tall foliage like a sail and blowing the plant over.

Replant in groups of three, five, or more and water them in thoroughly. Irises must not be planted too deeply; on an exposed site, it may help to pin down the rhizomes with hoops of galvanized wire, removing these when the plants have developed their own anchoring roots.

■ **Disbud dahlias** if you want larger blooms and support the flowering stems with canes or stakes. If you've recently joined a local gardening society then dahlias are definitely one of the best plants with which to enter the cut-throat world of showing. Any club organizing a show will issue its own strict rules on how flowers are presented and for dahlias this nearly always means growing single, large blooms on long, sturdy stems. Rules for flower arrangements may not be so precise, but some stunning dahlias always make a good centrepiece for a display.

All disbudding means is removing some of the sidebuds at the apex of the stems, leaving the larger bud in the middle to flower. Remove sideshoots lower down the

Dividing irises

1 Lift the clump of old, knobbly rhizomes and cut off small, healthy, young pieces that each have a clump of leaves attached.

2 Pull off dead foliage, then with a sharp knife cut across the fan of leaves. Replant the small divisions in a sunny spot, 8–15cm (4–6in) apart, the rhizome just below the surface.

stem, too, to get those long stems. Dahlias are normally supported with stakes, as there is a fair weight of top growth on the plants. Use one stake at planting time, and later put three or four canes around the plants as well and tie twine around all the supports. In this way the whole plant will be supported.

■ **While borders are in full bloom** it is a good idea to have a wander around the garden and look carefully at the display and decide which plants look out of place – perhaps colours clash – and which just haven't performed very well. Look out, too, for those overgrown plants that may need dividing during the autumn and winter. Dividing them may rejuvenate them, giving them a new lease of life. Take a notepad or gardening diary with you and note down all the things that need to be done, because by the autumn, if you have a memory like mine, you'll have forgotten everything.

■ **Continue to cut back faded flowers** on perennials if seed is not required. This will encourage new growth and more flowers

later in the summer. Plants like Oriental poppies and hardy geraniums can be cut back to ground level with a pair of shears, and taller perennials such as delphiniums should have their faded flower spikes cut back, to encourage new shoots that, hopefully, will produce more flowers later in the summer. Aquilegias can have the old flowering stems removed if seed is not required from the plants. All the old growth can be discarded on the compost heap. Give the plants a feed and a good watering if the weather is dry.

■ **Harvest seed from perennials.** Many perennials will be finishing flowering now and if they haven't been cut off, seed pods will be developing. A lot of seedheads will become ripe towards the end of the month and must be gathered before they open up and scatter the seeds. You will have to be vigilant if you want to catch them.

Seeds are best collected on a dry, sunny day when there will be less chance of rot getting in to them. When collecting the seeds, put the heads or pods into paper bags with the name of the plant written on

them. If the seeds are ripe and are beginning to come out of the seedhead, close the top of the bag and shake it to get all of the seeds out. If you cut off one corner of the bag, you should be able to trickle the seeds onto a sheet of paper, keeping most of the debris in the bag. If the heads aren't quite open, lay them out on a sheet of paper in a dry place until they begin to shed the seeds.

Carefully separate the seeds from any dirt and chaff using an old kitchen sieve, or by very gently blowing over them. The heavier seeds should stay in place while the chaff is blown away, but do it carefully.

Put the seeds into paper envelopes, seal, and label them. Store them somewhere cool and dry – the ideal place being in an air-tight container on the bottom shelf of the refrigerator.

■ **Herbaceous perennials in general,** and late-flowering ones like Michaelmas daisies (asters) and chrysanthemums, in particular, will benefit from a sprinkling of a general organic fertilizer now to give a boost to their growth for the rest of the summer. Hoe or lightly rake it in and if the weather is dry, water it in as well.

■ **Layer pinks and carnations.** Border pinks and carnations are delightful cottage-garden plants to have in the borders. After three or four years they can become a bit straggly, but they are easy to propagate. You can layer them by pegging stems into the ground, so that roots form on the stems and become new young plantlets. This can be a bit fiddly and sometimes not as successful as taking cuttings or "pipings", as they are called. However, the advantage of layering is that you need less space to grow on cuttings and young plants in pots, as the layers can be transplanted directly into their new site as soon as they have formed good roots, or even left in place until next spring, if you prefer. Some gardeners layer a few stems each summer, just to see what happens. You should get at least a new plant or two.

Alpines

■ **Save seeds from alpines** in exactly the same way as described for herbaceous perennials, though alpines require cold weather to break the seeds' dormancy, so they have to be left outside or in an unheated cold frame for the winter.

However, seeds of some alpines only remain viable for a relatively short time and these have to be sown now, straight after harvesting has taken place. These include primulas, cyclamen, androsaces, dionysias, and meconopsis.

If you are not sure of the correct time for sowing a particular variety of seed, sow some as soon as the seed is ripe, or in the autumn and then sow some in late winter or spring. This way you cover each period. Note down which seeds germinate best at which time for future seed sowing.

■ **Spot-treat any perennial weeds** that appear among alpines. If weeds grow between, or even through, alpines they can be difficult to uproot without disturbing the plants and impossible to spray with weedkiller, but all is not lost if this happens.

There are some weedkillers that come ready-prepared in the form of a gel, with a small brush built into the lid of the container. It is an easy matter to brush the weedkiller onto the foliage of the weed, using a piece of cardboard as a shield to protect the alpine plant and kill the weeds.

■ **Some alpines with a carpeting habit** can die off in the centre and look horrible. This problem can be remedied by infilling the centre of the plant with gritty alpine compost. This will encourage the plant to regrow, filling in the bare patch.

Layering pinks

1 Find a shoot that can be bent to touch the ground and remove all but the top few leaves.

2 Wound the stems to stimulate root formation by nicking the shoot with a very sharp knife at a leaf joint.

3 Use hoops or staples of galvanized wire to peg the shoot securely into the ground, at the point where you have made the wound.

BULBS

■ **Bulbs that were heeled** in in trenches for the foliage to die back can be dug up and stored until they are required for planting. Make sure they are dry and free from diseased material, so that they do not rot in store. Remove all dead foliage and flowering stems. Inspect the bulbs for disease or rotting, removing any that are affected. Lay the bulbs out in a single layer to dry off for a few days and then store in boxes or trays in a cool, dry, airy place.

■ **Plant autumn-flowering** bulbs now. These bulbs will flower through September, October and, if the weather is reasonable, into November. The flowers appear without foliage because the leaves have died down during the summer. The leaves will appear in the spring. Bulbs to choose are autumn-flowering crocus: *Crocus speciosus* with blue-purple and white flowers, *C. kotschyanus* with lilac-pink flowers, and *C. sativus*, with dark-veined lilac flowers. Plant them in full sun to a depth of 10cm (4in).

Nerines are wonderful plants from the warmer climes of South Africa. Like colchicums, the flowers appear before the leaves, with tall stems bearing up to nine blooms with pink, curling petals. They will need a warm, sunny, sheltered spot, preferably at the base of a south-facing wall or fence, and well-drained soil. *Nerine bowdenii* is the most widely known and the easiest to grow, but even this will need some protection in colder areas. In northern parts and very exposed, chilly gardens it may be best to grow nerines under cover. Plant the bulb to at least twice its own depth.

■ **Lilies should be looking gorgeous** now, but it's easy to brush against the flowers inadvertently. Pollen on the large stamens can cause stains, so cut the stamens off to prevent this, as florists often do.

ANNUALS AND BEDDING

■ **Maintain annuals and tender perennials** to keep the display going well into the autumn. Deadhead old flowers regularly to prevent the plants from setting seed unless, of course, you want to collect seeds from some plants. Do bear in mind, though, that hybrid plants such as "F1 hybrids" will not come true to type from seed. Plants such as pansies and petunias tend to get straggly now and picking off individual spent flowers from these plants can be tedious. An easy way to deadhead them is to cut them back with secateurs or shears. Cut them back quite hard, give a quick tonic with a high-potash fertilizer and new growth will soon be produced with flowers later in the summer.

■ **Finish planting out summer bedding** plants in baskets, containers, and borders. The sooner this job is done the better, as the plants will have time to settle in and flower for the rest of the summer.

■ **Continue to water plants** if the weather is dry. Give a good soaking once a week rather than a little each day. Regular feeding with a high-potash fertilizer will also help to prolong the flowering period. Hoe between plants, if they've not grown into each other, to keep down weeds.

July bedding planting Change tired plants and fill in any gaps in the border.

Cut flowers to dry

1 Cut everlasting flowers such as statice (*Limonium*) just as the flowers start to open. Cut low down to get the full length of stem.

2 Tie the flowers in small bunches and hang them upside down in an airy place, out of full sun, which will bleach the colour.

■ **Transplant biennial seedlings** that were sown in May and June. Seedlings of wallflowers, forget-me-nots (*Myosotis*), bellis, Canterbury bells (*Campanula medium*), and ornamental kales and cabbages can be transplanted to nursery rows to grow into larger plants before planting in their flowering positions in the autumn, when the summer bedding has finished. Water the seedlings an hour or so beforehand and lift them carefully. Replant about 15cm (6in) apart in rows in a corner. Water the seedlings well after transplanting to settle them in. Wallflowers tend to have one main, or tap, root with only a few fibrous roots, so to encourage more fibrous roots to grow, cut back the thicker tap root when transplanting them. Water the young plants regularly, keep them weeded throughout the summer by regularly hoeing between the plants and they should make fine plants to put in their flowering positions in autumn.

■ **Cut and dry everlasting flowers.** Flowers of plants like statice, *Xerochrysum*, and rhodanthe can be cut for drying and used for decorative displays in the home during the winter. They have to be picked just before they reach their peak, which is when they are almost fully open. They will open slightly more as they dry out. Tie them in bunches and hang them up in an airy place to dry out. Don't try to speed up the drying process by putting the flowers in a warm place, as they will shrivel up.

■ **Disbud tuberous begonias** growing in pots or as bedding. These large-flowered begonias produce three flower buds at the top of the stems. The central bud is the male flower and this should be kept for its frilly petals. The smaller buds either side are the less showy, single female flowers and these need to be removed to get a reasonable-sized double flower.

CONTAINERS

■ **Continue maintaining containers** to extend the colourful display well into autumn. Water and feed the containers regularly and perhaps even do it twice a day during very hot spells of weather. Containers will still need plenty of water even when it rains. The mass of roots inside the container and the foliage on top make rain penetration almost impossible and so watering with a watering can or hose is the only answer. Deadhead the plants regularly to keep the plants looking good and prevent them from setting seeds.

Plants crammed together in containers can sometimes begin to look a bit straggly towards late summer and it is a good idea to go over your containers occasionally, pruning off any straggly shoots and any that are crowding out other plants too much. You can always make some cuttings from the material you cut off.

Summer attention Water and feed your container plants regularly through the summer.

LAWNS

■ **Continue to mow** and trim edges once or twice a week to keep the lawn in good condition. During very dry weather, raise the blades of the mower and mow less often. The grass is best left a little longer during dry periods so that the plants retain more leaf area and can therefore cope better. The grass will also not be growing as vigorously, so the frequency of mowing can be reduced. Clippings left on the lawn act as a mulch, helping to retain moisture in the soil. When the grass gets going again in more moist conditions the blades can be gradually lowered to normal height.

■ **Don't water** unless absolutely necessary. If you have to water the lawn do it once a week, soaking it thoroughly. Established lawns will turn brown in hot weather, but it's not worth wasting water on them, as the grass will soon recover.

■ **Give the lawn a boost** with a liquid fertilizer unless you did so in June. Most lawns will benefit from a quick boost. There are many types of liquid fertilizer on the market.

New lawns

■ **Water new lawns** made in spring, either from seed or turf. It is vitally important not to let newly laid turf dry out: it shrinks when it dries and it's almost impossible to undo the damage when this happens.

■ **Get ahead.** If you are planning to make a new lawn, begin initial preparation now for sowing seed or laying turf in the autumn. The more time you give the soil to settle, the easier it is to achieve a level surface. Dig over the whole site and remove all perennial weeds, levelling it roughly. If the ground is weed-free, use a rotavator over large areas. The final levelling-off and raking down can be done nearer the time of sowing or laying the turf.

VEGETABLE AND HERBS

■ **Water all vegetables regularly.** If this is not done they will bolt and start producing seeds, making them inedible. The easiest way to water is by using leaky pipe or seephose laid along the rows or buried. This directs the water where it's most needed, preventing splashing, especially from large-leaved plants. The most efficient time to water is at night. Keep down weeds by continuing to hoe between the rows. Hoe on a dry day and the weed seedlings will shrivel up in the warm sun. Mulching the soil with a layer of dry grass mowings will also suppress weeds.

Harvesting

■ **Keep harvesting vegetables** as soon as they are ready. Most taste much better when they are young. Also, if you keep harvesting vegetables when they are young you are more likely to enjoy them fresh over a longer period.

■ **Early potatoes should be ready** to harvest. To see if they are, lift one plant and see how big the crop is. If there aren't many potatoes there that are more than marble-sized, leave the rest of the plants to develop further. To encourage the tubers to swell, water the plants once a week, giving them a good soaking.

■ **Begin harvesting shallots.** Shallots need dry, sunny weather to ripen properly. Lift the bulbs carefully, levering them out of the ground with a fork when the leaves turn yellow. In sunny weather they can be left on the surface of the soil to dry out. Or, to allow plenty of air to circulate around the bulbs, erect a temporary support by banging four low stakes into the ground and stretching a piece of chicken wire between the posts to create a sort of "hammock". Put the shallots on this and they will dry out quickly. If rain is forecast cover them with a piece of polythene. If the weather is very wet, put the shallots under cover, in a cold frame with the lid on, or lay them out in a greenhouse or shed with good light.

■ **Harvest onions when the leaves** begin to turn yellow and flop. Ease the bulbs out of the soil and leave them on the surface for a few days if the weather is warm and dry. As with shallots you can make a chicken wire support for them, allowing air to circulate freely. Once dry, onions can be stored in several ways. Tie them up to make an onion string, or put them into an old pair of tights and hang them up – or just lay them in a single layer in boxes.

■ **Harvest globe artichokes** before the scales begin to open. This is a striking architectural plant that can be grown in ornamental borders as well as in the vegetable garden. The bold foliage makes a perfect contrast to other finer-leaved plants in the garden. If the flower heads are left on, they open up to reveal the most beautiful thistle-like flowers.

Fat, round artichoke globes Pick these promptly or the scales will open.

Lift garlic Spread the bulbs in the sun to dry before storing.

■ **Harvest garlic planted last year** in exactly the same way as for shallots. If the bulbs have been healthy and shown no sign of virus, then some of the cloves can be kept for replanting.

Sowing and planting outdoors

■ **It's not too late** to be sowing vegetables for autumn harvesting. Whenever some ground becomes vacant, revitalize the soil with organic matter and sow vegetables such as lettuces, which will grow quickly as long as they don't dry out. An early variety, like 'Tom Thumb', is small and will mature quickly. Beetroot is another crop that can be sown now. 'Boltardy' is a good old reliable variety to try. Beetroot will be good for storing over winter. Carrots can still be sown, too, providing succulent young roots for immediate use and for storing. Turnips are very quick to mature and the leaves can also be used as greens.

■ **Sow autumn and winter salads.** Corn salad and rocket can be sown now. Both are happy in most situations. Claytonia (winter purslane) prefers lighter, sandy soils. Sow the seeds thinly in drills 23cm (9in) apart. These crops don't need to be thinned out; they can just be cut as required and will grow away again.

Oriental vegetables make an interesting addition to autumn salads and these can be sown now too. They are all very attractive to look at and can therefore be grown in with ornamental plants in borders as well as in the vegetable garden. Ones to look for are Chinese radish, mizuna greens, pak-choi, and spinach mustard. Sow in rows 30cm (1ft) apart and thin to 15–30cm (6–12in) between the plants.

■ **Continue sowing peas** until the end of the month. Use an early variety such as 'Douce Provence', which will mature quickly. Take out a trench about 5cm (2in) deep with a spade or a draw hoe and space-sow the seeds about 2.5cm (1in) apart. Water the drill if the soil is dry. Cover the seeds and tap down the soil firmly with the back of a rake. Then cover the row with fine netting or horticultural fleece. Support the plants with twiggy sticks as they grow.

■ **Finish planting out winter brassicas** sown in April and May. To make watering the plants in easier, now that it is so dry, take out a deep drill with a draw hoe and put the plants in with a dibber or a trowel, planting in the drill. A watering can or hose can then be run along the rows, with the drill keeping the water where it is needed. Remember to put collars at the base of the stems to prevent the cabbage root fly from laying its eggs there. And grow them under fleece to protect them from the cabbage white butterfly, which lays its small, yellow eggs on the leaf undersides.

■ **Sow spring cabbages** at intervals of a week to ten days. This vegetable is particularly welcome when there is little else to be harvested from the vegetable garden. Sow the seeds thinly in drills 15cm (6in) apart, watering the drills before sowing if the soil is dry. Follow the directions on the seed packet. Cover them with fleece to stop pigeons eating the seedlings and flea beetles making small holes in the leaves. When the young plants have made two or three true leaves, transplant to their cropping places.

Looking after crops

■ **Stop outdoor cordon tomatoes** when they have made four trusses of fruit. Outdoor tomatoes grown in temperate climates will not carry or ripen any more fruit than this because of relatively short summers. Pinch out the growing tip one leaf beyond the topmost flower truss. This allows plant foods to travel to the top truss, setting and ripening the fruit. Feed the plants with a high-potash fertilizer for a good crop and remove sideshoots from the leaf axils on cordon-grown varieties. Bush and trailing varieties can be left to their own devices; they fruit on sideshoots and there is no top truss of flowers.

■ **Endives can be blanched** to turn the foliage white and make it more palatable. Cover each plant with a plate, making sure you cover up any drainage holes in the bottom of pots so the plants are in total darkness. They should be ready to harvest after about ten days of blanching.

■ **Watch out for the tomato problems** blossom end rot and ghost spot. The symptoms of blossom end rot appear as a sunken brown patch on the fruit at the farthest end from the flower stalk. It is caused by a lack of calcium, brought on by a lack of water. It only needs the plant to be short of water for a brief time for this to happen. The way to prevent blossom end rot is to water the plants regularly and evenly, never allowing them to dry out.

Watering regularly will also prevent splitting, which happens after a dry spell if the plants are suddenly given a lot of water, the upsurge in water causing the skins of the fruits to split.

Ghost spot appears as small spots on the fruits, surrounded by a lighter ring. This fungal disease can usually be avoided by taking care not to splash the fruits with water when damping down or watering.

■ **Begin to earth up celery** growing in trenches. By now the stems should be about 30cm (1ft) high and ready for blanching. This makes the stems more succulent. To prevent soil getting into the centre of the plant and causing rot, make a newspaper collar, leaving the tuft of foliage exposed. The soil can be filled in from either side of

the trench. Self-blanching celery does not need earthing up and can be left to grow in its blocks.

■ **Look out for potato and tomato blight.** Blight on these crops is caused by a fungus-like pathogen whose spores are wind-blown and infect when conditions are wet. It causes rapid browning and collapse of leaves, brown blotches on fruit, and discoloration and rotting of tubers. Prompt removal and destruction of infected foliage may prevent spread to tubers. Regular sprays with a proprietary fungicide will provide protection. The new potato variety 'Mira' and others from the 'Sarpo' range show promising resistance.

■ **Water runner beans regularly** at the roots to help the flowers set and form pods. Many gardeners also recommend spraying the flowers with water daily. Adding a small handful of hydrated lime to a full two-gallon watering can and applying along the row at the bases will also help the flowers to set and produce more pods.

■ **Stop climbing beans** when they reach the tops of their supports – pinch out the tip of the leading shoot. This will encourage the plants to make more sideshoots lower down and therefore more beans will be produced. Be sure to pick regularly. If the pods are left on the plants too long they become tough and stringy. The more you pick them, the more you will get through the summer because plants will continue cropping for longer.

■ **Protect summer cauliflowers** by bending or snapping leaves over the flower heads. Keeping them in the dark by breaking leaves over them will keep the curds white and lengthen the time before they begin to open up.

Blanching endive

1 Put an upturned plate over the heart of the plant to exclude the light.

2 In a week or two, the inner leaves become pale and sweet to eat.

Herbs

■ **Pick herbs regularly** to maintain a supply of fresh, young shoots. It's almost like pruning the plant: the more you pick, the more young shoots, with the best flavour for cooking, will be produced. If herbs are not picked regularly they tend to become spindly. But if they have been neglected they can be brought back to bushiness again. Most herbs benefit from being trimmed to encourage new growth.

■ **Pick and dry herbs.** Sage, rosemary, and thyme can be cut now and hung up to dry. Do this in an airy place outdoors, where the herbs will be protected from the rain. Another easy way to store herbs is to freeze them.

■ **Take cuttings from herbs** such as lemon verbena, sage, and thyme – all the herbs that tend to become woody near the ground. To increase success, dip the bases of the cuttings in hormone rooting solution. The cuttings should root in four to six weeks, when they can be potted up individually. They can sit outside in a shady corner over the summer, provided that you remember to water regularly, and planted in autumn or overwintered in a cold frame.

Pinching out basil Nip out the tips of the shoots to make the plant bush out lower down.

FRUIT
Picking and storing

■ **Summer-fruiting raspberries** should ripen this month. If you have a surplus, they freeze very well, either singly or cooked gently to reduce to a purée.

■ **Blackcurrant bushes** can be partially pruned, if you like, as the crop is harvested, so you can take some whole branches into the kitchen and pick the fruits off with ease. Remove about one-third of the bush each year, taking from low down to encourage strong new shoots from the base of the plants. Pruning blackcurrants is a compromise between cutting out old wood and leaving enough new wood for fruiting the following year. It is inevitable that some new growth will be pruned out.

■ **Red- and whitecurrants are harvested** by pulling or snipping entire, long fruit clusters from the plant. Don't strip the berries off individually until you have got them indoors.

Pruning and training

■ **Summer-prune red- and whitecurrants** and gooseberries late in the month. Trim back all sideshoots made this year to three or four buds from their point of growth. Any crossing shoots and those growing into the middle of the bush can be removed at the same time. This allows air to circulate more freely around the bushes, lets more light in to ripen the fruits, and reduces disease; it also encourages the formation of fruit buds for fruiting again next year.

■ **Prune summer-fruiting raspberries** after all of the fruit has been picked. The old fruited canes are easily identifiable as they should have been tied to the supporting wires. If not, the wood of these canes is more brown in colour, there will be the remains of fruit clusters and the leaves

Summer-fruiting raspberries Prune out the fruited canes by cutting them at ground level.

tend to look a bit tatty by this time of year. By contrast, the younger canes that have been produced during the summer will have fresh, green foliage and the stems will still be green. First untie the old canes from the supporting wires and cut them out to ground level. The new canes can now be tied in, spacing them about 10cm (4in) apart. Only tie in good, strong canes; any weak ones should be pruned out completely. Any canes growing far out from the rows should be dug up or they will continue to creep outwards.

■ **Continue training new canes** of blackberries and other hybrid berries. Most of the hybrid berries have vicious thorns and if you don't tie them in regularly they will become quite a problem, getting tangled up in other plants. There are some thornless hybrid berries as well as the blackberry variety 'Oregon Thornless', which are better for family gardens – although it can mean that little fingers get to your crop before you do. As with raspberries, tie the new canes to the supports with twine, on the opposite side to the fruiting canes already there. There are many complicated ways of training hybrid berries, but this is the easiest way: fruiting canes to one side of the support, and new canes to the other, to form a fan.

■ **Continue training fan-trained fruits** like cherries, apples, and pears. Remove unwanted shoots that spoil the fan shape. Shorten back any side growths to about 7cm (3in) long, cutting just above a bud. If the "spokes" of the fan have reached the required size prune these back to two or three buds of the current year's growth. If required to extend the "spokes" leave until winter and prune by one-third to one-half.

■ **At the end of the month** begin summer-pruning trained apples and pears.

Looking after crops

■ **Ripening fruit of peaches and nectarines** will need protecting from birds and wasps. Trees trained against walls or fences are relatively easy to protect; you can easily drape horticultural fleece or fine mesh netting over them. Make sure that it is secured to the wall and that there are no gaps where birds can get in. Free-standing trees are more difficult to protect, but fleece draped over will give some protection, particularly if it can be secured at ground level.

■ **Thin out fruit on apples and pears.** Once the "June drop" is over (fruit trees naturally shed some fruit in June), it is safe to thin out any other fruits not required. Remove any very small, damaged, or diseased fruits in each cluster. To get apples and pears to grow to a reasonable size, thin the remaining fruits so that you leave one fruit every 10cm (4in) apart. It may seem disappointing to remove a lot of fruit from the tree at this stage, but the resulting crops in the autumn will be of far superior quality than if a lot of fruits are left on the tree.

■ **Support heavily laden fruit tree branches.** The weight of fruit on trees can be considerable at this time and it makes

sense to support the branches of some trees. Plum branches, in particular, will break very easily. A stake with a V-shaped notch in the end can be put under any vulnerable-looking branch to prop it up. Smaller shoots on some trees can be tied up to a cane lashed to the tree's stake, or just to a more mature branch, to support the weight of the crop.

■ **Inspect apples for woolly aphids** and spray with a suitable insecticide. Woolly aphids appear as white fluff on the shoots and branches and their feeding causes lumpy growths to appear on the younger shoots. Aphids of all kinds can also spread virus diseases and so it is important to control them. Be sure to spray only in the late evening, when there are fewer pollinating and other beneficial insects around. Light infestations can be controlled by squashing the aphids by hand. Some of the organic insecticides will harm not only pests, but also beneficial wildlife too.

■ **Remove old foliage from strawberries** once fruiting has finished. Old leaves become diseased and are of little use to

the plants. Remove them by going over the plants with a pair of shears. Any straw that was put around the plants to keep the fruits from being spoiled should be removed too. Lightly fork over the soil between the plants and take out any weeds. The plants will soon produce new foliage over the next few weeks. The old leaves and straw can be consigned to the compost heap or burned if diseased.

Planning ahead

■ **Prepare the ground** for new strawberry plants. After three years, the yield from strawberry plants tends to decline and the plants sometimes get virus disease. So it is better to replace plants after three cropping seasons. If the old plants have shown signs of virus, buy new ones from reputable nurseries, where you will be able to get healthy new stock certified virus-free. Choose a fresh patch for the new strawberries. Prepare the ground well, incorporating organic matter to improve soil structure and retain soil moisture.

Strawberries after cropping

1 After the last fruits have been picked, trim all the leaves off the plants with shears and put them on the compost heap.

2 Remove straw mulches or strawberry mats, clear all debris from the crowns of the plants, and weed and gently fork over the soil.

UNDER COVER

■ **Keep the greenhouse** and conservatory well ventilated in hot weather. Ventilators can be left open almost all of the time now, to help avoid temperature fluctuations. Damping down paths regularly with water will also help to reduce the temperature.

At the end of the month there may be the occasional colder night, when it is a good idea to make sure that the doors and ventilators are closed.

Glasshouse and house plants

■ **Start taking fuchsia cuttings.** Root them in exactly the same way as you would do for pelargonium cuttings. When the cuttings have rooted, pot them on.

■ **Train standard fuchsias from cuttings.** Growing standards is a very attractive way of growing these delightful plants. If you keep your greenhouse or conservatory heated over winter, then the young plants will continue to grow year-round, although growth will inevitably slow during winter.

Cuttings that have naturally developed with a single, definite, sturdy main stem are the best material to start with. As the cuttings grow, tie them to a cane regularly to keep the stem straight. Remove any sideshoots as they develop from the leaf axils. Pot the young plant on into progressively larger pots and keep it growing slowly over the winter in cool but frost-free conditions. You need only water very sparingly.

In spring, growth will pick up again. Once the plant has reached the height you want, pinch out the growing tip. The sideshoots that develop can be pinched out themselves when they have made three or four pairs of leaves. Do this another couple of times and you will have developed a good bushy head to the plant which will, in summer, be covered in flowers. Leaves on the clear stem should drop naturally, but remove any shoots.

■ **Take cuttings from regal pelargoniums.** These showy plants can be propagated by cuttings from now through the rest of the summer. Select non-flowering shoots about 10cm (4in) long and cut them from the plant. Remove the lower leaves, leaving two or three leaves at the tip of the cutting. In addition, remove the little scale-like structures at the base of the leaf stalks (stipules), as these may rot. They are particularly prominent on pelargoniums.

Trim the cuttings just below a leaf joint, so that each is about 8cm (3in) long. Dip the ends in hormone rooting solution and put into pots containing cutting compost. There is no need to cover them. Stand the pots on a well-lit bench or windowsill, but out of direct sunlight. The cuttings will take four weeks to root, when they can be potted up to grow on.

■ **Prick out seedlings of plants** sown earlier for winter-flowering pot plants, such as cinerarias and calceolarias. Prick out the seedlings when they are large enough to handle. This can be a tricky job with calceolarias, as the seedlings are small, yet cannot be left in the seed tray too long. Either prick out into trays spacing the seedlings about 5cm (2in) apart or pot them up individually into small pots. More seed can be sown now to produce a succession of flowers throughout the winter and into spring on plants that are kept in the warmth. Sow in trays or pots of seed compost and water the container before sowing.

Seeds of cinerarias and calceolarias are very small and can be sown on the surface of the compost and left uncovered. You may find it easier to sow them by first mixing a little silver sand with the seeds. This makes it a little easier to see where you have sown the seeds and helps distribute them evenly.

Sweet peppers Support them with canes and twine. Leave a short stalk when harvesting.

Crops under glass

■ **Continue to maintain indoor fruits and vegetables.** Tomatoes need to have any sideshoots that grow from the leaf axils removed. Remove them before they get too large, to minimize the shock to the plant. Keep feeding all crops under cover with a high-potash feed, applied weekly, and water regularly – every evening if possible. Aubergine and pepper plants may benefit from some support now that the fruits are forming. Like tomatoes, their stems are thick but fleshy and can snap easily.

■ **Start removing foliage from tomatoes** around the end of the month. This will allow more light to get to the ripening tomatoes and will also allow better circulation of air, reducing the incidence of diseases like leaf mould and botrytis. Start removing the older leaves at the bottom of the plants, some of which may be going yellow, especially around the first truss of tomatoes, which will be starting to ripen. Don't remove too many all at once.

■ **Watch out for tomato disorders** such as blossom end rot and ghost spot.

THE AUGUST GARDEN

August is traditionally the month for a well-earned break, but whether you're going away or just planning to put your feet up at home, make sure that the garden can cope with the summer heat. Continue with all the usual deadheading and pruning activities, make preparations for autumn-flowering bulbs and don't forget to keep your vegetables well watered this month.

THINGS TO DO

Feed and water all plants that need it regularly.

Make sure that the birds have enough water.

Trim hedges regularly.

Prune rambling roses after flowering.

Deadhead flowers as they fade and trim lavender plants after flowering.

Take cuttings from tender perennials such as pelargoniums and fuchsias.

Collect ripening seed from plants you wish to keep.

Layer pinks, rhododendrons, and clematis.

Water your vegetables and fruit regularly.

Lift and dry onions and cut and dry herbs to store.

Feed and water tomato plants regularly.

Prop up heavily laden fruit tree branches, and summer prune gooseberry and redcurrant plants.

Plant new strawberry plants and harvest the first apples and pears.

LAST CHANCE

Finish summer pruning apples and pears and other trained fruit trees.

Complete the summer pruning of wisteria.

Plant colchicums for winter flowering.

GET AHEAD

Start planting spring bulbs, especially daffodils.

Force hyacinths for Christmas.

Divide perennials towards the end of the month and prepare ground for making new lawns.

Sow parsley and pot up herbs for later use.

The month of plenty Vegetables such as tomatoes, climbing beans, and peas will all be ready for harvesting.

SAVOURING THE SUMMER

You will certainly get some hot, sultry days this month, so be prepared to water your garden regularly and make preparations if you are going away. When you are at home, take the time to enjoy your garden, but don't forget to get down to a few jobs such as routine weeding, saving seeds, and deadheading.

This is traditionally the holiday month, but don't forget to make plans for the garden before you go away. Some preparation carried out beforehand will pay dividends when you come back. It's all too easy to leave the garden, hoping it will take care of itself while you're away, but at this time of year it can so quickly become overgrown. There's a risk of returning from your break to find weeds everywhere and much of the hard work you put in earlier in the year wasted.

Try to keep ahead with all the routine jobs, such as deadheading, weeding, and watering, which have to be done. The lawn may need trimming if there has been a lot of rain and it is growing fast, but resist the temptation to cut it shorter than you would normally do as this will only encourage it to grow even faster while you are away.

Plants growing inside will need special attention. If you can, ask a neighbour or friend to call in and water all of your indoor plants. If this cannot be arranged, then put as many plants as possible outside in a cool, shady corner of the garden. Even better, if you can, is to plunge the pots into the ground; this way they will not dry out as quickly as when the containers are fully exposed to the sun.

Automatic watering and ventilating systems for greenhouses and conservatories are not overly expensive to buy from garden centres or specialist firms. Some types are controlled by a small computer. There are similar systems that can be set up to water plants in containers outdoors as well and these are invaluable if you have a patio or courtyard garden, or even a roof terrace or balcony, and rely very heavily on pots and baskets filled with plants. These systems are no more complicated to operate than your average central heating system and can save you a lot of time even when you're

A cottage garden border The differing heights of delphinium, *Nepeta, Robinia* 'Frisia', and *Achillea* 'Ptarmigan' are used to advantage in this border.

not on holiday – and you can go away at any time, at a moment's notice, knowing that your precious plants won't go short of water.

Home and dry

If you're not jetting off to some far-flung corner of the globe then take time to relax and enjoy the fruits of your labours earlier in the year. But make time, too, for some light summer maintenance in the garden to keep it looking its very best. As was the case in July, the early mornings and evenings are often the most comfortable and pleasant times to work.

The weather in August is often hot and sultry. In a prolonged dry spell, take care to conserve as much water as you possibly can, since many regions will have restrictions in place on the use of sprinklers, which seem to be enforced as soon as we get a glimpse of sunshine for a few days. There are ways to economize on the use of mains water – by reusing washing-up water on the soil around plants, for instance. This will do them no harm at all. Bath water, as long as you haven't used lashings of rich bath oil, can also be siphoned out of the bath, either directly onto the borders or into buckets. But do not use it on fruit and vegetables. The most needy plants – it can't be said often enough – are those that are growing in pots and hanging baskets and also trees and shrubs that were planted the previous winter and which are still getting their roots established in the soil. Fruiting vegetables, such as tomatoes, are also thirsty for water at this time of the year, as they need a regular supply to help their fruits swell.

Topping up water features

Keep an eye on the level of water in ponds during prolonged dry spells, as the water can evaporate at an alarming rate in these conditions. Oxygen levels in the water will also become low in still, hot weather, so make sure that you top up the pond regularly and if you can, spray water on the surface to increase the oxygen levels. This is particularly important if you are keeping fish in the pond, but all aquatic life will feel the benefit. Oxygenating plants also help keep the water clear and aerated, but at this time of year you are more likely to find that they are

Weather watch

August temperatures are similar to July's, often with hot, sultry days occasionally interspersed with thundery showers. Daily minimum temperatures are usually around 11–13°C in the south, and 8–10°C in the north. Maximum temperatures can, of course, be more than double this on bright, sunny days. High ground will always be slightly cooler and coastal areas are kept fresher by sea breezes.

Some winds and gales

There are very few gales in any parts of the country now, but there can be strong winds in coastal areas, especially in the north and west. Up to 0.5 days of gales may be experienced in the western isles of Scotland and parts of north-west England may have up to 0.4 days of gales.

Sunshine hours

Generally August is slightly duller than July, with more marked differences in the number of sunshine hours up and down the country – northern parts getting around 140 hours and southern parts on average 190 hours of direct sun. The amount of sunshine will always vary according to the locality, height above sea level and proximity to the coast, and the local topography.

Varying rainfall

The amount of rainfall this month will vary considerably depending on where you are. The south coast will typically receive around 50mm of rain this month; inland regions can experience higher rainfall, at around 60mm, due to the higher frequency of thunderstorms as clouds break over higher ground. In the Midlands, for example, thunderstorms occur on average on 15 days a year, but in the west and north this is reduced to around eight days a year.

No snow

There is generally no snow anywhere in the country save on the highest mountains, where patches linger in pockets for most of the year.

Ripening tomatoes These need plenty of water,
especially in hot weather.

becoming overgrown and need thinning, rather than not
having enough. One way to ensure that pond water
remains well oxygenated for fish is to install a small
fountain – this will help to move the water around. The
low, bubble-type fountains are by far the best for water
conservation as fine sprays will evaporate far too quickly.
You will need to run electricity outside to power the

pump. It's important to consult a professional about
installing electrical equipment outdoors, especially
where water is concerned. You could, as an alternative,
investigate self-contained solar-powered fountains.

Weeding wisely

It's vital to keep up with the weeding in all parts of the
garden at this time of year. Weeds not only compete for
precious space in the borders, but they also take up

valuable moisture from the ground. The best tool for weeding is the Dutch hoe. The technique is to slice off the tops of the weeds just below the surface of the soil and leave them on the surface to dry out in the sun. A dry, sunny day is best for this job. Weeding is well worth the effort because it not only keeps the garden looking attractive but it helps to maintain a loose, crumbly layer on the surface of the soil. By doing this, you are preventing the ground from cracking in hot weather and conserving moisture in the deeper layers.

Saving seeds

Watch out around now for seeds ripening on plants in the garden. Growing plants from seeds collected from your own garden is one of the most rewarding aspects of the gardening process. You will have to be vigilant, though; seed pods or heads may not look ready, but you can be sure that as soon as your back is turned the seeds will pop out and spread themselves over the border. This is no bad thing, of course, as many plants will freely seed themselves around the garden. But if there are some plants you particularly want seed from, then watch them carefully. Seed heads are usually ripe when they begin to turn brown; this is the time to cut them off and drop into paper bags, to be sorted and stored later on.

Savour the end of summer

This is the last month of summer and though it's hard to believe, with the abundance of flowers, fruits, and foliage around us, plant growth really starts to slow down from the end of August onwards. So you can complete summer pruning of fruit trees and wisterias and trimming of hedges this month, without fear of too much regrowth – although fast-growing conifers may well need a final going-over in the autumn. You can also look forward to spending less time weeding from the end of the month onwards as germination also slows down. And if you want an even sharper reminder that the seasons are about to change, remember that however hot and sultry the weather is right now, this is the month to start forcing pots of bulbs to flower at Christmas!

Picking strawberries Check your plants every day so that you can pick when the fruit are at their very best.

Dutch hoe Choose this tool for keeping up with the weeding. To save lots of work, simply slice the weeds and leave them on the surface of the soil to dry in the sun. This also helps to conserve moisture.

Cosmos atrosanguineus
Perennial with chocolate-scented flowers (*see p.289*)

Osteospermum jucundum
Sun-loving perennial with silvery leaves (*see p.314*)

***Buddleja davidii* 'Fascinating'**
Shrub with enormous wildlife appeal (*see p.280*)

***Hydrangea paniculata* 'Grandiflora'** ♀
Huge flower clusters; a lovely shrub for shade (*see p.302*)

Begonia* x *tuberhybrida
Tender perennial with huge, blowsy flowers (*see p.279*)

***Solenostemon* 'Brightness'**
Try bedding out these glasshouse favourites (*see p.330*)

***Aconitum* 'Bressingham Spire'** ♀
Lovely perennial, but toxic; site with care in a family garden (*see p.275*)

***Phygelius* x *rectus* 'Salmon Leap'** ♀
Slightly tender shrub for a sunny, sheltered spot (*see p.317*)

***Monarda* 'Mahogany'**
One of the most popular perennials with bees (*see p.311*)

***Penstemon* 'Apple Blossom'** ♀
Narrow-leaved perennial bearing pale-pink flowers (*see p.316*)

***Lavatera* 'Barnsley'** ♀
Reliable shrub; good even in poor dry soil (*see p.307*)

***Lobelia* Fan Series**
Dark-leaved perennial that enjoys damp soil (*see p.308*)

***Clematis* 'Ville de Lyon'**
Large-flowered climber, which bears carmine-red flowers (*see p.286*)

Nemesia caerulea
Woody-based, slightly tender perennial; good in containers (*see p.312*)

***Salvia coccinea* 'Lady in Red'** ♀
Vivid perennial that needs some winter protection (*see p.328*)

Lantana camara
Frost-tender shrubs for multicoloured summer display (*see p.306*)

***Echinacea purpurea* 'White Swan'**
Hardy perennial; looks good well into autumn (*see p.294*)

***Lathyrus odoratus* 'Colin Unwin'**
Brick-red sweet pea; an annual climber (*see p.306*)

Argyranthemum foeniculaceum
Tender sub-shrub that forms a flower-covered bush (*see p.278*)

Rhodochiton atrosanguineus ♀
Tender climber that can be grown annually for summer (*see p.322*)

Indigofera amblyantha ♀
Sun-loving shrub with pea-like flowers and elegant foliage (*see p.303*)

Euryops pectinatus ♀
Sun-loving, half-hardy perennial with cheerful daisy flowers (*see p.296*)

***Fuchsia* 'Auntie Jinks'**
A trailing variety of these popular half-hardy shrubs (*see p.298*)

***Scabiosa* 'Butterfly Blue'**
Cottage-garden perennial, popular with all flying insects (*see p.328*)

Pelargonium 'Apple Blossom Rosebud' ♀
Lovely form of this summer favourite (*see p.312*)

Scaevola aemula
Trailing tender perennial; good in hanging baskets (*see p.325*)

Perovskia 'Blue Spire' ♀
Dreamy subshrub with silvery stems and leaves (*see p.313*)

Tropaeolum speciosum ♀
Exotic-looking climber that prefers an acid soil (*see p.328*)

Dierama pulcherrimum
Graceful perennial with wand-like flower spires (*see p.289*)

Heliotropium 'Marine'
Tender shrub; good in dry soil and in pots (*see p.297*)

Crocosmia x crocosmiiflora 'Jackanapes'
Clump-forming, nearly hardy perennial (*see p.287*)

Geranium psilostemon ♀
Hardy perennial covered in flowers until late in the season (*see p.295*)

Abutilon 'Souvenir de Bonn' ♀
Spindly, sun-loving shrub; good against a wall (*see p.270*)

Verbena 'Showtime'
Tender perennial; a popular bedding and container plant (*see p.329*)

Kniphofia 'Green Jade'
Cool-coloured variant of a fiery perennial (*see p.301*)

Cotinus coggygria ♀
The smoke bush, with clouds of tiny flowers in summer (*see p.286*)

WHAT TO DO IN AUGUST

AROUND THE GARDEN

Use water wisely, but during hot weather make sure that bird baths and other containers that wildlife drink from are topped up regularly.

Be vigilant in watching for pests and diseases.
Warm, dry weather encourages diseases such as mildew (a white powdery coating on stems and leaves). Preventative fungicide sprays can be used, but by

ensuring the plants do not come under any stress – for instance, lack of water – the plants will stand up to any problems much better. There will be the usual army of aphids about; these can be kept in check by squashing them by hand. If you have a bad infestation, control them by using a suitable pesticide that is available from garden centres and spray in the evening when fewer beneficial insects are around.

In damp summers, slug damage to plants in the garden can be rather dispiriting. The lusher and greener foliage is, the more they like it. But there are ways to combat the onslaught without resorting to pellets. First of all, birds, ground beetles, and frogs all eat slugs, so the more they can be encouraged into the garden the better. Put down pieces of slate or wood in the border for the slugs to creep under. They like dark, cool, moist hiding places. These traps can then be turned over, exposing the slugs to any birds in the vicinity – or pick them up and dispose of them. Other traps that work well include beer traps. You could also try inverted hollow grapefruit or orange halves placed about the border or hollowed-out potatoes – these are often used as decoys by vegetable gardeners trying to protect a potato crop. Plants that are particularly prone to slug attack can be surrounded with a layer of crushed eggshells or grit. Slugs don't like the coarse surface and so are less likely to reach the plants.

Continue weeding borders regularly, while watching for any self-sown seedlings. It is surprising what you can find. Most hybrids and many cultivars of plants will not reproduce true from seed, but the seedlings that do emerge can throw up all sorts of variations in flower colour, plant growth habit, and even leaf colour. You never know when you might discover a winner of a plant in your own back yard.

Slugs and hostas Use a copper band around the rim of a terracotta pot to act as a barrier to slugs, which are particularly keen on hostas. A layer of vaseline is also worth trying – slugs don't like it because of its water-repelling properties.

TREES AND SHRUBS

■ **Continue to deadhead roses.** Remove the fading flowers to prevent plants putting energy into producing seeds. Instead, that energy will go into new growth and more flowers. Even when deadheaded now, modern roses can still produce new shoots that will flower before the end of the season. It is not uncommon these days, with milder winters, to see roses blooming into November or even later. Prune back to at least one or two leaves below the base of the flowered shoots, to a healthy, outward-facing bud. You may have to prune harder than this to find a good bud; the harder you prune, the more strongly the new shoot will grow.

Pruning and training

■ **Trim lavender lightly.** At this time, you want to remove the old flower spikes. Go over the plants with a pair of hand shears, cutting off the old flower spikes and about 2.5cm (1in) of the leafy growth at the tips of the shoots. This will encourage sideshoots to grow, keeping the plants bushy and compact.

Lavender rarely grows again from old wood and if plants have become old and straggly, it is best to either take cuttings from them or remove the old plants altogether and buy in new plants. If your soil is on the heavy side, with a high clay content, incorporate plenty of coarse grit before planting new lavenders. This will improve drainage, which they will enjoy.

Propagation

■ **Continue to take semi-ripe cuttings** from shrubs. These cuttings are taken when the bases of the young shoots are beginning to turn woody or ripen. Take the cuttings in the early part of the day or in the evening, when it is cooler.

Almost all of the popular garden shrubs we grow can be increased by taking these cuttings, although you need patience while they grow to maturity. Plants to try include berberis, buddlejas, box, ceanothus, choisya, cistus, cytisus, ericas, escallonia, hebes, lavenders, philadelphus, potentilla, pyracantha, santolina, and viburnums.

■ **Layer rhododendrons and azaleas.** These plants are difficult to root from cuttings, but they are easy to propagate by layering. Choose a flexible young shoot that is growing close to the ground, so that it can be bent easily into the soil. Then remove a few leaves 10–15cm (4–6in) from the shoot tip. Wound the shoot at the point that will be buried by cutting part of the way through it, or carefully twisting it until it just begins to crack.

Make a small depression in the soil and hold the shoot in place in the depression with a wire hoop. Cover up the stem with soil, insert a cane next to the shoot, and tie the shoot to the cane so that the tip of the shoot remains upright.

To conserve as much moisture as possible, place a brick or large stone over the stem in the soil. After about a year has gone by, the layer should have produced a good root system and it can be cut from the parent and planted out.

Hedges

■ **Most hedges** can be given their final trim towards the end of the month as they will not grow much after this, although conifers may need another going-over. If you want a level top to the hedge, fix a post at either end and tie twine between them at the required height. Trim the sides of the hedge first, working from the bottom up, whether using either a powered hedge trimmer or hand shears. The reason for working upwards is that as you cut, the trimmings will fall away and you will be better able to see where you are going.

Make the hedge wider at the base and narrower at the top. This way it will stand up to the weather better. The top can be trimmed last, using the twine as a guide.

You may have trimmed conifer hedges last month; if not, do it now. It is often recommended that conifer hedges only be trimmed with shears, because powered hedge trimmers bruise the growth. This can happen, but damage is so minimal that it doesn't really make any difference. The key point with conifer hedges is never to let them get beyond the height and width you want, as none will regrow if cut back into hard, old wood. The only exception is yew. It can be cut back to very old wood and will still grow again.

Large-leaved hedges such as spotted laurel (*Aucuba*) cannot be trimmed with shears or hedge trimmers, however, because these would cut through the large leaves, causing the edges to go brown. The way to cut these hedges is with a pair of secateurs. Put posts and string across the top, as described for other hedges and trim the sides first in the same way, starting at the base and working up. It can be a tiresome task, especially if you have a large hedge, but it is well worth the effort as the hedge will look so much better with no browned-off foliage.

Encourage your box hedge Create a good, manageable shape with regular, light pruning. Shears are the tool of choice for this task.

CLIMBERS

■ **Prune rambling roses** after they have flowered. Pruning of woody plants, most especially roses, can sometimes be portrayed as being very complicated and this may make you hesitant when it comes to doing the job. But pruning this kind of rose is, in fact, very easy. All you have to remember is that these roses produce flowers on wood produced the previous year. All sideshoots that have flowered can be pruned back to one or two buds from the main stems. Any new, strong growths can be tied in to replace older shoots and any very old stems can be pruned out to the ground, so encouraging more new shoots from the base of the plant.

■ **Propagate clematis by layering.** Select a shoot growing from near the base of the plant and lay it on the ground. To encourage the formation of roots, cut part-way through the stem at each of the leaf joints, being careful not to cut right through the stem. If you want to, you can apply some hormone rooting solution to each cut, but it's not essential. Make some wire hoops and peg each leaf joint to the surface of the soil. Each can be covered with a little soil if you wish. After a few weeks, roots will begin to form and new growth will appear from each leaf joint.

Clematis **'Lady Londesborough'**

Rambling roses Prune the flowered sideshoots hard to encourage more next year.

The new plants can then be separated from the parent plant, potted up individually and grown on.

■ **Complete the summer pruning of wisteria**, pruning all the long, whippy sideshoots to five or six buds from the main stems. This will encourage the plant to produce flower buds for next year's flowers. If you require any growth for tying in to extend the framework of the plant you can leave it unpruned.

One of the most common questions put to gardening experts is – why does my wisteria not flower? Lack of correct pruning is often the reason given, which rather puts the blame on the gardener. However, the main reason for wisterias not flowering is that they are not named hybrids and have not been grafted. To see if the plant has been grafted, look at the base of the stem to check that there is a slightly swollen area; the point where the plant was grafted. So always make sure you get a named variety. Often some garden centres and market stalls sell unnamed seedlings, which can take many years to flower, if at all.

PERENNIALS

■ **Chrysanthemums and dahlias** are terrific plants for displaying throughout late summer and autumn until the first frosts. They also last well as cut flowers. The more you cut dahlias (they make great arrangements in the house), the more flowers you get. But they both have one problem and that is that the flowers are irresistible to earwigs.

The best way to control these is to put upturned pots filled with straw or shredded newspaper on the top of canes among the plants. Earwigs love to crawl into dark places during the day. In the morning you can empty the pots of earwigs and dispose of them.

■ **Continue collecting ripening seeds** of perennials. Collecting and sowing your own seed is the most rewarding aspect of gardening. Collect the seedheads carefully into a paper bag. Spread the seeds on a sheet of paper and leave to dry. Separate the chaff from the seeds and store them in labelled paper envelopes.

Some seeds can be sown straight away as they germinate best if they are fresh (such as meconopsis, cyclamen, aconites, and delphiniums) and kept in a cold frame over winter; others can be stored in a cool, dark place until spring.

Ripening geranium seeds The seed pods all too readily spring open to disperse the seeds.

Penstemon cuttings Propagate these attractive perennials by taking stem-tip cuttings.

■ **Take cuttings of penstemons,** which do not divide easily like other perennials. Take the cuttings in the same way as for pelargoniums.

■ **Cut back perennials** that have collapsed or spread over the lawn and other plants in the border. In wet weather a lot of taller-growing perennials, especially achilleas, tend to flop over and smother other smaller plants. Trim them back from the smaller plants to give the latter a chance to recover and flower. The cut-back plants may also grow again and produce some flowers in the autumn.

You may find that perennials that have spread over the lawn will have killed off the grass in that area. Trim the perennials back off the lawn. Give this bare patch of grass a good watering and a dose of lawn fertilizer and it will very quickly regrow.

■ **Hardy geraniums** that were not cut back earlier should be cut back now to make them look neater. Again they will produce new growth, which may flower again later in the autumn. Feed and water them to encourage growth.

■ **Continue to propagate carnations** and pinks by layering. Once the layers produce roots, usually in five to six weeks, they can be separated from the parent plant and planted in their flowering positions. There is no need to use hormone rooting solution as the stems root easily. If you find nicking the stems a little tricky, slightly twist the stem between your fingers until you feel that it is beginning to crack and peg this part of the stem in the soil.

■ **Start dividing perennials** towards the end of the month. If the soil is dry, wait or water the plants thoroughly an hour or two before and afterwards.

Alpines

■ **Take cuttings of alpines.** Many alpines, such as aubrieta, *Phlox douglasii, P. subulata,* and the dwarf helianthemums, can easily be propagated from cuttings. Take small non-flowering shoot tips about 5cm (2in) long, removing the lowest leaves, and insert them into gritty compost – equal parts peat-free compost and perlite or vermiculite, with a handful of horticultural grit added.

Put the cuttings in a warm propagator, spray them daily with clear water to maintain a humid atmosphere and shade in hot, sunny weather, and in five or six weeks they should have rooted. If you're not sure whether they have rooted, give the cuttings the gentlest tug; if there is resistance then roots have formed. The cuttings can then be potted up.

■ **Continue to weed between alpines,** and top up with fresh grit. Grit or gravel around the plants not only makes them look terrific; it also stops rain splashing soil onto the plants, keeps down weeds, and retains moisture in the soil.

BULBS

■ **Plant daffodils and narcissi** before the end of next month. Daffodils look particularly good when they are planted in drifts, naturalized in grass. Bear in mind, though, that the grass will have to be left uncut for at least six weeks after the flowers are over, to allow the bulb to build up its flower bud for the following spring. Dwarf varieties also look good in rock gardens or in raised beds, where the flowers can be appreciated more easily.

If you are planting the bulbs in a border where you don't need to lift them, always mark them with a label; you may well forget where they are after the flowers and foliage have died down and it's all too easy to dig them up again.

The general rule for depth of planting for any bulb is to plant two to three times its own depth. If you're not sure, it's better to plant a little too deeply than too shallowly. If your soil happens to be a heavy clay, add some grit to the planting hole and sit the bulbs on this. Bulb-planting tools make the job of planting large quantities of bulbs much easier. Leave tulip bulbs until late October or November before planting.

Bulbs in a lawn Place bone meal, mixed with a little soil, into each prepared bulb hole.

■ **Plant colchicums** (often misleadingly called the "autumn crocus"). The flowers of this bulb appear before the leaves and it can look rather too startling on its own, so plant it in among other plants or naturalize it in grass.

■ **Plant madonna lilies** (*Lilium candidum*). Most lilies are planted from November until the spring, but the madonna lily is best planted this month as it is dormant. It will start into growth next month. The most likely source of these exquisite bulbs is from a bulb specialist and sent by mail order. Most of these companies advertise in the gardening press, so this is a good place to look.

Plant the bulbs in a warm, sunny spot in well-drained soil. These lily bulbs must not be planted as deeply as you would plant other lilies. Cover the bulbs with no more than 2.5–5cm (1–2in) of soil. Always feed them after flowering.

■ **Pot prepared hyacinths** and other bulbs such as 'Paper White' narcissi for flowers at Christmas. If you are planting them in bulb bowls that have no drainage holes, use bulb fibre; otherwise, any proprietary potting compost will do.

Plant several bulbs in a bowl or pot, close enough together so that they are almost touching. Then cover them with compost, leaving just the nose of the bulbs uncovered. Next "plunge" the containers outside, covering them with compost, or, alternatively, put them in a cool, dark place. After six to eight weeks have gone by, start inspecting the bulbs every day and when they have made about 2.5cm (1in) of growth they can be brought inside into cool conditions.

ANNUALS AND BEDDING

■ **Continue to deadhead annuals** in borders, to prevent the plants' energies going into producing seeds and extend the flowering period into autumn. However, no matter how regularly you deadhead, some of the earlier-sown hardy annuals will be over later in the month. These can be cleared away and consigned to the compost heap. Gaps in borders can be filled with larger plants in pots, either planting or plunging them, to be lifted easily in the autumn.

■ **This is the traditional month** for taking cuttings from pelargoniums, fuchsias, and other tender perennials. They can, of course, be taken at other times from spring through until autumn. But if they are taken later than September, then don't pot them up until the spring.

The cuttings are very easy to take, only those of pelargoniums differing in one or two ways. All cuttings should be removed from the parent plant by cutting off strong, non-flowering shoots just above a bud, leaving a cutting about 10cm (4in) long. Trim the lower leaves off and then trim the cutting immediately below a leaf joint. With all pelargoniums, remove the stipules – the little papery flaps – at the base of the leaf stalks. Pelargoniums do not need hormone rooting solution; they root

perfectly well without it. All other kinds of cuttings will benefit from being dipped in hormone rooting solution. Insert the cuttings around the edge of small pots containing cuttings compost (half peat-free compost, half perlite or vermiculite), and cover all kinds except pelargoniums with polythene; the fine hairs on the leaves will trap moisture and may cause the cuttings to rot. Place the pots on the windowsill or in a shady part of the greenhouse. The cuttings will root in about four weeks, when they can be potted on to overwinter under cover.

■ **Some hardy annuals** can be sown outside now and next month to overwinter and flower early in the summer next year.

■ **Collect seeds from hardy annuals.** Seed can be collected from most hardy annuals except the F1 hybrids, which will not come true to type. Harvest the seeds on a dry sunny day, into paper bags. Tip them onto a sheet of paper and sort them out from the chaff. This is well worth doing to get clean seeds. Any debris left in with the seeds may cause them to rot so an old flour sieve can be useful. Store the seeds in labelled paper envelopes. Store in a cool, dry place; an airtight box in the bottom of the fridge is ideal.

Drying seeds Spread seedheads on newspaper to dry out before you sift and sort them.

CONTAINERS

■ **Continue watering and feeding** bedding plants in hanging baskets, tubs, and other containers. Watering may have to be done several times a day when the weather is very hot. Feed at least once a week with a high-potash fertilizer to encourage the plants to bloom well into autumn.

■ **Remember also to feed permanent** plants such as shrubs, perennials, and trees in containers. These need looking after just as much as temporary summer bedding plants. They require regular feeding and watering and again, especially with woody plants, feed with a high-potash fertilizer to encourage ripening of the wood rather than the production of soft, sappy growth, which may be damaged in winter.

■ **Make sure containers** will be cared for if you are going on holiday. Before you go, group all the containers together in a shady spot, if this is possible. This will make it easier for the person watering, as well as benefiting the plants: a more humid atmosphere is maintained around the leaves where plants are clustered together. In normal circumstances this is not to be recommended, as crowded growth encourages diseases to spread. But it's fine for a week or two. Hanging baskets can be taken down and grouped with the others by perching them on buckets or on upturned pots.

Convenience food Feed plants in containers regularly to prolong the display. The simplest way is to add soluble fertilizer to the watering can.

LAWNS

■ **Continue to mow the lawn regularly,** raising the blades if the weather is very hot and dry. The frequency of mowing can also be reduced in hot, dry weather, as the grass won't be growing much.

■ **Grass clippings** can be left on the lawn in dry weather. Nobody likes grass clippings trailed into the house and this is easily done when they stick to your shoes in damp weather. But in dry spells, leave the grass box off the mower and the clippings will act as a mulch for the grass, helping to retain moisture in the soil and returning organic matter at the same time.

■ **Apply a fertilizer** with a high phosphate content. In late summer it is not advisable to apply a high-nitrogen fertilizer to a lawn as it will promote vigorous growth, which will not stand up to the rigours of the winter. Fertilizers high in phosphates will instead promote root growth, toughening up the grass for the winter ahead. Apply all fertilizers according to the manufacturer's instructions. A wheeled fertilizer spreader will take the guesswork out of applying the feed and saves the chore of marking out the area to do it by hand. You may be able to hire one from your local garden centre or hire shop.

Feed your lawn If you mark out rectangular areas to treat one at a time, this will help achieve an even spread.

■ **Don't water unless absolutely necessary.** There is no point in watering established lawns, as they will soon recover whenever rain does come. Grass has remarkable powers of recovery.

New lawns

■ **Continue to water** new lawns regularly.

■ **Prepare for sowing seed or laying turf** next month. To create a good lawn from scratch takes work, but done properly it is well worth the effort and you will be pleased with the results. Preparation is the key to success and autumn is a good time for making a new lawn. There is usually more moisture in the ground; heavy autumn dews making a contribution. New lawns need a lot of water. Seed must have water to germinate and grow and if turf dries out it shrinks. It's impossible to get rid of the cracks along the joins. With the warm, moist weather of autumn you should not need to water new lawns as frequently as during late spring and summer and the grass will establish before winter, ready to grow strongly in spring.

Dig over the area thoroughly, removing every trace of perennial weeds. Make sure all their roots are removed or they will grow again. Mowing keeps broad-leaved perennial weeds down in lawns if you are not too fussy about their appearance, but some cause other problems: nettles, for example, can ruin a lawn as a play area. Leave the soil for a few weeks to allow annual weeds to germinate and then hoe these off, removing them to the compost heap. Preparing the ground a few weeks before you sow seed or lay turf will also allow the cultivated soil to settle, making it easier to level, or you could let the weeds come up on prepared soil and then run over it with a glyphosate weedkiller.

VEGETABLES AND HERBS

■ **Sow green manure crops** on vacant ground. If you find it difficult to obtain enough garden compost or farmyard manure to pile on beds, a good substitute is to grow a green manure crop on ground that is vacant. Rape and mustard are fast-growing crops that can be dug in during the autumn, before the plants begin to flower and are killed off by frosts. Other green manures can be sown then to overwinter. These seeds are easily sown by broadcasting. Just lightly fork over the soil and rake it level, scatter the seeds, and rake them into the soil surface. This is an easy way to add organic matter to the soil, improve soil structure, and reduce the problem of nutrients being leached from bare ground. By covering the ground with a "living mulch" you also reduce the need to weed it.

Harvesting

■ **Harvest onions** when the foliage collapses, if they weren't ready last month. It is often recommended that you bend over the tops of onions to ripen them, but this happens naturally and there is no need to do it for the plants. Choosing a dry day if you can, gently ease the onions out of the soil to break the roots' hold. Leave the onions on the surface to dry. It's important that they are properly dry if they are to

Dry shallots You can place shallots on soil or a chicken-wire rack to dry them out.

Green manure This is a crop that is grown especially to be dug back into the soil.

store well. If the weather turns wet, cover them with a sheet of polythene or cloches, or lay them out in a shed or greenhouse.

■ **Keep harvesting crops** while they are young as vegetables have a much better flavour when they are picked young. As they age, flavour and texture become coarser. If marrows and courgettes are harvested regularly, the plants produce more flowers and fruits to continue the crop well into autumn. Summer cabbages should be ready to eat too now; cut them before pests get to them first.

■ **Harvest beans and freeze them.** Fresh vegetables direct from the plant to the kitchen and cooked within a short time have the best flavour of all, but there are times when you get a glut of some crops and can't cope with them all. Freezing is one way around the problem and most vegetables, including French and runner beans and podded broad beans, can be frozen. This is the perfect way to avoid wasting them. They will provide a welcome vegetable through the winter.

Sowing and planting outdoors

■ **Sow Japanese onions** to harvest in early summer next year. Japanese onions are also available as onion sets. Before sowing seeds or planting sets, rake down the soil and incorporate a general organic fertilizer. For seeds, take out shallow drills 30cm (12in) apart and water the drills if the soil is dry. Sow the seeds thinly along the drills and cover with dry soil. Thin out to 8–15cm (3–6in) in the spring. In colder areas it may be useful to cover the young plants with cloches during severe winter weather. Japanese onion sets can be planted a little later than seeds, in October or November. Onions of both sets and seeds should be ready to harvest in July the following year, giving an early harvest before other onions are ready.

■ **Sow some salad crops now.** This is the last month for sowing salad crops outdoors, but it is worth trying a few. Not all of them will mature, but you will at least get some fresh, young salad material in the autumn. Seeds to sow include lettuce, radish, salad onions, red chicory, and spinach. It's even worth trying some peas, sowing an early variety such as 'Douce Provence'. You may be lucky with good weather in the autumn. Don't expect to get a great crop, but some fresh peas are always welcome.

■ **Continue to sow spring cabbages** at intervals. Sow the seeds in wetted shallow drills, covering with dry soil. Transplant the seedlings when they are large enough to handle. Plant them 15cm (6in) apart in rows that are 30cm (1ft) apart.

Looking after crops

■ **Continue watering and weeding regularly.** The weather can often be very dry in August and it is important to keep vegetables well watered if they are not to bolt and run to seed. Plants such as celery and tomatoes need regular watering, or celery will bolt quickly and tomatoes will suffer problems such as blossom end rot (dark-brown patches on the base of the tomatoes) due to a lack of water. Irregular watering will also cause tomato skins to split; after a dry spell, if they are given a lot of water, the upsurge of sap in the stems causes the skins to rupture.

Weeds rob valuable moisture from crops. They also act as host plants to pests and diseases, so by keeping them down problems are reduced.

■ **Look out for pests** and use a physical barrier to prevent them getting at crops. A second generation of carrot fly is about now, so make sure vulnerable crops are protected. Crops can be grown under horticultural fleece from sowing to harvesting, as it lets in light and water, but protects plants from insects. Make sure it is tucked into the soil or weighted down, or insects will crawl under it.

■ **Continue earthing up celery.** Blanching makes tough stems more palatable and easier to cook. Draw earth up from either side of the rows until only foliage is showing. Each time this is done, put a collar of paper around the plant to prevent the soil getting into its heart, causing disease to set in. Self-blanching celery may be left to grow on normally.

■ **Marrows left to grow larger** for storing over winter are best raised off the ground slightly to expose them to the sun to ripen. This will also help to prevent rotting caused by the fruits sitting on damp earth. Support them on a block of wood or a couple of bricks. Remove some of the old leaves so that more sunlight can get at the fruits to ripen them. Harvest before the first frosts in autumn.

■ **Stop outdoor tomatoes** when they have produced four trusses of fruit, if this was

not done last month. The summer in this country is too short to get more fruits from outdoor-grown plants. Remove any sideshoots growing from the leaf axils. Any old foliage can be removed at the same time. Foliage clustered around the trusses of fruit can be thinned too. This will allow more light to fall on to and ripen the fruits and improve air circulation, thus reducing the risk of diseases such as botrytis getting a hold and spoiling the fruits.

Herbs

■ **Make a sowing of parsley** to last through the winter. Sow the seeds in shallow drills outside and thin the seedlings to about 15cm (6in) apart when they are large enough to handle. It is worth covering the seeds with fleece to protect them from the second generation of carrot flies, which will be around now. Parsley belongs to the same plant family as carrots and is therefore subject to the same range of pests. Cover the young plants with cloches later in the autumn to protect them from the worst of the winter weather. Alternatively, lift a few seedlings and pot them up and grow on in a cool greenhouse or on the windowsill in the kitchen and you will have a supply of fresh parsley to hand through the winter.

■ **Pot up other herbs such as chives** for use during the winter. Lift a clump of chives from the garden; if it is fairly large, split it into smaller clumps. This way you may get several pieces to pot up. Put each piece into a pot with general, multi-purpose compost, cut back the old foliage and water them in. Stand the pots on the windowsill or in a cool greenhouse or conservatory and in a few weeks you will have a fresh supply of chives.

■ **Take semi-ripe cuttings** from shrubby herbs like bay, hyssop, rosemary, and sage.

Pot up chives

1 **Dig up a clump of chives** from the garden with a spade or fork. Shake off the soil.

2 **Pull the clump apart into sections.** Use a knife to help if necessary.

3 **Pot up the small clumps** individually in small pots, using a peat-free compost.

4 **Cut back the leaves** to about 5cm (2in) and water by standing the pot in a dish or tray of water.

FRUIT
Picking and storing
■ **Harvest early apples and pears.** You can tell when the fruit is ready to harvest as there will be one or two fruits on the ground. A more reliable way is to cup it in your hand and gently twist it. If it is ripe the fruit should part from the tree, stalk intact, with almost no effort at all. If it does not part from the tree, leave it there for a few more days.

Early-cropping apples and pears don't store for very long and they are best used soon after picking. Damaged fruits should be used first if damage is not too severe, otherwise put them on the compost heap.

Looking after crops
■ **Pay attention to fruit trees** trained against walls. The base of a wall can be a very dry place indeed, especially if it is a house wall and there are overhanging eaves. So it is vital that these trees are watered regularly. It's amazing how quickly the soil dries out. After watering give the trees a thick mulch of organic matter to help retain the moisture.

Pruning and training
■ **Continue pruning summer-fruiting raspberries.** Cut out the old fruiting canes and tie in the new canes that have grown this year. Any that grow beyond the height of the topmost wire of the support can be pruned back to the top wire in the winter. Any weak canes should be pruned out rather than tied in as they will not bear much fruit. The old canes that have been pruned out can be shredded and then used as a mulch in other parts of the garden. If you haven't got a shredder, one can easily be found in your local hire shop.

■ **Summer-prune trained fruit trees.** Summer pruning of cordon and espalier forms of fruit trees couldn't be easier; try and get it all finished this month.

Testing ripeness Cup the fruit in your palm and twist it gently. It should drop into your hand.

■ Cordon apple and pear trees should have the side growths from the main stem cut back to 8cm (3in). Those shoots that were pruned in the same way last year will have produced sideshoots of their own and these need to be pruned back to 2.5cm (1in). This encourages formation of fruit-bearing spurs for next year. When the leading shoot extending the height of the cordon has reached the limit of the support, prune it like the sidegrowths.
■ Espalier and fan-trained trees should be pruned in the same way.
■ Trained forms of acid cherries, nectarines, and peaches need all the shoots growing from the main branches pruned to 10cm (4in), and sideshoots from these pruned to 5cm (2in).
■ For fan-trained plums, damsons, and sweet cherries, prune back by half all the shoots that have borne fruit.

■ **Finish off summer-pruning** cordon- and fan-trained gooseberries and redcurrants.

Planting
■ **Plant new strawberry plants** in ground prepared last month, provided that you are not in the middle of a drought: if so, wait until September. If your old plants are healthy and show no signs of virus disease, use some of their runners, or plantlets, which you may have pegged down into pots. But if there are signs of virus, which usually shows up as streaks through the foliage, then start afresh with strawberries from a specialist fruit grower, where you know the stock has been certified as being free from viruses.

Grow the strawberries on ground that has not grown them for a few years. You can move a strawberry bed in stages – if you have, say, three rows of fruit growing in the vegetable garden, renew one row each year.

Plant the new row to one side of the existing rows and remove the last old row on the other side. Do this each year and you will gradually work your way down the vegetable plot, planting new strawberries in fresh ground each year.

Keep newly planted strawberries well watered. Planting them now enables the plants to build up and get well established before the winter, but if they go short of water this will not happen.

Propagation
■ **Strawberry runners** that were pegged down last month can be cut from the parent plant, either to be planted out or potted up to be forced inside during the winter to get early fruit in the spring. Pot these plants up into 18cm (7in) pots and leave them outside for the rest of the summer. In autumn, lay the pots on their sides to protect them from the winter wet. After Christmas the pots can be taken inside in stages, to provide a succession of fruits whenever they are scarce and expensive in the shops.

UNDER COVER

■ **Check greenhouse heaters** are in working order. Winter may still seem a long way off, but the sooner this job is done the better. It is better to have portable heaters sent off for a professional service. Fixed electric-heating pipes and gas systems should be checked by a qualified electrician or engineer. Paraffin heaters need to have wicks trimmed or replaced as necessary and then be thoroughly cleaned.

■ **Damp down regularly** during hot, dry weather. It's been stated many times already, but it is a job that gives a good growing atmosphere to plants and helps to control pests like red spider mite. Soak the floor and under the staging and you will, almost immediately, feel the atmosphere cooling as the water evaporates. Do this several times a day in hot weather.

■ **Towards the end of the month** the nights can turn chilly, so it's worth closing ventilators and doors in the evening to maintain a little warmth. But remember to open up again early in the morning.

■ **At the end of the month,** remove shading. The days start to shorten at this time and plants under glass will need all the light they can get. Clean off shading wash with a dry duster, or remove mesh and shake it out and roll it up neatly for storage. Or consider investing in roller blinds for next year. It's an ideal time to make enquiries.

■ **Continue taking cuttings** from pelargoniums, fuchsias, and other tender perennials.

Glasshouse and house plants

■ **Start cyclamen now.** Those cyclamen that were rested in their pots during the summer can be started into growth now. They may already be under way and you will be able to see small buds growing. Start watering the plants now and scrape away some of the old compost from the surface, top-dressing with some new potting compost. This will give the plants a good start. Cyclamen don't require a lot of heat, so putting them in a cold frame for the rest of the summer is ideal; then bring them inside early next month. Occasionally they will produce an early flower or two, but these are best removed to allow the plant to build up strength before the main flowering period in the winter.

■ **Pot bulbs for flowers at Christmas.** The end of the month and early September are the latest times to plant prepared hyacinths and other bulbs to flower in time for Christmas. After about six to eight weeks inspect the bulbs and when they have made about 2.5cm (1in) of growth they can be brought inside to cool conditions. Then, after a few weeks bring them into the warmth to flower in time for Christmas.

■ **Start freesias and lachenalias** into growth. Freesias are beautifully scented flowers produced on wiry stems, ideal for winter flowering in a cool conservatory or greenhouse.

Corms of freesias can be planted from now at intervals over the next few weeks to provide a succession of blooms through the winter. Seven or eight corms can be planted in a 12cm (5in) pot containing multi-purpose compost. Cover the corms with about 2.5cm (1in) of compost. Plunge the pots outside and after about six weeks take them inside to flower. After flowering, feed the plants until the foliage begins to turn yellow and then rest the corms. Lachenalias are also good plants for cool greenhouses, grown in the same way as freesias.

■ **Continue to maintain house plants** by watering and feeding. Plants with large decorative leaves will benefit if the foliage is wiped over once in a while. It is amazing how much dust can settle on leaves, reducing the plant's capability to manufacture its foodstuffs from sunlight. This process of turning light into energy – photosynthesis – is essential for survival.

Crops under glass

■ **Continue to remove** old leaves from tomatoes and other greenhouse crops to aid ripening and air circulation. Yellowing leaves can be removed at the same time, otherwise they will encourage diseases like mildew and botrytis. All these leaves can be put on the compost heap. Tidiness in the greenhouse and conservatory will go a long way to reducing pests and diseases.

■ **Sow parsley for a winter crop.** Sow the seeds in pots or trays, watering compost before sowing and covering the seeds lightly with compost. Put in a sunny spot. When seedlings emerge, pot them up individually when they are large enough to handle and you will get a good crop of parsley to see you through the winter.

Sowing seeds in pots Be sure to label up your pots carefully to avoid confusion later. Seedlings are not always easy to recognize.

THE SEPTEMBER GARDEN

Throughout this month you will be gathering in the harvest and watching rich autumn colours develop – a hint of the glorious shades to come. There is a distinct chill in the morning air and northern parts may have their first frosts. With winter approaching, you can start to think about shaping your garden for next year, by planting new trees, shrubs, climbers, and perennials.

THINGS TO DO

Start clearing autumn debris to prevent pests and diseases overwintering.

Net ponds to keep out falling leaves.

Sow or turf new lawns, and scarify and aerate established ones.

Move evergreen shrubs.

Reduce feeding of plants in containers.

Take hardwood cuttings from roses.

Begin dividing overgrown perennials.

Plant spring-flowering bulbs, plant out spring-flowering biennials, and plant up containers with spring bedding.

Lift tender perennials and bring them under cover.

Harvest the last of the marrows and courgettes, and lift the maincrop potatoes.

Plant out spring cabbages and sow winter lettuce.

Continue to harvest apples and pears and pick autumn-fruiting raspberries.

Reduce watering and ventilation in the greenhouse.

LAST CHANCE

Force hyacinths and narcissi for Christmas flowering.

Plant onion sets and sow spring cabbages.

GET AHEAD

Start to prune climbing roses as the flowers finish.

Clean the greenhouse in preparation for winter.

Dig over heavy clay soil before the autumn rains make it less workable.

Sow hardy annuals to flower next year.

Autumn is just beginning Crops are ripening now and the last of the early-season apples, such as 'Discovery' and the first of the mid-season crops, will be ready for picking.

A WONDERFUL MONTH

Shortening days are a sure sign that the year is moving on. After you've completed autumn harvesting, storing tasks, and all the other jobs that need doing, why not think about putting up a greenhouse, if you have room? If you start now, you will find many uses for it throughout the winter.

September can often be a wonderful month in the garden. The sultry heat of high summer has gone and the air feels fresher. If there is high pressure over the country we may enjoy an Indian summer, lasting into October, but those clear, sunny days can also mean colder nights. And with heavy dew on the lawn in the mornings, it really is the start of the season of mists and mellow fruitfulness. There are apples, pears, and masses of vegetables to be harvested and stored over the winter months. And after the slight lull in activity in the garden over summer, there suddenly seems to be a lot to get on with.

Time to take cover

The effects of the shortening days are now quite noticeable. From now on the climatic differences in the different regions of the country will become more

Hyacinth bulbs Summer seems to be barely over before thoughts of next spring begin. Buy spring bulbs for the garden early to get the best choice of varieties.

obvious, with the north generally experiencing colder weather and frosts starting early this month. But even in the balmy south, frosts can start quite early. So it's time to move frost-tender plants indoors.

August and September are the usual months for taking cuttings from tender perennials, such as pelargoniums, fuchsias, and argyranthemums. The earlier in the month this is done the better, as the cuttings will form roots much more quickly before the cooler weather sets in. Normally these cuttings are first inserted around the edge of pots or in seed trays and then potted on when they have rooted, but if taken at this time of year it is better to leave them in their pots or seed trays over winter. The plants will get a better start by being potted on when the days begin to lengthen again.

Some people prefer just to give the old plants shelter over winter – for example, in a cool utility room – and then take cuttings when the plants shoot again in spring. It all depends on what sort of space you have for looking after plants over winter.

Give yourself a treat

If you're forever trying to find space for overwintering plants, pots, and trays of cuttings and seedlings, maybe it's time to indulge yourself and choose a greenhouse. It may seem rather odd to advise buying a greenhouse at this time of year, right at the end of summer. But it is, in fact, far better to choose one now and have it erected and ready, rather than wait until spring and miss out on all the fun you will have raising your own plants. You could make a start right now by sowing a few winter lettuces. Once you have a greenhouse you'll wonder how you ever managed without one.

Harvest your carrots As a rule, if you sow a mixture of early and maincrop varieties from May onwards, you should be able to harvest them from June until the end of the year.

Plants for a cold greenhouse

It is surprising what you can grow in even an unheated greenhouse. The most endearing plants for growing in a cold greenhouse are alpines. Many will not stand up to our damp winters as the wet causes them to rot off. A greenhouse with ventilators and doors open all winter to keep the air circulating is the ideal place.

All the spring-flowering bulbs will flower earlier if grown inside in pots. Hellebores are terrific too; under cover in pots, the beautiful flowers cannot be spoiled by rain. Hardy cyclamen also look good under glass. Winter-flowering shrubs can also be grown in a cold greenhouse, at least in their first year. Shrubs such as *Mahonia* x *media* 'Charity' and *Viburnum* x *bodnantense* 'Dawn' have a terrific scent and you can enjoy this to the full under

Weather watch

There can be occasional warm days this month, but on the whole it is cooler in all parts of the country and the first night frosts can be expected in cold and exposed areas. But the warm autumn days should be relished as the days get shorter and there is less time to work in the garden. Good weather will prolong the flowering display until well into autumn.

A windy month

September can be a windy month, but after the sultry heat of summer it comes as something of a relief. Gales increase in frequency again as autumn approaches and more low-pressure systems arrive over the country from the Atlantic Ocean: areas most prone to the first autumn gales are the western isles and the west coast. Although most prevailing winds come from the west, the wind direction can change quickly to colder directions like the north and east.

Direct sunshine

It is surprising just how much direct sunshine there can be this month, although this will depend on cloud cover. Parts of the north and west can experience over 100 hours of direct sunshine and the south and east as much as 150 hours. Days with clear, blue sky, bright sunshine and just a hint of a chill in a gentle breeze are a pure delight in autumn.

Increasing rainfall

It's not every year we can expect an Indian summer; the amount of rain falling generally increases this month. Again, the wettest parts are the north and west parts. The south and east will have the least rain, around 47–51mm falling on average, while the north and west experience anything from 90mm to over 200mm in north-west Scotland.

No snow

Snow rarely falls before the months of November or December. Only on the high peaks, such as Ben Nevis in Scotland, does the snow lie on the mountain top right through the summer.

Winter pansies Plants for winter colour and spring bedding will now be available from garden centres, nurseries, and market stalls.

glass. Stand well-grown new plants in the garden, then bring them in during late autumn and the flowers will soon open up. They can be planted out in spring.

The right greenhouse for you

The choice and size of greenhouse will depend on how deep your pockets are and how big your garden is. The specialist firms will be able to advise you on the best size for your garden, as well as the best position and aspect. But try to get the biggest you can. It is amazing just how soon the space will fill up. Make sure there is good provision for ventilation, with at least one roof ventilator and preferably one in the side. Most manufacturers will add more ventilators on request. It's also advisable to have utilities – a power source or an outside tap – put in at the same time as your greenhouse is built.

The manufacturers will arrange for your greenhouse to be erected, but there are some that are not so difficult to put up yourself. If you choose this option, then a greenhouse with a base will make the job much easier.

Don't forget the pests

Pests and diseases can still be a problem at this time of year and now is the time to clear up any diseased material in the garden. If it is left lying around it gives the spores

of fungal diseases and other harmful organisms a chance to overwinter in the soil and thus cause more problems the following year. The same applies to pests: they just love to crawl into a pile of leaves or into the cracks in tree trunks to hibernate over winter. Paradoxically, it is better if you can leave a small corner of the garden untidy for hibernating mammals such as hedgehogs and other beneficial insects. A small pile of leaves makes a perfect home for these friendly creatures. Birds are friends, too. Blackbirds and thrushes feast on slugs and snails, while many birds eat caterpillars and grubs. Although autumn is a time of plenty for the birds, winter is not far behind and they will need help to get them through these barren months. Keep bird feeders stocked up and buy (or make) a simple wooden bird table. They are available at many garden centres and nurseries.

Under glass at this time of year many of the biological controls will become less effective due mainly to the cooler temperatures – most require a minimum of around 10°C (50°F) – and the best thing you can do to prevent pests nestling down in the warmth of the greenhouse or conservatory is to give it a good clean before winter.

Plants to enjoy

There are still plenty of routine jobs, such as deadheading, in beds and borders, to be done. At this time of year deadheading is unlikely to extend the flowering performance of plants, but it will make the garden look tidier, setting off plants such as dahlias and chrysanthemums, which start looking good now. Many asters will be in flower too. They make a stunning show, if the weather is not too harsh, but some of them are prone to attack from mildew. So keep an eye on them and spray with fungicide before mildew gets a grip. By September most of the summer bedding plants are past their best and spring flowering plants and bulbs can be put in their place. If you haven't sown biennials earlier, then there is usually a good selection available. The sooner they are in and settled the better they will stand up to the winter and also flower better in the spring.

It may be the end of summer and the days may be drawing in, but in autumn there seems to be a special

Continuing sunshine So many of the late-summer and autumn-flowering perennials seem to come in warm shades, as if in preparation for the blazing autumn leaf colour that deciduous trees will soon display.

quality in the light. Early mornings in September can be wonderful, with a clear, blue sky and a freshness in the air. Put this together with beautiful autumn-flowering plants and plenty of fruit and vegetables to harvest and life doesn't get much better.

***Caryopteris* x *clandonensis* 'Kew Blue'**
Small shrub that enjoys sun and shelter (*see p.282*)

***Solidago* 'Goldenmosa'** ♀
Clump-forming perennial, good for cut flowers (*see p.330*)

***Viburnum opulus* 'Compactum'** ♀
Shrub with clustered white flowers, then bright fruits (*see p.334*)

Eryngium* x *tripartitum ♀
Prickly perennial with sea-green foliage (*see p.295*)

Clematis viticella ♀
The easiest type of clematis to prune; in spring (*see p.286*)

***Dahlia* 'Bishop of Llandaff'** ♀
Tender perennial with semi-double, bright-red flowers (*see p.292*)

Plumbago auriculata ♀
Sprawling shrub for a warm wall or conservatory (*see p.318*)

Stipa gigantea ♀
Silvery, purplish spikelets, which turn gold when they are ripe (*see p.331*)

***Sedum spectabile* 'Brilliant'** ♀
Perennial, whose flowers are a late treat for wildlife (*see p.329*)

***Agapanthus* 'Blue Giant'**
Tall bulbous perennial; perfect in a pot (*see p.275*)

***Aster novi-belgii* 'Peace'**
Michaelmas daisy; a reliable, tall, clump-forming perennial (*see p.278*)

***Rudbeckia* 'Herbstsonne'** ♀
Perennial; the flowerheads still look good when faded (*see p.327*)

WHAT TO DO IN SEPTEMBER

AROUND THE GARDEN

Buy or make a compost bin for all the autumn debris. It is essential to add plenty of organic matter to the soil to maintain it in good heart. Growing plants intensively, as we tend to do in small gardens, means that a lot of goodness is taken out of the earth in a relatively small area. It is therefore essential to put something back in order to continue to get the best out of the garden. Making your own compost is the ideal way of doing this and although there are plenty of bins to buy, you can make a simple one yourself. Remember to use a good mix of different materials, except woody and diseased material, to make the best compost. If you grow vegetables they will generate quantities.

Damage from pests and diseases will be slowing down at this time of year, but it is still necessary to be on the lookout to prevent pests overwintering and becoming a problem next year. Clear any debris in borders, consigning it to the compost heap or burning it if it is diseased. Yellowing leaves on plants should be removed as they will encourage mildew and botrytis. Any pests, such as aphids, still around can be dealt with by squashing. Shoot tips heavily infected with mildew or overwhelmed by aphids can become distorted under the attack. Trim these back to healthy growth and burn the prunings.

Take a notebook on rambles around the garden. Before the summer display is completely over for another year, it is a good idea to have a wander around, assessing how plants have performed and deciding whether they need to be moved or removed completely. Sometimes you have to be tough and if a plant just has not come up to expectations, then it has to go. There is no point in spending a lot of time and effort in growing something, to find that no matter what you try it just won't grow well. Perhaps some colours have clashed and plants need to be moved. It can be fascinating thinking up new plant colour themes and contrasts. Don't forget, too, that foliage plays an important part in any display and dramatic effects can

be created by putting together a range of different leaf shapes, colours, and sizes. Variety and continuity can be created with foliage alone.

Cultivating clay soil. This type of soil can be difficult to cultivate, especially if it has not been worked for several years. Now is a good time to dig it, while the soil is reasonably dry. This will give the winter weather plenty of time to help break down lumps of soil, ready for making seed beds or planting out in spring. Roughly dig the soil, incorporating plenty of organic matter and leave it rough for the winter. To permanently improve the drainage, dig in pea shingle. Combined with the organic matter, this will also raise the level of the soil slightly, making it drain more easily and helping it to warm up faster in spring.

Make your own bin Compost bins are easy to make and provide a great way to recycle kitchen and garden waste. Simply fix chicken wire to sturdy wooden posts, line the bin with thick cardboard to retain heat, and cover the contents with a piece of old carpet.

TREES AND SHRUBS

■ **Autumn and early spring** are good times to move evergreen shrubs, while the soil is still relatively warm. Dig around the plant as far away from its base as you can and as deep as you can, to take as good a root system as possible. If it's a large shrub you may have to enlist the help of a willing friend or family member.

Wrap the roots in hessian or polythene sheeting eased under the rootball to retain moisture. It may be necessary to rock the plant back and forth to work the sheeting under the roots, in which case you will certainly need to ask someone else to help you. Tie the sheet up and move the plant to its new location. Dig a hole big enough to take the root ball without having to cram the roots in. Be sure to plant to the same depth as before.

Put the plant in the hole, pull the wrapping out from under the roots, and gradually fill in the hole. Work the soil right in and gently firm with your boot as you go. Water in well and stake the plant if it is in an exposed place. If there are cold winds it's worth erecting a windbreak of hessian or fine plastic mesh on stakes on the windward side of the plant. This will help to reduce evaporation from the leaves.

Planting

■ **Planting container-grown trees and shrubs** in the autumn is beneficial in several ways. At this time of year the soil is still quite warm and moist. This means that the roots can become established before winter sets in and the plants will get off to a flying start in the spring. Because the soil is relatively moist there is no need to pay so much attention to watering in the early stages, saving on water and time. Plant them just as you would container-grown perennials, staking trees in addition. Planting of bare-root plants of deciduous trees and shrubs can start in November through to March.

Planting container-grown plants Check the depth of the hole you have prepared against the tree or shrub by using a bamboo cane.

Propagation

■ **Take hardwood cuttings of roses.** Roses are normally propagated by budding – grafting a bud of the chosen variety onto a rootstock. This is an easy and quick commercial way of propagating roses. It does, however, have a downside. The rootstock will often throw up suckers, which, if left unchecked, will take over the whole bush. Remove them when they are still small, when they can be torn from the plant quite easily. Tearing or pulling them off is better than cutting them out as they will then grow again. It's just like pruning them. However, there is a way to produce roses that don't throw up suckers and that is by taking hardwood cuttings.

Select a shoot of about pencil-thickness and about 30cm (12in) long. Remove the soft growing tip and all but the top three sets of leaves. Trim the base of the cutting immediately below a leaf joint, making the cutting about 23cm (9in) long. Make a slit trench in the ground and if your soil is heavy clay, put some sharp sand in the bottom of the trench to assist the drainage process. Set cuttings along the trench to two-thirds of their length and firm in. The cuttings will root ready to transplant to their flowering positions next autumn.

CLIMBERS

■ **Plant new container-grown climbers.**

■ **Start pruning climbing roses.** Do this when the flowers start to fade. If they are still going strong, wait until next month. To prune (see below), first of all remove any dead or diseased wood. Then look for any new shoots, especially those growing from the base of the plant, for tying in. If there aren't many new basal shoots, prune all the sideshoots from the existing framework of branches to two or three buds. If possible, remove entirely any very old stems, pruning them to near ground level. New shoots can be tied in to replace these.

Pruning climbing roses

First remove any dead, damaged, and unhealthy-looking stems and dispose of the prunings.

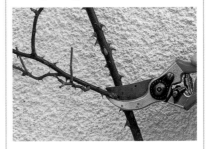

Tie in shoots that can extend the framework and prune others back to two or three leaves or buds.

PERENNIALS

■ **Plant new perennials.** This is a good time of year for planting new perennials. The soil is moist and still warm enough for the plants' roots to become established before the winter sets in. Garden centres should have a good selection of flowering and foliage herbaceous perennials available. It's fun going round deciding what plants to buy and taking them home. Perennials are generally not expensive – and, of course, the plants can be lifted and divided and cuttings taken, in years to come, so each plant then costs almost nothing.

Choose plants carefully, making sure they are right for your garden and for the position they are intended for. It's a waste of money to buy something just because it is appealing, only to find it struggles or even dies because it was a bad choice. Look for plants with strong, healthy growth, with the root balls showing plenty of roots, but not so packed that the plants are pot-bound. If you don't want to turn the plant out of its pot (though no good nursery should mind you doing this) then at least make quite sure that no roots are thrusting through the drainage holes at the bottom. Water the plants well before and after planting. If they seem rather dry when you buy them, plunge them in a bucket of water to ensure the root ball is moist right through.

■ **Keep collecting seeds from perennials** as they ripen. Be vigilant, otherwise the seeds will be spread as soon as your back is turned.

■ **Cut down and divide perennials** that have finished flowering and are not looking good. Most perennials look rather tatty when the flowers have gone over and the best thing to do is to cut them down and make the borders look tidier. At the same time, any clumps that are becoming old and bare in the centre need to be lifted and

Dividing perennials If you are using forks to prise tough clumps apart, push down on the metal hasps that form the lower part of the handle. This will avoid breaking the handle where the wood joins the hasp.

divided. Some plants, such as sedums, thrive on being divided every year and others, like peonies, really resent being disturbed. It's very difficult to give generalized advice. There are so many thousands, literally, of perennials now available to gardeners that it is well worth treating yourself to a really good reference book on the subject – or perhaps putting one on your Christmas list this year.

Clumps that need dividing can be lifted with a fork and placed on a sheet of polythene on the lawn. Divide large clumps with two forks back to back pushed into the centre of the clump, prising them apart. Smaller pieces can be pulled apart by hand. Revitalize the soil with plenty of organic matter and plant the smaller pieces in groups of three, five, or more, if you have the space.

If you haven't time to divide clumps of herbaceous perennials now, it can be done throughout the autumn and into spring, as long as the soil conditions are good enough to work. But if you can't get on with the

work, it is a good idea to go out and make notes about the plants to be divided or moved. Sometimes, no matter how expert we like to think we are, some plant associations just don't work. Colour combinations are easy to plan using photographs (though you can still occasionally miss getting the effect you were hoping for), but getting the heights and relative vigour of neighbouring plants right can be more tricky. The one advantage of growing herbaceous perennials is that they are easily moved if this happens and they don't take many years to get established.

■ **Tall-growing clumps of asters** will need support or they will be blown down in windy conditions. There are many different ways to support plants. The wire supports available from garden centres are popular and do a good job, but these have to be put in place while the plants are young and can grow through them. The easiest way to provide support now is by using canes and string. Put three or four canes around the plant and wind string around the canes to enclose all of the stems. If it's done carefully the canes and string will be almost hidden by the foliage of the plant.

Alpines

■ **Any plants that have outgrown their space** can be moved this month. This will give them plenty of time to settle in before the winter. Water the plants well before transplanting and lift them carefully, with a good ball of soil around the roots. Plant in the new position to the same depth as before, firm in well, and water in to settle the roots. If the weather is dry keep an eye on the plants and water them regularly (perhaps once a week) until they are established. Mulch the plants with grit to help winter rains drain away.

BULBS

■ **Continue planting spring-flowering bulbs** This is the main month for planting spring-flowering bulbs, except for tulips. Look out for chionodoxas, ornithogalum, scillas, puschkinia, and *Iris histrioides*, as well as corms of the many varieties of *Anemone blanda*. Grape hyacinths are essentials too.

■ **This is the latest month for planting bulbs** to flower at Christmas. But continue planting spring-flowering bulbs in pots.

Dwarf bulbs in pots are particularly appealing. There are plenty of daffodils to choose from, among them *Narcissus tazetta*, with yellow and white scented flowers; 'Jack Snipe', with creamy-yellow petals, and 'Minimus', with yellow flowers. Other dwarf bulbs to try include species tulips, such as *Tulipa tarda*; chionodoxas, crocus, and dwarf iris.

■ **Plant bulbs to naturalize in grass.** Bulbs always look pleasing growing in turf. All bulbs, with the exception of the tiniest alpines, are suitable. For smaller bulbs or corms like miniature daffodils and crocus, the easiest way to plant them is to lift a piece of turf and place the bulbs in groups on the soil, replacing the turf afterwards. With larger bulbs, use a bulb planter rather than trying to dig individual holes. To get an informal drift of bulbs in grass scatter a handful of bulbs over the area and plant them where they fall. The general rule is to plant them two to three times their own depth and add fertilizer.

■ **Towards the end of the month,** lift gladioli. When the leaves start to go yellow it is time to lift the corms before frost damages them. Lift them carefully as the corms are usually surrounded by cormlets and these can be saved and grown on if you are intending to increase your stock. Leave the old foliage on until it has dried

Scilla siberica

Anemone blanda 'Violet Star'

off and then cut it off 5–8cm (2–3in) above the new, main corm above the remains of the old one.

When the corms have dried twist off the old corm and dust the base of the new one with sulphur to prevent the spread of disease and store them in a cool, dry place. The cormlets can be separated out and stored in envelopes along with the other corms. These can be "sown" in trays in spring, just like seeds. It doesn't matter which way up they are; they are so small that the shoots will find their own way to the surface.

ANNUALS AND BEDDING

■ **Sow hardy annuals** for flowering next year. Some hardy annuals can be sown outside now for flowering next year. Sown now, the plants will flower from early May the following year. To sow, rake the soil to a fine tilth and mark out informal areas with a stick or sand poured out of an empty wine bottle. Take out shallow drills within each marked area and water them if the soil is dry. Sow the seeds thinly and cover with dry soil. When the seedlings are about 2.5cm (1in) high, thin them out to about 10cm (4in). In spring you may have to thin them again. Look on the back of seed packets for those annuals that can be sown outside in August and September; they include *Calendula officinalis*, *Centaurea cyanus*, *Limnanthes douglasii*, California poppies (*Eschscholzia*), and *Papaver somniferum*. If your soil is heavy clay seedlings may rot. Sow the seeds in modules and overwinter them in a cold frame, planting them out in the spring.

■ **Lift tender perennials** before autumn frosts begin. Plants like argyranthemums, gazanias, lantanas, osteospermums, pelargoniums, and arctotis will have to be lifted and taken under cover for protection. Give the plants a trim, removing yellowing leaves and spent flowers; if they are a bit large for the space, don't be afraid to prune quite hard. If space is really limited, pack them closely into boxes and cover the roots with compost. Otherwise pot them up and keep in a cool but frost-free place over winter. High temperatures will induce spindly growth. Keep them on the dry side, too, giving them just enough water to keep them ticking over until better weather and longer days come along. Some of the plants can be replanted next year just as they are. But others, like pelargoniums, are much better grown from cuttings each year. Cuttings can be taken either now or in the spring.

Clearing summer displays Bedding plants only have shallow roots so are easy to rake out.

■ **Plant out spring-flowering biennials, which have been** in nursery rows through the summer. Clear old summer bedding away when the flowers have gone over. This is the time to incorporate organic matter into the soil. Afterwards, rake the soil level and mark out informal drifts with a stick. Plant groups of each kind of plant in each drift for best effect. Make sure the crown of each plant is level with the soil and that you firm them in well. Water plants in to settle the soil around the roots. If you haven't been able to grow your own biennials, garden centres should have a selection available. Plants to look for are wallflowers, forget-me-nots (*Myosotis*), bellis, canterbury bells (*Campanula medium*), sweet Williams (*Dianthus barbatus*), foxgloves (*Digitalis purpurea*), anchusa, Iceland poppies (*Papaver nudicaule*), ornamental cabbages, and winter-flowering pansies.

Remember: don't grow wallflowers and ornamental cabbages in the same ground as last year. They belong to the brassica family and, like brassica crops, are subject to the disease clubroot (a swelling of the root system), which is very infectious and persists in the soil. Rotate them just as you would brassica crops.

CONTAINERS

■ **Continue to care for bedding plants** by deadheading and feeding to extend the display until the first frosts.

■ **Stop feeding permanent plants** growing in containers. Plants like shrubs, trees, and fruit trees growing in containers will, if fed, produce soft growth now, which may be damaged in winter. So stop feeding them with general fertilizers now. One last feed with sulphate of potash or rock potash will benefit them by ripening the wood, making it more able to stand up to the rigours of winter.

■ **Move pots of tender perennials** such as fuchsias and pelargoniums under cover, to be kept over winter in a cool frost-free greenhouse or conservatory.

■ **Once summer bedding plants in containers** have come to the end of their time they can be cleared out and spring bedding plants planted in their place.

Remove some of the old compost and put in some fresh. The choice of plants and colour schemes is entirely personal, so let your imagination run riot. If you haven't raised your own spring bedding like wallflowers, forget-me-nots, and bellis yourself, garden centres will have a wide range to choose from. Remember to plant bulbs in with the spring bedding too.

■ **Plant bulbs in containers.** There is no need to renew the compost when summer bedding has been pulled out, as bulbs will thrive well in the old compost. The most important time to feed bulbs is after they have flowered, when they are building up to flower again the following year. Pack the bulbs in as close to each other as you can, planting them between two and three times their own depth. Use one kind, or colour, of bulb for each container, to make a stunning show.

LAWNS

■ **Start mowing less frequently** as the growth of grass begins to slow down.

■ **Autumn maintenance.** Towards the end of the month, most gardeners start the annual round of work on the lawn to reinvigorate it. If you just have too much else to do in the autumn, it is quite alright to do it in the New Year instead.

■ **Remove thatch from the lawn.** Over a period of time, a layer of dead grass and other debris accumulates in any lawn; this is called "thatch". If it is left in the lawn over the years it restricts air movement around the grass and can cause problems with surface drainage, encouraging moss and other weeds to colonize the lawn. From late August through the autumn, begin to remove this thatch. It can be done in several ways, the most back-breaking method being to drag it out with a spring-tined rake. Use this tool to rake out the dead grass and moss. It can be very hard work and it is easier to use a powered scarifier if you have a large lawn. These can be hired and you will find it relatively easy to remove all the thatch with little effort. Be warned, the lawn will look an absolute mess when scarifying has been done, but it will do it the world of good and it will soon recover.

■ **The next job to be done is aeration.** Like any other plant, grass needs air and the surface of the lawn gets very compacted over the summer, with constant use and cutting every week. To relieve this compaction, aerate the lawn with a fork pushed into the ground, to a depth of 15cm (6in) at 15–18cm (6–9in) intervals over the whole area. Again, if you have a large lawn, machines can be hired to do this job too. Some of these remove a small core of soil, which is of particular benefit if you have a heavy clay soil.

■ **Top-dress immediately after aerating.** Top-dressing ensures that aerating holes stay open and revitalizes the upper layer of soil. A mix of three parts sieved garden soil, two parts sharp sand, and one part sieved garden compost (or old potting compost, if you have some) is the best top-dressing to use. If your lawn is a bit worn, mix in some grass seed with the top-dressing mix. Spread a 1–2cm (½–1in) layer over the lawn and work it in with a stiff broom or with the back of a rake. It will look a bit of a mess for a couple of weeks, but the grass will soon grow through again.

■ **Patches of broad-leaved weeds** can be treated with a lawn weedkiller in autumn or in spring. Make sure you use a selective weedkiller especially formulated for lawns, otherwise you will damage the grass. Always use these chemicals strictly according to the manufacturer's instructions on the packaging.

■ **Established lawns can be fed now,** unless you did so last month. Don't use up any high-nitrogen feeds that you were using earlier. At this time of year, it is better to use one of the low-nitrogen fertilizers sold as autumn-lawn feeds in garden centres, as you don't want to encourage soft, sappy growth.

■ **Reseed worn patches on the lawn** Small bare patches can be easily repaired by sowing seed. Rake out any thatch and then roughen the surface slightly with a fork to make a fine tilth and level it. Put the grass seed in a bucket and mix in an equal quantity of old potting compost or sieved garden compost. Spread this mix evenly over the bare patch and tamp it down with the back of a rake. To encourage quick germination, cover the area with polythene pegged into the ground. Keep the patch watered if it gets dry and the seed should germinate in two to three weeks. Remove the polythene covering as soon as the shoots begin to show.

New lawns
■ **Sow grass seed or lay turf.** Although grass seed can be sown and turf laid at almost any time of the year, by far the best time is in early autumn. If you have not already prepared the ground, do it as soon

Laying turf

1 Start from a definite edge, whether defined by a hard surface or a line. Butt the turves up closely together.

2 Lay the next row with staggered joints. Almost overlap the turves and press them down with your fingers.

3 Once all of the turves are laid, it is worth going over them, tamping down the joints with the back of a rake.

4 Cut edges as necessary with a hemispherical edging iron. Hosepipe or rope can be used to mark out curves.

5 Walking backwards, brush up the grass with a stiff broom to stimulate its growth, especially across joints.

6 Water really thoroughly with a sprinkler and keep the turf well watered until autumn rains come.

as you can now, digging over thoroughly and removing all trace of weeds. After that, preparation up to a certain point is the same, whether you are sowing seed or laying turf:

■ Roughly level the soil with a rake to break down the lumps.

■ Then tread the ground with your weight on your heels, keeping your feet close together.

■ Rake over the soil and then tread it again, this time shuffling across it at right-angles to the first time. Stand back and squat down to look across the soil surface and spot any hollows and bumps that should be taken out.

■ Finally, rake the soil to a fine tilth as if preparing any seedbed.

Now, either sow seed or lay turf:

■ Sow grass seed according to the specifications on the back of the packet. If you are sowing by hand you can mark out the area in square metres with string and canes to make it easier. Measuring the amount for each square metre into a small plastic cup once and using this as a guide will save a lot of time; you won't need to weigh out all the seeds each time. An even quicker way to sow is to use a fertilizer spreader. Detailed instructions for sowing seeds with this should come with the spreader.

■ Lay turf by rolling it out and butting it up close, so there are no gaps. Lay it in the same pattern house bricks are laid in, so that none of the joints line up. This ensures that a good bond is made when the turf knits together. Always work outwards, from boards placed across the turf that has already been laid. Water well and keep it watered if necessary, but keep off the new turf as much as possible for four or five weeks, to allow it to establish.

VEGETABLES AND HERBS

■ **Cut down asparagus foliage** now that it is turning brown. Be careful, as there are sharp spines on the stems. Then give the plants a generous mulch of organic matter. This is also a good time to prepare a site for planting new asparagus crowns next spring. If your soil is a heavy clay it is worth ordering grit to incorporate into the soil to improve drainage, as asparagus likes a well-drained soil.

Harvesting

■ **Harvest the last of the globe artichokes,** cutting only buds that have not started to open up.

■ **Pick marrows, pumpkins, and squashes.** Leave them in the sun for a couple of weeks, or put them in a greenhouse to ripen and dry off before storing them in a cool, dark place. They should keep until well after Christmas. Clear the old plants away as soon as the fruits have been picked, as they will by now almost certainly be mildewed.

■ **Begin lifting root vegetables** for storing. Vegetables such as beetroot, carrots, and turnips can be lifted and stored for use over the winter. Parsnips are best left in the ground as they taste better when they have had a bit of frost on them.

To store all the others, select only undamaged roots. Any damaged ones should be used straightaway and not stored, as they are liable to spread disease. Lift the roots and twist or cut off the foliage, leaving a few centimetres of stem. Put the roots in boxes between layers of sand or old potting compost. This precaution prevents them drying out too quickly and keeps them in the dark, discouraging growth. Make sure they are in a frost-free place. Inspect them regularly and throw out any that are showing signs of rotting.

Asparagus fern Female plants will produce bright berries among the ferny foliage.

■ **Lift maincrop potatoes** by the end of the month. Lift them on a warm, sunny day and leave them on the surface to dry out. Again store only undamaged ones, in paper sacks tied at the neck, in a frost-free dark place. Potatoes must be kept dark, otherwise they turn green.

■ **Get onions under cover.** Lift and dry any still in the ground and bring them into a cool, dry storage area before damp autumn weather sets in. In mild autumns, especially, if onions are left in the ground after the leaves have gone over, they often start to regrow.

Sowing and planting outdoors

■ **Sow a winter variety of lettuce.** Sow in shallow drills in the usual manner and cover with cloches. The seeds will germinate quickly and when the seedlings are large enough to handle, thin them out to about 15cm (6in) apart. Harvest from January onwards. A reliable old favourite is 'Winter Density'.

■ **Plant garlic.** Autumn is the traditional time for planting garlic as it needs a period of cold weather to grow well. To get good-quality crops buy bulbs specially cultivated for planting. Plant in a sunny site in well-drained soil. On heavy soil, dig in some horticultural grit to aid drainage. Break each bulb into individual cloves and plant each one 8–10cm (3–4in) apart, with 30cm (1ft) between rows. Plant so that the tips of the cloves are just below soil level.

To get the plants off to a quicker start, plant them in module trays with large cells and keep these in a cold frame for the winter, or place them at the base of a sheltered wall. The plants can then be put in the ground in the spring.

■ **Plant out spring cabbages** sown last month. These can be planted 15cm (6in) apart in rows 30cm (1ft) apart. Harvest every other plant as spring greens, leaving the others to heart up. Cover the plants with netting or fleece or the pigeons will have them eaten to the ground as soon as your back is turned.

There is still time to sow a fast-maturing variety like 'Duncan' or 'Pixie' under cover. To get them off to a good start sow the seeds in modules, so that when it comes to planting them out the roots are not disturbed and the plants will get away without a check to their growth.

■ **Earth up trench-grown celery** for the final time, leaving just a tuft of foliage poking out at the top. Blanching has the effect of making the stems more tender. Keep some straw or fleece handy and throw it over the tops of the plants if severe frost is forecast over winter. Harvest the last of the self-blanching celery before the first frosts.

■ **Plant autumn onion sets.** The sooner these go in and get growing before winter sets in the better. Varieties to look for are 'Radar' and 'Swift'. Plant them 8cm (3in) apart in drills deep enough to just cover

Planting onion sets

Make a shallow drill 2.5cm (1in) deep and position sets 8cm (3in) apart.

Firm the earth around each set so that the tips are only just visible.

the tip of the sets. Apply a general organic fertilizer in spring to boost growth.

■ **Lay tomato plants on a layer of straw** and cover with cloches to speed up ripening. It is rare in our short summers to ripen the whole crop from outdoor tomatoes. By laying the plants down and covering them you can maximize the ripening effect of late sunshine. Any fruits left unripe can be used to make green tomato chutney – or, place them into a drawer and put a banana in with them. The gases given off by the banana help the ripening process.

FRUIT
PICKING AND STORING

■ **Towards the middle and end of the month** autumn-fruiting raspberries come into their own. These late-fruiting varieties are delicious, often more concentrated in flavour than their summer counterparts. Once the fruit is picked, leave the canes unpruned until late winter or early spring.

■ **Blackberries ripen in succession** over a much longer period than other soft fruits and if you have only a few plants it can be frustrating trying to gather enough for a good meal all in one go. The trick is to freeze them in small batches until you have gathered enough together – currants, raspberries, blackberries, and hybrid berries all freeze very well.

■ **Continue harvesting fruit** as it ripens. Cooking varieties of apples and pears will not be ready for picking until near the end of the month and into October. Handle all fruits as gently as possible as the skins are easily bruised and this can adversely affect their keeping qualities. Store only those that are unblemished. Fruits showing damage should be used right away or kept away from the main storage area. Large crops of apples should be individually

Conserving apples Wrap apples or leave them unwrapped. However, if you leave them unwrapped make sure they are not touching.

wrapped in paper (old newspaper is handy for this purpose) and laid on trays in a single layer. Smaller quantities can be stored in polythene bags. Make a few holes in the bags with a skewer to let out gases given off by the fruits – this will hasten the ripening process. Pears are best left unwrapped, standing on slatted benches. Pick early dessert pears while they are still hard and let them ripen indoors.

Looking after crops

■ **Strawberries** that were planted last month need to be kept well watered.

■ **Protect ripening fruits** from birds and wasps, who like the sweet, ripening crops just as much as we do. Netting is the only way to keep birds off fruit trees, but it must be well secured to prevent them from getting trapped. If you can, grow all your fruit in a fruit cage made specially for the purpose. There are many different ones on the market, or you could make your own. Be wary of wasps as you pick up spoiled windfalls and scatter them on bare ground in the vegetable garden for wildlife. Plums are a favourite with butterflies, who love to feed on the sugary juice.

Fruit cages These are necessary to protect your crops from birds. You can buy cages in kit form or make your own by wiring sturdy stakes together and draping netting over.

■ **Prune off mildew-infected shoots** of apples and pears. Mildew often attacks trees at this time and once it has got a hold, spraying with a fungicide is next to useless. Fungicides should be used in the early part of the season before the mildew appears as a preventive measure. Now the only remedy is to prune off the infected shoots and burn them or put them in the bin. Don't shred them or throw them on the compost heap or the spores of the mildew will be spread around the garden.

Pruning and training

■ **Finish cutting out fruited canes** of summer-fruiting raspberries. Take care not to get them confused with the autumn-fruiting raspberries, which will be ripening this month.

■ **Prune blackcurrants.** From now through the winter blackcurrants can be pruned, if you wish. In the past the practice was to prune blackcurrants as soon as the fruits had been picked. But at that time the plants are still in full leaf, the foliage manufacturing plant foods. Early pruning takes off a lot of leaves, reducing the plants' capacity to manufacture this food; and it is also more difficult to see what you are doing. It is far better to leave the pruning until the leaves have begun to fall in the autumn and in winter, when you can see what you are doing more clearly.

Planting

■ **Finish planting new strawberry plants** before the end of the month. This is the latest they can be planted to allow them to become established before winter sets in. The plants must have time to establish and form a good root system to crop successfully the following summer. However, if they go short of water this will not happen and they will not be able to

Trimming When planting strawberries avoid bending or constricting the roots by trimming them first to no less than 10cm (4in).

fruit very well next year, so if the weather is dry, they need plentiful watering. Plants that are under stress through lack of water are also more prone to being attacked by pests and diseases.

Strawberries are not a permanent crop like other fruits, so if you can, grow them in the vegetable garden, where they can be rotated like the other crops.

■ **Plant container-grown peaches and nectarines** in a sheltered spot. Planting now, in the autumn, will give the plants a good chance to become established before winter. Prepare the soil by digging it over and incorporate plenty of farmyard manure or garden compost.

Dig out a hole big enough to take the root ball and deep enough to plant it at the depth it is in the container. Make sure the point at which the tree is grafted (a swollen part of the stem near the base of the tree) is above ground level.

The rootstock onto which the tree is grafted controls the vigour of the tree. Gently replace the soil in stages, firming as you go. Water in well and if the tree is being trained against a wall or fence, tie it to its supports.

UNDER COVER

■ **Remove shading** Clean off shading washes, give blinds a shake or brush before rolling them back, or fold and store shading curtains. From now on plants under cover need all the light they can get.

■ **Check the glass and puttying** in the greenhouse to see if repairs are needed. Replace broken panes of glass. It is surprising how much heat can be lost through cracks.

■ **Start preparing the glasshouse for winter.** Towards the end of the month, but before tender perennials are brought inside for the winter, take all the plants outside and thoroughly clean the place. Get it done this month, so that if it takes more than a day, the plants can be left outside overnight without fear of them being harmed by frosts. Make sure you get into every little corner, where pests hibernate and lay eggs. A hose-down with a jet of water, inside and out, is ideal initially; then, wash down with a weak solution of household bleach or a proprietary product. Then rinse down again. Be sure to cover power points and remove appliances. Switch off the power supply completely. If there are any problems, call out a professional before turning it on again.

■ **Reduce watering and ventilation.** Now the nights are getting cooler reduce watering and water early in the day. This allows the greenhouse to dry out before the cooler evenings, reducing the chances of diseases such as mildew and botrytis getting a hold. Ventilators should be closed now at night, but opening them on mild days to keep air circulating will help reduce disease infection.

■ **Bring in tender plants** to overwinter. Plants like pelargoniums, argyranthemums, and lantanas should all be brought inside now. With these plants inside, the greenhouse can seem as packed as it was in the spring, but most will be quite happy under the staging, where it is cool. Be careful when watering, giving just enough to keep the plants ticking over until the spring. Inspect them regularly and remove yellowing or diseased leaves before infection spreads.

Raising plants for outdoors
■ **Sow the last spring cabbages.** There is still time to sow fast-maturing spring cabbage varieties like 'Duncan' or 'Pixie'. They are best sown in modules.

Glasshouse and house plants
■ **Bring house plants indoors** that have been standing on the patio or on greenhouse shelves for the summer.

■ **Continue planting winter- and spring-flowering bulbs in pots.** Get prepared hyacinths and other bulbs in before the end of the month if they are to flower at Christmas, but non-prepared hyacinths and plenty of other bulbs will provide a continuity of blooms until spring. Plunge them outside under compost or leafmould, or put them in cool, dark place to form roots. The formation of a good root system first is the key to getting a good display from forced bulbs.

■ **Sow hardy annuals in pots** to flower under cover during spring. Sow your own seeds collected in the summer. Sow a few seeds thinly in each 12cm (5in) pot and cover with a thin layer of compost. The seeds will germinate fairly quickly and can be kept in a cool greenhouse over winter. Don't give them too much warmth or they will produce weak growth with the lack of light. Just keep them watered. If you sow at two-week intervals you will have a succession of flowers and a longer display.

Pick tomatoes Wait until your tomatoes fall easily from the trusss before you harvest.

Crops under glass
■ **Pick tomatoes, peppers, and aubergines.** Continue harvesting tomatoes as they colour up. Removing some of the leaves from around the trusses will let more light in, hastening ripening. This will also increase air circulation around the plants, reducing the possibility of botrytis. The leaves are removed easily: snap them off by putting your thumb under the leaf stalk close to the main stem and pushing upwards. Then give a sharp push down and the leaf will come away cleanly. Feed and water regularly or some fruits may split.

Harvest peppers regularly. They can be harvested green, so don't worry if they don't colour up. If you are growing the chilli type, the riper they get, the hotter they will be. If there are fruits still to ripen at the end of the month, remove the plants from the pots, shake the soil off the roots, and hang them in a warm place with fruits still attached; they will soon ripen.

Aubergines should be picked when the fruits are well coloured, but the skin still taut. If they are left longer and the skin begins to wrinkle, they will taste bitter. They are harvested by cutting the stalk at least 2.5cm (1in) away from the fruits. They don't keep for long.

THE OCTOBER GARDEN

Autumn colours are at their best this month in gardens, parks, and woodlands with only a short time to appreciate them before the leaves begin to fall. Before you know it, it will be winter again. If you have planted your garden with autumn and winter in mind, garden birds will be attracted to the bright fruits and berries on your trees and shrubs. It's good to share.

THINGS TO DO

Rake up fallen leaves and make leafmould.

Continue clearing up the garden and burn any diseased material.

Dig over empty areas of soil.

Lay turf to make new lawns.

Collect any leaves that have fallen in ponds.

Finish planting evergreen shrubs.

Take hardwood cuttings from shrubs.

Collect berries from trees and shrubs for sowing.

Give conifer hedges a last trim if needed.

Plant climbers, perennials, and lily and tulip bulbs.

Divide any overgrown perennials.

Protect alpines from winter wet.

Lift and store dahlias, gladioli, and summer-flowering bulbs, making sure you label them first.

Cut down the dying tops of perennial vegetables.

Lift and divide rhubarb.

Fix grease bands to apple and pear tree trunks.

Insulate the greenhouse and check heaters work.

LAST CHANCE

Sow grass seed in milder areas.

Finish planting spring bedding.

Harvest apples and pears before they are damaged.

Lift and store your potatoes and carrots.

GET AHEAD

Prepare the ground for planting bare-root stock.

Make early sowings of broad beans and sow sweet peas under cover.

A rich show The brilliantly coloured berries of *Cotoneaster salicifolius* 'Gnom' set against the shrub's dark-green foliage make a rich autumnal display in the garden.

AUTUMN RICHNESS

The nights are drawing in and temperatures dropping, but the garden still has much to keep us occupied. Now is the time to plant trees and shrubs, gather the harvest of fruits and vegetables, and collect and store seeds. And don't forget to clean and maintain your greenhouse.

October can bring a richness of colour to the garden, with the multitude of different hues displayed by autumn foliage. The night frosts and clear sunny days that we often get in October bring out the intensity of the colours in the leaves of trees and shrubs. There are many gardens open to the public that are famous for their autumn show, such as Westonbirt Arboretum in Gloucestershire. The colours will take your breath away.

Seeds and fruits The fluffy seedheads give clematis its common name – "old man's beard". Both the seeds and the succulent rose hips are a treat for garden birds.

Sharing with friends

Fruits and berries are an added attraction now, not only to us but to the birds as well. Shrubs such as cotoneaster and trees like the mountain ashes and crab apples are often covered in fruits. But the birds love them so much that often a whole tree can be stripped of berries quite literally overnight. I, for one, don't feel too aggrieved about sharing with these garden friends – though ask me that again in the spring when they've stripped an unprotected fruit tree of buds! Overall, though, garden birds are a joy, not only when they eat up pests for us, but also when you witness their feeding and bathing antics and especially when they honour your own green sanctuary by raising their young in it.

Because frosts are quite common now, any tender plants in the borders that you want to keep over winter must now be lifted, potted up, and put into a frost-free greenhouse or conservatory – or if you have room, overwinter cuttings taken from them on the windowsill.

Shortening days

There is less time to garden in the evenings now, so for most people that means most of the work outdoors must be done at the weekends. This leaves little time to get on with things, depending on the size of your garden, of course. With some jobs, the earlier they are done in autumn the better. One such is winter digging, especially if you have heavy clay soil. The more time this type of soil gets for the winter weather to break it down the better, so dig it as early as you can. Don't underestimate the effect wind, rain, frost, and snow will have in improving this type of soil. After a winter of pounding

Pumpkin time Whether destined for the table, for show, or for Halloween Jack-o'-lanterns, pumpkins benefit from being harvested in advance. Leave them in the sun for a few days to harden, or "cure", the skins and dry off the fleshy stalks.

by the elements, in spring you will be able to break down the clods easily to make good seed beds. Incorporate as much organic matter as you can into the soil as this will also help to improve its structure. If you don't have a compost heap of your own then look in your local directory for riding stables and go along and get a load of horse manure. It's wonderful stuff and most riding stables will either charge a very small fee or be only too glad to see the back of it. It's not as difficult to get these days as many people imagine.

Time for planting

This is a good month to start planting trees, shrubs, and herbaceous plants, while the soil is still warm enough for the roots to get a hold before winter sets in. Any plants that are on the borderline of hardiness are better not bought until spring, when they will have a better chance of survival.

Choose hardy plants that give a good show right now, such as asters, with their daisy-shaped blooms and crocosmia, which has strappy leaves and tall stems of bright red, orange, or yellow flowers. Mix these with evergreen grasses, such as bronze carex, to inject colour throughout the autumn and winter. These plants not only give the garden an instant autumn lift, but will continue to perform year after year.

Weather watch

There is a significant drop in temperatures now, with frosts more likely on clear nights. But October can have warm, sunny days too. A still, frosty start to a bright, sunny day definitely increases the intensity of autumn leaf colour in deciduous trees.

High winds

The number of gales tends to increase now that we are well into autumn. A pity, because high winds blow the leaves off the trees, spoiling the beautiful autumn display. Gales are now most likely in western coastal areas and will occur on average 3–4 days in the month. Southern and eastern areas generally get between 0.1 and 1.3 days in the south-west.

Decreased sunshine

The amount of direct sunshine is now on the decrease, but there can be some fine days in October. The northern Highlands of Scotland compare favourably with parts of central England: around Wick on the north coast of Scotland the average is 88 hours of sun and in Nottingham, 86. The south coast always fares better, averaging 107 hours this month.

More rainfall

October inevitably brings more rain for all parts of the country, most noticeably in the north and west. The north of England and central Scotland receive similar amounts of rainfall, ranging from 93mm in north-west England to 115mm in the Glasgow area. The farther north you go the more rain falls, with Highland areas getting about 216mm this month. The driest places are East Anglia and north-east England. In these areas typical October rainfall is 47–67mm.

Snow on high ground

Snow begins to fall this month, but only on high ground in the north. Northern areas of Scotland and Ireland have on average 0.1 days of snow on ground above 30m. In the north-east this may increase to 0.3 days on ground above 300m. In these areas, make the best of good weather before winter really sets in.

Give your greenhouse staging a thorough scrub-down to help discourage pests and prevent disease. Tackle all surfaces, particularly any wooden benches. Use disinfectant, diluted as stated on the packaging, before rinsing down with a hose.

Bringing in the harvest

Now is the time to gather in any remaining fruits, such as apples and pears, before they are damaged by frost. It is easy to tell if a fruit is ripe and ready for picking. Carefully cup the fruit in your hand and with a gentle upward movement the fruit should part from the tree easily; if it's not ripe, leave it for a few days and try again. Only store fruit that is not damaged in any way. Storing damaged or diseased fruit will only encourage diseases to spread through the other fruits more quickly, reducing the time they will keep over the winter.

Elbow grease in the glasshouse

Now is a good time to get the greenhouse and conservatory thoroughly cleaned out before the onset of winter. Most plants can still be left outside for the day and this will make the process of cleaning much easier. Thoroughly clean the glass inside and out to admit the maximum amount of light during the shorter days of winter. Scrub down benches with a disinfectant and, finally, hose the whole place down, paying particular attention to all the corners where pests can lurk and hibernate for the winter.

You may have frost-tender plants that will need some heat at night, so check now to see that all your heaters are in working order. Be careful with electrical heaters; if you are unsure about anything or you suspect there is a problem with your heater, then contact a qualified electrician. And always use an ELCB (earth leakage circuit breaker). This will cut the current in a fraction of a second if there is a problem with the electrical supply – much quicker than a fuse alone would do.

Seedheads to save

Keep on watching out for ripening seeds to propagate and collect them before they are shed. Dry the seeds off and put them in paper envelopes, storing these in turn in an airtight container, which you can place on the bottom shelf of the fridge. If you're not sure when to sow the seeds you've collected, it's a good idea to sow half of them now, but store the other half and sow those when spring arrives.

Even if you're not on the lookout for seeds to collect, so many plants now have seedheads and pods as beautiful as their flowers. While autumn is a time for tidying up the borders, it's also perfectly possible to clear up at ground level without cutting down the tall stems of plants like achillea and acanthus. If bad weather threatens to knock them down, you can always cut the stems for drying and displaying indoors. But if the weather holds, October can be a lovely month in the garden – so savour it before the onset of winter.

Maple in autumn colour Maples, or acers, provide some
of the most brilliant foliage tints in autumn – from burning
yellows through rich reds to bronze-purples.

Nerine bowdenii ♀
Spring-like flowers at the end of the season (*see p.312*)

Sorbus commixta
Deciduous tree with white flowers followed by scarlet berries (*see p.330*)

Prunus sargentii ♀
Flowering cherry tree with fine autumn colour (*see p.320*)

Colchicum cilicicum
Perennial whose funnel-shaped flowers appear before the leaves (*see p.287*)

***Malus* 'John Downie'** ♀
Narrow, conical tree bearing orange and red fruit (*see p.310*)

Rhus typhina ♀
The stag's horn sumach; a spreading deciduous tree (*see p.323*)

Acer palmatum 'Corallinum'
A slow-growing tree with long, brilliant-pink leaves in spring (*see p.274*)

Schizostylis coccinea 'Sunrise' ♀
An exotic but hardy perennial (*see p.329*)

Anemone x hybrida 'Max Vogel'
Perennial with pink flowers that fade to white (*see p.273*)

Amelanchier lamarckii ♀
Shrub or small tree with spring and autumn interest (*see p.277*)

Cotinus 'Grace'
Smoke bush with brilliant autumn colour (*see p.286*)

Rosa rugosa
Shrub rose with purple-pink flowers and large hips (*see p.327*)

WHAT TO DO IN OCTOBER

AROUND THE GARDEN

Pests are generally on the decline now that the weather is turning cooler, but diseases such as botrytis and mildew are still quite prevalent because of the generally damp weather in autumn. Practising good garden hygiene will go a long way to avoiding problems. Don't leave rubbish lying around; either compost it or put it in the bin. Diseased material should be burned or put in the bin and never composted. Clear weeds, as they act as host plants to many pests and diseases.

It's not worth using chemical sprays for mildew and botrytis at this time; they are more effective as a preventative early in the year. Plants like courgettes and marrows are particularly prone to both at this time of year. Burn the infected parts as they come to the end of their cropping time.

Rake up fallen leaves at regular intervals from the lawn and among plants in the borders. If leaves are left in a thick layer on the lawn they will kill off the grass. Fallen leaves left lying over and around plants can encourage slugs and snails.

Raking up Use a rake with long tines to gather up all the fallen leaves. Raking will help improve the lawn as well.

Make a container for fallen leaves. Autumn leaves piled up and left to decompose for a year or two will make the most wonderful organic matter to use as a mulch or a soil conditioner, known as leafmould. Leaves can, of course, be mixed with other material and put on the compost heap, but if you want leafmould, then they will need a heap of their own. Make a container with four stakes and chicken wire. Bang the four posts into the ground to make a square and nail the netting around the posts to form the container. The netting helps to keep the leaves in one place. Larger leaves take longer to rot down, but after about 18 months to two years you should have good friable leafmould. Use it as a mulch or dig it into the soil as you would do with garden compost.

Dig empty areas of soil. Digging sounds like hard work and so it can be if you do it all day long, day after day. But it needn't be like that. By this time of year the soil is moist, but not too sticky and the weather, generally, is not too warm or too cold – perfect for some exercise. The first point to make about digging is not to rush at it. Take it easy and work at a steady, but not hectic, pace. Work for short periods, perhaps for half an hour at a time and then take a break or do something else that does not involve bending. Then go back to the digging for another half an hour, and so on.

Use a good spade that is well balanced. Always pick tools up and handle them for a while before buying. If you can afford it, choose a stainless-steel spade, as it should last a lifetime, with little need for maintenance. Don't lift too much soil at a time as this will only cause backache.

You can sow green manure crops to cover and condition soil that will otherwise be bare over winter. Green manures that will stand through winter, to be dug in in spring, include winter rye, field beans, and tares.

TREES AND SHRUBS

■ **Move evergreen shrubs.** This is still a good time to move evergreens, while the soil retains some warmth. At this time of year there will be less need to water plants that have been moved as there would be in hot weather. In exposed areas it is worth erecting a wind barrier on the windward side of the transplanted shrub, as winter winds can cause evaporation from the leaves. This can cause browning, known as "scorch". Deciduous trees and shrubs should be moved when dormant.

■ **Rake up fallen leaves from roses** to prevent black spot spores from overwintering in them. Do this regularly and burn the leaves or put them in the bin. Don't add them to the compost heap, as the heat may not be sufficient to kill off the black spot spores.

Pruning and training

■ **Tall shrubs such as lavateras** and *Buddleja davidii*, which will be pruned hard in the spring, can be cut back now by about half their height to prevent wind rock. If plants have a lot of top growth to catch the wind, they can be blown about, rocking them to and fro. When this happens a hole forms in the soil at the base of the stem, where water collects, causing the stem to rot. In hard weather the water can freeze,

Lavatera 'Barnsley'

damaging roots further. Check all newly planted trees, shrubs, and hedging plants and if they are loose, firm them in again carefully and, if necessary, provide a stake.

Planning ahead

■ **Prepare ground for planting** bare-root trees and shrubs next month. If you want long-lasting plants, it is worth preparing the ground well.

If you are planting a border of shrubs and trees, dig over the entire area, removing roots of perennial weeds. Don't leave even tiny portions of roots behind as they will grow again. Dig in plenty of organic matter. If the soil has not been cultivated before "double-dig" it. Take out a trench at one end of the area and barrow the soil to the other end. Then break up the soil in the bottom of the trench with a fork, without bringing the poorer subsoil to the surface. Put organic matter into the trench and mix it in. To make the next trench, throw the soil forward onto the first trench, covering the organic matter. Continue the process until the area has been dug. The soil you barrowed to the end when you began goes in the last trench.

For planting trees and shrubs in an existing border, take out a hole big enough to take the roots without cramping them. Drive a stake into the hole before planting, so as not to damage the roots. Fork over the bottom of the hole to break up the subsoil. Plant the tree or shrub to the same depth. Work soil back in among the roots and gradually fill in, firming as you go. Then rake the soil level and water in. Finally, tie the trunk to the stake using an adjustable tree tie.

Propagation

■ **Take hardwood cuttings of deciduous shrubs.** Take out a slit trench by pushing a spade into the soil and then pushing and pulling the handle to and fro. If your soil is

heavy clay, trickle in some sharp sand to improve drainage. Remove shoots of the current season's growth, about 30cm (12in) long. For each, trim off the soft growing tip and trim the base of the cutting below a bud. Dip the base into hormone rooting solution. Place the cuttings in the trench to about two-thirds of their length and firm in gently. Label the row and the cuttings will root and be ready to plant out next autumn.

Plants to try from hardwood cuttings include buddleja, cornus, escallonia, forsythia, leycesteria, philadelphus, roses, and weigela.

■ **Collect berries from trees and shrubs.** They generally don't need warm conditions to germinate and most need to go through a period of cold weather to break the seed dormancy. This is called "stratification".

First remove the berries. Separate the seeds and dry them off and store in a cool place. Sow the seeds in trays or small pots of multi-purpose compost, covering the seeds with grit. Place the container outside in a cold frame, or in a sheltered place covered with a sheet of glass or plastic to keep excessive rain out. Alternatively the seeds can be stratified or given a chilling period, artificially. Mix the seed with moistened vermiculite or sharp sand in a plastic bag and place it in a refrigerator. Generally up to six weeks will be required. Check the seeds regularly and when you see signs of germination take them out and sow in trays or pots. Some trees and shrubs to grow from berries: cotoneasters, *Rosa rugosa*, gaultheria, and all sorbus.

Hedges

■ **Trim conifers again if necessary.** Leyland cypress can regrow after trimming in late summer, but can now be trimmed again. Be sure not to cut into old wood, as most conifers will not regenerate.

Planting a mixed hedge A mixture of flowering and berrying, evergreen, and deciduous shrubs planted close together are very wildlife-friendly. They need little or no pruning.

■ **Plant hedges of evergreen and deciduous plants.** Evergreen plants for hedging should be put in as soon as possible this month; if not, wait until spring. Deciduous hedging can be planted all through the winter if soil conditions allow. Prepare a trench 90cm (3ft) wide along the length of the proposed hedge. Dig in generous amounts of organic matter and add a dressing of bonemeal, according to the instructions on the package. Peg out a line along the trench to plant to. Deciduous hedging, such as beech, is usually planted at around 45cm (18in) apart and conifers about 90cm (3ft) apart. Plant firmly to the same depth as they were previously planted and water them in well if the soil is dry.

If you live in an exposed part of the country, protect conifers with a screen of plastic mesh stapled between strong posts for the first year after planting. Make sure all new hedges are watered regularly during their first year, while they get established, and feed them with an organic fertilizer in the spring.

CLIMBERS

■ **Prune climbing roses** and get them tied in before autumn gales pick up. Rose stems are stiff compared to those of other climbers and can be snapped by high winds. Clear up all fallen leaves around them carefully and also any leaves that ramblers have dropped. Rose leaves can harbour diseases such as black spot: it is safer to bin them rather than putting them on the compost heap.

■ **Plant container-grown climbers,** provided that they are hardy plants that will stand up to their first winter when young. All are planted in the same way as container-grown trees and shrubs, then tied into their support to get going. Dig a deep hole and work some organic matter into the bottom – leafmould and a sprinkle of bonemeal is ideal, as it will condition the soil without adding too much nitrogen at this time of year.

Ensure that climbers are planted so that the surface of the root ball is level with the soil's surface, with the exception of clematis.

Most clematis varieties are rather prone to a disease called "clematis wilt", which is noticeable when a plant suddenly begins to wilt for no apparent reason. To overcome this problem it is advisable to plant clematis deeper than is normally suggested for most plants, with part of the stems below the surface of the soil. Plant so that the top of the root ball is up to 15cm (6in) below soil level.

If the plant is then affected by wilt, cut it down completely. The portion of stem below ground will have unaffected buds that may send up new shoots from the base of the plant, so giving a better chance of survival.

PERENNIALS

■ **Cut back perennials** that have finished flowering. This will make the garden look much tidier and discourage diseases from attacking old growth. If on some plants the flowers have finished, but the foliage is still quite green and attractive, leave it until it is really blackened by the frosts. Cutting everything down can leave unsightly gaps in the borders and this should be avoided until as late in the autumn as possible. Any soft growth cut down, such as that of hardy geraniums, can be consigned to the compost heap. Other growth that is semi-woody will take longer to break down on its own. But the process can be speeded up by shredding the material rather than burning it, which is the more usual practice. Shredded material can be added to the compost heap to rot down further, or used as a mulch on the borders in spring.

■ **Plant new herbaceous perennials** while the soil is still warm and moist. Prepare the soil well by incorporating plenty of organic matter and adding some bonemeal. There is a wide range of perennials to choose from and attractive displays can be made for little outlay. Perennials will last for many years if they are propagated regularly, by dividing them up and replanting, collecting seed and sowing it, and by taking cuttings and growing them on.

Perennials always look best when they are planted in groups of three or more plants, but if your budget is limited, buy one of each of the varieties you want and then propagate them yourself using whichever methods are most appropriate, so building up the numbers over two or three years.

■ **Lift and divide overgrown clumps of perennials.** Older clumps are easily spotted, as all the young, vigorous growth is towards the outside of the clump and the centre is bare. Dividing can be done from now through until spring as long as soil conditions allow. If the soil is so wet that it sticks to your boots then keep off it; likewise later on if it is frozen. Late-flowering perennials like asters (Michaelmas daisies) are best left until the spring before being divided.

Lift the clumps and separate larger ones with two forks pushed into the centre of the clump back to back, pushing the handles apart to separate the roots. Smaller pieces can be separated out by hand. Replant the new pieces after revitalizing the soil with organic matter. Water in well after planting.

■ **Dahlia tubers** will have to be lifted and stored now. Cut the plants from their supports and cut the stems back to about 10cm (4in) from ground level. Label each plant before you lift it and forget which variety it is. Use a garden fork to dig carefully around the plant so as not to damage the tubers underground. Shake off as much of the old soil as you can and then use a hose to rinse off the tubers to get rid of the rest.

The stems of dahlias are hollow and if moisture collects at the base of the stems while the tubers are in store it will cause them to rot. So the tubers and stems must be turned upside down and left like this for a couple of weeks in a cool, dry place so that any moisture is allowed to drain from the stems.

After that, box up the tubers in peat-free compost, making sure the crowns of the tubers (the point where the stems meet the tubers) are not buried in compost. Small embryo buds are located here and if they are buried in compost they may rot off. You can cover the surface of the compost with something loose and dry, such as bark chippings, as an extra

Lifting and storing dahlias

1 Cut down all of the top growth from the plants (here blackened by an early frost). Lift the tubers and shake or rinse off all soil.

2 Stand them upside-down in wooden trays in a cool, dry place so that they dry off thoroughly.

3 Store them for winter in boxes of dry, peat-free compost. To save space, they can be packed more tightly. Make sure the stem is above the surface and space out in spring.

precaution. Keep them in a cool frost-free place over winter. They can be started back into growth in the spring and will provide cuttings for you to increase your stock before they are planted out.

Alpines

■ **Clear leaves from around alpines.** Leaves collecting in among alpines will encourage rots and other diseases to affect the plants. Pick out leaves from around the plants at regular intervals during the autumn. Plants that are particularly susceptible to rotting are those with grey, woolly foliage, but it's best to keep all plants clear of leaves. A layer of leaves on plants will also exclude any light, making the plants turn yellow and eventually killing them. Don't let leaves lie on top of any plants for any length of time.

■ **Protect alpines from wet.** This is the time of year when alpines will appreciate protection from the wet weather. It's not the cold alpine plants mind but the damp. This is why some alpines are grown in alpine houses, where there is no heat in the winter and plenty of ventilation. Proper alpine houses have extra ventilators fitted to keep a good through-flow of air at all times, but an ordinary unheated greenhouse, or even a cold frame, will make a perfectly good home for alpines.

Of course not all alpines have to be grown in an alpine house and those growing outside can be protected from the rain quite easily by using a cloche, with the ends left open for ventilation, or a piece of glass or rigid clear plastic supported on bricks. Then weight the sheet down with extra bricks to prevent it being lifted off by winds. If you have a raised alpine bed, then with a little improvisation you can make a mini-greenhouse with open sides to protect the plants through the winter.

BULBS

■ **Plant tulip bulbs** towards the end of this month and next month, though they can be planted as late as mid-December. Tulips are more prone to disease than other bulbs and are planted later. The depth of planting is about twice to three times their own depth. On heavy clay soils, put a layer of grit in the hole and sit the bulbs on this.

■ **Lift and store tender summer-flowering bulbs.** In sheltered gardens and warm regions, slightly tender bulbs like galtonias may survive *in situ*, but in cold areas bulbs such as these and eucomis, and certainly tigridias, should be lifted, dried, and stored in pots or boxes of dry sand. Lift, clean up, and dry the bulbs just as you would spring-flowering bulbs.

■ **Finish planting all spring-flowering bulbs now.** The bulbs will start to send out roots. Planting them late just means they will flower that bit later than others – perhaps no bad thing to give continuity.

■ **Examine bulbs being forced** in darkness to see if any top growth is being made. If so, bring them into the light in a cool place. But first knock them out of their containers to see the root system. If there aren't many roots put them back in the dark for a few more weeks.

■ **Plant lily bulbs** this and next month. Plant them in well-prepared soil in sun or partial shade. If your soil is heavy, sit the bulbs on a layer of coarse grit to aid drainage. Plant the bulbs at two and a half times their own depth. Lilies can also be planted in pots, in multi-purpose compost and on a layer of grit, from now until late winter. Leave the pots outside to allow a good root system to form. When new growth has been made, take some pots inside and the lilies will flower early. After flowering these bulbs can be planted out.

ANNUALS AND BEDDING

■ **Finish lifting any tender perennials** in order to protect them from frost. If you don't have anywhere suitable to keep them, cuttings can still be taken. Those taken earlier than this may need potting up now, but don't pot up any cuttings you take now until the spring.

■ **Half-hardy fuchsias** need a rest period over winter and should be potted up, if necessary, and taken under cover, either storing them with other tender perennials or keeping them on benches in gently heated glasshouses or cool rooms. The leaves will still drop off now, but these plants will start into growth and produce the earliest shoots for cuttings.

The plants should be kept cool and on the dry side, but don't let them dry out completely. Just give them enough water from time to time to keep them alive. It's difficult to say how often plants kept over winter should be watered, as it depends on how warm the plants are kept. It really is a matter of experience and practice.

■ **Finish planting spring bedding plants** this month. It is important to get this job done, especially if you have a heavy clay soil, before the soil cools down too much. In some parts of the country summer-bedding plants may still be flowering, but you will have to take the bull by the horns and get them out if you want to get spring bedding in.

On light, sandy soils you may get away with planting spring bedding later, as these soils warm up much quicker in the spring. If planting late, add a little fertilizer that is high in phosphates such as bonemeal, seaweed meal, or hop manure to the soil rather than a general feed. This encourages root growth, which is what we are aiming for at this time of year. Soft growth made now will be more easily damaged during winter.

Sowing hardy annuals

1 Use a bamboo cane to create some straight drills in which to sow the seed – press the cane lightly into the soil.

2 Transfer a little seed to the palm of your hand and gently tap it with your finger to trickle the seed into the drill.

3 Water well, using a watering can with a fine rose. A sprinkling is less likely to disturb the seed.

■ **Sow overwintering hardy annuals** outside if this was not done last month. If you act fast, there is still time to do this in milder parts of the country.

CONTAINERS

■ **Continue planting containers** with spring-bedding plants and bulbs in order to achieve a worthwhile display in the spring. The sooner that this job is completed, the sooner the plants will establish before the winter sets in.

■ **Don't forget perennials and shrubs for winter colour.** You don't have to limit your choice of plants for containers to bedding plants. Many evergreen shrubs will provide colour and interest all the year round. Variegated shrubs are particularly good value and will brighten up a dull or bare corner at any time of the year. There are many to choose from, but look out for *Euonymus japonicus* 'Marieke' and 'Aureopictus'.

There are also varieties of variegated box and dwarf conifers in a wide variety of shapes and colours.

Other plants to brighten up containers throughout the winter include hardy cyclamen and heathers, which also have a wide range of foliage hues. Winter-flowering pansies will give a bright, cheerful display from now right into the early summer.

Autumn colour Heather makes a colourful display, whether in a bed or a container.

LAWNS

■ **Reduce the frequency of mowing now.** Established lawns should be mown less frequently now as growth slows right down. In addition to this, raise the height of the cutting blades in the mower. Grass that is cut too short over the winter will not stand up to the poorer weather conditions and will be more likely to become infested with moss and weeds, since it is weaker.

■ **Rake out thatch, aerate, and top-dress lawns.** This autumn overhaul of your lawn will make a great difference to the grass after a summer of hard use. If you have larger lawns to deal with, powered machines can easily be bought or hired to help with all of these jobs.

■ **Reseed any bare or worn patches.**

New lawns

■ **Make new lawns.** Turf can be laid at almost any time of the year as long as the soil is not frozen or waterlogged. Be sure to keep the new turves well watered until you get the chance to lay them.

There is still time to sow grass seed if it is done early enough in the month. The soil is still reasonably warm and moist and germination should be fairly quick. If you have doubts about the weather and the area sown is not too big, cover it up with polythene; this will encourage even more rapid germination. Remove the polythene as soon as you spot the first seedlings coming through.

■ **New lawns made earlier** may need cutting, but again, don't cut them too short. About 2.5cm (1in) is the closest to cut newly sown lawns and newly laid turf for the last cut before winter.

VEGETABLES AND HERBS

■ **Cut down the tops of Jerusalem artichokes.** It is the swollen roots, rather like potatoes, of these plants that are eaten. The tops can grow to over 2m (6ft), making this an excellent plant to use for screening ugly structures such as the shed or the compost heap in summer; occasionally they produce quite attractive yellow flowers. But by this time of year, the plants will be dying back and just look a mess. Cut them down to ground level. Shred the old stems and use them for mulching borders, or mix them in with other garden compost. Although it makes a good screen, Jerusalem artichokes can be invasive, so keep a close check on them and harvest the swollen roots regularly. As with potatoes, even the smallest tuber left in the ground will regrow.

■ **Cut down asparagus fern** now that it has turned yellow, if you didn't do it last month. After cutting down the foliage, top-dress over the crowns with garden compost or well-rotted farmyard manure.

■ **Empty compost bins** of well-rotted compost and use it for mulching and digging in to improve the soil. Well-made garden compost will do the soil a power of good and using it up will free the compost bin for more material. If you haven't got much compost, it is better to give adequate amounts to a smaller area, rather than trying to spread it too thinly over all of the ground. With a good crop-rotation system going you should plan to incorporate organic matter into at least a third of the vegetable garden each year.

■ **As soon as ground is cleared,** dig it over if necessary. The sooner soil cultivation in the vegetable garden can be done the better. Heavy clay soils, in particular, will benefit from being broken up and exposed to winter weather conditions for as long as possible. Rain, snow, and frost all play a vital part in breaking down soil particles, enabling us to make good seed and planting beds in the spring. Dig for short periods at a time and do other jobs in between to prevent damage to your back.

The easiest way to dig a large area of the vegetable garden is to take out a trench at one end of the plot and barrow the soil to the other end. Put organic matter into the bottom of the trench. Then take out the next trench with your spade and throw the soil forward into the first one, covering the organic matter. Carry this out over the whole area and fill in the last trench with the soil taken out at the start of the process.

■ **Dig in green manure crops** sown earlier in the autumn. Green manure crops are a good substitute for well-rotted garden compost or farmyard manure if you cannot get a good supply of organic matter. They will condition the soil and some, like clover and field beans, also "fix" nitrogen for use by the plants that follow.

To dig them in, take out a trench and skim the surface of the neighbouring soil, scraping the tops of the plants into the bottom of the trench. Throw the soil containing the roots forward into this first trench to cover them, so that you make the next trench in the process. Repeat until the job's done. You can also sow green manures now to overwinter.

■ **Cover some ground with polythene** to keep the worst of the rain off. Hold the polythene in place with bricks or long pieces of wood. It is surprising just how much water will be kept off the land by covering it and how early you can start planting and sowing by replacing the polythene sheeting with cloches in late winter and early spring.

Harvesting and storing

■ **Pick the last of the runner beans.** No matter how quickly you pick runner beans there comes a point when they seem never-ending. If they are not too big they can be frozen; overgrown pods can be composted as they will be old and stringy. If you want to collect your own seed, leave some pods on the old plants until they turn brown. Otherwise, cut the plants from their supports and compost them, but leave the roots in the ground. Runner beans, like broad beans and peas, return valuable nitrogen to the soil. In the crop-rotation system, beans can be followed by leafy crops such as brassicas, which have a high demand for nitrogen, and less nitrogen will have to be applied to the soil in the form of synthetic feeds.

■ **Finish lifting maincrop potatoes.** Leave them on the surface of the soil for a couple of hours to dry out. If it is a damp day, put them in a cold frame or a greenhouse to dry. They must be dry before you put them into storage. Store only undamaged potatoes, using those that are damaged first. Store them in paper or hessian sacks, ensuring no light gets to them, as this will turn them green and poisonous.

Potatoes Be careful how you dig; above-ground stems give no indication of how many you'll find.

■ **Continue lifting carrots and beetroot** for storing and only store sound produce. Any that is damaged should be used first and not stored. Store these crops in boxes in layers separated with moist sand or old potting compost. Store all root crops in a cool, dark, and frost-free place. Check through at regular intervals during winter. If any show signs of rotting discard them.

■ **Make a clamp to store root vegetables.** This is an old method of storing root crops; ideal if you haven't got much room indoors. You will have to get some straw. Put a thick layer on the ground and start laying the dry roots on it. Build up the crops in a cone shape, tapering towards the top. Next put a layer of straw around the mound of roots, building it up to the top and making sure it goes right over the top. Next start covering the straw with soil, digging it from around the mound and again building it up to the top until the entire mound is covered, except at the very tip. Leave some straw poking out, to let air in.

Sowing and planting outdoors

■ **Plant out spring cabbages** if this was not done last month. This is the latest month for planting spring cabbages, and the sooner the better.

■ **Finish planting autumn onion sets.** Plant them 8cm (3in) apart in well-prepared soil. Japanese onion sets can also be planted, a little later than seeds are sown, in October or November. Japanese onions from both sets and seeds should be ready to harvest in June or July the following year, giving an early harvest before other onions are ready.

■ **Plant garlic** if you didn't do it last month. If the soil is too wet to plant outside then grow the cloves in modules and plant out in late winter or early spring.

Put one clove in each cell, with the tip of each clove just sticking out of the compost. They don't need any warmth, so keep them in a well-ventilated cold frame or outside under the shelter of a wall, just to keep the heaviest of the rain off them.

Planting garlic

1 Break up the head to separate the individual cloves.

2 Make holes with a dibber – roughly twice the depth of the cloves and 18cm (7in) apart.

3 Plant cloves individually, pointed end uppermost.

■ **Sow broad beans outside** and cover with cloches in colder parts of the country. Take out a shallow trench, about 5cm (2in) deep, with a spade, or a draw or onion hoe. The seeds are quite large and can be spaced at intervals of 15cm (6in). Cover with soil and tamp it down with the back of a rake. Cover with a cloche or fleece, principally to stop mice digging them up.

Looking after crops

■ **Earth up celery** for the last time, if not done last month. Leave a tuft of foliage at the top uncovered. If hard frost is forecast keep some straw or fleece handy to cover the plants. Straw can be held in place with chicken wire or plastic netting pegged into the ground; fleece is easily kept in place with a few bricks. Start harvesting the celery as and when necessary.

■ **Remove yellowing leaves from Brussels sprouts** and other winter brassicas such as cabbages, cauliflowers, and broccoli. Old yellowing leaves are of no use to the plants; they will just encourage diseases such as grey mould (*Botrytis*) to invade, reducing the overall crop yield.

Planning ahead

■ **Prepare a bed for planting asparagus** in the spring. Asparagus likes well-prepared soil enriched with plenty of organic matter, but drainage must be good. Drainage can be improved permanently, especially on heavy soils, by incorporating pea shingle when digging in the organic matter. This will raise the level of the bed, but this is no bad thing as a raised bed will also help to improve drainage. If your soil is very heavy clay, which asparagus really doesn't thrive on, there is still a way of growing it; in high raised beds with strong sides to retain the soil. Make sturdy wooden surrounds with planks and posts, about 60cm (2ft) deep and as long and

wide as you want, but 1.2m x 1.2m (4 x 4ft) is a good size. Make up a compost mix to fill the beds, ideally of equal parts garden compost and grit; if you don't have enough compost, buy in bagged products.

Beat the seasons

■ **Force chicory.** Chicory, such as Witloof, which has been growing through the summer, can be lifted in batches and forced for a succession of pointed, tight-leaved "chicons". The roots can be potted up in old potting compost. Cover the pot with another upturned pot, ensuring you cover drainage holes. To get the best chicons, place the pots in a minimum temperature of 10°C (50°F).

■ **Force seakale.** This perennial can be forced from now until January. Cut the plants down, cut off yellowing leaves and clear debris from the base. In cold areas put a 10cm (4in) layer of straw over the crowns as insulation. Cover the plants with a bucket or large pot, covering drainage holes to exclude light. The stems will be ready to harvest in about three months.

Herbs

■ **Lift parsley and mint** for winter use. A few pots of herbs will provide you with valuable additions to winter meals. Dig up a few roots of each and remove yellowing leaves. Pot each piece in small pots of compost, water them in, and stand on a bright kitchen windowsill. You will then have fresh herbs at your fingertips all through the winter.

■ **Basil outdoors will not survive now** and growing it outside after September is usually difficult, if not impossible. If grown in pots, you could bring it into a greenhouse or conservatory – or, harvest all the leaves and freeze in ice-cube trays topped up with water.

FRUIT
Picking and storing
■ **Finish picking maincrop apples.** Varieties like 'Spartan' and 'Sunset' and the cookers will be ready for harvesting around now. Pick them when they are ripe and only store sound fruit. Damaged fruit can be used straight after picking, if it is ripe. If fruits are ripe they should part from the tree easily. If they don't, leave them for a little longer. If stored properly they will last most of the winter. Apples can be eaten straight from store, but pears may need a few days in a warm room to ripen fully.

Looking after crops
■ **Clean up strawberry beds.** Remove yellowing foliage and old runners that were overlooked and generally weed the area to tidy up and lessen the risk of pest and disease problems next year. Older plants showing signs of virus infection should be taken out and put in the bin. New plants can be bought in and planted in the spring. Young plants put in during the spring should not be cropped in the first summer as they need time to build up a crown to produce good crops in subsequent years.

■ **Keep newly planted strawberries well watered.** Planting strawberries now enables them to get established before winter so that plants develop well, but if they go short of water this will not happen and they will not fruit well next year.

■ **Spray peaches and nectarines** against peach leaf curl. Trees that were sprayed with copper fungicide earlier in the year to prevent peach leaf curl need another application now, just as the leaves begin to fall. When the leaves have fallen, covering the trees with polythene supported on a wooden framework will also reduce the incidence of peach leaf curl disease, as its spores need water to infect.

Pruning blackberries Untie all the old fruited canes and cut them to the ground.

Pruning and training
■ **Blackberries and hybrid berry fruits** should be pruned after the fruit has been harvested. Cut out all the old fruited canes and tie in the new ones. It is easier to cope with training these fruits if the new canes are tied to one side of the support, then the canes that will grow next year and fruit the following one can be trained to the other side.

■ **Prune blackcurrants.** These can be pruned now, but better to wait until winter.

Planning ahead
■ **Order new fruit trees.** This is a good time to choose new fruit trees. There will be a selection of varieties available, on different rootstocks. This means that the top part of the tree that bears the fruit has been grafted at an early stage onto the roots of a different tree. The chosen rootstock will affect the vigour, and thus the eventual size, of your fruit tree, and also the age at which it bears fruit. Various rootstocks are available and each one gives a different size of tree.

■ **Prepare the ground for new fruit trees.** It's a good idea to do this in advance. If you're planting several trees, dig over the whole area, incorporating plenty of organic matter. If just one or two trees are being planted, prepare generously sized individual holes. Break up the bottom of the hole to loosen the subsoil, without bringing any subsoil to the surface. Put plenty of muck in the hole and work it into the bottom of it.

Propagation
■ **Take hardwood cuttings** of blackcurrants, red- and whitecurrants, and gooseberries. The preparation of the cuttings for all of these plants is the same. Take shoots around 30cm (12in) long, cutting just above a bud on the parent plant. Remove the top 5cm (2in) of softer growth at the tip of the cutting and trim the base just below a bud. Now dip the base in hormone rooting solution. Make a slit trench. If your soil is a heavy clay, trickle sharp sand into the bottom of the trench and then line out the cuttings. If the blackcurrants have shown any signs of reversion virus or big bud mite don't propagate from them.

The new plants will have rooted by next autumn, but you can leave them for another year before moving to their permanent positions, as they will not fruit when young.

Order new fruit trees Dwarf trees like these pear pyramids are perfect in small gardens.

UNDER COVER

■ **Thoroughly clean** the glasshouse or conservatory if you didn't do so last month.

■ **Continue ventilating** on warm days, but close the vents in mid-afternoon to conserve heat. It is important to keep air circulating indoors to keep diseases such as mildew and botrytis at bay, as they flourish in warm, moist, still conditions.

■ **Buy bubble polythene** to insulate the greenhouse or conservatory. You can do a lot to keep bills down by lining the structure with bubble polythene. Although it may cut down on some of the light getting in, it is well worth installing it for the warmth it keeps in. It can be taken down again in the spring.

■ **Take more care with watering** at this time of the year. With the shorter days and cooler temperatures, watering has to be done with much more care now. If diseases such as botrytis are not to thrive, it is better to get watering done as early as possible in the day, so that the place has a chance to dry out before nightfall. Watering in early morning is preferable. Try to avoid getting water on the plants' leaves too, as this can take time to dry out. Most plant growth will have slowed down now, so only water plants when you can see they really need it.

■ **Check plants over regularly** and remove any yellowing leaves and fading flowers. Don't leave these lying around as they will encourage diseases to set in and attack your cherished plants. A look around the greenhouse once a week is quite a pleasant job when the weather is bad outside. It also gives you an opportunity to spot pests that may be lurking and deal with them quickly and easily. It is surprising how many pests you can find overwintering in the warm conditions inside.

Raising plants for outdoors

■ **Sow sweet peas for next spring.** With the luxury of space in a greenhouse, you can sow sweet peas now, though a cool, light windowsill will accommodate a few pots too. Sow just as you would in spring, but sowing five or six seeds to a 12cm (5in) pot rather than using long tubes and the young plants can be potted up individually in spring.

Glasshouse and house plants

■ **Lift a few herbaceous perennials** for some early flowers inside. Naturally early-flowering plants like hellebores, doronicum, and pulmonarias can be potted up and they will flower even earlier. You can do this when dividing them. Pot them in pots containing John Innes or another soil-based compost and water them in. Stand them outside and bring them in from January onwards. They make unusual pot plants and can be planted out afterwards.

■ **Citrus fruit trees** and any other tender shrubs in pots, such as bay and oleander, which have been outside for the summer, should be brought in now. Keep them in cool but frost-free conditions, opening ventilators or a window whenever the weather is mild to give them some fresh

Citrus crop You can grow oranges in the greenhouse very successfully.

air. Feeding and watering will have to be done carefully, as citrus trees will be coming into flower. Some will already have fruits on them as well and these should ripen over the winter.

Crops under glass

■ **Clear out old tomato, aubergine, and pepper plants** and all their debris as they finish cropping. Any green tomatoes can be brought indoors to ripen on the windowsill, clearing the space so you can give the greenhouse a clean before winter.

■ **Grow radishes, mustard, and cress** for winter salads in growing bags used previously for tomatoes and other crops. Some lettuces (see below) will also do well. Give them a liquid feed regularly, as the previous plants will have used up the nutrients in the compost. It is a good way of making full use of these growing bags. And when these crops have finished, the compost can be used again, to improve the soil in the garden. Avoid adding the compost from tomato growing bags to beds where you will be growing potatoes or outdoor tomatoes next year, as diseases common to both may be passed on.

■ **Sow a few winter lettuces** in a cold greenhouse, or grow a few in pots on the kitchen windowsill. Sow the seeds in small pots or trays and place them in a propagator, maintaining a temperature of 16°C (61°F). The seeds will germinate in a few days, when they can be either potted up in small pots of peat-free compost, or planted in the border soil of a greenhouse or in used growing bags. Water the lettuces carefully as they are very prone to botrytis and rotting off. Always err on the cautious side when watering in the winter. The lettuces will be ready to harvest in early spring. Varieties to try are 'All the Year Round' and 'Winter Density'.

THE NOVEMBER GARDEN

November can be a damp, raw month. Flowers may be scarce in the garden, but there are many berries, evergreen foliage, and trees with decorative bark to add interest on the dullest of days. You can warm yourself up by tidying the garden and preparing for the winter ahead. It's also a good time to check your tools, catch up on greenhouse maintenance, and begin planning your spring display.

THINGS TO DO

Wash or discard any old pots and trays that you're not intending to reuse.

Clean out nesting boxes and put food out for the birds on a regular basis.

Check for hibernating creatures before lighting a bonfine.

Have the lawnmower serviced and check tools.

Keep off the lawn in frosty weather.

Install heaters in the greenhouse and insulate if necessary.

Press on with winter digging.

Plant bare-root trees, shrubs, and roses.

Protect all tender and newly planted shrubs from frost and wind, and the alpines from winter rain.

Insulate pots that will remain outside during winter.

Plant fruit trees and bushes, and winter-prune established plants.

Lift and divide rhubarb crowns.

Heel in a winter supply of home-grown leeks by the back door, ready to use.

LAST CHANCE

Lift and store your dahlias if not already done.

Start off amaryllis bulbs to flower for Christmas.

GET AHEAD

Order seed catalogues.

Begin winter-pruning deciduous trees and shrubs.

Renovate hedges, and prune glasshouse vines.

Vibrant autumnal shades Acers display a startling range of autumn foliage colours, which are guaranteed to brighten up your garden at this time of year.

LAST DAYS OF AUTUMN

Make the most of any late-autumn foliage colour in the garden this month. There is quite a bit of seasonal variation, so rich displays may go on and the weather may well stay good for a while. Take advantage of this by cracking on with winter-preparation tasks while there's still the chance.

By this month there is still some colour in the garden, especially from the asters – or Michaelmas daisies – if the weather has been reasonable. Nerines will also be in flower and if you are lucky there will still be a few roses to pick. You may also still have some late-autumn foliage colour. The main period for autumn colour is usually in October, but due to seasonal variations, the peak of the autumn display can vary by several weeks from year to year. So there may well be gardens to visit where you can still enjoy the richness of colourful foliage.

Where leaves have fallen, clear them up. A blanket of sodden leaves on lawns and around the bases of plants will do no good at all and wet leaves on paths and steps are a real safety hazard. Fallen leaves will rot down into a really good soil conditioner – leafmould – in time, so heap them up or make a chicken-wire container for them to stop them blowing about. If you don't have enough leaves to make a good pile, then either put them on the compost or stuff them into a plastic rubbish bag with some holes pierced in it. If you choose the latter option, then remember that the leaves must be wet to rot down, so either bag them on a damp day or pour in some water.

Prickly, green fruits The horse chestnut splits to reveal shiny, brown seeds, known as "conkers"; a familiar sight in large gardens and parks.

Make leafmould You don't need a compost bin or lots of space. Pierce plastic bags, fill them with wet leaves, and give them plenty of time to rot down.

Using the better days

Some of the more exposed northerly parts of the country may experience wintry spells now, while other more sheltered parts will often be quite mild right through the month. Snowfalls in November seem quite rare and any snow that does fall usually clears as quickly as it came down. There can often be beautiful days in November, but there's no doubt that it can sometimes be a dreary month weatherwise. Before the real winter weather sets it's good to take advantage of any good spells to crack on with the work so that you don't fall behind in the spring. Many people regard this as the end of the gardening season, but it is really the beginning. Work done now can save a lot of time and effort when spring comes around.

Revamp the veg plot

The earlier any winter digging is done the better, as this will allow rain, snow, and frost to break down the clods of soil, improving its structure and making it much easier to cultivate in the spring. One major project, which if done now will save you lots of work, not only next spring but in many years to come, is to convert your vegetable plot to the deep-bed system. This is a way of growing vegetables that acknowledges the "no-dig" approach to gardening, popular with many organic gardeners. The theory is that if you cultivate and improve the soil once, really thoroughly, you will encourage a population of soil-dwelling creatures, especially earthworms, that in subsequent years will take a mulch of organic matter down into the soil for you, aided and abetted by the ongoing processes of planting and harvesting. So there's no need for digging and turning to interfere with the soil's structure and, because beds are made small, there's never a need to tread on the soil and compact it. You'll have to sacrifice some of your plot to create more paths from which you can work and weed, but on the other hand, you'll find that with this system you can plant much more closely, so it shouldn't affect yields.

You can make beds long and narrow, or create a checkerboard effect with small, square beds intersected by paths; a design that shows off the ornamental potential of many of the crops.

Weather watch

Some November days can be damp and raw, especially with low cloud cover. Frosts can be quite frequent at night, especially when it is calm and clear. Cold winds, especially those from the east, will make it feel much colder than it really is.

Autumn gales

Gales increase this month, now that we're in the middle of autumn. In England, most hit the south-west, with on average two days of gales being driven in from the Atlantic. Inland it's generally calmer, but eastern coastal areas can turn very cold when the wind comes from mainland Europe. However the worst gales are suffered on the west sides of Scotland and Ireland – up to five days in some parts.

Bright sunshine spells

It is surprising just how much direct sunshine there can be this month, although this will depend on cloud cover. Parts of the north and west can experience over 100 hours of direct sunshine, and the south and east as much as 150 hours. Days with clear, blue sky, bright sunshine, and just a hint of a chill in a gentle breeze are a pure delight in autumn.

High rainfall

Rainfall is on the increase and November can be a soggy month. The wettest parts of the country are the Highlands of Scotland and Ireland. Here rainfall can be as much as 267mm, compared to eastern parts of England, where it can be as little as 47mm. Get on with soil cultivation as soon as the weather permits and cover some ground with polythene sheeting to protect it from the wet.

Some snow

Snow is definitely on the agenda now in north-eastern parts. Braemar in Aberdeenshire can expect, on average, five days of snow on the ground. Other parts of the country may see some snow, but it is rare and can range from none at all in the south to 1.7 days in the central belt of Scotland.

A welcome display *Viburnum* x *bodnantense* 'Charles Lamont' sports a welcome display of bright-pink blossoms from as early as late autumn into the spring.

Routine tasks

Tidying borders by clearing away old stems and dead foliage and lightly forking over the ground around plants will transform the appearance of the garden, making it neat for the rest of the winter. Leave a few plants like

Sedum spectabile and ornamental grasses such as *Carex pendula* and miscanthus uncut, as frost on these plants looks extremely decorative.

During all this clearing up you will inevitably generate a lot of material, most of which can be composted, but some of the woody and semi-woody material will take a long time to rot down. The usual way to get rid of this woody material is to have a bonfire, but although a fire can be cheery and satisfying, it's a terrible waste of material that can be recycled in the garden. Therefore, if you can, invest in a garden shredder. There are many different makes available, powered by petrol or electricity. These machines will shred up all woody material into fine pieces that can then be used as a mulch – or they can be mixed with other composted material to make the best compost you'll ever have. And, of course, these machines can also be hired if you don't want to buy one.

Planting and transplanting

November is a good time to plant new trees, shrubs, and roses. And if you have been walking around the garden with your notebook in hand earlier in the year, making notes of any changes to be made, then this is a good month to move plants, because there is still some warmth in the soil left from the summer. Larger plants are best moved first, with as much soil around the roots as possible. And if they are large trees or shrubs, remember to stake them again if you garden in an exposed place. Water plants well after moving them and mulch with a thick layer of organic matter; remember to keep watering them well throughout the next season.

Stars among the sleepers

This is the month when most plants become dormant and everything, as far as plant growth goes, shuts down for the winter; but there are some plants that begin to flower around now and carry their blooms throughout the winter months. Plants such as *Viburnum* x *bodnantense* will produce exquisite pink flowers from as early as October right through the season. The flowers borne by this shrub are also powerfully and sweetly scented, and will fill the air around them with fragrance even on the coldest and dullest November days. The winter-flowering autumn

***Miscanthus sinensis* 'Graziella'** This perennial grass, makes a delightful autumnal display, with its arching leaves and graceful spikelets.

cherry, *Prunus* x *subhirtella* 'Autumnalis', produces its white blossom intermittently throughout the winter. For a change in colour try the pink-flowering variety, 'Autumnalis Rosea'.

Ordering early

When the weather makes it difficult to do any work outside, having a look through seed catalogues is not just a pleasurable occupation for a dank autumn day. If you get your seed order in early, you are less likely to be disappointed, because the seed companies often quickly run out of popular lines of seeds. This applies especially to any plants highlighted at flower shows, on TV programmes, and in the gardening magazines earlier in the year. And you'll get your seeds earlier, too, and can therefore get a head start in the spring.

Vitis coignetiae ♀
Clinging, very vigorous climber; at its finest in autumn (*see p.335*)

Cimicifuga simplex 'White Pearl'
Autumn-flowering herbaceous perennial (*see p.284*)

Libertia ixioides
Slightly tender perennial with brown-edged, white flowers (*see p.307*)

Pyracantha 'Golden Charmer' ♀
Spiny shrub ideal for wall training (*see p.321*)

Euonymus alatus ♀
Dense, bushy deciduous shrub with bright fruits and leaves (*see p.296*)

Lonicera fragrantissima
Shrubby honeysuckle with richly scented flowers (*see p.308*)

Chrysanthemum 'Glowing Lynn'
Hardy perennial; can be left in the garden all winter (*see p.284*)

Chelone obliqua
Herbaceous perennial that enjoys heavy, damp soil (*see p.283*)

Clematis GOLDEN TIARA
One of the last clematis of the year to flower (*see p.287*)

Rosa moyesii
Shrub rose, with distinctive bullet-shaped hips (*see p.326*)

Cortaderia selloana 'Sunningdale Silver' ♀
Pampas grass; an old favourite back in vogue (*see p.288*)

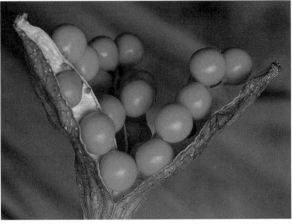

Iris foetidissima ♀
The stinking iris, with insignificant flowers but vivid fruits (*see p.804*)

WHAT TO DO IN NOVEMBER

AROUND THE GARDEN

There will be few pests around now, but it is best to be on your guard as some will be hiding in corners. The best way to avoid problems is to practise good hygiene and this includes keeping sheds and equipment clean and tidy as well as the borders. Any dirty pots and seed trays should be thrown out or recycled, or washed in a weak solution of garden disinfectant and stored for the winter. Clean the ends of stakes and canes before storing as pests often lurk there.

Clean out bird boxes of old nesting material; this will encourage birds to nest in them again next year. Do this as soon as possible, as birds will soon be looking for winter roosts. If they are already familiar with a box by spring, they are more likely to select it as a nesting site.

Protect young plants from rabbits. Rabbits can do an enormous amount of damage, but a few simple precautions will prevent some of it. Surrounding young plants with chicken wire will give them a little protection.

Have a bird box Attracting birds into the garden is an important way to help replace disappearing countryside habitats.

Tree trunks can be surrounded similarly, or there are special rabbit guards that wrap directly around the trunks to stop rabbits eating the bark. If you can afford it, putting chicken wire around the perimeter of the garden, sinking it at least 15cm (6in) into the ground, is the best deterrent of all. Bend another few inches at the base of the netting in the trench outwards, to prevent the rabbits from digging down and then underneath.

Continue to gather up fallen leaves. Use a rake, though the job can be made much easier by using a vacuum for awkward corners. You can either buy one from the garden centre or hire one from your local hire shop. There are both electric and petrol-driven models available. Some have a blowing facility so that leaves can be easily blown out from around the bases of plants.

Continue sowing green manure crops on bare ground, especially in the vegetable garden. Winter rye can be sown well into November. These crops can be dug in during the spring and they will return valuable organic matter to the soil, improving the soil structure and its organic content.

Cold frames are endlessly useful, but they can also be insulated for warmth and even heated, either with small heaters or electric-heating cables on the base and around the sides on the inside. However, to install any electrical wiring, especially outdoors, call in a qualified electrician to do the job.

Bubble polythene can be used to insulate the top of the frame and polystyrene slabs cut to size for the sides. Insulation alone will help to keep out several degrees of frost, enabling some tender plants to be overwintered there if space in the greenhouse or conservatory is limited. More protection can be given on very cold nights by covering the cold frame with a piece of old carpet or another sheet of polystyrene held in place with bricks.

TREES AND SHRUBS

■ **Protect tender and newly planted trees and shrubs** from frosts and cold winds. Bitter winds damage foliage by dehydrating it and strong winds in freezing temperatures can cause more harm to plants than a severe frost on its own. Use a windbreak made from netting supported by posts. Evergreen shrubs and hedging plants are more prone to wind damage than deciduous ones, so these are the more important ones to give protection to. Smaller shrubs and those that are newly planted can be protected from the frost by packing straw or bracken around them and holding it in place with netting. Polythene can also be used for temporary protection, but it must not touch the foliage of evergreen plants as any moisture condensing out on the polythene will freeze and damage the foliage. Support the polythene by nailing it onto a framework of canes or onto wooden battens.

■ **Check tree ties and stakes.** These should be checked regularly to see that the stakes are sound and that ties are not cutting into the trunks of the plants; if they are, they will eventually strangle the plant as the trunk expands outwards.

■ **Clear any snow off conifers** and other shrubs. Heavy snow lying on branches will

Staking trees These angled stakes give support low down, where it is needed, and can be inserted without damaging the root ball of container-grown plants.

weigh them down, spoiling the shape of the plants. Although it looks very pretty, shake the snow off the plants as soon as you can to avoid branches being broken under the weight of snow. It is surprising just how heavy a layer of snow can be.

Planting

■ **At this time of year** bare-root stock of most deciduous trees and shrubs will become available and can be planted throughout the dormant season (that is, from now until at the latest, March), whenever soil conditions allow. They are cheaper than container-grown plants, but do take a look at the root systems before you buy, to ensure that they have been lifted with care and are not dried up. Make sure they are well wrapped before transporting them and plant as soon as possible. If the plants arrive by post, phone the supplier straight away if the plants do not seem satisfactory.

To plant (see right), prepare the ground well. Dig a hole large enough to take the root system without cramping the roots. Put a stake in first for trees and tall shrubs, on the windward side so that the plant is blown away from the stake (this prevents rubbing). Then plant the tree or shrub to the same depth as it was planted before at the nursery (you can see this easily – the darker part of the stem near the roots), fill in the hole and firm in gently with your boot.

Make sure all newly planted trees and shrubs are well staked and tied. The stake should come at most about one-third of the way up the trunk and often even shorter stakes are recommended. The only exception is when staking top-grafted standards such as dwarf, weeping trees, when the stake should reach the graft point. But for all other trees, a low stake allows the top of the tree to flex in the wind, strengthening the trunk. Make sure

Planting bare-root roses

1 Dig a generous hole so as not to cramp the root system. Incorporate organic matter into the hole and add a small handful of bonemeal.

2 Place the rose in the hole with the roots well spread out. Lay a cane across the hole to check that the graft union will be below soil level.

3 Fill in the hole by gradually working soil in around the roots with your hands and pressing down firmly. Lightly tread the soil and water well.

the tree is secured to the stake using a tree tie. Check as the tree grows and loosen ties as the trunk expands.

Container-grown trees and shrubs can also be planted all through the year. The soil will require the same thorough preparation as for bare-root trees and shrubs. If container-grown plants look a little pot-bound it is a good idea to tease out some roots, otherwise they will continue to grow round in circles, forming a weak root system.

■ **Plant new roses.** Bare-root roses should be available from this month through to March. They are slightly cheaper than container-grown plants and they do establish better. For roses to give off their best thorough preparation of the soil is essential. Cultivate as large an area as you can or dig as large a hole as possible and work in plenty of organic matter.

Never allow the roots to dry out and if the roses have arrived by mail order and the roots are dry, put them in a bucket of water. Plant the rose deep enough so that the point at which it was grafted is about 5cm (2in) below ground level. Work soil in among the roots well and firm as you go. Mulch the surface with well-rotted garden compost or manure.

If you are planting new roses to replace old ones, you may have problems. New roses planted in soil that has grown roses for a number of years are prone to a disease known as "rose sickness". Take out as much of the old soil as possible and replace it with fresh soil from another part of the garden that has not grown roses.

Pruning and training
■ **Begin winter-pruning deciduous trees and shrubs.** Don't prune, however, if nothing needs doing, however satisfying a job it is hacking away at woody growth. Unnecessary pruning weakens growth and

the fewer wounds you make the better, as each is a potential entry point for disease. Ornamental cherries (*Prunus* species) are susceptible to the same disease, silver leaf, that is so dangerous to plum and cherry trees if pruned in winter and it may be wise to delay pruning of ornamental cherries until the summer.

However, on most deciduous trees, dead, diseased, and damaged wood should be removed now, as although the pruning will create wounds these are less risky than leaving the unhealthy wood on the plant. Any further cuts you make will probably be more cosmetic, but consider the effect before removing anything substantial – it's not only the effect of removing growth that you must envisage, but also the direction in which the new growth that will come from the point of pruning will grow.

Propagation
■ **Continue sowing seeds of berried shrubs and trees.**

■ **Hardwood cuttings taken last autumn** should have rooted by now and these can be lifted and planted in permanent positions. Hardwood cuttings are an easy way to propagate plants as they don't require special conditions, being happy outside unprotected. There is still plenty of time to take more hardwood cuttings.

Hedges
■ **Continue planting hedging plants.**

■ **Carry out any renovation of deciduous hedges.** From now until spring major renovation in the form of hard pruning can be carried out on deciduous hedges. However, you can leave evergreen hedges until spring.

CLIMBERS
■ **Tie in long, whippy shoots** of climbers and wall shrubs to prevent them from being blown about and possibly damaged during any bad weather. If there doesn't seem to be a suitable gap in the framework to secure the shoot to, try pruning it back to five or six buds.

■ **Continue planting** new climbers in the same way as for other container-grown woody plants.

■ **Complete autumn planting** of hardy climbing plants so that they can establish their roots before the onset of winter. Plants that were propagated from semi-ripe or hardwood cuttings earlier in the year can also be planted out now, if big enough. It is worth preparing the planting position well before you start.

Mix well-rotted organic matter with the soil that you have removed to make the hole. Water the plant thoroughly before you remove the plant from the pot.

Add a good dusting of bonemeal and plant the climber so that the top of the root ball comes level with the surface of the soil and firm it in well (use a stake to assess depth). Water well after you have completed planting and apply a mulch with a 5–8cm (2–3in) layer of organic matter.

Protecting slightly tender plants Blanket them with a thick mulch.

PERENNIALS

■ **Pot up some lily-of-the-valley rhizomes** to force them into flower early. A cool, frost-free greenhouse or conservatory will allow the plants to grow at their own pace, but if you want to hurry them on a bit it's a good idea to give them warmer conditions. The plants can be put back in the garden after flowering and will flower again the following year.

■ **Protect kniphofias (red-hot pokers)** from frost. In colder parts of the country kniphofias may not be reliably hardy, especially when young, but they can easily be given some protection. Gather up the foliage and tie it together quite firmly. This will protect the crown of the plant, so if the foliage is damaged by hard frosts the crown should be unaffected.

Protect other slightly tender herbaceous plants like penstemons too. Bracken or straw placed over the plants and held in place with netting, or a layer of a dry, loose mulch such as leafmould or bark chippings, will give a good degree of protection from hard frosts. Check the plants from time to time through the winter to ensure no diseases have set in.

■ **Clear leaves that have accumulated** on top of clumps of perennials. If the leaves are left there for any length of time the plants will eventually suffer through lack of light and the dark, moist conditions will attract slugs and snails. Don't burn the fallen leaves; you can either add them to the compost heap or make a separate leaf heap to make leafmould.

■ **Take root cuttings** of perennials from now until late winter.

■ **If dahlias have not yet been lifted** do so when the foliage has been blackened by frost. Dry and pack them into boxes and fill in with old potting compost, leaving the crown uncovered and keep them in a frost-free place. Cuttings can be taken from the tubers in the spring.

■ **Continue lifting and dividing** herbaceous perennials as the weather and soil conditions allow. The earlier this is done in the month the better, as the newly divided plants will have time to settle in before the harsher winter weather.

■ **The routine job of cutting down old growth** can continue, but if you live in colder parts it may be better to leave some of the old growths on now so that they can provide protection for the plants during severe weather. Some of the more attractive or architectural dead stems can look quite stunning when covered with frost or snow.

■ *Helleborus niger*, the Christmas rose, rarely actually flowers in time for Christmas, but it can be encouraged to flower a little earlier if you cover it with a cloche. Covering it will also help prevent the flowers being splashed with soil in heavy winter rain. Also, you could try lifting one or two plants and potting them up and forcing them in gentle heat, or just in a cold greenhouse. Then the full beauty

Helleborus niger

Cutting back bamboo Use long-handled loppers to do a really efficient job.

of the flowers can be enjoyed without having to go out in the cold.

■ **Cut back ornamental grasses** and bamboos. Those that are not ornamental in winter are best cut back now as they can often look messy in winter. Some bamboos, if their canes are thick enough, can be cut, cleaned up, and stored and used for supporting plants next season. You can thin out ornamental canes on bamboos, so that congested clumps are opened up and the canes displayed to their best advantage.

Alpines

■ **Continue to remove fallen leaves** from around alpines. If the leaves are left they will keep light off the plants and encourage rotting, slugs, and snails. At the same time clear any weeds growing in between the plants and give the rock garden a general tidy-up before winter.

■ **Cover vulnerable alpines** to protect the crowns of the plants from the rain, or take alpines in pots under cover. Plants that are most susceptible to winter wet are those with grey, woolly leaves, such as erinus, lewisias, and edelweiss.

BULBS

■ **Continue planting lilies** until the spring.

■ **Remember to examine bulbs** that are being forced for early flowering. When they have made about 2.5cm (1in) of growth, move them into a cool greenhouse or a cold frame. If you have a cool windowsill, this would also serve as an ideal spot. When hyacinths and narcissi such as 'Paper White' and 'Soleil d'Or' begin to form flower buds, bring them into warmer conditions so that they flower in time for Christmas.

■ **Continue to check** all stored bulbs, corms, and tubers. Any that are showing signs of rotting should be thrown away. If only small parts of the bulb, corm, or tuber are affected you may get away with cutting out the infected part with a sharp knife and dusting the cut surface with flowers of sulphur.

   However, it's important to keep them separate from the others in store, just in case any infection is spread.

■ **Protect slightly tender bulbs** left in the ground, such as nerines and agapanthus, with a thick mulch of garden compost. If possible grow them in a sheltered part of the garden, at the base of a south-facing wall or fence.

■ **If you want hippeastrums** (amaryllis) in flower at Christmas, start them into growth at the beginning of the month. Pot up and water the bulbs and put in a warm place to get them going quickly. Some people start them off in an airing cupboard, but check them regularly if you do this as they grow so rapidly that they may be a couple of feet tall before you know it. Over a radiator (a place most house plants hate) is also ideal.

■ **Plant tulips this month.** By planting tulips late, after the other spring-flowering bulbs are in, there is a better chance of preventing the bulbs being infected with the fungal disease, tulip fire. Try to get them in before the end of the month. Tulips flower better in a sunny situation and if your soil is heavy clay, lighten it by digging in coarse grit. You can, of course, grow tulips in pots as well as other spring-flowering bulbs. One advantage of growing them in pots is that they can be planted, pot and all, in any part of the garden lacking colour in the spring and then are easily lifted out again when the flowers are over. Plant tulips in borders and pots just as you would other bulbs, at two to three times their own depth. Plant the bulbs on a layer of coarse grit to prevent them rotting off. It is always better to plant tulips a little more deeply than too near the surface.

Overwintering dahlia tubers Label up individual tubers with tags.

Tulipa **'Dreamboat'**

Tulipa **'Spring Green'**

Tulipa **'Giuseppe Verdi'**

Tulipa **'Dreaming Maid'**

ANNUALS AND BEDDING

■ **Protect seedlings of hardy annuals**
Keep an eye on the weather forecast and if it turns very cold, protect those hardy annuals sown earlier in the autumn. Cover them with cloches, or have some horticultural fleece handy to throw over the plants. It would be rare indeed for these plants to be killed by frost, but it does no harm to have some protection to hand for really severe weather.

■ **Tuberous begonias** that were bedded out for the summer should be lifted and brought inside before the frost gets at them. Allow them to dry out under a greenhouse bench or other frost-free place. Once the old stems have parted from the tubers, clean these up and store them in boxes in a cool place.

■ **Finish planting spring bedding plants.**
If the planting of wallflowers, forget-me-nots, bellis, and sweet Williams has not been completed by now, get it done as soon as possible so that the plants have a little time to become established before the winter sets in.

Wispy protection Carefully hang lengths of horticultural fleece between stems to protect the plant from frost.

CONTAINERS

■ **Insulate pots that are too large to take indoors.** The roots of plants growing in containers outside tend to be more prone to suffering from frost damage than plants that are growing in the open ground and they need some protection from hard frosts. Insulate them by wrapping bubble polythene or hessian sacking securely around the pots.

Tie up the leaves of plants such as cordylines to protect the growing tip from excess winter wet, which will rot it, and wrap in fleece.

Containers can be moved together for mutual protection. Modern plastic or terracotta containers are generally frost-proof, but older terracotta pots may not be, so even if they are empty, wrap them or take them indoors for the cold winter months. Ensure that containers are lifted off the ground slightly to improve their drainage. There are decorative "feet" that you can buy from garden centres designed for this very purpose.

■ **Finish planting containers** with spring bedding plants.

Insulate pots Even if the plant is hardy, the root system exposed above ground may be vulnerable.

LAWNS

■ **Keep off the lawn during wet weather.**
If you have to walk over the lawn to reach borders when it is extremely wet, then put down some planks to step on, but ideally try to keep off the grass altogether. Don't walk on the lawn when it is frosted, either, otherwise you may leave marks.

■ **In dry weather, rake up fallen leaves** on the lawn. Don't just burn them or throw these away – instead, use them to make leafmould, which makes an excellent soil conditioner, mulch, and ingredient in potting composts.

■ **Send the lawn mower away for sharpening and servicing.** All machines do a far better job if they are maintained properly. Service agents are relatively quiet at this time of year because a lot of people leave it until the last moment in spring to have mowers serviced and this causes a rush.

Don't forget, though, to give the lawn an occasional light trim through the winter so that you can keep it looking neat. Just take the tops off and don't do it if the lawn is very wet or frozen.

New lawns

■ **Continue to dig over areas for new lawns** and to lay turf on prepared ground when the soil is not excessively wet or frozen. This month may be the last chance you have to lay turf in the current year, as the weather may turn bad next month. The one advantage of laying turf at this time of the year is that it won't have a chance to dry out. Always work from boards when you are laying turf so that you don't compact the soil in places and make the lawn uneven.

VEGETABLES AND HERBS

■ **Press on with winter digging** as the weather allows. The soil should not be so wet that it actually sticks to your boots when you walk on it. You can cover ground with polythene sheeting to keep off the worst of the rain. Pull it back on a fine day to dig and cover the soil again when you are finished.

■ **Check all stored crops** for signs of disease. It is better to do this regularly so that any rotting doesn't get a chance to spread. It's a good job to carry out when it is too wet to work outside.

Harvesting

■ **Lift parsnips.** Parsnips taste better when they have had a touch of frost on them, but they can be lifted and stored in the same way as carrots. Pack them in boxes of sand and they will keep through the winter. An alternative, if you haven't much room available for storing crops, is to heap them up outside the back door and cover them with a thick layer of straw. Hold this in place with some netting pegged into the ground.

■ **Heel in a supply of leeks** by the back door. Severe frosts will make it impossible to dig up crops for the kitchen, so lift a supply and re-bury them horizontally with the tops sticking out, close to the house in a sheltered part of the garden.

■ **Begin harvesting Brussels sprouts.** Start harvesting from the bottom of the plant upwards, since the largest sprouts form at the base of the plant first of all. Very tall plants that look as if they might blow over in high winds can be staked and tied to a cane.

Sowing and planting outdoors

■ **Finish planting garlic** by the end of the month. The sooner it is in, the better it will

Stand on a plank Spread your weight evenly over beds while you are digging.

grow. If the weather is too wet to plant outside, start the cloves off in modular trays and overwinter these in a cold frame.

■ **Broad beans and peas** can still be sown outside this month, covered with cloches, but the difference between the cropping times of these and sowings made in the spring is negligible. These sowings will, however, be greatly appreciated by all the mice in the neighbourhood, so make sure the cloches are firmly in place and the ends closed properly so there are no gaps.

To make some cheap, improvised cloches, get a length of polythene and some galvanized fencing wire. Cut the wire to make hoops and stick these, at intervals, into the ground. Stretch the polythene over the hoops and bury it in the soil at both ends. These cloches will also be useful for protecting crops sown and planted early in the spring.

Looking after crops

■ **Net all brassicas** if you haven't done this by now. As the weather gets colder and there is less food around, pigeons will be increasingly attracted to the winter crops in your garden. There are many different types of bird scarer on the market, but by

far the best way to protect the crops is by covering them. Make sure traditional netting is properly secured at ground level so that small birds don't get caught up in it; a safer alternative for birds is the very fine mesh sheeting used as a barrier to pests like carrot fly, or even spare pieces of horticultural fleece. Whatever you use as a cover, you must hold it up off the plants with cane supports or the birds will peck through it. Remember to shake it after any heavy falls of snow, or the weight may bring supports down or rip the netting, making it useless.

■ **Protect the curds of cauliflowers** to keep them white and delay the time when the flowers will open. The inner leaves can be tied or snapped and bent over the curd.

Beat the seasons

■ **Force chicory and seakale**.

Herbs

■ **Terracotta pots containing herbs** may have to be wrapped carefully with insulating material if it is impossible to move them indoors.

■ **Lift clumps of chives** and grow them in pots on a windowsill.

Medium-gauge netting This will keep birds off brassicas. A finer mesh is not necessary at this time of year.

Deep beds for vegetables

Deep beds can be any length, as long as they are no more than about 1.2m (4ft) wide, so that they can be tended from each side without treading on them. However, here we suggest a design using square beds intersected by paths that makes a really good-looking, as well as productive, kitchen garden, combining potager-style traditional formality with an up-to-date, labour-saving way of producing your crops.

The design uses a herb garden with a bay tree as the centrepiece and all of the vegetable beds are built in exactly the same way. First, dig and turn the soil thoroughly and then make timber-framed square-raised beds. Finally, add a top layer of soil mixed with compost or soil-based John Innes-type compost. This is the last time you will need to dig these beds. The soil will sink and settle over time, making room for a good top-dressing

of well-rotted manure or garden compost and a feed with an organic fertilizer every winter – and that's it!

Remember to rotate the crops around the beds just as you would in allotment rows. Path materials are up to you. Beaten earth is serviceable, although it can become muddy. A thick layer of straw with planks laid on top for the wheelbarrow is traditional and clean. Old, mucky straw can go onto the compost heap in spring.

Crop rotation

Move crops to different beds each year on a four-year rotation (right). Crops that do not fall into traditional rotation groups, such as salad leaves, sweetcorn, and also potatoes and tomatoes (as long as ground has not been recently manured) can replace any crop in any year (do not follow potatoes with tomatoes, or vice versa). Strawberries and perennial vegetables could also occupy beds on a longer-term basis.

Year 1	1, 2	3, 4	6, 7	8, 9
Year 2	8, 9	1, 2	3, 4	6, 7
Year 3	6, 7	8, 9	1, 2	3, 4
Year 4	3, 4	6, 7	8, 9	1, 2
Year 5	1, 2	3, 4	6, 7	8, 9

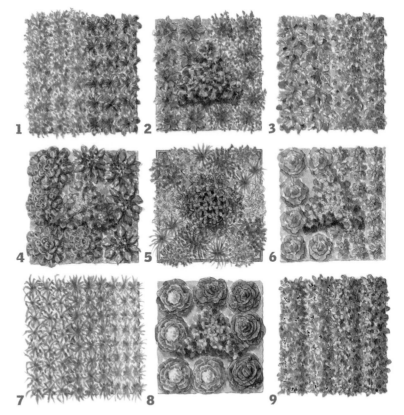

Bed 1 Beetroot and carrots
Bed 2 Turnips, celeriac, and a wigwam of runner beans
Bed 3 Kohl rabi and parsnips
Bed 4 Brussels sprouts and broccoli, with a wigwam of peas and sweet peas
Bed 5 (central bed) Bay tree, sage, thyme, chives, and basil
Bed 6 Lettuce and radishes, with a wigwam of peas and sweet peas
Bed 7 Onions, shallots, and salad onions
Bed 8 Cabbages and cauliflowers, with a wigwam of runner beans
Bed 9 Dwarf runner beans and broad beans

FRUIT
Picking and storing
■ **Check fruits in store regularly** and remove any showing deterioration.

Pruning and training
■ **Start winter-pruning** established apple and pear trees. Winter-pruning of established trees consists mainly of pruning back the leaders of branches by about one-third. Long sideshoots can be spur-pruned to two or three buds to form fruiting spurs on spur-bearing trees. Tip-bearing apples produce fruiting buds on spurs and on the tips of branches, so limit spur-pruning. Short shoots of about 23cm (9in) or less, should be left unpruned and longer shoots can be spur-pruned. The leading shoots of the branches can be tipped, pruning off the top three or four buds, to encourage them to produce more sideshoots. Older branches that are crossing and rubbing should be cut out to prevent damage and keep the centre open.

■ **Blackcurrants** produce shoots from the base and you will have to cut out older shoots to ground level every year to stimulate new shoots from the base. Aim to remove about a third of the bush each year. You will remove current year's growth when pruning, but it is necessary to encourage new shoots from the base.

Hard prune Established blackcurrant bushes need pruning to take out unproductive stems.

When pruning, make your cuts clean Trim any torn or ragged edges. In winter, when the tree is dormant, wounds should heal without becoming infected.

■ **Prune gooseberries and redcurrants** in a similar way to apples and pears. The intention with pruning young bushes is to build up a framework of four or five main branches, each with plenty of fruiting spurs to produce a lot of succulent fruits.

On established frameworks, any shoots not summer-pruned in late summer should be pruned back to two or three buds from the previous year's growth. Leading shoots can be pruned by one-third to half. Dead, crossing, or diseased wood can be cut out. Opening up the centre of the bush to allow air to circulate helps to prevent disease.

Planting
■ **Plant fruit trees and bushes** whenever the soil is not frozen or too wet. Bare-root trees and bushes are planted during the dormant season, from now until March. Container-grown plants can be planted at any time. Make sure the ground has been well prepared by incorporating plenty of organic matter. If just one or two trees are being planted the preparation can be done at planting time. Dig a generous hole to accommodate the roots. Loosen the soil at the bottom of the hole with a fork, without bringing it to the surface. Add a general-purpose fertilizer and water in well.

The planting technique is the same for all trees and shrubs, with the trees always being planted at the same depth as previously. With grafted fruit trees the point of grafting should always be kept above ground level. Otherwise the variety part of the tree will begin to root into the soil and so any control over the vigour of the tree will be lost. So, never plant deeply: put the tree in at the same level as before. Gradually fill in, working the soil between the roots and firm gently. Level off and water in thoroughly and tie to the stake with a tree tie. Then mulch with a thick layer of organic matter. Garden compost or well-rotted manure is ideal; straw is also good in sheltered spots.

■ **Blackcurrants are a slight exception** to the planting rules above in that they should be set lower in the planting hole, with 8–10cm (3–4in) of stem below ground level. This encourages new growth from the base of the plant. The newly planted bushes should then be pruned to 10cm (4in) from the ground to produce strong growth for future fruiting.

■ **Prune newly planted young apple and pear bushes and trees.** Trees bought when three years old or more should not need pruning, but young trees that are to be freestanding will benefit from pruning to form a good shape. Crossing branches or those which make the tree misshapen should be pruned out first. What you do then depends on the age of the tree.
■ Maiden (one-year-old) trees should have the main stem pruned back to 75cm (30in) from the ground, cutting to a bud. This will

encourage branches to form lower down.
- For a two-year-old tree, prune the sideshoots to half of their length. These will form the primary branches. Cut the main stem back to the topmost sideshoot, keeping the centre of the tree open.
- In the third year, prune the leaders that will form the main branches by about half again, cutting to a bud facing in the direction you wish the branch to extend. Any sideshoots growing from these branches should be pruned to one or two buds to form fruiting spurs. In the fourth year formative pruning should be finished and the tree will be cropping.

Propagation

- **Propagate rhubarb.** Lift a large root and split it into smaller pieces, so that each piece has at least one bud. Plant the divided portions 90cm (3ft) apart in soil that has been previously enriched with organic matter.

- **Young strawberry runners** that were potted up for forcing and left outside should be put on their sides to prevent them from getting too wet. Or put them in a cold frame, but keep it well ventilated so as not to start them into growth too early.

- **Take hardwood cuttings** from your redcurrants, whitecurrants, blackcurrants, and gooseberrries.

- **Take cuttings from vines.** Now is a good time to propagate vines from eye cuttings. Make each cutting about 3cm (1½in) long, with each having one bud or "eye". On the opposite side, make a shallow, sloping cut just underneath the bud and dip the cut part into hormone rooting solution. Put the cutting horizontally, bud facing upwards, into a small pot of cutting compost, lightly covered. Keep in a propagator at 24°C (75°F).

UNDER COVER

- **Some heating will be required now** if you are keeping frost-tender plants inside. The most convenient heaters are thermostatically controlled electric ones, although there are gas and paraffin heaters as well. Heating large greenhouses can be expensive. To save on heating bills:
- Separate off a smaller part of the greenhouse with bubble plastic.
- Insulate the greenhouse with bubble plastic to reduce the heating costs.
- If your greenhouse has glass to the ground, the lower half can be insulated with bubble plastic plus polystyrene.

- **Ventilate whenever possible.** It is vital to keep air circulating. Good circulation, without draughts, is vital to keep down diseases such as botrytis. Close the ventilators in the early afternoon to conserve precious heat.

- **Clean pots and seed trays.** If this job is done now it will save a lot of rushing around trying to find clean containers for seed-sowing and taking cuttings in spring. Also, trays left lying around with bits of

Seed trays and pots When you have given them a thorough clean, group pots according to size, ready for sowing seeds under cover.

dead plants and old compost in them will harbour pests and diseases, making propagation less successful. Using clean containers is an important step towards success in propagating plants.

- **Water all plants more carefully now.** With shorter days and cooler temperatures, plant growth will be slowing down. So it is important to be more careful with watering. Wait until plants look as if they really need watering.

Glasshouse and house plants

- **Pot up some lily-of-the-valley** rhizomes for an unusual and fragrant houseplant.

- **Sow cyclamen now** to give the plants a long growing period before flowering, not this coming Christmas, but the following one, giving them 14 months to make good plants with plenty of flowers. Soak the seeds prior to sowing to soften the seed coat, then sow in a pot or tray filled with seed compost and cover lightly with compost or vermiculite. A temperature of 12–15°C (54–60°F) is required for germination. When the seedlings are large enough to handle, prick out into small pots and water in well. A winter temperature of 10°C (50°F) is needed to keep the young plants growing. A final potting into a 12–15cm (5–6in) pot will be required in the summer. The plants can go outside once the threat of frost has gone. Feed and water the plants regularly. Bring them inside again in September.

Crops under glass

- **Begin pruning indoor vines** by cutting all the fruited shoots back to one or two buds from the main stem. Vines can be pruned through to late winter, but those under glass are best pruned early to admit light for other plants under cover. Cuttings can be made from the prunings.

THE DECEMBER GARDEN

Any sunshine there is in December will be weak, but sunny days can be quite pleasant, and if you wrap up well you can have a good day in the garden, digging or catching up with other clearing-up jobs. Now's your chance to carry out any repairs and maintenance jobs that have been piling up during the year, and make the most of any good weather by pruning and protecting plants for the winter.

THINGS TO DO

Feed birds in cold weather.

Prevent ponds, water features, and bird baths freezing over.

Continue winter digging, incorporating organic matter into the soil.

Repair lawns, sheds, and fences when the weather conditions allow.

Prune woody ornamental plants, fruit trees and bushes, ornamental vines. and grape vines.

Shake snow off trees, shrubs, and hedges.

Reduce watering of plants that are overwintering under cover to avoid the risk of them rotting.

Winter-flowering houseplants will need attention but avoid overwatering dormant pot plants.

Lift and heel in celery so that you have plenty of winter supplies, and earth up tall Brussels sprout stems to support them.

Spray fruit trees and roses with a plant oil winter wash to reduce pest and disease problems.

LAST CHANCE

Protect plants and pots that are vulnerable to frost damage.

Insulate garden taps and exposed pipes to stop them freezing.

Prune tall bush roses to guard against wind rock.

Bring in Christmas bulbs for flowering.

GET AHEAD

Sow pelargonium seeds under cover.

Sow some early crops under cover for the first plants to put out in the new year.

Witch hazel (*Hamamelis* x *intermedia* 'John') makes a lovely display to enliven a winter garden. There are cultivars of witch hazel with red, yellow, or orange flowers.

COLD, CRISP, CLEAR DAYS

Clear skies can mean cold, sunny days – so time in the garden can be enjoyable. Colour can be found, too, to cheer up the short winter days. Look out for bright berries, subtle heathers, and the gardener's friend, the red-breasted robin. There are plenty of jobs to be done – especially winter pruning.

December can be a wonderful month in the garden. The days may be short, but on the whole the weather is usually not too bad, with wonderfully clear, frosty, sunny days, when it can be a pleasure to be out. It really is much better for you than snoozing in front of the fire! Make the most of these days as they may be few and far between.

Plants can look charming with a light covering of snow on them and the bare stems of trees and shrubs can be transformed with a silvering from a sharp frost. But be

Winter stems Dogwood underplanted with winter creeper (*Cornus alba* 'Sibirica' and *Euonymus fortunei* 'Silver Queen') gives the garden a festive glow.

aware; overly heavy falls of snow will damage trees and shrubs, so thick layers will have to be knocked off before they cause any harm.

The winter scene

It's not a completely bleak month for colour in the garden. Plants such as the winter-flowering heathers and *Jasminum nudiflorum* should be in flower. *Hamamelis mollis* and *Iris unguicularis* can also be relied on to cheer up December days. There should still be berries on trees and shrubs, too, if the birds haven't eaten them all during spells of bad weather when other food is scarce.

There is still plenty to do outside, although the pace of work will be more gentle now. Gardening in winter can be relaxing, having none of the urgency of spring and summer. With borders tidied up, it is an ideal opportunity to give borderline-hardy plants such as penstemons protection against hard frosts. Over the years, milder winters and nurseries selecting and breeding more robust cultivars, have meant that plants, including penstemons, once always lifted for winter protection, now stay happily outdoors all year round. However, winters are not reliably mild and these plants are not immune to the harshest weather, so it is worth covering them as winter enters its coldest phase. The easiest way of doing this is by covering the plants with a cloche; many ornamental cloches are available today in either glass or plastic. More utilitarian cloches can be made with plastic sheeting stretched over wire frames. Alternatively, use horticultural fleece or a layer of straw held in place with pegged-down netting.

Winter-pruning of fruit trees is a satisfying job to be undertaken now. It's also a good time to do any major pruning of ornamental deciduous trees and shrubs, not only because the plants are now in their dormant period, but also, with the leaves now off the plants, it's much easier to see what you are doing. It's also easier to identify dead and diseased wood, which can then be cut out. Of course, shrubs such as the dogwoods (*Cornus*) and willows grown for their ornamental bark should be left until spring. If you prune them now you will lose the colourful stems – the very reason why they are grown.

Company in the garden

Winter digging can continue this month whenever weather conditions allow; that is, when the soil is not excessively wet or frozen. While digging you will probably be accompanied by a robin, eagerly waiting for a worm or other insects to be uncovered by your work. They can be too friendly at times, getting so close that you may fear trampling on them. But it's certainly a reminder to feed garden birds now that the weather is getting harsher. A varied selection of food put out regularly from now on will help see them through the winter and keep them in the neighbourhood of your garden, rather than trying their luck elsewhere. If you have decided to replant part

Feed the birds Fat balls and well-stocked bird feeders will encourage birds to keep visiting your garden during the winter months when insects are hard to find.

Weather watch

Although there can be a few relatively mild December days, it's a cold month and there's no getting away from it. One exceptionally bitter Christmas in my home town near Glasgow the temperature fell to -19°C for several days. With sharp frosts and driving winds, some days the temperature will rarely get above freezing. However the cold can be beneficial in the garden, by killing off pests and diseases.

Winds and gales

Definitely a windy month, with bitingly cold winds at times. But it can be calm, especially in frosty weather. The most intense gales are likely in western coastal areas close to the Atlantic Ocean as weather depressions are driven across from America. Northern areas can expect from two to five days on average of gale-force winds. Southern areas experience up to two days of gales.

Limited sun

The north of the country comes off worst in the sunshine stakes this month: only 13 hours in the far north, up to about 50 hours in the north-east. Southern parts can expect up to 54 hours.

A wet month

It can be quite wet this month too, with all areas seeing increase in rainfall. All coastal areas can be wet, as well as hilly areas like the Highlands of Scotland. Here you can expect around 275mm of rain, whereas in the south the average is 53mm. Keep off sodden soil or you will do more harm than good.

Some snow

There is an increased chance of snow this month, but rarely does it last, or lie on the ground, for long. We may hope for a white Christmas, but it rarely happens these days. A good covering of snow can turn the garden into a winter wonderland, but do be aware that it can also damage plants. Snow on trees and shrubs can break the branches, so shake it off before the damage occurs.

Frost-hardy Brussels sprouts These come into their own this month and their taste may even be improved after a cold spell of weather. You need to harvest them when they are still quite small, starting to pick from the bottom and working upwards.

of the garden, you can do much to encourage birds by including plants that attract them. All the berrying trees and shrubs will attract birds and if you have room, a mixed, informal hedgerow of flowering and fruiting trees and shrubs will give them sustenance and shelter. Bare-rooted hedging plants will be available throughout the winter and can be planted whenever weather conditions are favourable. It's also a good time to take hardwood cuttings of trees and shrubs; a free and easy way of propagating some plants. Your spring plans could also include a water feature, will bring birds to your garden to drink and bathe in shallow water.

Conserving warmth

Inside there will be a lot to do if you haven't yet cleaned out the greenhouse or conservatory. After doing this, insulate with bubble polythene to reduce the cost of

Use this quiet time to sort out your tools and tidy the shed, ready for spring. While you're at it, you could make a list of anything you need and put it on your Christmas list. If your tools always end up in a heap on a shelf, why not ask for a tool tidy. You can then store your tools permanently in the box, making them easier to find.

Plants for winter display

Garden centres are now packed with winter-flowering pot plants and there will be a wide variety to choose from. In very cold weather, make sure the plants are properly wrapped when you buy them, as even a short period exposed to the cold can affect the growth and flowering of these plants. A good selection includes azaleas, poinsettias, winter cyclamen, and *Solanum capsicastrum* (the winter cherry). These will fill your home with colour over the holiday period. They are living decorations, so they will last longer given a little care and attention.

Another way to have colour in the home at this time is by cutting shoots from winter-flowering shrubs and putting them in water; the flowers will open up in the warmth of the greenhouse, conservatory, or home. If you can do this early in December the flowers will open in time for Christmas.

Armchair gardening

If the weather is just too bad to do any work outside then it is a good idea to plan ahead and consider the plants you want to grow and the features to be created in your garden for next year. It's a pleasant occupation, leafing through seed and plant catalogues by the fireside. Getting orders off early will ensure that you get the plants you want before the nursery runs out of them. There are many specialist plant nurseries around the country and most of them produce catalogues. These can be a mine of information and you will often come across some little treasures. Vegetable seed catalogues are also a fine source of inspiration. With memories still fresh of the crops that did and didn't do well this year for you, all of the information that the best brochures give on the strengths and weaknesses of the various cultivars will probably have you planning next year's menus, never mind plantings, well in advance.

heating. Quite a dramatic reduction in heating costs can be achieved by insulation and it will enable you to get your plants off to a good start early in the New Year. If you don't have a greenhouse and don't have room for one either, consider investing in a cold frame. You'll be surprised at how much scope it will give you for sheltering plants during the winter months, sowing early crops, propagating plants, and hardening off seedlings in the spring.

Mahonia x media 'Charity'
Evergreen shrub with honey-scented flowers (*see p.309*)

Hippeastrum 'Apple Blossom'
One of the most spectacular bulbs to grow as a house plant (*see p.302*)

Viburnum x bodnantense 'Dawn' ♀
Beautifully scented flowers on bare winter branches (*see p.334*)

Elaeagnus x ebbingei 'Gilt Edge' ♀
Variegated evergreen shrub to give a splash of colour (*see p.294*)

Ilex aquifolium 'Handsworth New Silver' ♀
Variegated female holly, bearing bright berries (*see p.303*)

Cyclamen coum ♀
Perennial that can be grown in pots for an indoor display (*see p.291*)

Cotoneaster frigidus 'Fructu Luteo'
Yellow-berried shrub, popular with birds (*see p.290*)

Aucuba japonica 'Variegata'
Hedging stalwart puts on a winter show (*see p.279*)

Rhododendron 'Inga'
Compact azalea, ideal as a winter pot plant (*see p.322*)

Salix x rubens 'Basfordiana'
Prune this willow hard each year for bright stems (*see p.328*)

Jasminum nudiflorum ♀
A straggly but welcome winter-flowering climber (*see p.305*)

Clematis armandii 'Apple Blossom' ♀
Evergreen clematis with scented winter flowers (*see p.285*)

WHAT TO DO IN DECEMBER

AROUND THE GARDEN

There are few pests around in the garden now, but it always pays to be vigilant, as milder winters lead to many surviving the winter when they would normally be killed.

Move plants. Whether they are deciduous trees, shrubs and climbers, or herbaceous perennials, all can be moved if they are growing in the wrong place or have become too big for their current position – provided that soil conditions permit. Always take as big a root ball as you can cope with when lifting larger plants. Remember to revitalize the soil where the plant was taken from and in its new position. Stake tall plants to prevent wind rock and provide a windbreak shelter to protect from cold winds.

Protect plants vulnerable to frost. Take in any plants that have been overlooked. Plants *in situ* such as penstemons will benefit from a layer of protection, particularly in colder parts. Herbaceous perennials are very easy to protect now that plants have died back – though it won't harm them even if they are in leaf. Just put a thick layer of straw or bracken over the crown of the plant and hold it in position with some wire netting. Taller shrubs can be "lagged" with straw held in place with hessian or sacking. Don't use plastic since even when plants are dormant they still need to breathe.

Winter is pruning time for ornamental and fruiting woody plants. Consider shredding the prunings rather than burning them. Shreddings make a terrific mulch, or they can be added to the compost heap. If your garden is mostly shrubs and lawn, keep a pile of shreddings to mix in with grass clippings in the summer. These need plenty of air in them if they are to rot down properly and not form a slimy, stinking mess. Don't shred any diseased material because the disease will be spread.

Wrap insulation around outside taps. As ice forms, water expands and this can easily burst pipes, which could affect the water supply to the house. You can insulate taps by binding them in several layers of hessian, or there are products on the market especially for insulating outside taps. If possible, turn off the supply to outside taps and drain the pipe during the winter. This way you will avoid any possibility of burst pipes.

Continue winter digging of new planting areas and empty vegetable beds for as long as the weather permits. If the soil is so wet that it sticks to your boots, then keep off it until it dries out a bit. If you have to walk on the soil when it's wet, use planks to get across. Trodden soil is compacted by your weight and, particularly if the soil is a heavy clay, the air will be driven out of it. When it does eventually dry out it will set as hard as concrete. To prevent excessive wet in the soil, especially if you have to get on with the work, cover at least part of the ground with polythene to keep off the worst of the rain. When you want to work the soil, pull it back and when you're finished cover it up again.

Keep composting Woody prunings and leaf litter decompose faster when shredded. Try running the lawn mower over piles of fallen leaves, then collect them up and add them to the compost bin.

TREES AND SHRUBS

■ **Early in December** cut a few shoots from winter-flowering shrubs such as *Viburnum* x *bodnantense* and *Prunus* x *subhirtella* 'Autumnalis'. Put the shoots in water and keep them in a cool place indoors. Soon the buds will begin to open and the beautifully scented flowers can be added to the holiday decorations.

■ **Holly trees with their red berries** are very attractive at this time of year and they provide excellent Christmas decorations for the home. But birds love to eat the berries just as much as we like to look at them. While we mustn't begrudge birds their food in harsh winter weather, it is wise to cover at least part of a holly tree with some netting to save some of the berries for the Christmas festivities. Make sure the netting is secured firmly so that birds don't get caught up in it.

■ **Check newly planted trees and shrubs,** including roses, to see if they have been loosened by winds or lifted by frost. When this happens, gaps form around the roots, causing them to dry out because they are not in close contact with the soil. If you see cracks around the plant, gently firm in with your feet. Be careful on heavy clay soils not to tread too heavily, or all the air will be driven out of the soil.

■ **Put a windbreak** around newly planted evergreens. Strong cold winds can have a devastating effect on recently planted leafy shrubs. Plants are continuously losing water from their leaves (known as "transpiration") and the rate of water loss increases with high winds passing over the surface of the leaves – just as a windy day dries washing more quickly. The edges of the leaves dry out faster than the plant can replace the water and so cells die off. It's known as "wind scorch". To reduce damage, erect a shelter around the plants.

Ilex aquifolium **'Madame Briot'**

It can be made from any material stretched between posts, from hessian sacking to polythene, or fine net mesh made specially for the purpose. If you haven't got enough to go right around the plant, make sure it is at least on the windward side.

■ **Shake snow off trees and shrubs.** It is rare that we get a lot of snow in December, but it is best to be aware that although plants look terrific with a layer of snow on them, it can be a considerable weight and will easily bring down a branch or two. As long as the layer of snow hasn't frozen hard, brush it off as soon as possible and the damage will be slight.

Small to medium conifers that have been planted as specimen trees and need to be kept in shape can be protected by tying thin wire or strong string around them, preventing the branches opening up when the snow falls on them. Don't worry about snow lying over low plants: it actually gives them protection against cold, blanketing them from frost.

Pruning and training

■ **Prune deciduous trees and shrubs** for health and to shape. Have a look at all of the deciduous trees and shrubs in your garden to see if any need attention to improve the health or shape of the plant. At this time of year, with no leaves in the way, it is easier to see what you are doing. You will need a good pair of secateurs, a pair of loppers, and a pruning saw for cutting off larger branches. Chainsaws can be hired from local hire shops, but unless you are familiar with these machines they are best left to the experts; they can be extremely dangerous in inexperienced hands. Likewise, on no account saw through large branches, or branches high up in a tree, yourself. These are jobs for a trained tree surgeon. And check with your local council before doing any pruning on established trees to make sure they are not subject to a tree preservation order.

■ First remove any dead or diseased wood and any crossing branches that are rubbing together, cutting out whole shoots to a joint whenever possible rather than just tipping them back.

■ If the plant is taking up too much room in a small garden then it can be trimmed. The main point to remember is that the harder you prune, the stronger will be the resulting growth, so when restricting size, light pruning will have a much more satisfactory effect than hacking away. Don't just give freestanding plants an all-over "haircut", as when trimming a hedge. Try to open up the centre of the plant to allow air to circulate and reduce the amount of shadow cast on lower-growing plants in the border.

■ Take your time when pruning. Stand back and look at the plant often and consider what effect removing a branch will have on the appearance of the plant before making the cut. You can't stick a branch back on once it's been pruned off.

■ Most woody material can be put through a shredder to make a mulch for borders. Any diseased material should be put in the bin, taken to the local household waste tip

Cutting off a low branch

1 First reduce the weight of the branch so that the final cut is easier to make cleanly. To prevent downward tearing, make an undercut.

2 Supporting the weight of the branch, cut downwards straight through it about 5cm (2in) beyond the undercut.

3 Now cut back the stub cleanly, cutting just beyond the swollen ring or the "branch collar", at the point where it meets the trunk.

or burned. Composting it will more than likely spread the disease.
■ Feed after pruning and mulch with organic matter.
■ Most plants will tend to produce a mass of young shoots from the points where they were pruned. Keep an eye on this regrowth through spring and summer and remove unwanted shoots while they are still young.

■ Prune tall bush roses by half to prevent wind rock. If plants are rocked about by wind a hole will form at the base of the plant, where water will collect and cause the roots to rot. In frosty weather the water may freeze, resulting in further damage to the root system.

Planting
■ **Continue planting trees, shrubs and climbers.** As long as the soil is not frozen or waterlogged, press on with planting, as weather conditions can change quickly and short days mean there is less time to work in the garden. Heel in plants if soil conditions are not suitable for planting. Plants will keep for quite a long time if planted temporarily in a corner of the garden.

Propagation
■ Continue taking hardwood cuttings.

Hedges
■ **Brush any heavy snow off** evergreen hedges before the weight of it splays out branches and causes damage.

■ **Prune overgrown deciduous hedges** like beech and hornbeam. No matter how often we trim hedges through the summer, they imperceptibly creep outwards, taking up more space and becoming more difficult to cut. Now, while the plants are dormant, is a good time to reduce the hedge to a manageable size. On an old, established

hedge you may need loppers or a pruning saw to cut some of the larger branches.
Cut back the sides until the hedge is no more than 45–60cm (18–24in) wide at the top, tapering it so that the bottom of the hedge is wider. This shaping will protect the hedge from damage by heavy snowfalls. The top can be trimmed to whatever height you want. To get the top level, you may need to put up a line at the height required.

■ **Taking hardwood cuttings** is an ideal way of producing quantities of hedging plants for free. The cuttings will have rooted by next winter, when you will be able to dig them up and plant them in their permanent positions.
Alternatively, grow a deciduous hedge from hardwood cuttings *in situ*. Prepare a trench along the line of the proposed hedge as the planting area and line out cuttings along it, about 30cm (1ft) apart. Put a few more in at the end of the row as spares in case some of the cuttings don't root. It may take a few years to grow, but you will end up with a bargain hedge.

Clearing snow Use a sturdy broom to knock snow off hedges to avoid spoiling their shape.

CLIMBERS

■ **Brush snow off** dense evergreen climbers and wall shrubs. When heavy snow accumulates on these it can not only break stems but also puts strain on any ties and supports.

■ **Early in December** cut a few shoots from winter jasmine. Put the shoots in water and keep them in a cool place indoors. Soon you'll find the buds will begin to open and you will be able to use the beautifully scented flowers to add to your Christmas decorations.

■ **Ornamental vines** can be pruned now to keep them from completely taking over the garden. Vines can produce growths up to 3m (10ft) or more in one season and over several years; if they are not pruned, you will end up in a mess. Thin out any overcrowded shoots and then prune sideshoots to two buds from the main stems kept as a framework.

■ **Take hardwood cuttings of deciduous climbers.** Remove strong, woody shoots about 30cm (1ft) long from the plant, cutting just above a bud. Trim the base to just below a bud and cut off the tip just above a bud to leave a section of stem about 22.5cm (9in) long. Dip the cut end into hormone rooting solution. Make a slit trench in a corner of the garden with a spade, to the depth of the spade.

On heavy clay soils put some grit in the base of the trench to help improve the drainage. Put the cuttings in to two-thirds their depth and carefully firm them in with your boot. The cuttings will have rooted by next winter, when you will be able to dig them up and plant them out in their permanent positions.

PERENNIALS

■ **Continue to cut down dead growth** on herbaceous perennials and generally weed and tidy borders. The sooner this is done, the less work there will be left in the busy spring period. But robust stems with seed heads, as on sedums, can be left uncut until the spring because they look beautiful when rimed with a layer of frost, especially on a clear, sunny morning.

■ **During reasonable periods of weather** when the ground is not frozen or excessively wet, you can continue to lift and divide herbaceous perennials.

■ **Root cuttings** of perennials can be taken through the winter.

Alpines

■ **Continue to clear fallen leaves** from the rock garden. Alpine plants will not enjoy this natural mulch and will suffer if they are left covered with a damp layer of leaves for any length of time.

In their native mountainous regions, alpines are usually protected by a blanket of snow, which actually keeps them relatively dry. The snow generally melts quickly and the plants are then exposed to the fresh alpine air.

■ **Sow alpine seeds.** This may seem an odd time of year to do this, but in the wild, alpine seeds have to go through a period of cold weather to break the seed's dormancy. This can be imitated at home by sowing the seeds in a pot and standing the pot outside to let the seeds freeze from time to time; put a sheet of glass over the them to protect them from excessive wet. The seeds will germinate in the spring. If you choose to sow them later when it gets warmer, you will need to put the seeds in the fridge for six to eight weeks before sowing, to break dormancy.

Sow the seeds in pots containing alpine compost, consisting of equal parts' loam, sharp grit, and peat-free compost. Water the compost before sowing and sow the seeds thinly on the surface. Cover them with horticultural grit. This will reduce the problem of algae growing on the compost, as the seeds can take some time to germinate. They may also germinate at different times so don't throw away the pots until you have your full complement of plants. Grow the plants on in the same type of compost. Alpines don't need a lot of fertilizer, so little feeding is necessary.

Covering alpine seeds

1 Cover the seeds when sown with a layer of clean, fine grit.

2 The grit lets water drain away from the crown of young plants, which are prone to rot in the wet.

BULBS

■ **Check bulbs, corms, and tubers** in store for signs of disease. Botrytis and rotting can quickly spread. If diseases start to show, remove the affected bulb or tuber – or if only part of it is affected, cut out the diseased portion and treat it with a proprietary fungicide.

■ **Bring bulbs being forced for Christmas** into light and warmth. Bulbs such as prepared hyacinths and daffodils that were plunged outside in the autumn and then brought into cool conditions a few weeks ago, can be brought into the warmth to encourage them into flower for Christmas. Hyacinths are a particular favourite as they fill the room with their scent.

■ **Bulbs that have been plunged** for forcing into flower in spring should also be inspected regularly. Check to see if they need watering. Don't overwater, especially if the bulbs are growing in bulb bowls that have no drainage holes, or rot will set in.

When the bulbs have made about 2.5–5cm (1–2in) of growth they should be taken indoors to a cool greenhouse or conservatory, or placed on the windowsill of a cool room. A few weeks later the bulbs can be moved to a warmer room to flower and fill the room with spring cheer. Too much warmth too early causes them to grow thin and straggly, and they don't then produce the best flowers. Turn them regularly to make sure they grow up straight. Tall narcissi often benefit from some support; a few twiggy sticks, especially bare stems of twisted hazel or willow, look attractive.

■ **Continue to pot up lilies** for a succession of blooms. Put four or five bulbs into an 18cm (7in) pot containing coir compost, covering the bulbs with about 10cm (4in) of compost. Water them in and wait for the stunning flowers in spring.

ANNUALS AND BEDDING

■ **Get seed catalogues** and plan border designs and colour schemes for next year. Even on a cold winter's day, you can dream of the summer to come. It's exciting to try some new varieties each year and by ordering early you have the best chance of getting the varieties you want and having them in good time for sowing. Many people leave it to the last minute to order their seeds and get caught up in the rush of spring orders to seed companies.

■ **Sow pelargonium seeds** this month. It may seem early to be starting seeds into growth, but these bedding plants do need a relatively long growing period to flower the first year after sowing.

Whether you have a greenhouse or not, the ideal way to start off the seeds is in a propagator. This cuts down on the cost of having to heat a whole greenhouse. Place the propagator on the windowsill to get the maximum amount of light during the short days of winter.

A temperature of 18°C (65°F) is needed for the seeds to germinate successfully. The seeds can be sown in small pots of peat-free compost, watering the compost before sowing. Lightly cover them with sieved compost or vermiculite and place them in the propagator. Pot up the seedlings into larger pots when they are large enough to handle.

If you haven't got the room to germinate your own seeds, then you can order seedlings or young plants ("plug plants") from seedsmen for delivery in spring, so reducing the expense and the time needed to grow the plants at home. But do send off for them quickly as they are very popular and usually sell out fast.

CONTAINERS

■ **Permanent plants in containers** should be checked over regularly and any debris cleared out. Fallen leaves can get in around the base of plants in containers, encouraging disease and also giving pests somewhere to hibernate. They also make the plants look untidy.

■ **Move pots of borderline hardy plants** inside if you did not do this earlier. It is rare, in fact, that we get very severe weather in December, but there can often be sharp frosts this month. Move plants into an unheated or cool greenhouse or conservatory. Very little heat is required, otherwise the plants will tend to put on too much growth, which will be very straggly due to the lack of light.

Water the plants carefully, giving them enough to keep them alive. Don't overdo it as the plants may be killed off. Whenever possible ensure there is plenty of air circulating around the plants and open the ventilators on reasonably mild days. Be aware that damp, still air encourages diseases, such as botrytis, to set in.

Clear out debris Don't leave fallen leaves trapped around the stems of container plants.

LAWNS

■ **Keep off the lawn** if it is frosted or wet or put down some planks to walk on. If you walk on a frozen lawn, yellow patches will appear when it thaws.

■ **Repair lawns with turves.** Any worn areas of the lawn can be returfed now, working from boards to distribute your weight if the ground is very wet. Leave the turf a little higher than the surrounding lawn in order to allow it to settle. If you can't get hold of a small quantity of turf, or at least one that in any way resembles your own, the trick is to swap the damaged part with a sound patch taken from somewhere where the damaged one will be less noticeable – just as one can covertly move stained carpet tiles around. Damaged patches on the edges of neat

lawns should always be repaired by returfing, not sowing, to give the required clean, firm edge. This is another place where you can swap turves around.

■ **Rake up any fallen leaves** that have been left lying on the lawn. If they are left the grass will die off due to lack of light, and diseases may set in due to a lack of air circulation. If a lawn has been neglected under a layer of leaves for any length of time, spiking the lawn after clearing the leaves will help to improve aeration again, especially to the roots.

New lawns

■ **If weather conditions allow** – that is, the soil is not sodden or frozen – you may continue preparing ground and laying turf.

Mending a broken edge

1 Check lawn edges regularly. Damaged patches are unsightly and exposed earth becomes weedy.

2 Cut out a generous rectangle. Undercut as evenly as possible, lifting the turf with at least 2.5cm (1in) soil.

3 Rotate and re-lay the turf, so that the broken patch faces inward.

4 Fill the hole with top-dressing and work into the joins. Sprinkle seed.

VEGETABLES AND HERBS

■ **Cover bare beds** with polythene to protect the soil from winter rain. This will allow you to dig in the New Year without being held up by bad weather.

■ **Make a hotbed** from fresh horse manure. This is a Victorian idea, but it is still perfectly valid today. It makes good use of horse manure piled up to rot down. A lot of heat is given off by manure as it breaks down and this can easily be harnessed to produce some early crops. Fresh horse manure is not as difficult to obtain as most people think. There are many riding stables in towns or on the edges of cities and towns these days and all too often they are glad to pass it on to gardeners. Some establishments may ask a modest price, but it is well worth the expense. You will almost certainly have to transport it home yourself, unless you live close to the stables.

A hotbed can be made as a free-standing heap, but the heat will be retained better in a container – a wooden compost bin is ideal. Pile it in until it is mounded above the topmost timbers. Then cap the manure with a soil mix of seven parts loam, three parts spent mushroom compost and two parts coarse grit. Mix it well and spread a good layer on top of the heap.

Put a cold frame on top and leave it for about a week to allow the temperature to build up. It is surprising how hot it gets – something you can test by sticking a cane into the heap and pulling it out after a few days. You'll be able to see how much heat is being generated. In two or three weeks, when it has cooled a little, you can sow lettuces, carrots, radishes and turnips, and spinach for early crops.

Once these crops have finished, you can grow trailing tomatoes, cucumbers, or even melons on the heap. At the end of the season you will be left with a fine pile of well-rotted manure to dig into the soil.

Swelling crowns You can lift celeriac throughout the winter. In frosty conditions, protect the stems with a straw mulch.

Harvesting

■ **Keep harvesting winter crops.** Sprouts and parsnips are festive meal essentials.

■ **Lift celery as required.** If severe weather is forecast, it is worth lifting some and heeling it in in a sheltered part of the garden – close to the back door is ideal, as it will then stay fresh and be handy for the kitchen. Plants left in the ground can be protected from severe frost by covering the tops with a thick layer of straw or bracken, held in place with chicken wire and wire hoops pushed into the ground.

Looking after crops

■ **Earth up spring cabbages** and other winter brassicas to give them better anchorage in strong winds. Tall-growing Brussels sprouts are particularly prone to being blown over. It may also be necessary to put in canes and tie the plants to them. Remove yellowing leaves regularly, as these encourage fungal diseases. Spring cabbages are normally planted in the autumn at a distance of about 15cm (6in) apart. During the winter, cut every other one as winter greens, leaving the others to grow on and heart up in the spring.

Sowing indoors

■ **Sow some early crops.** If you have space, you could sow a few pots or module trays of lettuce, summer cabbages and cauliflowers, radishes, round varieties of carrots, spinach, salad onions, and turnips. These seeds don't require high temperatures to germinate; about 13°C (55°F) is adequate, so a windowsill is fine if you don't have a propagator. If you sow in pots or seed trays you will need to prick the seedlings out, spacing them about 2.5cm (1in) apart into another tray. Grow the young plants on in good light, watering regularly. They will be ready to put out under cloches or horticultural fleece in February for the very earliest crop.

Herbs

■ **Bay trees grown in pots** should be taken indoors if there is a likelihood of cold weather, or they can be moved to the most sheltered part of the garden.

Potted bay tree This attractive display can be recreated next year, so move the vulnerable bay to a more sheltered spot, or even indoors.

FRUIT
Picking and storing

■ **Continue to inspect stored fruit** for signs of rotting and throw any that are rotten onto the lawn or vegetable garden for the birds to feed on. It will be a welcome treat for them in harsh weather.

Looking after crops

■ **Check apple and pear trees** for any signs of canker.

■ **Check tree stakes and ties are sound.** Tree ties can easily break after a few years, so check them regularly. Also bear in mind that as a tree grows the stem expands, making the tree tie tighter around the trunk. So on your regular inspection tours check that ties are not too tight or they will strangle your trees.

■ **Spray fruit trees and bushes** with a winter wash. Many pest and disease problems can be reduced if fruit is given an annual plant oil winter wash, which destroys overwintering eggs of many pests. It has to be done when the plants are completely dormant, as the spray will harm any green foliage it comes into contact with.

If the trees are growing in grass or there are other plants under the trees, it is worth covering them with a sheet of polythene, otherwise they will be harmed by the spray. Be sure to spray thoroughly, getting into all the little cracks and crevices on the tree. These are the places where the pests love to hibernate. The product you need is readily available from garden centres. Follow the instructions on the packaging with care and be sure to wear gloves and old or protective clothing. Spray on a still day to minimize drift.

Pruning and training

■ **Winter-prune apple and pear trees.**

Pruning vines First cut all of the fruited shoots back to two or three buds from the main stem.

■ **Finish pruning currants and gooseberries** through the winter.

■ **Prune grape vines.** Vines should be pruned when dormant as they "bleed" sap copiously if cut when in growth, weakening the plant. All the laterals (sideshoots made in one season) should be pruned back to two or three buds, leaving you with long, stumpy main stems, which you can also cut back in length if they are overgrown.

You may feel that you are being a bit ruthless pruning so hard, but vines produce a lot of extremely vigorous growth and you'll need to keep them in check. The new shoots that grow from the stumpy stems will grow long and bear fruit all in one season next year. You can make some prunings into cuttings. Grape vines under glass should also be pruned this month.

Planting
■ **Plant fruit trees and bushes** whenever the soil is not frozen or too wet.

Propagation
■ **Take hardwood cuttings** of redcurrants, whitecurrants, blackcurrants, and gooseberries. All are taken in exactly the same way (*see October*).

UNDER COVER
■ **Tidy plants in the greenhouse and conservatory** regularly, removing yellowing and fallen leaves and fading flowers. The warm, moist atmosphere and short days are perfect breeding conditions for moulds and other fungal diseases. Any dead plant material left lying around will encourage them.

■ **Check greenhouse heaters** are working efficiently. If not, take them to a service agent or call in an electrician.

■ **Water all plants carefully** as their growth is reduced to a minimum, unless they are winter-flowering plants such as cyclamen and indoor azaleas. Do all the watering during the early part of the day, if this is at all possible. This will give the greenhouse or conservatory time to dry out before nightfall. Cooler, damp conditions overnight are the perfect breeding ground for diseases such as grey mould (*Botrytis*). Try to ventilate the greenhouse for an hour or two on mild days to keep air circulating, for exactly the same reason.

Raising plants for outdoors
■ Sow pelargonium seeds.

■ **Keep houseplants in good light.** During the short days of winter plants need all the light they can get, especially house plants that often get light from only one side. Keep them on a bright windowsill and turn them every few days so they don't grow to one side – plants tend to stretch for the light. If you have a heated conservatory or greenhouse so much the better; you can move them there for the midwinter period. Clean the leaves of large foliage plants such as rubber plants. When dust gathers on them, it can dramatically reduce the amount of light getting to the leaf surfaces and they suffer as a result.

Pot plants make very popular presents and can be quite expensive, but they often don't last for very long. A few simple points kept in mind can keep them looking their best and prolong their shelf life. All need slightly differing conditions in order to get the best out of them.

The ever-popular winter-flowering *Cyclamen persicum* needs a cool room and good light. When watering, try not to splash the corm and the foliage with water. It is best to water the plant from below, standing the pot in a shallow saucer.

Poinsettias, with their spectacular red, pink, or white bracts are actually a type of euphorbia native to warm countries, where they make tall trees. They need quite warm rooms and should be kept moist, but dislike being waterlogged, so check to see if the soil is dry before you water.

Azaleas are pretty flowers and given sufficient light and a cool place, they will bloom for weeks. But they dislike warm rooms and should never be allowed to dry out – not even slightly – so keep them well watered all the time.

Cyclamen persicum

A-Z PLANT DIRECTORY

This directory gives siting and growing information for all of the "Star Plants" featured month by month throughout the book, arranged here in alphabetical order for ease of reference. We also recommend other good species and cultivars, and suggest "Perfect Partners" to look out for, to help you plan planting schemes and groupings.

H = Height. Trees and shrubs may take many years to reach the height given.

S = Spread. To obtain planting distances between two plants, add spreads together and divide by two.

♈ = The plant holds the RHS Award of Garden Merit. To get it the plant must be: excellent for ordinary use in appropriate conditions; widely available; of good constitution; essentially stable in form and colour; and reasonably resistant to pests and diseases.

A gorgeous display Orange heleniums, flat, yellow-headed achilleas, daisy-like echinaceas, and pink *Liatris* form a beautiful natural summer planting with drifts of tall perennials and grasses.

A

Abelia 'Edward Goucher'

Abelia

A moderately vigorous, semi-evergreen shrub with arching branches. H 1.5m (5ft), S 2.5m (8ft).

■ **Seasonal highlights** Bears a mass of trumpet-shaped, lilac-pink flowers from summer to autumn.

■ **Value at other times** The glossy, dark-green leaves are bronzed when young.

■ **Ideal site** Excellent in a shrub border.

■ **Cultivation** Best in fertile, well-drained soil in full sun, but tolerates light, dappled shade. Protect from cold winds. Prune after flowering. Deadhead and shorten to a strong bud any shoots that spoil the outline.

■ **Also recommended** *Abelia x grandiflora* ♀.

■ **Perfect partners** *Abelia triflora*, taller with fragrant white flowers; *Jasminum humile*, evergreen shrub with yellow flowers from spring to autumn.

Abutilon 'Souvenir de Bonn' ♀

Indian mallow

Evergreen shrub or small tree. H 3m (10ft), S 2–3m (6–10ft)

■ **Seasonal highlights** From spring to autumn, it has hanging, bowl-shaped orange flowers with darker veins.

■ **Value at other times** Pale-green leaves with creamy-white margins all year.

■ **Ideal site** A sunny border, warm wall, or conservatory.

■ **Cultivation** Under glass, grow in loam-based compost (eg John Innes No 2). Grow in fertile, well-drained soil outdoors. It is best in a sheltered spot in full sun, but will tolerate dappled shade. Bring indoors for the winter in cold areas, as it will not tolerate frost.

■ **Also recommended** *Abutilon megapotamicum* ♀ with plain green leaves and yellow and red flowers.

■ **Perfect partners** All kinds of summer bedding.

Acer palmatum

Japanese maples

Acer palmatum cultivars are deciduous, mostly mound-forming, shrubs or small trees with lobed or finely cut leaves.

■ **Seasonal highlights** All are valued for their habit and vibrant autumn colours.

■ **Value at other times** Most have small, beautifully tinted spring flowers and winged fruits in autumn.

■ **Ideal site** A sheltered shrub border or in decorative containers.

■ **Cultivation** Grow in full sun or dappled shade, in leafy, moist but well-drained soil. Mulch annually in autumn. Shelter from cold winds and spring frosts.

■ **Perfect partners** Conifers, heathers, and epidemiums (underplanting).

Acer 'Bloodgood' ♀ has red-purple leaves that turn scarlet in autumn. H & S 5m (15ft)

Acer 'Chitose-yama' ♀ has crimson-green leaves with red-purple autumn colour. H 2m (6ft), S 3m (10ft)

Acer 'Corallinum' has red-pink young leaves that are green in summer, then red, orange, and yellow in autumn. H 2m (6ft), S 3m (10ft)

Acer 'Garnet' ♀ has finely cut, red-purple leaves. H 2m (6ft), S 3m (10ft)

Acer 'Sango-kaku' ♀ has coral-red shoots and orange-yellow young leaves that turn yellow in autumn. H 2m (6ft), S 3m (10ft)

Acer 'Linearilobum' has deeply cut leaves that turn yellow in autumn. H 2m (6ft), S 3m (10ft)

Acer pensylvanicum 'Erythrocladum'
Moosewood

A deciduous tree with an upright habit of growth. Also known as striped maple. H 12m (40ft), S 10m (30ft)

■ **Seasonal highlights** The bark on young shoots is a striking, brilliant coral-pink in winter, fading to orange-red with greyish-white stripes at maturity.

■ **Value at other times** In spring, clusters of yellow-green flowers hang beneath fresh green leaves, which turn yellow in autumn.

■ **Ideal site** Use as a specimen or grow in a woodland garden.

■ **Cultivation** Thrives in any fertile, well-drained soil in sun or dappled shade. Provide shelter from cold winds and late frosts.

■ **Also recommended** *Acer platanoides* 'Crimson King' ♀ has leaves of the deepest red-purple.

■ **Perfect partners** Conifers and heathers.

Achillea 'Fanal'
Yarrow

A moderately vigorous, clump-forming, herbaceous perennial with fragrant leaves. H 75cm (30in), S 60cm (24in)

■ **Seasonal highlights** Throughout summer, it bears flat heads of bright-red flowers with yellow centres.

■ **Value at other times** The flowers fade with age, but can be dried for winter flower arrangements.

■ **Ideal site** A sunny, mixed or herbaceous border.

■ **Cultivation** It prefers an open site in sun, but tolerates light, dappled shade. Grow in moist, but well-drained soil. Lift and divide every three or four years to maintain vigour.

■ **Also recommended** *Achillea millefolium* 'Cerise Queen' has heads of magenta-pink flowers with white centres. There are many cultivars.

■ **Perfect partners** Phlox, hemerocallis.

Aconitum 'Bressingham Spire' ♀
Monkshood, Aconite

A clump-forming, herbaceous perennial of upright growth. All parts are toxic if ingested. H to 1m (3ft), S 30cm (1ft)

■ **Seasonal highlights** Bears tall, tapered spires of deep violet-blue flowers from midsummer to autumn.

■ **Value at other times** It has pretty, glossy, dark-green foliage from spring to autumn.

■ **Ideal site** A mixed or herbaceous border.

■ **Cultivation** Best grown in partial shade, but tolerates full sun. Grow in moist, fertile soil enriched with organic matter. Divide the plants every three or four years in spring or autumn.

■ **Also recommended** *Aconitum carmichaelii* 'Arendsii' ♀ has branched spires of clear-blue flowers in autumn.

■ **Perfect partners** *Aconitum* 'Ivorine', with ivory-white flowers in late spring and early summer.

Agapanthus 'Blue Giant'
African blue lily

A clump-forming herbaceous perennial of upright habit. H 1.2m (4ft), S 60cm (2ft)

■ **Seasonal highlights** Has rounded clusters of bell-shaped, rich-blue flowers from mid- to late summer.

■ **Value at other times** Large, strap-shaped, deep-green leaves.

■ **Ideal site** A sunny border, or a tall, shapely container.

■ **Cultivation** Best in sun, but will tolerate light, dappled shade. Grow in moist but well-drained soil. In cold areas, mulch in winter to protect fleshy roots from frost.

■ **Also recommended** *Agapanthus campanulatus* has pale- to dark-blue, occasionally white, flowers from mid- to late summer.

■ **Perfect partners** The strap-shaped foliage contrasts well with the bold, rounded leaves of hostas.

Alcea rosea Chater's Double Group
Hollyhock

A short-lived perennial of vigorous, upright growth. H to 2.5m (8ft), S 60cm (2ft)

■ **Seasonal highlights** In summer, it bears peony-like flowers, ranging from white, yellow, apricot, and red to lavender and purple. It attracts butterflies and bees.

■ **Value at other times** Attractive leaves for most of the year.

■ **Ideal site** The back of a sunny border, especially in cottage gardens.

■ **Cultivation** Flowers best in sun, but tolerates dappled shade. Grow in any fertile, well-drained soil. Stake in exposed sites. Treat as annuals or biennials to limit hollyhock rust.

■ **Also recommended** *Alcea rosea* 'Nigra', with single, chocolate-maroon flowers.

■ **Perfect partners** Other tall herbaceous plants such as delphiniums.

A

Alchemilla mollis ♀
Lady's mantle

A vigorous, clump-forming, herbaceous perennial.
H 60cm (24in), S 75cm (30in)
■ **Seasonal highlights** Bears loose clusters of tiny greenish-yellow flowers from early summer to autumn.
■ **Value at other times** The hairy, soft-green leaves look especially good spangled with droplets of rain or dew.
■ **Ideal site** The front of a herbaceous border, or in paving crevices.
■ **Cultivation** Thrives in sun or partial shade. Grow in any moist, humus-rich soil. Deadhead after flowering, or it will seed itself all over the garden.
■ **Also recommended** *Alchemilla alpina* is similar but lower-growing and mat-forming.
■ **Perfect partners** It associates well with most other herbaceous perennials, but looks especially good with penstemons.

Allium hollandicum ♀
Ornamental onion

A moderately vigorous, bulbous perennial.
H 1m (3ft), S 10cm (4in)
■ **Seasonal highlights** In summer it produces dense, rounded heads of many star-shaped, purplish-pink flowers.
■ **Value at other times** The attractive seedheads of autumn can be dried for flower arrangements.
■ **Ideal site** The perfect highlight in a sunny, mixed border.
■ **Cultivation** Ideally grow in full sun, but will tolerate light shade. Grow in any fertile, well-drained soil. Plant bulbs 5–10cm (2–4in) deep in autumn.
■ **Also recommended** *Allium caeruleum* has intense, bright-blue flowers.
■ **Perfect partners** Excellent with hemerocallis and achilleas, providing good contrasts of form and colour.

Alopecurus pratensis '*Aureovariegatus*'
Foxtail grass

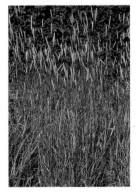

A spreading perennial grass.
H 1.2m (4ft), S 40cm (16in), often more, but not invasive
■ **Seasonal highlights** It produces dense, cylindrical heads of pale-green to purple flowers from mid-spring to midsummer.
■ **Value at other times** Has narrow, green leaves that are striped rich yellow and arranged in basal tufts.
■ **Ideal site** A sunny mixed border or wild garden.
■ **Cultivation** Best in full sun, but it will tolerate light shade. Grow in fertile, well-drained soil. Cut back to ground level in spring for the freshest-coloured foliage in summer.
■ **Also recommended** *Alopecurus lanatus* has silver-grey leaves.
■ **Perfect partners** *Hakonechloa macra* '*Aureola*' ♀ and *Carex elata* '*Aurea*' ♀ for contrasting golden foliage.

Alstroemeria '*Orange Glory*' ♀
Peruvian lily

An upright, moderately vigorous, herbaceous perennial. H 1m (3ft), S 60cm (2ft)
■ **Seasonal highlights** For many weeks in summer, it bears showy, orange-yellow flowers with darker speckles. They are excellent for cutting.
■ **Value at other times** It has grey-green foliage.
■ **Ideal site** A mixed border or one devoted to flowers for cutting.
■ **Cultivation** Ideally, grow in full sun; it tolerates light shade. Plant carefully in late summer or early autumn in any moist but well-drained soil; the fleshy roots are fragile and resent disturbance. In cold areas, apply a dry winter mulch.
■ **Also recommended** *Alstroemeria hookeri*, pale-pink flowers; *A*. '*Parigo Charm*' in salmon.
■ **Perfect partners** Roses, sunflowers, and tall border phlox.

Amaranthus caudatus
Love-lies-bleeding

Also known as tassel flower. A vigorous, bushy, upright perennial, usually grown as a frost-tender annual.
H 1–1.5m (3–5ft), S 45–75cm (18–30in).
■ **Seasonal highlights** From summer to autumn, it produces long, hanging tassels of crimson-purple flowers.
■ **Value at other times** Lush leaves with red or purple stems. Flowers are good for dried arrangements.
■ **Ideal site** An annual or cutting border.
■ **Cultivation** Grow in full sun in humus-rich soil in a sheltered spot. It tolerates poor soils. Sow seeds under glass in early spring and plant out when the threat of frost has passed.
■ **Also recommended** *Amaranthus caudatus* '*Viridis*' has green flowers that fade to cream.
■ **Perfect partners** Grow amid annual bedding as a dot plant.

Amelanchier lamarckii ♀
Snowy mespilus

Also known as Juneberry. A moderately vigorous, deciduous shrub or small tree, with upright stems. H 10m (30ft), S 12m (40ft)
■ **Seasonal highlights** In mid-spring, a profusion of star-shaped, white flowers.
■ **Value at other times** The young leaves are bronzed, turning to green, then to shades of orange and red.
■ **Ideal site** A sunny shrub border, in an open glade in a woodland garden, or as a specimen plant.
■ **Cultivation** Will tolerate light, dappled shade. Grow in lime-free soil that is moist but well-drained and enriched with organic matter. Tolerates hard pruning.
■ **Also recommended** *Amelanchier x grandiflora* 'Ballerina' ♀ is smaller, but similar.
■ **Perfect partners** Combine with a late, large-flowered clematis, such as 'Ville de Lyon', with bright carmine-red flowers, or 'Rouge Cardinal' with velvety crimson flowers.

Anemone blanda 'Violet Star'
Mountain windflower

A moderately vigorous, spreading, tuberous perennial. H & S to 15cm (6in).
■ **Seasonal highlights** In spring it produces clear-amethyst flowers with a white reverse to the petals.
■ **Value at other times** The dark-green leaves are pretty but fade away during summer dormancy.
■ **Ideal site** Excellent when naturalized in turf or woodland and good at the front of a border.
■ **Cultivation** Plant tubers 5–8cm (2–3in) deep in autumn, in humus-rich, well-drained soil, in sun or dappled shade.
■ **Also recommended** *Anemone blanda* 'White Splendour' ♀ has large, white flowers that are pink on the reverse.
■ **Perfect partners** Create a spring tapestry of bloom with dwarf narcissus and crocus.

Anemone x hybrida 'Max Vogel'
Japanese anemone

A vigorous, spreading, herbaceous perennial of upright growth. H 1.2–1.5m (4–5ft), S indefinite
■ **Seasonal highlights** From late summer until late autumn, it bears single, light-pink flowers that become paler as the flower ages.
■ **Value at other times** The lobed, dark-green leaves make good ground cover.
■ **Ideal site** A mixed or herbaceous border, or woodland garden.
■ **Cultivation** Prefers a moist, humus-rich soil and thrives in sun or dappled shade. It is invasive, but easily controlled by digging out unwanted pieces.
■ **Also recommended** *Anemone x hybrida* 'Honorine Jobert' ♀ has white flowers.
■ **Perfect partners** Use with roses and other perennials. It looks good in an open woodland glade.

Antirrhinum majus 'Trumpet Serenade'
Snapdragon

A bushy, upright, moderately vigorous perennial that is grown as an annual. H & S 30cm (12in)
■ **Seasonal highlights** From summer to autumn it bears spikes of open trumpet-shaped, bicoloured flowers in a mixture of pastel shades.
■ **Value at other times** Has attractive, lance-shaped, semi-glossy leaves.
■ **Ideal site** Good for bedding, containers, and for children's plots.
■ **Cultivation** Best in full sun, but it tolerates light shade and thrives in any fertile soil. Sow seeds in late winter under glass. Set out when risk of frost has passed.
■ **Also recommended** *Antirrhinum majus* 'Jamaican Mist' is early and long-flowering in a range of pastel colours.
■ **Perfect partners** Snapdragons associate well with a wide range of annual bedding plants.

Aquilegia vulgaris 'Nora Barlow' ♀
Granny's bonnet

Also known as columbine. A robust, upright, moderately vigorous perennial. H 90cm (36in), S 45cm (18in)
■ **Seasonal highlights** From late spring to early summer, it bears pompon-like flowers with narrow, spurless petals in pale green and red.
■ **Value at other times** Has pretty, dark greyish-green foliage in spring and summer.
■ **Ideal site** A sunny border, especially in a cottage garden.
■ **Cultivation** Grow in full sun or light shade, in any fertile, moisture-retentive soil. Increase is easy by division in spring, or seed sown in spring or autumn and self-sown seedlings come fairly true to type.
■ **Also recommended** *Aquilegia alpina* is shorter with clear-blue flowers.
■ **Perfect partners** Roses, lupins, delphiniums, and other perennials.

A

Arctotis x hybrida 'Red Devil'
African daisy

Argyranthemum foeniculaceum
Marguerite

Artemisia alba 'Canescens' ♀
White sage

Arundo donax var. versicolor
Giant reed

Aster novi-belgii 'Peace'
Michaelmas daisy

Moderately vigorous, semi-erect perennial that is grown as a half-hardy annual. H 45–50cm (18–20in), S 30cm (12in)
■ **Seasonal highlights** Throughout summer, it bears dark-centred, red flowerheads.
■ **Value at other times** Felted, silvery-green leaves are good for foliage contrasts.
■ **Ideal site** Sunny banks and borders, gravel gardens, and containers.
■ **Cultivation** Grow in sun, in well-drained soil. Will tolerate light, part-day shade. Sow seed under glass in early spring and set young plants out when risk of frost has passed.
■ **Also recommended** *Arctotis x hybrida* 'African Sunshine' has orange-yellow flowerheads.
■ **Perfect partners** Gazanias and other sun-loving, annual bedding plants.

A compact, fairly vigorous subshrub, evergreen but frost-tender.
H & S to 80cm (32in)
■ **Seasonal highlights** It bears single, white, daisy-like flowerheads with yellow centres, continuously from summer to autumn.
■ **Value at other times** Fine, blue-grey leaves all year.
■ **Ideal site** Sunny borders and containers.
■ **Cultivation** Prefers full sun, but tolerates light shade. Grow in well-drained soil. Pinch out stem tips to keep plants bushy and deadhead regularly. In cold areas, overwinter under glass.
■ **Also recommended** *Argyranthemum frutescens* is similar, with less finely cut leaves.
■ **Perfect partners** *Argyranthemum* 'Jamaica Primrose' ♀ with primrose-yellow flowerheads; *A.* 'Vancouver' ♀ with pink, anemone-centred blooms.

A vigorous, bushy, semi-evergreen perennial. H 45cm (18in), S 30cm (12in)
■ **Seasonal highlights** It is grown mainly for its beautiful, aromatic, silver-grey leaves, which are very finely cut.
■ **Value at other times** In late summer it bears yellow-brown flowerheads, but most gardeners prefer to remove them.
■ **Ideal site** A hot, sunny border or gravel garden.
■ **Cultivation** Grow in any well-drained soil in sun or light, part-day shade. Dig coarse grit into heavy clay soils to improve drainage. They grow a bit less leggy and are therefore more attractive in dappled shade, especially 'Powis Castle'.
■ **Also recommended** *Artemisia arborescens* ♀ has finely dissected, silver-white leaves.
■ **Perfect partners** Argyranthemums and bold foliage plants, such as irises and yuccas, contrast well with the fine foliage of artemisias.

A vigorous, half-hardy, perennial grass. H 1.8m (6ft), S 60cm (24in)
■ **Seasonal highlights** The arching, white-striped leaves are attractive all summer.
■ **Value at other times** In late summer it bears dense heads of creamy spikelets.
■ **Ideal site** At the back of a border or in containers in a conservatory.
■ **Cultivation** Any well-drained soil is suitable and it tolerates light shade, but grows best in sun in reliably moist soil. Protect from cold winds and hard frost. Cut to the base in spring for the best-coloured foliage.
■ **Also recommended** *Arundo donax* is taller, hardier, and has plain, bluish-green leaves.
■ **Perfect partners** *Pennisetum villosum* ♀, with feathery, pale buff-purple flowerheads; *Stipa gigantea* ♀, very tall with airy, glistening, golden spikelets.

An upright, moderately vigorous, herbaceous perennial. H 1.2m (4ft), S 90cm (36in)
■ **Seasonal highlights** From late summer to mid-autumn, it bears masses of single, yellow-centred, mauve flowerheads, 7cm (3in) across.
■ **Value at other times** Attractive lance-shaped leaves.
■ **Ideal site** Indispensable in a late summer and autumn border.
■ **Cultivation** Grow in sun or light shade. Well-cultivated, moisture-retentive soil, full of organic matter, is best. Divide every three or four years. Cut down the old stems after flowering.
■ **Also recommended** *Aster amellus* 'Sonia' is shorter with pale-pink flowerheads.
■ **Perfect partners** Rudbeckias and sedums, which also bring useful colour to the garden during late summer and autumn.

Astilbe 'Bronce Elegans' ♀
Astilbe

A moderately vigorous, clump-forming herbaceous perennial of upright growth. H 30cm (12in), S 25cm (10in)
■ **Seasonal highlights** In late summer it produces plumes of red-pink flowers.
■ **Value at other times** The red-stemmed, dark-green leaves are good ground cover.
■ **Ideal site** A bog garden, waterside plantings, or a shady border.
■ **Cultivation** Best grown in boggy soil in sun, but will tolerate slightly drier conditions in partial shade. Cut down old foliage in late autumn. Divide every three to four years.
■ **Also recommended** *Astilbe* 'Aphrodite' has sprays of red flowers and bronze leaves.
■ **Perfect partners** Hemerocallis, ferns, and grasses, such as squirreltail grass (*Hordeum jubatum*) with silky, beige flowerheads.

Astrantia major
Masterwort

A moderately vigorous, upright herbaceous perennial. H 30–90cm (12–36in), S 45cm (18in)
■ **Seasonal highlights** In early and midsummer, it bears heads of tiny green, pink, or purplish-red flowers surrounded by white bracts.
■ **Value at other times** The flowerheads can be used for dried arrangements.
■ **Ideal site** A mixed or herbaceous border, especially in cottage gardens.
■ **Cultivation** Ideally, grow in full sun, but it will tolerate light shade. Plant in a humus-rich soil that doesn't dry out. Cut down dead stems when flowering is over. This plant self-seeds quite prolifically.
■ **Also recommended** *Astrantia major* subsp. *involucrata* has green-tipped white bracts.
■ **Perfect partners** Astilbes, rudbeckias, asters.

Aubrieta 'J.S. Baker'
Aubretia

A spreading, mat-forming perennial of dense, moderately vigorous growth. H 5cm (2in), S 60cm (24in)
■ **Seasonal highlights** In spring, it produces single, white-eyed, purple flowers in profusion.
■ **Value at other times** The greyish-green leaves form dense ground cover.
■ **Ideal site** A rock garden, drystone wall, sunny bank, or border front.
■ **Cultivation** Grow in well-drained, preferably neutral to alkaline soil, enriched with organic matter. Cut back hard after flowering to maintain neat, compact plants.
■ **Also recommended** *Aubrieta* 'Joy' has double mauve flowers.
■ **Perfect partners** *Aurinia saxatilis* ♀, with yellow flowers and most arabis, which have flowers in white or shades of pink.

Aucuba japonica 'Variegata'
Spotted laurel

A vigorous, evergreen shrub of dense, bushy growth. H & S to 3m (10ft)
■ **Seasonal highlights** Attractively variegated foliage all year round.
■ **Value at other times** Upright clusters of small, red flowers appear in mid-spring; on female plants, like this cultivar, they are followed by bright-red berries.
■ **Ideal site** Grows almost anywhere, but good in dark, shady corners, in containers, or as hedging.
■ **Cultivation** Exceptionally tolerant of a range of difficult sites, from deep, dry shade to coastal cliffs. It grows in any but waterlogged soil. Prune or trim hedges in spring. Very tolerant of hard pruning.
■ **Also recommended** *Aucuba japonica* 'Crotonifolia' ♀ has yellow-speckled leaves.
■ **Perfect partners** Potentillas, rhododendrons.

B

Begonia x tuberhybrida
Tuberous begonia

Tuberous, moderately vigorous, frost-tender perennials that die down in winter. H & S 23cm (9in)
■ **Seasonal highlights** Throughout summer, they bear showy, mostly double, flowers, in vibrant shades of red, pink, white, and yellow. Upright and trailing cultivars are available.
■ **Value at other times** Large, glossy leaves.
■ **Ideal site** Bedding and containers.
■ **Cultivation** Best in full sun, but tolerant of partial shade. Grow in fertile, moist but well-drained soil. Bring into growth in warmth in early spring. Plant when the threat of frost has passed. Lift in autumn and store dry.
■ **Also recommended** *Begonia* Semperflorens Cultorum Group cultivars are compact, with masses of small flowers throughout summer.
■ **Perfect partners** Petunias and asters.

B

Bellis perennis Tasso Series
Double daisy

Moderately vigorous, rosette-forming perennial, usually grown as a biennial. H & S 5–20cm (2–8in).

■ **Seasonal highlights** From late winter until late summer, bears double-daisy flowers in red, pink, or white.

■ **Value at other times** Attractive spoon-shaped, semi-glossy, dark-green leaves.

■ **Ideal site** Bedding, border edging, and containers.

■ **Cultivation** Grow in any fertile, well-drained soil, in sun or light shade. Sow seeds outside in early summer or indoors in early spring. Deadhead to encourage more flowers and prevent self seeding.

■ **Also recommended** *Bellis perennis* 'Pomponette' ♀ has double flowers with quilled petals.

■ **Perfect partners** Tulips, wallflowers, and forget-me-nots.

Bergenia 'Sunningdale'
Elephant's ears

Clump-forming herbaceous perennial. H 30–45cm (12–18in), S 45–60cm (18–24in)

■ **Seasonal highlights** Rich lilac-magenta flowers on red stems appear in early and mid-spring.

■ **Value at other times** Bold, glossy, dark-green leaves, which turn copper-red in winter.

■ **Ideal site** Front of a border, containers, in a woodland garden.

■ **Cultivation** Best in sun in well-drained soil enriched with plenty of organic matter, but tolerant of partial shade and poor soils. Lift and divide every three to five years to maintain vigour.

■ **Also recommended** *Bergenia* 'Ballawley' ♀ has crimson flowers and bronze-purple winter leaves.

■ **Perfect partners** Roses, hostas, fuchsias, and other herbaceous perennials.

Betula papyrifera
Paper birch, Canoe birch

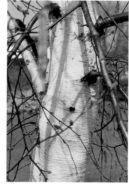

A deciduous, fairly vigorous tree of conical outline. H 20m (70ft) or more, S 10m (30ft)

■ **Seasonal highlights** The peeling white bark reveals pale orange-brown bark beneath and is beautiful when leafless in winter.

■ **Value at other times** Dark-green leaves turn yellow and orange in autumn. Long, yellow catkins appear in spring.

■ **Ideal site** A fine specimen, especially in damp soils by streams or pools.

■ **Cultivation** Grow in fertile, humus-rich soil in sun or dappled shade. In winter, prune out lowest branches when very small to create a clear trunk.

■ **Also recommended** *Betula pendula* 'Youngii' is dome-shaped and weeping. The most popular type for white bark is the silver Himalayan birch.

■ **Perfect partners** *Griselinia littoralis* 'Dixon's Cream', rowans (*Sorbus*), willows (*Salix*), and conifers.

Borago officinalis
Borage

A very vigorous branching annual, used as a culinary herb. H 60cm (24in), S 45cm (18in)

■ **Seasonal highlights** Throughout summer, it bears bright-blue, star-shaped flowers.

■ **Value at other times** Mounds of white, bristly, matt green leaves and hairy stems.

■ **Ideal site** Herb gardens, dry, sunny sites.

■ **Cultivation** Best in sun, in well-drained soil, but tolerates light shade. On heavy clay soils, dig in plenty of coarse grit to improve the drainage. Self-seeds freely.

■ **Also recommended** *Borago pygmaea* is mat-forming and bears hanging, clear-blue, bell-shaped flowers.

■ **Perfect partners** Mints, sage (*Salvia officinalis*), and feverfew (*Tanacetum parthenium*).

Buddleja davidii 'Fascinating'
Butterfly bush

A vigorous, deciduous shrub with arching branches. H 3m (10ft), S 5m (15ft)

■ **Seasonal highlights** From summer to autumn, it bears dense, arching spires of lilac-pink flowers.

■ **Value at other times** Attractive mid-green to grey-green foliage. It is excellent for attracting butterflies.

■ **Ideal site** Shrub or mixed borders and wildlife gardens.

■ **Cultivation** It tolerates dappled shade, but flowers best and attracts more butterflies, in full sun. Grow in any fertile, well-drained soil, rich in organic matter. Prune back the previous year's growth to a woody framework in early spring.

■ **Also recommended** *Buddleja davidii* 'White Profusion' ♀ has white flowers. There are many other cultivars.

■ **Perfect partners** Hypericum, berberis, and tree peonies.

Buddleja globosa ♀
Orange ball tree

Vigorous, deciduous, or semi- evergreen shrub. H & S 5m (15ft)
■ **Seasonal highlights** In early summer, it bears rounded clusters of fragrant, orange-yellow flowers.
■ **Value at other times** The dark-green, deeply veined leaves are handsome.
■ **Ideal site** A shrub or mixed border.
■ **Cultivation** Best grown in sun, in any fertile garden soil enriched with organic matter. It will tolerate light shade. Keep pruning to a minimum, but when mature, occasionally remove some of the oldest flowered shoots at the base, after flowering.
■ **Also recommended** *Buddleja* x *weyeriana* 'Sungold' ♀ has dark orange-yellow flowers.
■ **Perfect partners** Hypericum, berberis, and tree peonies.

C

Caltha palustris ♀
Kingcup, Marsh marigold

A vigorous, creeping, rhizomatous perennial. H 40cm (16in), S 45cm (18in)
■ **Seasonal highlights** In spring it bears glossy, yellow, cup-shaped flowers, often with a second flush of bloom later in the year.
■ **Value at other times** The heart-shaped leaves are attractive for most of the year.
■ **Ideal site** A bog garden, at the waterside, or in a damp border.
■ **Cultivation** Best in full sun, but tolerates light shade. Grow in boggy, permanently moist soil at the water's edge, or in planting baskets, in water to 23cm (9in) deep.
■ **Also recommended** *Caltha palustris* 'Flore Pleno' ♀ has double flowers.
■ **Perfect partners** Water lilies, *Mimulus luteus*, *M. ringens*.

Camassia cusickii 'Zwanenburg'
Camassia

An upright, moderately vigorous, bulbous perennial. H 60–80cm (24–32in), S 10cm (4in)
■ **Seasonal highlights** In late spring it bears spires of starry, deep-blue flowers.
■ **Value at other times** The grass-like leaves are ornamentally insignificant.
■ **Ideal site** A herbaceous border or wildflower meadow.
■ **Cultivation** Plant bulbs 10cm (4in) deep in autumn. Flowers best in full sun, but tolerates light shade. Grow in deep, fertile, moisture-retentive soil. Mulch in winter in cold, frosty areas.
■ **Also recommended** *Camassia cusickii* has pale to deep steely-blue flowers.
■ **Perfect partners** Alliums (ornamental onions), cowslips (*Primula veris*).

Camellia x williamsii 'Anticipation' ♀
Camellia

A moderately vigorous, evergreen shrub of narrowly upright growth. H 4m (12ft), S 2m (6ft)
■ **Seasonal highlights** The beautiful, peony-like crimson flowers appear from mid-winter to mid-spring.
■ **Value at other times** The lustrous, dark-green foliage is delightful all year.
■ **Ideal site** Shrub borders, woodland gardens, and containers.
■ **Cultivation** Thrives in sun or dappled shade, but needs shade from early morning sun, which may damage flowers in frosty weather. Grow in humus-rich, lime-free (acid) soil, or in ericaceous compost in pots. Trim lightly to shape after flowering, if necessary.
■ **Also recommended** *Camellia* x *williamsii* 'Donation' ♀ has semi-double, pink flowers. There are many other cultivars.
■ **Perfect partners** Rhododendrons and azaleas.

Campanula lactiflora
Milky bellflower

A moderately vigorous, upright herbaceous perennial. H 1.2–1.5m (4–5ft), S 60cm (24in)
■ **Seasonal highlights** Clusters of bell-shaped flowers from early summer to early autumn are white to pale blue, lilac-blue, or violet.
■ **Value at other times** Attractive leaves from early spring to late summer.
■ **Ideal site** A mixed or herbaceous border, or woodland garden.
■ **Cultivation** Thrives in sun, but flower colour is better preserved in light shade. Grow in fertile, well-drained, neutral-to-alkaline soil. It may need staking in exposed gardens.
■ **Also recommended** *Campanula lactiflora* 'Prichard's Variety' ♀ has violet-blue flowers.
■ **Perfect partners** Roses, *Campanula lactiflora* 'Loddon Anna' ♀ with lilac-pink flowers, *C.* 'Elizabeth', cream flowers.

C

Carex flagellifera
New Zealand sedge

A moderately vigorous, tuft-forming, arching sedge. H 1.1m (3½ft), S 90cm (3ft)

■ **Seasonal highlights** Grass-like, reddish-brown leaves all year.

■ **Value at other times** Tall stems bear light-brown flower spikes in summer.

■ **Ideal site** A mixed border, gravel plantings, or containers.

■ **Cultivation** Grow in sun or partial shade in any soil that is not too wet or too dry. In cold areas, protect with a winter mulch.

■ **Also recommended** *Carex siderosticha* 'Variegata' has pink-flushed, pale green-and-white-striped leaves.

■ **Perfect partners** Use *Carex oshimensis* 'Evergold' ♀, or *Hakonechloa macra* 'Aureola' ♀ for contrasting shades of green and gold.

Carex oshimensis 'Evergold' ♀
Golden sedge

A vigorous, evergreen, mound-forming sedge. H 30cm (12in), S 35cm (14in)

■ **Seasonal highlights** The arching, dark-green leaves have a central creamy-white stripe and remain attractive all year round.

■ **Value at other times** In mid- to late spring, tall spikes of brown flowers appear.

■ **Ideal site** A mixed border, gravel plantings, or containers.

■ **Cultivation** Thrives in sun or partial shade. A fertile, moist but well-drained soil is required.

■ **Also recommended** *Carex elata* 'Aurea' ♀ has rich-yellow leaves.

■ **Perfect partners** *Polystichum setiferum* (soft shield fern) and hostas form good foliage contrasts.

Carex pendula
Weeping sedge

A vigorous, clump-forming, evergreen sedge. H 1.4m (4½ft), S 1.5m (5ft)

■ **Seasonal highlights** In late spring and early summer, arching stems bear catkin-like, dark-brown flower spikes that are erect at first, then droop with age.

■ **Value at other times** Shiny mid-green leaves that are blue-green beneath.

■ **Ideal site** Poolsides, damp borders, and woodland gardens.

■ **Cultivation** Grow in sun or partial shade. Plant in moist, fertile soil.

■ **Also recommended** *Carex grayi* (mace sedge) is shorter; its green flower spikes give rise to spiky seedheads.

■ **Perfect partners** Use hostas to form a broad-leaved contrast to the narrow leaves of the sedge.

Caryopteris x clandonensis 'Kew Blue'

A moderately vigorous, arching, deciduous shrub. H 1m (3ft), S 1.5m (5ft)

■ **Seasonal highlights** From late summer to early autumn, it bears spires of deep-blue flowers.

■ **Value at other times** The dark grey-green leaves are silvery beneath.

■ **Ideal site** A mixed or shrub border, gravel plantings, hot, dry sites.

■ **Cultivation** It flowers best in full sun, but will tolerate light dappled shade. Prefers light, fertile, well-drained soil. In areas with cold winters and cool summers, plant against a warm, sheltered wall. In early spring, cut back to a permanent woody framework.

■ **Also recommended** *Caryopteris* x *clandonensis* 'Worcester Gold' ♀ has golden foliage and lavender-blue flowers.

■ **Perfect partners** Lavatera, fuchsias, potentillas.

Centaurea hypoleuca 'John Coutts'
Knapweed, Cornflower

A vigorous, spreading, clump-forming herbaceous perennial. H 60cm (24in), S 45cm (18in)

■ **Seasonal highlights** In summer, it bears fragrant, deep rose-pink flowers that attract bees and butterflies.

■ **Value at other times** The divided, grey-green leaves are grey-white beneath.

■ **Ideal site** An herbaceous border, especially in a cottage garden.

■ **Cultivation** Grow this drought-tolerant plant in full sun in any well-drained soil. Regular deadheading results in more flowers later in the season. Divide every three to four years to maintain vigour.

■ **Also recommended** *Centaurea dealbata* 'Steenbergii' has carmine-pink flowerheads.

■ **Perfect partners** *Centaurea macrocephala*, *Lythrum*, border phlox, and other herbaceous perennials.

Chaenomeles speciosa 'Phylis Moore'
Flowering quince

Also known as japonica. A vigorous, deciduous shrub with wide-spreading branches. H 2.5m (8ft), S to 5m (15ft)
■ **Seasonal highlights** In spring, before, and with the new leaves, it bears large clusters of semi-double, almond-pink flowers.
■ **Value at other times** Aromatic yellow fruits appear in autumn; they can be cooked in jellies or preserves.
■ **Ideal site** Shrub borders, sunny or shaded walls, and hedging.
■ **Cultivation** Grow in any fertile, well-drained soil in sun or partial shade. After flowering, shorten flowered shoots to strong buds. When mature, take out one in five of the oldest shoots.
■ **Also recommended** *Chaenomeles speciosa* 'Moerloosei' ♀ has apple-blossom-pink flowers.
■ **Perfect partners** Forsythia, pyracantha and *Ribes sanguineum* (flowering currant).

Chaenomeles x superba 'Knap Hill Scarlet' ♀
Flowering quince

Also known as flowering quince and japonica. A vigorous, rounded, spiny-stemmed, deciduous shrub. H 1.5m (5ft), S 2m (6ft)
■ **Seasonal highlights** From spring to summer it bears clusters of large, scarlet flowers with golden anthers.
■ **Value at other times** Later in autumn it produces golden-yellow fruits.
■ **Ideal site** Shrub borders, sunny or shaded walls, and hedging.
■ **Cultivation** Grow in any fertile, well-drained soil in sun or partial shade. After flowering, shorten flowered shoots to strong buds. When mature, take out one in five of the oldest shoots.
■ **Also recommended** *Chaenomeles x superba* 'Nicoline' ♀ has large, often semi-double, scarlet flowers.
■ **Perfect partners** Forsythia, pyracantha, and *Ribes sanguineum* (flowering currant).

Chelone obliqua
Turtlehead

A vigorous, upright, herbaceous perennial. H 40–60cm (16–24in), S 30cm (12in)
■ **Seasonal highlights** From late summer to mid-autumn, it bears dark-pink or purple flowers with yellow beards on the lower lip.
■ **Value at other times** It has attractive, lance-shaped, boldly veined leaves.
■ **Ideal site** Mixed or herbaceous borders, bog gardens.
■ **Cultivation** Grow in full sun or partial shade. A deep, fertile soil that retains moisture is ideal. Mulch well in spring before growth begins. Will tolerate heavy clay soils.
■ **Also recommended** *Chelone lyonii* is similar but taller.
■ **Perfect partners** *Coreopsis verticillata*, *Crocosmia* 'Lady Hamilton'.

Chimonanthus praecox
Wintersweet

A spreading, moderately vigorous, deciduous shrub. H 4m (12ft), S 3m (10ft)
■ **Seasonal highlights** On bare winter shoots, it bears nodding, very fragrant, soft-yellow flowers.
■ **Value at other times** The leaves are rather coarse, but this shrub is an ideal host for late-flowering clematis.
■ **Ideal site** As a specimen, in a shrub border, against a warm wall.
■ **Cultivation** Grow in full sun or partial shade. Grow in any fertile soil. Prune after flowering, removing misplaced shoots to maintain a good shape.
■ **Also recommended** *Chimonanthus praecox* 'Grandiflorus' ♀ has larger, deeper-yellow flowers.
■ **Perfect partners** *Jasminum nudiflorum* ♀ (winter jasmine), *Mahonia x media* 'Charity'; both have yellow flowers in winter.

Chionodoxa forbesii 'Pink Giant'
Glory of the snow

A moderately vigorous, bulbous perennial. H 10–20cm (4–8in), S 3cm (1¼in)
■ **Seasonal highlights** In early spring it bears spikes of starry, white-centred, pink flowers.
■ **Value at other times** Dies back after flowering.
■ **Ideal site** A rock garden, raised bed, beneath shrubs, in containers.
■ **Cultivation** Plant in autumn 8cm (3in) deep. Grow in any well-drained soil in sun or dappled shade. Lift and separate the bulbs after four to five years if they become congested.
■ **Also recommended** *Chionodoxa forbesii* has white-eyed, blue flowers.
■ **Perfect partners** Grow as a carpet beneath a forsythia, with dwarf daffodils.

C

Choisya 'Aztec Pearl' ♀
Mexican orange blossom

Chrysanthemum 'Glowing Lynn'
Chrysanthemum

Cimicifuga simplex 'White Pearl'
Bugbane

Cistus x cyprius ♀
Rock rose, Sun rose

Clarkia amoena
Satin flower

A bushy, fairly vigorous, evergreen shrub.
H & S to 2.5m (8ft)
■ **Seasonal highlights** In both late spring and late summer, it bears clusters of pink-tinted white flowers, often with a few in autumn.
■ **Value at other times** Beautiful aromatic leaves, divided into narrow, glossy dark-green leaflets.
■ **Ideal site** A shrub border, or against a warm or lightly shaded wall.
■ **Cultivation** It flowers best in sun, but will tolerate partial shade. Grow in any good garden soil. Trim after flowering in spring to improve the second flowering.
■ **Also recommended** *Choisya ternata* ♀ has broader leaves and white flowers.
■ **Perfect partners** *Choisya ternata* SUNDANCE ('Lich') ♀ has golden foliage if grown in sun, but seldom flowers.

A bushy, upright, moderately vigorous herbaceous perennial. H & S 45cm (18in) or more
■ **Seasonal highlights** It bears masses of double, red-bronze flowers in late summer and autumn. They make excellent cut flowers.
■ **Value at other times** Aromatic dark-green leaves.
■ **Ideal site** Borders and containers.
■ **Cultivation** Grow in full sun in fertile, well-drained soil. Plant out in late spring and pinch out the growing tips to encourage plentiful flowers. Except in very cold areas, it can be left outdoors in winter; protect the crown with a deep, dry mulch. Bring potted plants under glass for winter.
■ **Also recommended** *Chrysanthemum* 'Peach Margaret' has sprays of pale-salmon-pink flowers.
■ **Perfect partners** *Aster novi-belgii* (Michaelmas daisies), dahlias, rudbeckias.

A robust, upright, herbaceous perennial. H 60–90cm (24–36in), S 60cm (24in)
■ **Seasonal highlights** From early to mid-autumn, it bears spires of white flowers that open from green buds.
■ **Value at other times** The divided, pale-green leaves form dense, weed-smothering ground cover.
■ **Ideal site** Damp borders and woodland gardens.
■ **Cultivation** Grow in moist, fertile, humus-rich soil in partial shade. May need staking in exposed gardens.
■ **Also recommended** *Cimicifuga simplex* var. *simplex* 'Brunette' has purplish-brown foliage and purple-tinted, white flowers.
■ **Perfect partners** *Aster* 'Violet Queen', *Salvia* x *superba*.

A moderately vigorous, bushy evergreen shrub.
H & S to 1.5m (5ft)
■ **Seasonal highlights** During summer, it bears clusters of white flowers with crimson blotches at the bases of the petals.
■ **Value at other times** Forms a neat mound of rather sticky, dark-green leaves with wavy margins.
■ **Ideal site** Sunny banks, borders, hot, dry sites, and containers.
■ **Cultivation** Tolerant of poor and alkaline soils. Grow in well-drained soil in full sun. Set out new plants in spring, when the risk of frost has passed. Pinch out stem tips to keep the plant bushy, but don't prune hard.
■ **Also recommended** *Cistus* x *dansereaui* 'Decumbens' is low and spreading with red-blotched, white flowers.
■ **Perfect partners** Roses and lavenders.

A moderately vigorous, upright, hardy annual.
H 75cm (30in), S 30cm (12in)
■ **Seasonal highlights** Throughout summer, it bears clusters of satin-textured, lilac to red-pink flowers.
■ **Value at other times** Of no real value at other times. They last for the summer only.
■ **Ideal site** Annual borders and containers.
■ **Cultivation** Best in sun in slightly acid, moist but well-drained soil, but tolerates light shade. Rich soils encourage leafy growth at the expense of flowers. Sow seeds in the flowering site in spring or autumn. Protect late-sown seedlings with cloches overwinter.
■ **Also recommended** *Clarkia amoena* 'Sybil Sherwood' has salmon-pink flowers.
■ **Perfect partners** A wide range of hardy annuals.

Clematis alpina 'Frances Rivis' ♔
Alpine clematis

A vigorous, deciduous, twining climber. H 2–3m (6–10ft), S 1.5m (5ft)
- **Seasonal highlights** In spring or early summer, it bears hanging, blue flowers with slightly twisted petals.
- **Value at other times** Has attractive foliage all summer and fluffy seedheads in late summer and autumn.
- **Ideal site** Walls, trellis, or scrambling through late-flowering shrubs.
- **Cultivation** Tolerates sun or dappled shade, but the roots should be shaded. Grow in fertile, well-drained soil enriched with plenty of organic matter. After flowering, remove dead or damaged shoots and shorten others to confine to bounds.
- **Also recommended** *Clematis alpina* 'Pink Flamingo' has pale-pink flowers.
- **Perfect partners** Sturdy shrubs, like *Buddleja globosa* or *Phlomis fruticosa*.

Clematis armandii 'Apple Blossom'
Clematis

A vigorous, slightly frost-tender, evergreen climber. H 3–5m (10–15ft), S 2–3m (6–10ft)
- **Seasonal highlights** In early spring, it bears fragrant, pink-tinted white flowers with pink undersides.
- **Value at other times** Attractive foliage all year.
- **Ideal site** A sheltered wall, through shrubs and trees, or, in cold areas, as a conservatory plant.
- **Cultivation** Grow in sun or dappled shade in fertile, humus-rich, well-drained soil, with the roots in shade. After flowering, remove dead or damaged shoots and shorten others to confine to bounds. Use a fertile, loam-based compost for pot-grown plants and enjoy the scent at close quarters.
- **Also recommended** *Clematis armandii* has white flowers.
- **Perfect partners** Camellias make good hosts.

Clematis
Early-flowering clematis

These vigorous, deciduous clematis bloom in late spring and early summer, often with a second flush later in summer
- **Ideal site** Walls, trellis, arbours, pergolas; over shrubs, trees, or hedges.
- **Cultivation** Grow in fertile, well-drained soil enriched with well-rotted organic matter. They flower best with top-growth in sun and roots in shade, but darker colours bleach in sun, so these are better in partial shade. Plant with 10–15cm (4–6in) of stem below soil level to reduce danger of clematis wilt. Shade the roots with stone slabs or with nearby plants. In spring, before growth begins, cut out twiggy, dead, or damaged growth and trim remaining shoots back to strong buds.

Clematis **'Fireworks'** blue-violet with a central red-purple bar, in early and late summer. H 2.5m (8ft), S 1m (3ft)

Clematis **'Niobe'** ♔ free-flowering with velvety deep-red flowers. H 2–3m (6–10ft), S 1m (3ft)

Clematis **'Nelly Moser'** ♔ pinkish-mauve flowers with darker central bands, in early and late summer. H 2–3m (6–10ft), S 1m (3ft)

Clematis **VINO ('Poulvo')** pinkish-mauve flowers with darker central bands, in early and late summer. H 2–3m (6–10ft), S 1m (3ft)

Clematis **'Lasurstern'** ♔ blue flowers with cream anthers, in early summer. H 2.5m (8ft), S 1m (3ft)

Clematis **'Vyvyan Pennell'** double flowers with central lavender-blue petals; later flowers are single. H 2–3m (6–10ft), S 1m (3ft)

C

Clematis

Late-flowering clematis

The late-flowering clematis include large- and small-flowered cultivars, as well as species, which extend the flowering season from midsummer well into autumn.

■ **Cultivation** Late-flowering clematis are grown as for early-flowered, but are pruned differently. Cut back all of the previous year's stems to strong buds 23–45cm (9–18in) above the ground, just as the buds begin to break in spring. If new shoots are trimmed lightly when they reach 30–50cm (12–20in), they flower later, extending the season.

■ **Perfect partners** Since many of this group bloom well in autumn, the last of their flowers will complement autumn colours. The creamy- and white-flowered ones, like 'Huldine', look especially good with purple-leaved shrubs such as *Cotinus coggygria*.

Clematis **'Ville de Lyon'** bears bright carmine-red flowers with darker margins and yellow anthers. H 2–3m (6–10ft), S 1m (3ft)

Clematis viticella is a slender but tough species and bears blue to purple and red flowers. H 2–4m (6–12ft), S 1.5m (5ft)

Clematis **'Jackmanii'** ♀ has large, velvety, dark-purple flowers with light greenish-brown anthers. H 3m (10ft), S 1m (3ft)

Clematis **'Comtesse de Bouchaud'** ♀ bears its large, single, bright mauve-pink flowers from late summer on. H 2–3m (6–10ft), S 1m (3ft)

Clematis **'Etoile Violette'** ♀ has violet-purple flowers with contrasting yellow anthers. H 3–5m (10–15ft), S 1.5m (5ft)

Clematis **'Hagley Hybrid'** has large, single flowers with pinkish-mauve sepals and red anthers. H 2m (6ft), S 1m (3ft)

Clematis cirrhosa 'Freckles' ♀

Winter clematis

A vigorous, slightly frost-tender, evergreen climber. H 2.5–3m (8–10ft), S 1.5m (5ft)

■ **Seasonal highlights** In late winter and early spring, it bears creamy-white, red-speckled flowers.

■ **Value at other times** Has bronzed leaves all year and silky seedheads in summer.

■ **Ideal site** A sheltered wall, or through shrubs and trees.

■ **Cultivation** Grow in sun or dappled shade in fertile, humus-rich, well-drained soil, with the roots in shade. Protect from cold wind. After flowering, remove dead or damaged shoots; shorten others to confine to bounds.

■ **Also recommended** *Clematis cirrhosa* var. *balearica* has fragrant, red-brown speckled, cream flowers.

■ **Perfect partners** Large mahonias make good host shrubs.

Clematis macropetala 'Markham's Pink' ♀

Clematis

A vigorous, deciduous climber. H 2–3m (6–10ft), S 1.5m (5ft)

■ **Seasonal highlights** From spring to early summer, it bears soft sugar-pink flowers.

■ **Value at other times** Pale-green foliage and silver seedheads in summer.

■ **Ideal site** Prefers sun, but will tolerate dappled shade.

■ **Cultivation** Grow in sun or dappled shade in fertile, well-drained soil, enriched with organic matter. Site with the roots in shade. After flowering, remove dead or damaged shoots and shorten others to confine to allotted space.

■ **Also recommended** *Clematis macropetala* 'White Swan' has white flowers with creamy-white centres.

■ **Perfect partners** Forsythias, larger philadelphus, and lilacs are excellent host shrubs.

Clematis montana *f. grandiflora* ♀
Clematis

A very vigorous, deciduous climber. H 10m (30ft), S 4m (12ft)
■ **Seasonal highlights**
Single, white flowers with cream anthers are produced for about four weeks in late spring and early summer.
■ **Value at other times**
Attractive foliage all summer.
■ **Ideal site** A wall, fence, or large tree.
■ **Cultivation** Grow in sun or dappled shade in fertile, well-drained soil, enriched with organic matter. Site with the roots in shade. After flowering, remove dead or damaged shoots and shorten others to confine to allotted space.
■ **Also recommended**
Clematis montana 'Elizabeth' ♀ has scented, pale-pink flowers.
■ **Perfect partners** Conifers, old fruit trees, and beech (*Fagus sylvatica*) are good hosts; they must be vigorous to carry the weight.

Clematis GOLDEN TIARA ('Kugotia')
Late-flowering clematis

Vigorous deciduous climber. H & S 2–3m (6–10ft)
■ **Seasonal highlights**
From late summer until autumn, it produces open lantern-flowers in bright golden yellow, followed by fluffy seedheads that persist into early winter.
■ **Value at other times**
Attractive foliage all through the summer.
■ **Ideal site** Walls and fences of any aspect; climbing through deciduous trees.
■ **Cultivation** Grow in moderately fertile soil enriched with organic matter. Plant deeply and shade the roots. Prune to 30cm (12in) from the ground in spring.
■ **Also recommended**
Clematis 'Bill Mackenzie', similar if a little more vigorous.
■ **Perfect partners**
Clematis flammula, flowering in white at the same time; amelanchiers and crab apples.

Cleome hassleriana 'Colour Fountain'
Spider flower

A vigorous, half-hardy annual. H 1.2m (4ft), S 45cm (18in)
■ **Seasonal highlights**
Throughout summer, it bears dense heads of scented flowers with delicate petals, in shades of pink, violet pink, or white.
■ **Value at other times**
Pretty, divided leaves of fresh green.
■ **Ideal site** An annual or cutting border, or to fill seasonal gaps in a herbaceous border.
■ **Cultivation** Best in sun, but tolerates light dappled shade. Grow in light, free-draining soil. Sow seeds under glass in warmth in spring and plant out when the threat of frost has passed. Cut or deadhead regularly to prolong the flowering period.
■ **Also recommended**
Cleome hassleriana has white, pink, or purple flowers.
■ **Perfect partners**
Clarkias and rudbeckias.

Colchicum cilicicum
Autumn crocus, Naked ladies

Upright, low-growing, cormous perennials. H 10cm (4in), S 8cm (3in)
■ **Seasonal highlights**
In autumn, it bears funnel-shaped, purplish-pink flowers. They appear before the leaves.
■ **Value at other times**
The leaves are not ornamentally significant.
■ **Ideal site** Beneath deciduous shrubs or naturalized in grass.
■ **Cultivation** Best in an open site in full sun, but will tolerate light shade. Plant corms 10cm (4in) deep in late summer or early autumn, in fertile, well-drained soil. If grown in grass, allow the foliage to die down naturally before mowing.
■ **Also recommended**
Colchicum autumnale has lavender-pink flowers.
■ **Perfect partners**
Hydrangeas, *Viburnum* x *bodnantense* 'Deben' ♀.

Convallaria majalis ♀
Lily-of-the-valley

A vigorous, spreading, upright perennial with fleshy roots. H 23cm (9in), S 30cm (12in)
■ **Seasonal highlights** In late spring, arching stems of small, nodding, waxy, white flowers appear. They are strongly scented.
■ **Value at other times**
The attractive leaves make dense ground cover.
■ **Ideal site** A shady border, woodland garden, or in containers, especially for forcing.
■ **Cultivation** Tolerates deep or partial shade. Grow in damp, leafy, fertile soil. A top-dressing of leafmould in autumn is beneficial. Pot some up in autumn and grow under glass for a scented display indoors.
■ **Also recommended**
Convallaria majalis 'Flore Pleno' has double flowers.
■ **Perfect partners** Azaleas, dwarf rhododendrons, and narcissus.

C

Cornus
Dogwoods

The dogwood includes several vigorous, deciduous shrubs that are valued for their brightly coloured leafless stems, which bring interest to the winter garden.

■ **Value at other times** They bear clusters of white flowers in spring and white or blue-black fruit in autumn.

■ **Ideal site** A shrub border, winter garden, or beside pools and streams.

■ **Cultivation** Grow in any moderately fertile soil. Tolerate shade, but stems show their colour best in the sun. For the best effect, prune the stems back to the base each year in early spring.

Cornus alba **'Aurea'** ♀ has yellow leaves, and red winter stems.
H & S 3m (10ft)

Cornus alba **'Sibirica'** ♀ has glossy, bright-red winter stems.
H & S 3m (10ft)

Cornus alba **'Elegantissima'** ♀ has grey-green, cream-margined leaves and red winter stems. H & S 3m (10ft)

Cornus sanguinea **'Winter Beauty'** has bright orange-yellow and red winter shoots.
H 3m (10ft), S 2.5m (8ft)

Cornus stolonifera **'Flaviramea'** ♀ has bright yellow-green shoots.
H 2m (6ft), S 4m (12ft)

Cornus stolonifera **'Kelseyi'** is compact with red-tipped, yellow-green shoots.
H 75cm (30in), S 1.5m (5ft)

Cornus mas
Cornelian cherry

Spreading, moderately vigorous, deciduous shrub or small tree. H & S 5m (15ft)

■ **Seasonal highlights** In late winter, it bears small but profuse clusters of yellow flowers on bare branches.

■ **Value at other times** The dark-green leaves turn red-purple in autumn. It sometimes produces small bright-red fruits in autumn.

■ **Ideal site** Winter garden, shrub borders, or as a specimen plant.

■ **Cultivation** Any fertile, well-drained soil, including chalky ones. Best in an open, sunny site, but will tolerate light shade. Keep pruning to a minimum.

■ **Also recommended** *Cornus mas* 'Variegata' ♀ has white-margined leaves.

■ **Perfect partners** *Eleagnus angustifolia* 'Quicksilver', *Chimonanthus praecox*, *Viburnum* x *bodnantense* 'Dawn' ♀.

Cortaderia selloana 'Sunningdale Silver' ♀
Pampas grass

A vigorous perennial grass. H 3m (10ft) or more, S 2.5m (8ft)

■ **Seasonal highlights** In late summer and autumn, it sends up feathery, silvery-white flower plumes that are very weather-resistant.

■ **Value at other times** Clumps of arching bluish-green leaves all year round.

■ **Ideal site** As a specimen, at the back of a border, in woodland gardens.

■ **Cultivation** It prefers an open, sunny site, but tolerates dappled shade. Grow in fertile, well-drained soil. In late winter or early spring, carefully cut or comb out old foliage; the leaves have viciously sharp edges.

■ **Also recommended** *Cortaderia selloana* 'Albolineata' has yellow-margined leaves.

■ **Perfect partners** *Stipa gigantea, Arundo donax* var. *versicolor*.

Corydalis flexuosa
Fumewort

A slowly spreading, summer-dormant, herbaceous perennial. H 30cm (12in), S 20cm (8in) or more
■ **Seasonal highlights** From late spring to summer, it produces dense clusters of slender-tubed, brilliant-blue flowers with white throats.
■ **Value at other times** Fern-like, bluish-green leaves. Dies back after flowering.
■ **Ideal site** Shady borders, rock gardens, and woodland gardens.
■ **Cultivation** Grow in a cool site in partial or dappled shade, in a humus-rich, fertile, moist but well-drained soil.
■ **Also recommended** *Corydalis fumariifolia* has azure-blue, sometimes purple, flowers.
■ **Perfect partners** *Corydalis lutea*, with yellow flowers.

Corylopsis glabrescens
Corylopsis

A moderately vigorous, deciduous shrub of open, spreading habit. H & S to 5m (15ft)
■ **Seasonal highlights** In mid-spring, it produces hanging tassels of fragrant, pale-yellow flowers.
■ **Value at other times** It has oval leaves that are pale to dark green on top and blue-green beneath.
■ **Ideal site** Shady shrub borders, woodland gardens.
■ **Cultivation** Grow in partial or dappled shade. It prefers well-drained, humus-rich, acid soil, but will tolerate deep soils over chalk. Prune out or shorten badly placed shoots after flowering.
■ **Also recommended** *Corylopsis pauciflora* has cowslip-scented, pale-yellow flowers; it does not tolerate chalky soils.
■ **Perfect partners** *Corylus avellana* 'Contorta', magnolias, *Salix lanata*.

Corylus avellana 'Contorta'
Corkscrew hazel

A fairly vigorous, deciduous shrub with twisted shoots. H & S to 5m (15ft)
■ **Seasonal highlights** The twisted shoots look good in winter, especially when snow-covered. Yellow catkins hang from bare branches in late winter or early spring.
■ **Value at other times** The heart-shaped, wrinkled leaves are also twisted.
■ **Ideal site** As a specimen or at the back of a shrub border.
■ **Cultivation** Thrives in any good garden soil in sun or partial shade. Remove any suckers that grow from the base and carefully prune out any misplaced shoots in winter.
■ **Also recommended** *Corylus maxima* 'Purpurea' ♀ has purple leaves and purple-tinted catkins.
■ **Perfect partners** Magnolias, *Salix lanata*.

Cosmos atrosanguineus
Chocolate cosmos

A spreading, herbaceous perennial with tuberous roots. H 75cm (30in), S 45cm (18in)
■ **Seasonal highlights** From midsummer to autumn, velvety, dark-maroon flowers open to release an elusive, dark-chocolate fragrance.
■ **Value at other times** Clumps of divided, fresh-green foliage.
■ **Ideal site** Warm, sheltered borders.
■ **Cultivation** Grow in fertile, well-drained soil in full sun. Deadhead regularly to prolong flowering. In cold areas, lift tubers before the first frosts and store in a dry, frost-free place.
■ **Also recommended** *Cosmos bipinnatus* is a tall annual, with white, pink, or crimson flowers of similar form.
■ **Perfect partners** Achilleas, border phlox. Grey foliage and bright flowers form a good contrast to the flowers of *Cosmos atrosanguineus*.

Cosmos bipinnatus Sensation Series
Annual cosmos

A vigorous, erect, freely branching, half-hardy annual. H to 90cm (36in), S to 45cm (18in)
■ **Seasonal highlights** Large pink or white flowers are produced freely through summer and autumn. They are good for cutting.
■ **Value at other times** Has feathery foliage all summer.
■ **Ideal site** Annual and cutting borders, or as gap-fillers in mixed or herbaceous borders.
■ **Cultivation** Best in full sun, but tolerates dappled shade. Grow in any well-drained, moderately fertile, soil. Sow seeds under glass in early spring, or in the flowering site in late spring. Deadhead regularly.
■ **Also recommended** *Cosmos bipinnatus* Sonata Series are dwarf and good in containers.
■ **Perfect partners** Clarkia, *Chrysanthemum carinatum*.

C

Cotinus coggygria 🏆
Smoke bush

A vigorous, mound-forming deciduous shrub. H & S 5m (15ft)

■ **Seasonal highlights** Plumes of tiny buff-purple flowers become smoky grey by late summer, giving rise to the common name.

■ **Value at other times** The oval green leaves turn yellow to orange and finally flaming red in autumn.

■ **Ideal site** As a specimen, or in a mixed or shrub border.

■ **Cultivation** Grow in any moderately fertile, moist, but well-drained soil. For larger, brighter-coloured foliage, prune back hard in spring, but allow the plant to become established before doing so.

■ **Also recommended** *Cotinus coggygria* 'Royal Purple' 🏆 has dark red-purple foliage and vivid red autumn colour.

■ **Perfect partners** Berberis, escallonias, weigelas.

Cotinus 'Grace'
Smoke bush

A vigorous, deciduous shrub or small tree. H 6m (20ft), S 5m (15ft)

■ **Seasonal highlights** A haze of tiny purple-pink flowers appear in summer, giving the plant the common name of smoke bush.

■ **Value at other times** Oval purple leaves that turn a brilliant translucent red in late autumn.

■ **Ideal site** As a specimen, or in a mixed or shrub border.

■ **Cultivation** Grow in any moderately fertile, moist but well-drained, soil. To get larger, brighter-coloured foliage, prune all shoots back hard in spring, but let plants become well-established before doing so.

■ **Also recommended** *Cotinus coggygria* 'Notcutt's Variety' has wine-red foliage. The superb variety 'Flame' has good autumn colour.

■ **Perfect partners** Berberis, escallonias, weigelas, *Pittosporum tenufolium* 'Irene Paterson'.

Cotoneaster frigidus 'Fructu Luteo'
Cotoneaster

A moderately vigorous, erect then spreading, deciduous tree or large shrub. H & S to 10m (30ft)

■ **Seasonal highlights** Large clusters of tiny white flowers appear in summer, followed by creamy-yellow fruits in autumn. The flowers attract bees; fruits are eaten by birds in hard winters.

■ **Value at other times** Has peeling bark.

■ **Ideal site** At the back of a shrub border, or as a specimen.

■ **Cultivation** Tolerates almost any soil, including dry ones, but best in moderately fertile, well-drained soil in full sun. Prune lightly to shape in winter, if necessary.

■ **Also recommended** *Cotoneaster franchettii* is semi-evergreen with bright orange-red fruits. There are many types and cultivars.

■ **Perfect partners** *Cotoneaster horizontalis*, shrubby potentillas, ceanothus.

Crambe cordifolia 🏆
Crambe

A vigorous, clump-forming herbaceous perennial. H 2.5m (8ft), S to 1.5m (5ft)

■ **Seasonal highlights** In early to midsummer, tall, strong stems arise bearing clouds of honey-scented white flowers.

■ **Value at other times** Forms a mound of glossy, puckered, dark-green leaves that die down in late summer.

■ **Ideal site** At the back of a mixed or herbaceous border.

■ **Cultivation** Grow in deep, fertile soil in full sun. Will tolerate partial shade. Shelter from strong winds. Is best increased by root cuttings in winter.

■ **Also recommended** *Crambe maritima* is shorter with blue-grey, puckered, twisted, wrinkled leaves and white flowers.

■ **Perfect partners** Old garden roses, philadelphus.

Crataegus laevigata 'Rosea Flore Pleno' 🏆
Midland hawthorn, May

A very hardy, deciduous tree with a rounded crown. H & S to 8m (25ft)

■ **Seasonal highlights** Clusters of double pink flowers appear in late spring.

■ **Value at other times** Red fruits (haws) are produced in autumn.

■ **Ideal site** As a specimen, especially in small gardens, or as hedging.

■ **Cultivation** Tolerates sun and partial shade and a wide variety of soils. Needs minimal pruning to maintain the shape and to cut out dead or damaged wood in winter.

■ **Also recommended** *Crataegus laevigata* 'Paul's Scarlet' 🏆 has double, deep-pink flowers.

■ **Perfect partners** Acers, fastigiate beech (*Fagus sylvatica* 'Dawyck' 🏆), tulip tree (*Liriodendron tulipifera* 🏆).

Crocosmia x crocosmiiflora 'Jackanapes'

Also known as montbretia. A moderately vigorous, upright cormous perennial. H 40–60cm (16–24in), S 8cm (3in)

■ **Seasonal highlights** In late summer it produces arching sprays of orange-red and yellow flowers.

■ **Value at other times** Handsome, sword-shaped leaves for most of the year.

■ **Ideal site** Mixed or herbaceous borders.

■ **Cultivation** Ideally grow in full sun, but it will tolerate partial shade. Plant the corms 8–10cm (3–4in) deep in fertile soil. On heavy clay, plant on a layer of coarse grit. Lift and divide every three or four years, in spring.

■ **Also recommended** Crocosmia 'Emberglow' has dark-red flowers in summer. There are many cultivars, including the bright-red 'Lucifer'.

■ **Perfect partners** Crocosmia 'Golden Fleece', with lemon-yellow flowers, asters, rudbeckias.

Crocus tommasinianus ♀
Early crocus

A robust, cormous perennial. H 10cm (4in), S 2.5cm (1in)

■ **Seasonal highlights** In late winter or early spring, slender, goblet-shaped flowers appear. They come in white, lilac, and red-purple, often with silvery overtones.

■ **Value at other times** No real value at other times.

■ **Ideal site** Naturalize in turf, in borders, rock and woodland gardens.

■ **Cultivation** Best in full sun, but will tolerate dappled shade. Grow in fertile, well-drained soil. Plant corms in the autumn, 8–10cm (3–4in) deep.

■ **Also recommended** Crocus tommasinianus 'Albus' has starry, white flowers with golden anthers.

■ **Perfect partners** Snowdrops (Galanthus) and winter aconites (Eranthis hyemalis ♀).

Crocus vernus 'Pickwick'
Dutch crocus

Robust, cormous perennial. H 12cm (5in), S 5cm (2in)

■ **Seasonal highlights** From early to late spring it produces white flowers, striped pale and dark lilac, with dark-purple bases.

■ **Value at other times** No real value at other times.

■ **Ideal site** Naturalized in turf, in borders, rock and woodland gardens, and in containers.

■ **Cultivation** Grow in sun or light dappled shade, in fertile, well-drained soil. Plant corms in autumn, 8–10cm (3–4in) deep.

■ **Also recommended** Crocus vernus 'Remembrance' has glossy, violet flowers.

■ **Perfect partners** Snowdrops (Galanthus), winter aconites (Eranthis hyemalis ♀), narcissi.

Cyclamen coum ♀
Hardy cyclamen

Hardy cyclamen are spreading and low-growing perennials that grow from underground tubers. There are several species that flower in late summer or in autumn and winter, providing carpets of colour when most other plants have faded. Some flower before the leaves and others with them, but all have a delicacy that belies their tough constitution. Most self-seed freely, forming extensive colonies with time.

■ **Ideal site** Naturalized in turf, in shady borders, beneath shrubs and trees, including conifers.

■ **Cultivation** Grow in moderately fertile well-drained soil, ideally beneath a canopy of trees or shrubs to protect them from excessive summer rain when dormant. Cyclamen purpurascens ♀ needs soil that does not dry out and prefers alkaline soils. Plant tubers 3–5cm (1¼–2in) deep in autumn, or in early spring

C. coum Pewter Group ♀
Hardy cyclamen

for C. purpurascens ♀. Plants can be bought in flower and planted directly if the soil is not frozen or too wet. Give a deep, dry mulch of leafmould as the leaves wither.

■ **Recommended cyclamen** Cyclamen coum ♀ bears neat little blooms in white and shades of pink or carmine-red in winter or early spring, above shiny, deep-green leaves that are often marked with silver. C. coum Pewter Group ♀ has completely silvered leaves. H 8cm (3in), S 10cm (4in) Cyclamen hederifolium ♀ has small flowers in shades of white or pink in mid- to late autumn. Rounded, dark, grey-green leaves, often patterned with silver, appear after the flowers. H 13cm (5in), S 15cm (6in) Cyclamen purpurascens ♀ bears sweetly scented, pale to deep carmine-red flowers in mid- to late summer, with the shiny, dark-green leaves. H & S 10cm (4in)

C

Cytisus x *praecox* 'Warminster' ♀
Warminster broom

A moderately vigorous, arching evergreen shrub. H 1.2m (4ft), S 1.5m (5ft)

■ **Seasonal highlights**
In mid- and late spring, each stem is wreathed in pea-like, creamy-yellow flowers.

■ **Value at other times**
Arching wand-like shoots bear small dark-green leaves.

■ **Ideal site** Shrub borders, sunny banks, hot, dry sites.

■ **Cultivation** Grow in a moderately fertile, well-drained soil in full sun. Tolerates poor acid soils and deep soils over chalk. After flowering has taken place, cut back the flowered shoots to buds lower down green young wood. Don't cut into old wood.

■ **Also recommended**
Cytisus nigricans bears yellow flowers in late summer.

■ **Perfect partners**
Choisyas, camellias, and other broad-leaved evergreens.

D

Dahlia 'Bishop of Llandaff' ♀
Dahlia

A vigorous, tuberous, frost-tender perennial. H 1.1m (3½ft), S 45cm (18in)

■ **Seasonal highlights**
From late summer until late autumn, it produces peony-like, semi-double, velvety, glowing-red flowers.

■ **Value at other times**
It also has very attractive dark-red, almost black, leaves.

■ **Ideal site** Bedding and mixed borders.

■ **Cultivation** Best in full sun. Dahlias are gross feeders and need a fertile, well-drained soil enriched with well-rotted organic matter. Set out in early summer when all risk of frost has passed. Lift tubers when the foliage has been blackened by autumn frosts. Store in a cool, dry place.

■ **Also recommended**
Dahlia 'Alloway Cottage' has soft-yellow flowers. There are many other cultivars.

■ **Perfect partners**
Chrysanthemums.

Daphne mezereum
Mezereon

An upright, deciduous shrub. All parts are highly toxic. H 1.2m (4ft), S 1m (3ft)

■ **Seasonal highlights**
From late winter until early spring, it produces clusters of pink to purplish-pink flowers on bare branches.

■ **Value at other times**
Fleshy red fruits in summer.

■ **Ideal site** Shrub borders and woodland gardens.

■ **Cultivation** Grow in sun or partial shade. Prefers a slightly alkaline, humus-rich, moist but well-drained soil. Mulch to keep the roots cool. Prune only to take out dead or damaged wood, after flowering.

■ **Also recommended**
Daphne mezereum 'Bowles's Variety' has white flowers with yellow fruit to follow. *Daphne bholua* varieties also have a lovely scent, such as 'Jacqueline Postill'.

■ **Perfect partners**
Mahonias, *Viburnum* x *bodnantense* 'Dawn' ♀.

Delphinium Black Knight Group
Delphinium

A moderately vigorous, upright, herbaceous perennial. H 1.7m (5½ft), S 75cm (30in)

■ **Seasonal highlights**
From early to midsummer, it bears long spikes of black-eyed, deep-purple flowers.

■ **Value at other times**
Has attractive, deeply lobed, mid- to light-green foliage.

■ **Ideal site** A sunny border, especially in cottage gardens.

■ **Cultivation** Grow in full sun in fertile, well-drained soil enriched with plenty of organic matter. Needs staking in exposed gardens. Cut back in autumn when foliage has withered.

■ **Also recommended**
Delphinium 'Emily Hawkins' ♀ has semi-double, lilac flowers.

■ **Perfect partners**
Achilleas, lupins, oriental poppies (*Papaver orientalis*).

Dianthus 'Little Jock'
Alpine pink

A low-growing, cushion-forming, evergreen perennial. H & S 10cm (4in)

■ **Seasonal highlights**
In summer, it bears clove-scented, double, pale-pink flowers with a maroon eye and fringed petals, just above the foliage.

■ **Value at other times**
Neat mounds of grey-green foliage all year.

■ **Ideal site** Rock gardens, troughs, and other containers.

■ **Cultivation** Prefers an open, sunny spot, in sharply drained, gritty, slightly alkaline soil. On clay soils, dig in plenty of grit. Good drainage is essential.

■ **Also recommended**
Dianthus alpinus 'Joan's Blood' ♀ has deep magenta-pink flowers with crimson centres.

■ **Perfect partners**
Aurinia saxatilis ♀, *Saponaria caespitosa*, alpine phlox, thymes.

Diascia barberae 'Blackthorn Apricot' ♀
Diascia

A moderately spreading, mat-forming, evergreen or semi-evergreen perennial. H 25cm (10in), S 50cm (20in)
■ **Seasonal highlights** From summer until autumn, it bears a profusion of apricot flowers in loose spikes.
■ **Value at other times** The mats of heart-shaped, mid-green foliage are present for most of the year.
■ **Ideal site** A sunny bank or border, in a rock garden, or raised bed.
■ **Cultivation** Grow in full sun in fertile, moist but well-drained soil. Deadhead regularly to induce more flowers. May not survive very cold, wet winters. Take stem cuttings in summer and overwinter young plants under glass.
■ **Also recommended** *Diascia rigescens* ♀ is trailing with deep-pink flowers.
■ **Perfect partners** *Veronica prostrata* ♀, *V. spicata*.

Dicentra spectabilis ♀
Bleeding heart, Dutchman's breeches

Now more commonly referred to as *Lamprocapnos spectabilis*, this plant is a vigorous, clump-forming, herbaceous perennial. H 1.2m (4ft), S 45cm (18in)
■ **Seasonal highlights** In late spring and early summer, arching stems bear hanging, heart-shaped flowers with rose-pink outer petals and white inner ones.
■ **Value at other times** Ferny, pale-green leaves.
■ **Ideal site** Shady borders and woodland gardens.
■ **Cultivation** Best in partial shade, but tolerates part-day sun, if soils are reliably moist. Grow in damp, fertile, preferably neutral to slightly alkaline soil. Divide every three or four years to maintain vigour.
■ **Also recommended** *Dicentra spectabilis* f. *alba* bears white flowers over longer periods.
■ **Perfect partners** Bold foliage plants such as hostas.

Dierama pulcherrimum
Angel's fishing rod

Vigorous, upright, evergreen, cormous perennial. H 1–1.5m (3–5ft), S 60cm (24in)
■ **Seasonal highlights** In summer, it produces tall stems bearing bell-shaped, pale to deep magenta-pink flowers on very slender stalks.
■ **Value at other times** Grass-like, grey-green leaves for most of the year.
■ **Ideal site** At the front of a sunny border, or by a pool.
■ **Cultivation** Best in full sun in leafy, fertile, well-drained soil. Keep well watered in dry weather. Plant corms 5–7cm (2–3in) deep in spring. Divide every three or four years. Divisions may take a season to flower.
■ **Also recommended** *Dierama* 'Miranda' is shorter with bright-pink flowers.
■ **Perfect partners** Acanthus, penstemons, salvias.

Digitalis x mertonensis ♀
Perennial foxglove

An upright, fairly vigorous herbaceous perennial. H 90cm (36in), S 30cm (12in)
■ **Seasonal highlights** Tall spires of tubular, pinkish-buff flowers rise above the foliage in spring and early summer. They attract bees.
■ **Value at other times** Mounds of crinkled, deeply veined, dark-green leaves.
■ **Ideal site** Woodland gardens or mixed and herbaceous borders.
■ **Cultivation** Prefers partial shade and humus-rich soils, but tolerates most aspects and soils if not too wet or dry. Deadhead after flowering; it self-seeds but seedlings are variable.
■ **Also recommended** *Digitalis grandiflora* ♀ has brown-veined, pale-yellow flowers and the classic *Digitalis purpurea* should not be overlooked.
■ **Perfect partners** *Digitalis obscura*, with yellow flowers; dicentras.

Doronicum x excelsum 'Harpur Crewe'
Leopard's bane

A vigorous, upright, and bushy herbaceous perennial. H & S to 60cm (24in).
■ **Seasonal highlights** In spring, branched stems each bear 3–4 golden-yellow, daisy-like flowers.
■ **Value at other times** Has attractive, soft-green, hairy, heart-shaped leaves.
■ **Ideal site** Shady borders or naturalized in woodland.
■ **Cultivation** Best in partial or dappled shade, but tolerates a more open aspect if soils are not too dry. Grow in a fertile, moisture-retentive soil. Lift and divide every four to five years to maintain vigour.
■ **Also recommended** *Doronicum columnae* 'Miss Mason' has large, bright-yellow flowers.
■ **Perfect partners** Narcissus, pulmonarias, polyanthus primulas.

E

Echinacea purpurea 'White Swan'
Coneflower

A vigorous, upright, clump-forming herbaceous perennial. H 60cm (24in), S 45cm (18in)

■ **Seasonal highlights** From midsummer until early autumn, it bears large, single, white flowers with orange-brown centres.

■ **Value at other times** Has clumps of narrow, roughly hairy basal leaves.

■ **Ideal site** Late-summer borders.

■ **Cultivation** Best in full sun, but tolerates light, part-day shade. Grow in fertile, humus-rich, well-drained soil. Cut back the flowering stems as the blooms fade, to encourage a second flush of flowers.

■ **Also recommended** *Echinacea purpurea* 'Robert Bloom' has mauve-crimson flowers with orange-brown centres. There are many cultivars in various colours.

■ **Perfect partners** Achilleas, chrysanthemums, border phlox.

Elaeagnus x *ebbingei* 'Gilt Edge' ♥
Elaeagnus

A dense, bushy, moderately vigorous evergreen shrub. H & S to 4m (12ft)

■ **Seasonal highlights** All year round it has lustrous dark leaves with gleaming, creamy-yellow margins.

■ **Value at other times** The autumn flowers are fragrant but insignificant.

■ **Ideal site** Shrub borders and hedges.

■ **Cultivation** The leaves colour best in sun, but it tolerates dappled shade. Grow in any fertile soil that is not too dry or wet; it does not thrive on shallow, chalky soils. Prune lightly to shape in mid- to late spring; cut out shoots with all-green leaves.

■ **Also recommended** *Elaeagnus pungens* 'Frederici' has yellow-centred, shining, green leaves, and is slow-growing.

■ **Perfect partners** Dark-leaved shrubs like hollies (*Ilex*), escallonias, and *Viburnum tinus*.

Epimedium x *warleyense*
Bishop's mitre

Also known as barrenwort. A vigorous, clump-forming, evergreen perennial. H 50cm (20in), S 75cm (30in)

■ **Seasonal highlights** From mid- to late spring, it bears sprays of nodding, yellow and orange-red flowers.

■ **Value at other times** The leaves are tinted red in spring and autumn and form good ground cover.

■ **Ideal site** Shady mixed borders and woodland gardens.

■ **Cultivation** Best in partial shade, but tolerates some sun if soil is moist. Grow in fertile, moist, well-drained soil. Shelter from cold winds. Cut back old foliage in late winter to get best flowering displays.

■ **Also recommended** *Epimedium* 'Versicolor' has dark-red and yellow flowers. There are many cultivars, some of which complement the colours of Japanese maples very beautifully and so make good underplanting.

■ **Perfect partners** *Epimedium* x *perralchicum* ♥ (bright-yellow flowers); dwarf narcissi.

Eranthis hyemalis ♥
Winter aconite

A vigorous perennial with small, knobbly tubers. H 5–8cm (2–3in), S 5cm (2in)

■ **Seasonal highlights** In late winter and early spring, bright-yellow flowers appear above a ruff of dissected, bright-green leaves.

■ **Value at other times** No great value at other times. The foliage dies back after flowering.

■ **Ideal site** Beneath deciduous trees and shrubs or naturalized in grass.

■ **Cultivation** Grow in full sun, in any fertile soil that isn't very dry in summer. Plant tubers 5cm (2in) deep in autumn, or, buy plants "in-the-green" and plant when the soil is not too wet or frozen.

■ **Also recommended** *Eranthis pinnatifida* has white flowers.

■ **Perfect partners** Snowdrops, crocus, hardy cyclamen.

Erica carnea 'Springwood White' ♥
Winter heath

A vigorous, spreading, slightly trailing evergreen shrub. H 15cm (6in), S 45cm (18in)

■ **Seasonal highlights** From winter to mid-spring, it is covered with small, dense spires of white flowers.

■ **Value at other times** Bright-green foliage makes good ground cover all year.

■ **Ideal site** Rock gardens, especially with dwarf conifers.

■ **Cultivation** Best in an open, sunny site in well-drained acid soil; it will tolerate slightly alkaline soils. After flowering, trim off the old flowers with shears and top-dress with leafmould, garden compost, or similar.

■ **Also recommended** *Erica carnea* 'Springwood Pink' has rose-pink flowers.

■ **Perfect partners** Dwarf conifers and dwarf rhododendrons, shrubby potentillas, and gaultherias.

Erica x darleyensis 'Arthur Johnson' ♀
Darley Dale heath

A dense, bushy, vigorous evergreen shrub. H 1m (3ft), S 75cm (30in)
■ **Seasonal highlights** From midwinter until spring it bears long, dense spikes of mauve-pink flowers.
■ **Value at other times** Young foliage has cream and pink tips in spring; it makes good ground cover all year.
■ **Ideal site** Rock gardens, especially with dwarf conifers.
■ **Cultivation** Best in an open, sunny site in well-drained acid soil; it will tolerate slightly alkaline soils. After flowering, trim with shears and top-dress with leafmould or garden compost.
■ **Also recommended** *Erica x darleyensis* 'Darley Dale' has cream-tipped leaves in spring and shell-pink flowers.
■ **Perfect partners** Dwarf conifers and dwarf rhododendrons, shrubby potentillas, and gaultherias.

Eryngium x tripartitum ♀
Sea holly

An upright, clump-forming herbaceous perennial. H 60–90cm (24–36in), S 50cm (20in)
■ **Seasonal highlights** From midsummer until early autumn, it bears branching stems of violet-blue flowers with narrow, grey-blue bracts; they are good for drying.
■ **Value at other times** Basal clumps of shiny, slightly spiny, dark-green leaves.
■ **Ideal site** Sunny borders, seaside and gravel gardens.
■ **Cultivation** Grow in full sun in poor, dry, gritty soil. It may need protection from excessive winter wet, especially in cold or exposed gardens.
■ **Also recommended** *Eryngium giganteum* ♀ is a taller, self-seeding biennial with steel-blue flowers and silver bracts.
■ **Perfect partners** *Yucca gloriosa* ♀, *Y. filamentosa* ♀.

Erysimum cheiri Bedder Series
Wallflower

Upright, bushy, compact perennials grown as biennials. H 30cm (12in), S 23cm (9in)
■ **Seasonal highlights** Over long periods in spring, bear short spikes of sweetly scented, golden-yellow, orange or scarlet-red flowers.
■ **Value at other times** They are usually discarded after flowering.
■ **Ideal site** Spring bedding or containers.
■ **Cultivation** Grow in sun in well-drained, poor to moderately fertile, well-drained soil. Rich soils encourage leafy growth with fewer flowers. Sow seed in a seedbed in late spring or early summer. Prick out into a nursery bed. Plant in the flowering sites in the autumn.
■ **Also recommended** *Erysimum cheiri* 'Blood Red' has luminous, deep-red flowers.
■ **Perfect partners** Forget-me-nots (*Myosotis*), tulips, polyanthus primulas.

Erythronium 'Pagoda' ♀
Trout lily, Pagoda flower

Upright, vigorous, clump-forming, bulbous perennial. H 15–35cm (6–14in), S 10cm (4in)
■ **Seasonal highlights** In spring, it bears heads of nodding, brown-marked, sulphur-yellow flowers.
■ **Value at other times** Has bronze-mottled leaves that die down in summer.
■ **Ideal site** Beneath deciduous shrubs, rock and woodland gardens, or naturalized in turf.
■ **Cultivation** Grow in partial shade in fertile, reliably moist, humus-rich soil. Plant bulbs 10cm (4in) deep in autumn. Do not let bulbs dry out before planting, or when dormant.
■ **Also recommended** *Erythronium revolutum* ♀ has lilac-pink flowers and brown-mottled, dark-green leaves.
■ **Perfect partners** Crocus and narcissus.

Eschscholzia californica ♀
California poppy

A moderately vigorous, mat-forming hardy annual. H 30cm (12in), S 15cm (6in)
■ **Seasonal highlights** From summer to autumn, it bears satiny-orange, yellow, white, or red flowers.
■ **Value at other times** The flowers are followed by long, curving seed pods.
■ **Ideal site** Annual borders, dry, sunny banks, gravel gardens.
■ **Cultivation** Grow in poor, well-drained soil in full sun. Sow the seeds outdoors in early spring and thin out to about 15cm (6in), when the seedlings are large enough to handle. Deadhead regularly to prolong the flowering period.
■ **Also recommended** *Eschscholzia caespitosa* is dwarf, with scented, bright-yellow flowers.
■ **Perfect partners** Shirley poppies (*Papaver rhoeas* Shirley Series).

E

Euonymus alatus ♥

Winged spindle

A dense, bushy, vigorous deciduous shrub. H 2m (6ft), S 3m (10ft)

■ **Seasonal highlights**
The leaves turn brilliant crimson in autumn, setting off the red-purple fruits that split to reveal orange seeds.

■ **Value at other times**
The stems have corky "wings" and the dark-green leaves are attractive all summer.

■ **Ideal site** A mixed or shrub border.

■ **Cultivation** Autumn colour is best in full sun, but it will tolerate partial shade. Grow in any well-drained soil. Prune in winter, if necessary, to shape and to remove any wayward, or dead and damaged shoots.

■ **Also recommended**
Euonymus alatus 'Compactus' ♥ is similar but smaller and more dense.

■ **Perfect partners**
Euonymus fortunei 'Emerald 'n' Gold' ♥, with gold and green leaves.

Euonymus fortunei 'Silver Queen' ♥

Euonymus

A very hardy, vigorous, bushy, mounded, evergreen shrub. H 2.5m (8ft), S 1.5m (5ft); H to 6m (20ft) if climbing

■ **Seasonal highlights**
The shiny-green leaves with white, often pink-flushed margins make good ground cover all year round.

■ **Value at other times**
Tiny, greenish-white flowers in summer, followed by pink fruits with orange seeds.

■ **Ideal site** Herbaceous or mixed borders, walls, and containers.

■ **Cultivation** Foliage colour is best in full sun, but it tolerates light shade. Grow in any well-drained soil. Trim in mid- to late spring; remove any all-green shoots as soon as seen.

■ **Also recommended**
Euonymus fortunei 'Emerald Gaiety' ♥ has white-variegated leaves.

■ **Perfect partners**
Euonymus europaeus 'Red Cascade' ♥ has red autumn leaves and fruit.

Euphorbia x martinii ♥

Spurge

Upright, moderately vigorous, herbaceous perennial. H & S 1m (3ft)

■ **Seasonal highlights**
From spring to midsummer, it bears heads of clustered, yellow-green flowers with dark-red nectar glands.

■ **Value at other times**
Red stems and narrow green leaves that are often purple-tinged when young.

■ **Ideal site** Mixed or herbaceous borders.

■ **Cultivation** Best in full sun, but tolerant of light, dappled shade. Grow in a light, well-drained soil enriched with organic matter. On clay soils, dig in some grit to improve drainage.

■ **Also recommended**
Euphorbia mellifera ♥ is evergreen and much taller, with honey-scented, red-brown flowers. The classic *Euphorbia characias* subsp. *wulfenii* and cultivars should not be forgotten.

■ **Perfect partners** The broad, glossy leaves of bear's breeches (*Acanthus*).

Euphorbia polychroma ♥

Spurge

A vigorous, bushy, clump-forming, herbaceous perennial. H 40cm (16in), S 60cm (24in)

■ **Seasonal highlights** From mid-spring to midsummer, it bears long-lasting, bright yellow-green flowers at the stem tips.

■ **Value at other times**
Forms a dense mound of dark green, sometimes purple-tinted, leaves.

■ **Ideal site** Herbaceous borders and decorative containers.

■ **Cultivation** Best in full sun, but tolerant of light, dappled shade. Grow in a light, well-drained soil enriched with organic matter.

■ **Also recommended**
Euphorbia rigida ♥ has thick, arching stems with grey-green leaves and yellow flowers in spring and early summer.

■ **Perfect partners** *Stachys byzantina* 'Primrose Heron'.

Euryops pectinatus ♥

South African daisy

An upright, bushy, vigorous, half-hardy evergreen perennial. H & S 1m (3ft)

■ **Seasonal highlights** From early summer to mid-autumn, it bears bright-yellow, daisy-like flowers.

■ **Value at other times**
It has grey, hairy fern-like foliage all year round.

■ **Ideal site** As a filler in herbaceous borders or in decorative pots.

■ **Cultivation** Grow in full sun, in sharply drained, moderately fertile soil. Trim after flowering to keep compact. Take stem cuttings in summer; overwinter young plants and potted plants under glass.

■ **Also recommended**
Euryops acraeus ♥ is more compact and cold-tolerant, with yellow flowers and silver-grey leaves.

■ **Perfect partners**
Penstemons, osteospermums.

Exochorda x macrantha 'The Bride' ♈

Also known as pearl bush. A vigorous, mound-forming, deciduous shrub. H 2m (6ft), S 3m (10ft)

■ **Seasonal highlights** In late spring and early summer, the arching stems are wreathed in white flowers.

■ **Value at other times** Has attractive, light-green leaves from spring to autumn.

■ **Ideal site** A shrub or mixed border.

■ **Cultivation** Grow in full sun or partial shade, in any fertile, well-drained soil. Will tolerate shallow, chalky soils. Shorten flowered shoots to strong buds after flowering.

■ **Also recommended** *Exochorda racemosa* is taller, with upright clusters of white flowers in late spring.

■ **Perfect partners** Camellias as a dark-leaved backdrop; *Berberis thunbergii* 'Rose Glow', *Magnolia stellata* ♈.

F

Forsythia x intermedia
Forsythia

A vigorous, strongly upright, deciduous shrub. H & S to 1.5m (5ft)

■ **Seasonal highlights** In spring, it bears bright, deep-yellow flowers all along the bare branches.

■ **Value at other times** Undistinguished in summer, but a good host for clematis.

■ **Ideal site** Shrub and mixed borders, or as informal hedging.

■ **Cultivation** Thrives in any fertile soil in sun or light, dappled shade. Shorten flowered shoots to strong buds after flowering; when established, cut out one in four of the oldest stems to encourage new growth from the base.

■ **Also recommended** *Forsythia* x *intermedia* 'Lynwood Variety' ♈ has rich-yellow flowers in great profusion.

■ **Perfect partners** Create a blue carpet beneath forsythias with *Scilla siberica*.

Freesia 'Imperial Red'
Freesia

An upright, half-hardy, bulbous perennial. H 40cm (16in), S 5cm (2in)

■ **Seasonal highlights** Bears scented, pinkish-red, creamy-throated flowers from late winter to spring.

■ **Value at other times** Is grown only for its flowers.

■ **Ideal site** A cool greenhouse or conservatory; prepared bulbs are summer-flowering and can be grown outdoors.

■ **Cultivation** Plant bulbs in pots of loamy compost with added grit, in autumn. Keep temperature below 13°C (55°F). Give a balanced liquid feed weekly when the flower buds appear. Dry off after flowering and rest for the summer.

■ **Also recommended** *Freesia* 'Oberon' with lemon-yellow and red flowers.

■ **Perfect partners** Cinerarias (*Pericallis*), paper white narcissus (*Narcissus papyraceus*).

Fremontodendron 'California Glory' ♈
Flannel bush

A vigorous, upright then spreading, evergreen shrub H 6m (20ft), S 4m (12ft)

■ **Seasonal highlights** A long succession of saucer-shaped, deep-yellow flowers appear from late spring to mid-autumn.

■ **Value at other times** The lobed, dark-green leaves have tawny down beneath.

■ **Ideal site** A warm, sunny, sheltered wall.

■ **Cultivation** Grow in fertile, well-drained soil. Protect from cold winds. To wall-train, tie in the main stems to a support of wires or trellis. Keep pruning to a minimum; just shorten outward-growing shoots on wall-trained plants after the first flush of bloom and trim out damaged or dead wood.

■ **Also recommended** *Fremontodendron* 'Pacific Sunset' has yellow flowers with pointed petals.

■ **Perfect partners** *Clematis* 'Ascotiensis'.

Fritillaria imperialis
Crown imperial

A robust, strongly upright, bulbous perennial. H to 1.5m (5ft), S 25–30cm (10–12in)

■ **Seasonal highlights** In late spring or early summer, at the tips of stout stems, bears large, nodding, orange, yellow, or red flowers crowned by leafy bracts.

■ **Value at other times** Of no real value at other times.

■ **Ideal site** A sunny border or raised bed.

■ **Cultivation** Grow in full sun in fertile, well-drained soil. Plant bulbs in autumn, at four times their own depth, setting on a layer of sharp sand to improve drainage. The bulbs will rot in wet soils.

■ **Also recommended** *Fritillaria imperialis* 'Lutea' has bright-yellow flowers.

■ **Perfect partners** Mid-season and late-flowering tulips.

F

Fritillaria meleagris
Snake's head fritillary

An upright, slender bulbous perennial. H 30cm (1ft), S 5–8cm (2–3in)
■ **Seasonal highlights** In spring, it bears hanging, bell-shaped flowers in delicate, chequered shades of pink, purple, or white.
■ **Value at other times** No real value at other times.
■ **Ideal site** In a rock garden, or naturalized in turf.
■ **Cultivation** Grow in fertile, humus-rich, moisture-retentive soil. Plant the bulbs in autumn at two to three times their own depth and the same distance apart. If grown in grass, delay the first mowing until the leaves have faded naturally.
■ **Also recommended** *Fritillaria acmopetala* ♥ has pale-green, maroon-marked flowers.
■ **Perfect partners** Narcissus, camassias.

Fuchsia 'Auntie Jinks'
Fuchsia

A trailing, moderately vigorous, half-hardy shrub. H 15–20cm (6–8in), S 20–40cm (8–16in)
■ **Seasonal highlights** From early summer until late autumn, it bears masses of single flowers with pink-red tubes, cerise-margined white sepals and purple corollas.
■ **Value at other times** Of no value during winter.
■ **Ideal site** Containers, including hanging baskets, or mixed borders.
■ **Cultivation** Tolerates sun or light shade. Grow in fertile, well-drained soil or potting mix. Plant out when the threat of frost has passed. Bring indoors for the winter. Deadhead regularly. Cut back hard in spring.
■ **Also recommended** *Fuchsia* 'Celia Smedley' ♥ has pink and currant-red flowers. There are many other cultivars.
■ **Perfect partners** Argyranthemums, osteospermums, pelargoniums.

G

Galanthus plicatus subsp. byzantinus
Snowdrop

A vigorous perennial bulb. H 20cm (8in), S 8cm (3in)
■ **Seasonal highlights** In late winter or early spring, it bears nodding, honey-scented, white flowers with green markings on the inner petals.
■ **Value at other times** Of no value at other times.
■ **Ideal site** Woodland gardens, beneath trees and shrubs, or naturalized in turf.
■ **Cultivation** Grow in dappled shade in any fertile garden soil that does not dry out in summer. Lift and divide the bulbs when congested, after flowering but before the leaves have faded. May self-seed.
■ **Also recommended** *Galanthus nivalis* ♥ has white flowers with a V-shaped green mark on each petal.
■ **Perfect partners** Winter aconites (*Eranthis hyemalis*), hardy cyclamen.

Garrya elliptica
Silk tassel bush

A dense, vigorous, bushy evergreen shrub. H & S 4m (12ft)
■ **Seasonal highlights** From midwinter to early spring, it bears swags of silky, hanging, grey-green catkins.
■ **Value at other times** Glossy, wavy-margined, dark greyish-green leaves all year.
■ **Ideal site** Shrub or mixed borders and shady walls.
■ **Cultivation** Grow in any fertile, well-drained soil in sun or partial shade. Shelter from cold wind. After flowering, shorten any shoots that spoil the shape, or grow away from, or into the wall, if wall-trained.
■ **Also recommended** *Garrya elliptica* 'James Roof' ♥ has dark sea-green leaves and very long catkins.
■ **Perfect partners** *Jasminum nudiflorum* ♥, *Mahonia* x *media* 'Charity'.

Gazania Chansonette Series
Gazania

Vigorous, half-hardy perennial often grown as an annual. H 20cm (8in), S 25cm (10in)
■ **Seasonal highlights** Throughout summer, it bears daisy-like, dark-zoned flower heads in bronze, orange, rose-pink, salmon-pink or red.
■ **Value at other times** The glossy, dark-green leaves have silky white hair beneath.
■ **Ideal site** Bedding, containers, hot, sunny borders, seaside gardens.
■ **Cultivation** Sow seeds in warmth in spring and plant out young plants when the risk of frost has passed. Grow in full sun in light, well-drained soil. Deadhead regularly to prolong flowering.
■ **Also recommended** *Gazania* Daybreak Series has white, yellow, orange, and pink flowers.
■ **Perfect partners** Pelargoniums, French marigolds.

Genista aetnensis ♀
Mount Etna broom

A vigorous, deciduous shrub or small tree with upright, then weeping, shoots.
H & S to 8m (25ft)

■ **Seasonal highlights**
Fragrant, yellow, pea-like flowers are borne at the stem tips in mid- to late summer.

■ **Value at other times**
The weeping shoots are bright green and give an evergreen appearance.

■ **Ideal site** Sunny walls, banks, or borders.

■ **Cultivation** Grow in full sun in light, poor, very well-drained soil. After flowering, shorten flowered shoots to strong buds on green wood; don't cut into old wood.

■ **Also recommended**
Genista hispanica is dense, spiny and much smaller with golden-yellow flowers in late spring and early summer.

■ **Perfect partners** *Cytisus nigricans*.

Geranium himalayense
Himalayan cranesbill

A vigorous, mound-forming herbaceous perennial.
H 30–45cm (12–18in),
S 60cm (24in)

■ **Seasonal highlights**
In early summer, it bears a profusion of white-centred, violet-blue to deep-blue flowers, and then blooms sporadically into autumn.

■ **Value at other times**
The lobed, soft-green leaves colour well in autumn.

■ **Ideal site** Mixed or herbaceous borders.

■ **Cultivation** Grow in any fertile, well-drained soil, in sun or partial shade. Trim after the first flush of flowers to encourage more in the autumn. Divide every three or four years in spring.

■ **Also recommended**
Geranium endressii ♀ has silvery-pink flowers all summer. There are many cultivars, but 'Rozanne' cannot be too highly recommended.

■ **Perfect partners** *Hosta sieboldiana*, achilleas, hemerocallis, border phlox.

Geranium psilostemon ♀
Armenian cranesbill

A vigorous, clump-forming herbaceous perennial.
H 60–120cm (2–4ft),
S 60cm (24in)

■ **Seasonal highlights**
From early until late summer, it bears sprays of upturned, brilliant-magenta flowers with black centres and veins.

■ **Value at other times**
The leaves are tinted crimson in spring and red in autumn; they make good ground cover.

■ **Ideal site** Mixed or herbaceous borders, especially in cottage gardens.

■ **Cultivation** Grow in sun or light shade, in any fertile soil. Deadhead regularly to encourage continuous blooming.

■ **Also recommended**
Geranium 'Ann Folkard' is similar but more spreading.

■ **Perfect partners**
Achilleas, border phlox, hemerocallis.

Geum 'Borisii'
Avens

A vigorous, clump-forming, herbaceous perennial.
H 30–50cm (12–20in),
S 30cm (12in)

■ **Seasonal highlights**
From late spring to late summer, it bears long-stemmed clusters of bright, brick-red flowers with a boss of golden-yellow stamens.

■ **Value at other times**
Basal mounds of divided, fresh green leaves.

■ **Ideal site** The front of sunny, mixed, or herbaceous borders, especially in cottage gardens.

■ **Cultivation** Grow in any fertile, well-drained soil in full sun or light, part-day shade. Lift and divide the plants every three or four years to rejuvenate.

■ **Also recommended**
Geum 'Red Wings' has semi-double, scarlet flowers.

■ **Perfect partners**
Geum 'Lady Stratheden' ♀ with yellow flowers.

Gunnera manicata ♀
Gunnera

A massive, very vigorous, herbaceous perennial.
H 2.5m (8ft), S 3–4m (10–12ft)

■ **Seasonal highlights**
The enormous, prominently veined, bright-green leaves have red prickly stems and reach 2m (6ft) long.

■ **Value at other times**
In summer, it bears fat spikes of tiny greenish-red flowers, followed by orange-red fruit.

■ **Ideal site** Pool- and streamsides, damp borders. For large gardens only.

■ **Cultivation** Grow in sun or partial shade in deep, permanently moist, soil, enriched with plenty of organic matter. In cold areas, protect the crown in winter with a deep, dry mulch of straw or leafmould.

■ **Also recommended**
Gunnera tinctoria ♀ is similar but more compact.

■ **Perfect partners** *Iris sibirica*, *Rheum palmatum* 'Atrosanguineum'.

H

Hakonechloa macra 'Aureola' ♀
Hakonechloa

A spreading, mound-forming, deciduous grass. H 35cm (14in), S 40cm (16in)

■ **Seasonal highlights**
The narrow, arching leaves, striped bright-yellow and green, are present for much of the year. Pale-green flower spikes appear from late summer to autumn.

■ **Value at other times**
Leaves turn red in autumn and often persist into winter.

■ **Ideal site** The front of a border, in containers, in rock gardens, or woodland gardens.

■ **Cultivation** Grow in full sun, or for the best leaf colours, in partial shade. Grow in fertile, moist, but well-drained soil.

■ **Also recommended**
Carex elata 'Aurea' ♀, with golden, grass-like leaves.

■ **Perfect partners**
Miscanthus sinensis 'Gracillimus' has blue-green leaves that turn bronze in autumn.

Hamamelis x intermedia 'Arnold Promise' ♀
Hamamelis

Also known as witch hazel. Slow-growing, deciduous shrub of vase-shaped outline. H & S to 4m (12ft)

■ **Seasonal highlights**
Bare branches are spangled with fragrant, spidery, yellow flowers in early to midwinter.

■ **Value at other times**
The leaves turn yellow before falling in autumn.

■ **Ideal site** A woodland garden, as a specimen, in a shady border.

■ **Cultivation** Needs a fertile, humus-rich, moisture-retentive, neutral to acid soil and a sheltered spot in sun or partial shade. Keep pruning to a minimum, but remove crossing or damaged shoots after flowering.

■ **Also recommended**
Hamamelis x *intermedia* 'Jelena' ♀ has coppery-orange flowers.

■ **Perfect partners**
Mahonias, *Viburnum* x *bodnantense* 'Dawn' ♀.

Hebe 'Gauntlettii'
Hebe

Bushy, upright, fast-growing, half-hardy evergreen shrub. H & S to 1m (3ft)

■ **Seasonal highlights**
From late summer until late autumn, it bears hanging clusters of small, pink flowers.

■ **Value at other times**
Has glossy, rich-green leaves.

■ **Ideal site** Sunny mixed or shrub borders, decorative containers.

■ **Cultivation** Grow in fertile, well-drained, neutral to alkaline soil in sun or dappled shade. Shelter from cold winds. It may not survive outdoors in very cold areas; bring pot-grown plants into a cold greenhouse for the winter. Trim lightly to shape in spring.

■ **Also recommended**
Hebe 'Great Orme' ♀ is hardier, with bright-pink flowers.

■ **Perfect partners**
Bamboos, cotoneasters, shrubby potentillas.

Helianthemum 'Raspberry Ripple'
Rock rose, Sun rose

A spreading, low-growing, evergreen shrub. H 20cm (8in), S 30cm (12in)

■ **Seasonal highlights**
The white flowers, irregularly marked with raspberry-pink, appear over long periods from late spring to midsummer.

■ **Value at other times**
Dark greyish-green leaves.

■ **Ideal site** will tolerate sunny banks, borders and raised beds, hot, dry sites.

■ **Cultivation** Grow in full sun, in well-drained, neutral to alkaline soil that is not too fertile. Too rich a soil produces fewer flowers and soft growth that is more susceptible to cold damage. After flowering, trim back flowered shoots to strong young growth.

■ **Also recommended**
Helianthemum 'Rhodanthe Carneum' ♀ has flesh-pink flowers.

■ **Perfect partners**
Alpine pinks, *Phlox subulata.*

Helianthus annuus 'Teddy Bear'
Sunflower

A vigorous, upright, hardy annual. H 90cm (3ft), S 30cm (12in)

■ **Seasonal highlights**
In summer, it bears large, double, shaggy, golden-yellow flowerheads, 13cm (5in) wide.

■ **Value at other times**
Is discarded after flowering.

■ **Ideal site** Sunny annual borders; good for children's plots.

■ **Cultivation** Grow in full sun in fertile, well-drained soil, in a warm, sheltered site for most prolific flowering. Sow seeds under glass in small pots in early spring, or in the flowering site in late spring.

■ **Also recommended**
Helianthus annuus 'Sun Spot' is shorter, with larger, bright-yellow flowerheads. There are many cultivars, so it is a good idea to experiment with different ones each year.

■ **Perfect partners**
Dahlias, chrysanthemums.

Helictotrichon sempervirens ♀
Blue oat grass

A mounded, evergreen perennial grass. H to 1.4m (4½ft), S 60cm (2ft)

■ **Seasonal highlights**
In early and midsummer, stiff, upright stems bear airy, straw-coloured, purple-flushed flowering spikes.

■ **Value at other times**
Spiky mounds of grey-blue leaves all year.

■ **Ideal site** The front of a border, a rock garden, or gravel garden.

■ **Cultivation** The leaves colour best in full sun, but it tolerates light, dappled shade. Grow in poor, well-drained, preferably alkaline, soil. Remove dead leaves and old flower spikelets in spring. Divide in spring.

■ **Also recommended**
Leymus arenarius, a grass with bright blue-grey leaves.

■ **Perfect partners**
Purple sage (*Salvia officinalis* 'Pupurascens' ♀), and grey-leaved *Helichrysum splendidum* ♀.

Heliotropium 'Marine'
Heliotrope, Cherry pie

A bushy, upright, frost-tender, evergreen shrub, usually grown as an annual. H to 1.2m (4ft), S 35–40cm (12–18in)

■ **Seasonal highlights**
Over long periods in summer, it bears dense heads of sweetly scented, deep violet-blue flowers; they attract butterflies and bees.

■ **Value at other times**
It has wrinkled, dark-green, purple-tinted leaves.

■ **Ideal site** Bedding and containers.

■ **Cultivation** Grow in any fertile, moist but well-drained soil in sun or partial shade. Sow seeds under glass in spring and plant out when the threat of frost has passed.

■ **Also recommended**
Heliotropium 'Chatsworth' ♀ has deep-purple, very fragrant, flowers.

■ **Perfect partners** African and French marigolds.

Helleborus niger 'Potter's Wheel'
Christmas rose

A robust, upright perennial, also known as hellebore. H 30cm (12in), S 45cm (18in)

■ **Seasonal highlights**
From winter to early spring, it bears bowl-shaped white flowers with green "eyes".

■ **Value at other times**
Leathery, dark-green leaves on purple-marked stems.

■ **Ideal site** Shady borders, or naturalized in woodland gardens.

■ **Cultivation** Grows best in dappled shade, but tolerates a more open aspect if soil doesn't dry out. Grows in fertile, preferably heavy, neutral to alkaline soil. Will tolerate clay soils. Trim away old leaves before flowers emerge for the best display.

■ **Also recommended**
Helleborus purpurascens has purplish or slate-grey flowers that are pink-flushed pale green inside. There are many cultivars in various colours.

■ **Perfect partners** Ferns, snowdrops (*Galanthus*), winter aconites (*Eranthis*).

Helleborus orientalis
Lenten rose

A vigorous, upright, evergreen perennial. H & S 45cm (18in)

■ **Seasonal highlights**
From midwinter to spring, it bears stout-stemmed, white, or creamy-green flowers that flush pink with age.

■ **Value at other times**
Leathery, divided, deep-green basal leaves persist all year.

■ **Ideal site** Mixed or herbaceous borders, woodland gardens.

■ **Cultivation** Grows best in dappled shade, but will tolerate sun if the soil is reliably moist. Grow in any good garden soil. Tolerates clay soils. Trim away old leaves before flowers emerge to display them at their best.

■ **Also recommended**
Helleborus orientalis subsp. *guttatus* has creamy-white flowers spotted maroon within.

■ **Perfect partners**
Ferns, snowdrops (*Galanthus*), winter aconites (*Eranthis*).

Hemerocallis 'Gentle Shepherd'
Daylily

A moderately vigorous, semi-evergreen perennial. H 65cm (26in), S 1.2m (4ft)

■ **Seasonal highlights**
The ivory-white flowers with green throats appear over long periods in midsummer.

■ **Value at other times** The slender, arching green leaves often persist through winter and make good ground cover.

■ **Ideal site** Sunny borders, gravel gardens.

■ **Cultivation** Prefers full sun, but tolerates light, dappled shade. Grow in fertile, moist but well-drained soil. Mulch in autumn. Divide every three or four years, in spring, to maintain vigour.

■ **Also recommended**
Hemerocallis 'Chorus Line' has bright-pink, yellow-marked flowers with dark-green throats.

■ **Perfect partners**
Achilleas, border phlox, monardas.

H

Hippeastrum 'Apple Blossom'
Amaryllis

A robust, bulbous perennial. H 30–50cm (12–20in), S 30cm (12in)

■ **Seasonal highlights** In winter, it bears large, white, funnel-shaped flowers with pink-flushed petal tips.

■ **Value at other times** Has little value at other times.

■ **Ideal site** In a well-lit spot in the home or in a warm conservatory.

■ **Cultivation** Plant the bulbs in autumn, with "neck and shoulders" above soil level. Water little until growth is well under way then water freely and feed every two weeks with a balanced liquid fertilizer. After flowering gradually reduce watering as the leaves begin to die down.

■ **Also recommended** *Hippeastrum* 'Picotee' has white flowers with red-rimmed petals.

■ **Perfect partners** Early, forced narcissus, such as *Narcissus papyraceus* and hyacinths.

Hordeum jubatum
Squirrel tail grass

A moderately vigorous, annual or perennial grass. H 50cm (20in), S 30cm (12in)

■ **Seasonal highlights** In early and midsummer, erect stems bear nodding heads of silky, long-bristled, pale-green spikelets. They are flushed red or purple and turn buff as they age.

■ **Value at other times** Has tufts of narrow, light-green leaves. The flowerheads are good for drying.

■ **Ideal site** A wild garden or an annual, mixed or herbaceous border.

■ **Cultivation** Prefers full sun, but will tolerate light, dappled shade. Grow in any well-drained soil.

■ **Also recommended** *Stipa tenuissima* has narrow, feathery, buff-coloured flowerheads in summer.

■ **Perfect partners** *Stipa gigantea*, *Lagurus ovatus* (hare's tail grass).

Hyacinthoides non-scripta
Bluebell

A vigorous, clump-forming perennial bulb. H 20–40cm (8–16in), S 8cm (3in)

■ **Seasonal highlights** In spring, sturdy stems bear nodding, sweetly scented, violet-blue flowers amid glossy, dark-green strap-shaped leaves.

■ **Value at other times** Dies back in summer.

■ **Ideal site** Woodland gardens and shady borders.

■ **Cultivation** Grow in dappled shade, in any fertile soil that does not dry out in summer. Plant the bulbs 8cm (3in) deep in autumn. May self-seed to form extensive colonies.

■ **Also recommended** *Hyacinthoides hispanica* (Spanish bluebell) is taller, with unscented blue flowers.

■ **Perfect partners** *Erythronium* 'Pagoda' ♀, *Fritillaria cirrhosa*.

Hyacinthus orientalis 'City of Haarlem' ♀
Hyacinth

A vigorous, upright bulb. H 20–30cm (8–12in), S 8cm (3in)

■ **Seasonal highlights** In late spring, sturdy stems arise bearing dense spikes of highly scented, soft primrose-yellow flowers.

■ **Value at other times** Of no value at other times.

■ **Ideal site** Spring bedding, pots indoors.

■ **Cultivation** Best in full sun. Plant bulbs in autumn, 10cm (4in) deep, in fertile, well-drained soil. Use prepared bulbs for winter flowers indoors. Plant in bowls of bulb fibre with the tip of the bulb exposed. Keep in a cool, dark place for six weeks. When shoots are about 2.5cm (1in) long, bring into light and warmth.

■ **Also recommended** *Hyacinthus orientalis* 'Jan Bos' has cerise-red flowers.

■ **Perfect partners** Narcissus, tulips.

Hydrangea paniculata 'Grandiflora' ♀
Hydrangea

A vigorous, deciduous shrub. H 3–7m (10–22ft), S 2.5m (8ft)

■ **Seasonal highlights** In late summer and early autumn, it produces large, conical heads of white flowers that flush pink with age.

■ **Value at other times** Handsome dark-green leaves. Flowers are good for drying.

■ **Ideal site** A shrub or mixed border or a woodland garden.

■ **Cultivation** Grow in fertile, humus-rich, moisture-retentive soil in partial shade or sun. Shelter from cold, dry winds. Needs minimal pruning, but for larger flowers, in late winter, cut back all sideshoots to within 5–8cm (2–3in) of the main stems.

■ **Also recommended** *Hydrangea paniculata* 'Floribunda' has narrower flowerheads. There are many other cultivars.

■ **Perfect partners** Hypericums, hostas.

I

Ilex aquifolium 'Handsworth New Silver' ♀

Known as English holly. A dense, vigorous, evergreen shrub of columnar outline. H 8m (25ft), S 5m (15ft)

■ **Seasonal highlights** Bright-red berries in winter.

■ **Value at other times** All year, its dark-purple stems bear glossy dark-green leaves with spiny, cream margins.

■ **Ideal site** In a shrub border, woodland garden, or as a specimen.

■ **Cultivation** Full sun produces the best variegation, but it will tolerate dappled shade. Grow in any fertile, well-drained soil. Prune to shape, if necessary, in early spring.

■ **Also recommended** *Ilex* x *altaclerensis* 'Lawsoniana' ♀; gold-and-green leaves and red-brown berries. There are many other cultivars.

■ **Perfect partners** *Mahonia* x *media* 'Charity', *Viburnum* x *bodnantense* 'Dawn' ♀.

Impatiens Super Elfin Series

Busy Lizzie

Compact, frost-tender perennials grown as annuals. H & S to 25cm (10in)

■ **Seasonal highlights** Throughout summer, bears a mass of flat, spurred flowers in violet, orange, lipstick-pink, red and various pastel shades.

■ **Value at other times** Can be grown as a pot plant to flower through the winter.

■ **Ideal site** Summer bedding, containers.

■ **Cultivation** Sow seeds in warmth in early spring. Plant out when the threat of frost has passed, into moisture-retentive, fertile soil in partial or dappled shade.

■ **Also recommended** *I. walleriana* 'Starbright' has red, orange, rose-pink, and violet-blue flowers, each with a central white star.

■ **Perfect partners** Pelargoniums and Semperflorens begonias.

Indigofera amblyantha ♀

Indigofera

A vigorous, deciduous shrub with arching branches. H 2m (6ft), S 2.5m (8ft)

■ **Seasonal highlights** From early summer until early autumn, it bears slender, upright clusters of pale-pink, pea-like flowers.

■ **Value at other times** From spring to autumn, it has elegant bright-green leaves.

■ **Ideal site** A shrub border or as a specimen on a warm wall.

■ **Cultivation** Grow in full sun in fertile, moist but well-drained soil. In late winter or early spring, trim overlong, badly placed, or damaged shoots. In very cold areas, if severely damaged by cold, prune all stems back hard to a woody framework.

■ **Also recommended** *Indigofera heterantha* ♀ has purplish-pink flowers and grey-green leaves.

■ **Perfect partners** *Kalmia latifolia* ♀ (on acid soils), escallonias.

Ipomoea tricolor 'Heavenly Blue'

Morning glory

A vigorous, twining, frost-tender annual climber. H to 4m (12ft), S 15cm (6in)

■ **Seasonal highlights** From summer until autumn, it bears white-throated, funnel-shaped, deep sky-blue flowers.

■ **Value at other times** It has heart-shaped, bright-green leaves. It is usually discarded after flowering.

■ **Ideal site** Train through shrubs, on poles and pyramids, or in decorative containers.

■ **Cultivation** Prefers a warm, sheltered site, in moderately fertile well-drained soil. It needs sun but with shade from strong midday sun. Sow seeds in spring at 18°C (64°F); grow on in warmth and set out when risk of frost has passed.

■ **Also recommended** *Ipomoea lobata* has narrowly tubular, red and yellow flowers.

■ **Perfect partners** *Tropaeolum peregrinum*.

Iris danfordiae

Dwarf iris

A small, sturdy perennial bulb. H 10–15cm (4–6in), S 5cm (2in)

■ **Seasonal highlights** Solitary yellow flowers with greenish-yellow markings appear in late winter and early spring amid a sheaf of narrow greyish-green leaves.

■ **Value at other times** No real value at other times.

■ **Ideal site** Rock gardens, raised beds, troughs, beneath deciduous shrubs.

■ **Cultivation** Best in full sun. Plant bulbs at twice their own depth in late summer or early autumn in well-drained soil. Add coarse grit to heavy clay soils to improve drainage.

■ **Also recommended** *Iris histrioides* 'Major' has deep-blue flowers.

■ **Perfect partners** Snowdrops (*Galanthus nivalis* ♀), winter aconites, (*Eranthis hyemalis* ♀), winter-flowering heaths (*Erica carnea*).

I

Iris foetidissima ♀
Stinking iris, Stinking gladwyn

A vigorous, rhizomatous evergreen perennial.
H & S 30–90cm (1–3ft)
■ **Seasonal highlights**
In early summer it bears subtly coloured dull-purple flowers suffused with yellow.
■ **Value at other times**
In autumn, the seed pods split to reveal bead-like scarlet seeds. The strap-shaped, dark-green leaves give off an unpleasant scent if crushed.
■ **Ideal site** Dry, shady borders.
■ **Cultivation** Grow in any well-drained soil in sun or shade.
■ **Also recommended**
Iris foetidissima var. *citrina* has lemon-yellow flowers.
■ **Perfect partners** Lily turf (*Liriope muscari* ♀), with sheaves of strap-shaped leaves and spikes of bead-like violet-mauve flowers in autumn.

Iris germanica ♀
Bearded iris

A vigorous, rhizomatous perennial. H 60–120cm (2–4ft), S 30cm (12in)
■ **Seasonal highlights**
In late spring or early summer, upright stems bear blue-violet flowers with yellow beards.
■ **Value at other times**
Fans of sword-shaped, grey-green leaves.
■ **Ideal site** Herbaceous or mixed borders, especially in cottage gardens.
■ **Cultivation** Grow in full sun or light, part-day shade in any moderately fertile well-drained soil.
■ **Also recommended**
Iris germanica 'Florentina' has scented white flowers.
■ **Perfect partners**
The broad foliage of acanthus and hostas; *Centaurea montana.*

Iris 'Harmony'
Dwarf iris

A small, sturdy perennial bulb. H 10–15cm (4–6in), S 5cm (2in)
■ **Seasonal highlights**
Yellow-marked, royal-blue flowers appear in late winter amid a sheaf of narrow leaves.
■ **Value at other times**
No real value at other times.
■ **Ideal site** Rock gardens, troughs or other containers, or beneath deciduous shrubs.
■ **Cultivation** Best in full sun. Plant bulbs at twice their own depth in late summer or early autumn in well-drained soil. Add coarse grit to heavy clay soils to improve drainage.
■ **Also recommended**
Iris 'Joyce' has deep sky-blue flowers.
■ **Perfect partners**
Snowdrops (*Galanthus nivalis* ♀), winter aconites, (*Eranthis hyemalis* ♀), *Erica carnea* 'Springwood White' ♀.

Iris 'Katharine Hodgkin' ♀
Dwarf iris

A small but vigorous, bulbous perennial. H 12cm (5in), S 5cm (1in)
■ **Seasonal highlights**
In late winter, it bears pale-blue flowers, delicately patterned in blue and yellow.
■ **Value at other times**
No real value at other times.
■ **Ideal site** Rock gardens, troughs or other containers, or beneath deciduous shrubs.
■ **Cultivation** Best in full sun. Plant bulbs at twice their own depth in late summer or early autumn in well-drained soil. Add coarse grit to heavy clay soils to improve drainage.
■ **Also recommended**
Iris 'Natascha' has very pale blue-grey flowers.
■ **Perfect partners**
Snowdrops (*Galanthus nivalis* ♀), winter aconites, (*Eranthis hyemalis* ♀), winter heaths (*Erica carnea*).

Iris unguicularis ♀
Algerian iris

A vigorous, rhizomatous, evergreen perennial. H 30cm (12in), S 5cm (2in)
■ **Seasonal highlights**
In late winter and early spring, it bears scented, pale-lavender to deep-violet, yellow-marked flowers with contrasting veins.
■ **Value at other times**
Has tough, grass-like leaves throughout the year.
■ **Ideal site** Sunny borders, or at the base of a warm wall
■ **Cultivation** Grow in full sun in poor to moderately fertile, very freely draining, neutral to alkaline soil in a sheltered spot. Once planted, leave undisturbed; they flower with increasing freedom as they settle in.
■ **Also recommended**
Iris unguicularis 'Alba' has yellow-marked cream flowers.
■ **Perfect partners**
Interplant with autumn-flowering *Nerine bowdenii* ♀.

J

Jasminum mesnyi ♀
Primrose jasmine

A vigorous, scrambling, half-hardy evergreen shrub. H 2.5m (8ft), S 3m (10ft)
■ **Seasonal highlights** In early spring and early summer, it bears fragrant, bright-yellow flowers.
■ **Value at other times** The divided, glossy, deep-green leaves persist all year.
■ **Ideal site** A warm, sheltered wall in mild areas, or a conservatory.
■ **Cultivation** Grow in full sun, in fertile, well-drained soil or potting compost. Tie in shoots to a support as growth proceeds. After flowering, thin out the oldest flowered shoots and shorten the remainder to strong buds.
■ **Also recommended** *Jasminum humile* is similar but hardier.
■ **Perfect partners** *Jasminum officinale* 'Argenteovariegatum' ♀ has grey-green leaves with creamy-white margins and very fragrant white flowers.

Jasminum nudiflorum ♀
Winter jasmine

A vigorous, very hardy, deciduous, scrambling shrub. H & S to 3m (10ft)
■ **Seasonal highlights** In winter and early spring, it bears masses of bright-yellow flowers on bare branches.
■ **Value at other times** The green shoots and dark-green leaves persist for most of the year.
■ **Ideal site** Tied in to supports on a sunny or lightly shaded wall, or sprawling over a sunny bank.
■ **Cultivation** Grow in any fertile garden soil. After flowering, cut back flowered shoots to strong buds. Every three or four years, take out some of the oldest growths at the base.
■ **Also recommended** *Jasminum officinale* ♀ bears fragrant white flowers from summer to autumn.
■ **Perfect partners** *Daphne mezereum*, *Garrya elliptica*.

K

Kerria japonica 'Picta'
Kerria

An upright, moderately vigorous, deciduous shrub. H 1.5m (5ft), S 2m (6ft)
■ **Seasonal highlights** In mid- and late spring it bears golden-yellow flowers.
■ **Value at other times** It has grey-green leaves with margins of creamy white.
■ **Ideal site** A mixed or shrub border.
■ **Cultivation** Grow in sun or partial shade, in any well-drained soil enriched with organic matter. After flowering, cut back flowered shoots to strong sideshoots or buds.
■ **Also recommended** *Kerria japonica* 'Pleniflora' ♀ is more vigorous with pompon-like, double, yellow flowers.
■ **Perfect partners** Purple-leaved berberis; *Ribes sanguineum* 'Pulborough Scarlet' ♀ (flowering currant).

Kniphofia 'Green Jade'
Red-hot poker

A vigorous, clump-forming evergreen perennial. H 1.5m (5ft), S 60–75 cm (24–30in)
■ **Seasonal highlights** In late summer and early autumn, it bears tall spikes of green flowers that fade to cream and then white. They are attractive to bees.
■ **Value at other times** Has broad, grass-like, greyish green leaves all year.
■ **Ideal site** Mixed or herbaceous borders, gravel gardens.
■ **Cultivation** Grow in full sun in light, fertile, humus-rich, well-drained soil. Protect the crowns, of young plants especially, with a dry mulch.
■ **Also recommended** *Kniphofia* 'Prince Igor' has deep orange-red flowers.
■ **Perfect partners** Hemerocallis, *Knautia macedonica*.

L

Laburnum x watereri 'Vossii' ♀
Golden rain

A vigorous, deciduous tree with a spreading crown. H & S to 8m (25ft)
■ **Seasonal highlights** In late spring and early summer, it produces long, hanging chains of golden-yellow flowers.
■ **Value at other times** It has lustrous, dark-green leaves from spring to autumn.
■ **Ideal site** As a specimen or trained over a pergola.
■ **Cultivation** Grow in full sun in any moderately fertile soil. Prune in late winter to remove dead and damaged wood and badly placed shoots.
■ **Also recommended** *Laburnum anagyroides* is similar with shorter flower clusters.
■ **Perfect partners** *Crataegus laevigata* 'Rosea Flore Pleno' ♀, rhododendrons and azaleas (on acid soils).

L

Lachenalia aloides 'Nelsonii'
Cape cowslip

A vigorous, frost-tender perennial bulb. H 30–40cm (12–16in), S 5cm (2in)
■ **Seasonal highlights** In winter or early spring, it produces dark-stemmed spikes of hanging, tubular, golden-yellow flowers.
■ **Value at other times** It has clumps of strap-shaped, smooth, green leaves.
■ **Ideal site** As a house plant or in a greenhouse or conservatory.
■ **Cultivation** Plant bulbs 10cm (4in) deep in autumn, in fertile potting compost. Grow in full light and water moderately when in growth. Reduce watering as the leaves fade and rest in dry conditions in summer.
■ **Also recommended** *Lachenalia aloides* has tubular, yellow flowers with scarlet tips.
■ **Perfect partners** *Cyclamen persicum* (but not in the same pot).

Lagurus ovatus ♀
Hare's tail grass

Upright, tufted, moderately vigorous annual grass. H 50cm (20in), S 30cm (12in)
■ **Seasonal highlights** Throughout summer, it has dense heads of softly hairy, purple-tinted, pale-green flower spikelets that age to creamy white.
■ **Value at other times** The flowerheads can be dried and used for arrangements indoors throughout the year.
■ **Ideal site** A mixed or annual border.
■ **Cultivation** Grow in full sun in light, well-drained soil. Sow the seeds in the flowering site in spring, or in containers in a cold frame in autumn.
■ **Also recommended** *Hordeum jubatum* has long-bristled, silky flowerheads.
■ **Perfect partners** *Carex elata* 'Aurea' ♀.

Lantana camara cultivars
Lantana

Vigorous, frost-tender, evergreen shrubs, often grown as annual summer bedding. H & S 1–2m (3–6ft)
■ **Seasonal highlights** From late spring to autumn, they bear rounded heads of small white, yellow, salmon-pink, red or purple flowers.
■ **Value at other times** The prickly stems bear finely wrinkled, deep-green leaves.
■ **Ideal site** As bedding, or in containers for patios and conservatories.
■ **Cultivation** Grow in full sun in fertile, moist but well-drained soil. Sow seeds in warmth in spring. Plant out when the risk of frost has passed. Bring patio plants under glass in autumn. Prune back shoots to strong buds in late winter.
■ **Also recommended** *Lantana camara* 'Snow White' has pure-white flowers.
■ **Perfect partners** Petunias and clarkias.

Lathyrus odoratus 'Colin Unwin'
Sweet pea

A hardy, vigorous annual that climbs with twining tendrils. H 2.5m (8ft), S 45cm (18in)
■ **Seasonal highlights** From early to midsummer, it bears frilled, soft-red flowers; many more cultivars are available, with usually fragrant flowers in white, red, pink, or blue. Flowers are good for cutting.
■ **Ideal site** In mixed borders or cottage gardens, on poles or wigwams.
■ **Cultivation** Grow in sun in fertile, well-drained soil enriched with plenty of organic matter. Sow seeds under glass in late autumn or late winter, or in the flowering site in spring.
■ **Also recommended** "Old-fashioned" sweet peas have small but intensely fragrant flowers. There are many other cultivars.
■ **Perfect partners** Grow with lavenders and pinks, or with runner beans in the kitchen garden.

Lavandula angustifolia 'Munstead'

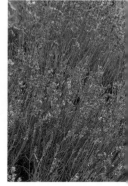

Commonly named lavender. A compact, evergreen shrub. H 45cm (18in), S 60cm (24in)
■ **Seasonal highlights** From mid- to late summer, it bears long-stemmed, very fragrant, blue-purple flowers.
■ **Value at other times** It has aromatic, narrow, grey-green leaves.
■ **Ideal site** Sunny, mixed, or herbaceous borders, in containers on a patio, in gravel gardens, as low hedging.
■ **Cultivation** Grow in full sun in any moderately fertile, well-drained soil. On heavy clay incorporate plenty of grit to improve drainage. In mid-spring, cut back the previous year's growth by about 5cm (2in) to strong pairs of buds. Don't cut into old wood.
■ **Also recommended** *Lavandula angustifolia* 'Loddon Pink' ♀ has soft-pink flowers. 'Hidcote' is a perenially popular variety and is very reliable.
■ **Perfect partners** Roses, cistus.

Lavatera 'Barnsley'
Tree mallow

A very vigorous, bushy, semi-evergreen shrub. H & S to 2m (6ft)
■ **Seasonal highlights** Throughout summer it produces open funnel-shaped, red-eyed, white flowers that flush soft pink with age.
■ **Value at other times** It has attractive lobed, grey-green leaves.
■ **Ideal site** A sunny shrub or mixed border, or as a specimen.
■ **Cultivation** Prefers an open, sunny site. Grow in any reasonably fertile, well-drained soil. Shelter from cold winds in exposed gardens. In spring, cut back hard to good buds low down on the shrub and apply a balanced fertilizer.
■ **Also recommended** Lavatera cashemiriana has clear rose-pink flowers.
■ **Perfect partners** Escallonias, lavenders, roses.

Liatris spicata 'Kobold'
Gayfeather

A delightful perennial with tightly packed flower spikes in shades of reddish purple. H 1.5m (5ft), S 45cm (18in)
■ **Seasonal highlights** The attractive flowers are produced from late summer until autumn.
■ **Value at other times** The flowers are good for cutting and the attractive sword-like foliage lasts until the first frosts.
■ **Ideal site** Grow in a sunny, herbaceous or mixed border, or in containers.
■ **Cultivation** Grow in light, reasonably fertile, moist but well-drained soil in full sun. Liatris spicata needs soil that is reliably moist. In heavy soils, plant on a layer of coarse gravel to improve drainage or plants may rot in winter.
■ **Also recommended** Liatris spicata 'Alba', L. pycnostachya.
■ **Perfect partners** To accentuate their form grow alongside perennials with open flowers such as erigerons, coreopsis, and geums.

Libertia ixioides
Libertia

An upright, moderately vigorous evergreen perennial. H & S to 60cm (24in)
■ **Seasonal highlights** In late spring and early summer, slender stems arise bearing dense clusters of small, white flowers.
■ **Value at other times** Clusters of orange-brown seeds follow the flowers and the narrow, leathery, dark-green leaves turn orange-brown in autumn.
■ **Ideal site** A sunny mixed border.
■ **Cultivation** Grow in moist, but well-drained soil in full sun. Protect with a dry mulch in winter, especially in cold areas.
■ **Also recommended** Libertia grandiflora ♀ is similar, but taller with white flowers.
■ **Perfect partners** Asphodelus albus, Scilla peruviana.

Ligularia 'The Rocket' ♀
Ligularia

This clump-forming perennial is a striking architectural plant grown for its handsome spikes of flowers and large mid-green leaves. H 1.8m (6ft)
■ **Seasonal highlights** From early to late summer it produces tall "candles" of orange-yellow flowers and attractive toothed leaves with purple veins.
■ **Value at other times** In some seasons the flowers can last into autumn. The foliage is attractive in its own right and will last until the frosts.
■ **Ideal site** Grow at the back of a sunny herbaceous or mixed border.
■ **Cultivation** Grow in reasonably fertile, deep, and reliably moist soil, in full sun or partial shade. Provide shelter from strong winds. May need staking with twiggy sticks. Divide in spring or after flowering.
■ **Also recommended** Ligularia 'Greynog Gold' ♀, L. przewalskii
■ **Perfect partners** Grow with other moisture-loving perennials such as astilbe and hemerocallis.

Lilium 'Sun Ray'
Lily

A vigorous, perennial bulb. H 1m (3ft), S 15cm (6in)
■ **Seasonal highlights** From early to midsummer, it bears bowl-shaped, glossy yellow flowers with brown dots on the petals.
■ **Value at other times** No value at other times.
■ **Ideal site** Sunny borders and in containers on a patio.
■ **Cultivation** Grow in sun but shade the roots from hot sun. Best in fertile, well-drained soil enriched with leafmould or well-rotted organic matter. Plant the bulbs in autumn at twice their own depth. On clay soils, plant on a layer of grit.
■ **Also recommended** Lilium 'Sterling Star' has scented, brown-speckled, cream-flushed-white flowers. There are many cultivars.
■ **Perfect partners** Looks good with peonies, poppies, and roses.

L

Lobelia
Fan Series
Lobelia

Vigorous half-hardy annual with a mix of rose, red, orchid, and scarlet flowers. H 50–60cm (20–24in) S 30cm (12in).
■ **Seasonal highlights**
Flowers are produced in succession from midsummer until the frosts in autumn in beautiful colours.
■ **Value at other times**
The fresh bronze-red foliage will last well into autumn.
■ **Ideal site** Grow with annuals or in a mixed border in sun or part shade.
■ **Cultivation** Sow seeds indoors in a temperature of 18–20°C (65–70°F) 10–12 weeks before the last frosts. When large enough to handle transplant into 7.5cm (3in) pots and grow on indoors. Transplant outdoors after hardening 30cm (12in) apart when the risk of frost has passed. Harmful if eaten.
■ **Also recommended**
Lobelia x *gerardii* 'Vedrariensis' has violet-purple flowers.
■ **Perfect partners**
Summer bedding such as antirrhinums, pelargoniums.

Lobelia
Waterfall Series
Lobelia

These are mound-forming annuals covered with masses of flowers through summer. H 26cm (10in) S 30cm (12in).
■ **Seasonal highlights** From midsummer to late autumn the plants are covered in small, star-shaped flowers in blues, light blues, or white.
■ **Value at other times**
Of little value at other times.
■ **Ideal site** Grown with other annuals in borders or in containers in a sunny position.
■ **Cultivation** Sow seeds indoors in spring in a temperature of 18-20°C (65–70°F) 10–12 weeks before the last frosts. When large enough to handle transplant into 7.5cm (3in) pots and grow on indoors. Transplant outdoors when the threat of frost has passed in a sunny position and around 15cm (6in) apart.
■ **Also recommended**
Lobelia erinus Cascade Series are trailing, with carmine-red, pink, blue, or white flowers.
■ **Perfect partners**
Alyssum (*Lobularia maritima*), begonia, marigolds.

Lonicera
fragrantissima
Winter honeysuckle

Bushy, spreading, moderately vigorous, semi-evergreen shrub. H 2m (6ft), S 3m (10ft)
■ **Seasonal highlights**
In winter and early spring, it bears very fragrant flowers.
■ **Value at other times**
It has dark-green leaves that are blue-green beneath.
■ **Ideal site** A shrub border or against a warm wall; it flowers more freely in warmth with shelter.
■ **Cultivation** Grow in any fertile, well-drained soil in sun or light shade. After flowering, prune back flowered shoots to strong buds or shoots lower down the stems.
■ **Also recommended**
Lonicera x *standishii* is similar and flowers from late autumn to early spring.
■ **Perfect partners**
Jasminum nudiflorum; use a late-season clematis like *Clematis* 'Ernest Markham' ♀ for interest in late summer.

Lonicera
x *heckrottii*
Honeysuckle

A vigorous, semi-evergreen, twining climber. H 5m (15ft), S 3m (10ft)
■ **Seasonal highlights**
From mid- to late summer, it bears clusters of fragrant coral-pink flowers that are orange-yellow within.
■ **Value at other times**
Has dark-green leaves with blue-green undersides and sometimes bears glossy, red berries in autumn.
■ **Ideal site** A wall, fence, or trellis.
■ **Cultivation** Grow in any fertile, moist but well-drained soil. In early spring, shorten shoots to strong buds or shoots lower down the stems.
■ **Also recommended**
Lonicera periclymenum 'Graham Thomas' ♀ has yellow flowers.
■ **Perfect partners**
Clematis 'Huldine' ♀, *Clematis* 'Ville de Lyon'.

Lonicera
x *purpusii*
Winter honeysuckle

A moderately vigorous, semi-evergreen or deciduous shrub. H 2m (6ft), S 2.5m (8ft)
■ **Seasonal highlights**
In winter and early spring, it bears small clusters of very fragrant white flowers with conspicuous yellow anthers.
■ **Value at other times**
It has purple shoots and dark-green leaves for the summer.
■ **Ideal site** A shrub border, or against a warm wall; it flowers most freely in warmth with shelter.
■ **Cultivation** Grow in any fertile, well-drained soil in sun or dappled shade. After flowering, cut back flowered shoots to strong buds, but only to confine to bounds.
■ **Also recommended**
Lonicera x *purpusii* 'Winter Beauty' ♀ is very free-flowering.
■ **Perfect partners**
Daphne mezereum, mahonias, sarcococca.

Lupinus 'The Page'
Lupin

A vigorous, clump-forming herbaceous perennial. H 90cm (36in), S 75cm (30in)
■ **Seasonal highlights** It produces dense spires of pea-like, carmine-red flowers in early and midsummer.
■ **Value at other times** Cut back after the first flush for a few more flowers later in summer. The attractive foliage fades after flowering.
■ **Ideal site** A mixed or herbaceous border, cottage gardens.
■ **Cultivation** Grow in light, fertile, well-drained, preferably slightly acid soil in sun; it tolerates part-day shade. Take basal cuttings in mid-spring; lupins are often short-lived.
■ **Also recommended** *Lupinus* 'Chandelier' has bright-yellow flowers. There are many other cultivars.
■ **Perfect partners** Delphiniums, Oriental poppies (*Papaver orientalis*), pyrethrums.

Lychnis chalcedonica ♀
Maltese cross

A moderately vigorous, herbaceous perennial. H 0.9–1.2m (3–4ft), S 30cm (12in)
■ **Seasonal highlights** In early and midsummer it produces rounded clusters of cross-shaped, scarlet flowers at the tips of upright stems.
■ **Value at other times** Has basal clumps of bright-green leaves.
■ **Ideal site** A mixed or herbaceous border.
■ **Cultivation** Grow in any fertile, moist but well-drained soil in sun or light shade. Provide support. Deadhead to prolong flowering. Divide in spring or autumn. Self-seeds freely.
■ **Also recommended** *Lychnis coronaria* ♀ has grey leaves and magenta flowers.
■ **Perfect partners** Aquilegias, lupins, Oriental poppies (*Papaver orientalis*).

Lysichiton americanus ♀
Skunk cabbage

A very vigorous, spreading herbaceous perennial. H 1m (3ft), S 1.2m (4ft)
■ **Seasonal highlights** In early spring, before the leaves appear, it bears club-like spikes of tiny green flowers surrounded by large, glossy, yellow spathes.
■ **Value at other times** The large, paddle-shaped leathery, green leaves elongate after flowering.
■ **Ideal site** Pool- or streamsides.
■ **Cultivation** Grow in full sun or light, dappled shade in moist, fertile, humus-rich soil. Allow plenty of room for the leaves to grow.
■ **Also recommended** *Lysichiton camtschatcensis* ♀ has creamy-white flower spathes.
■ **Perfect partners** *Caltha palustris* ♀.

M

Magnolia stellata ♀
Star magnolia

Compact, bushy, slow-growing, deciduous shrub. H 3m (9ft), S 4m (12ft)
■ **Seasonal highlights** In early and mid-spring, the silky buds open to star-shaped, white flowers.
■ **Value at other times** Has a neat habit and attractive leaves for the summer.
■ **Ideal site** As a specimen, or in a shrub or mixed border.
■ **Cultivation** Grow in moist but well-drained, fertile, humus-rich soil in sun or dappled shade. It tolerates slightly acid and slightly alkaline soils. Shelter from cold winds and late frosts, which may damage the flowers. Little or no pruning is required.
■ **Also recommended** *Magnolia stellata* 'Waterlily' ♀ has larger, double, white flowers.
■ **Perfect partners** Camellias, flowering quince (*Chaenomeles*).

Mahonia x *media* 'Charity'
Mahonia

An upright, bushy, vigorous evergreen shrub. H to 5m (15ft), S 4m (12ft)
■ **Seasonal highlights** From late autumn to early spring, it bears long spikes of fragrant, deep-yellow flowers.
■ **Value at other times** During the rest of the year, it has attractive, glossy dark-green, sharply toothed leaves.
■ **Ideal site** In a shrub border, woodland garden, or as a specimen.
■ **Cultivation** Grow in moist but well-drained, humus-rich soil, in partial shade or in sun if soils are reliably moist. It needs little pruning; if it becomes leggy or outgrows its allotted space, prune after flowering.
■ **Also recommended** *Mahonia repens* 'Rotundifolia' is shorter and spreading with dark-yellow flowers in spring.
■ **Perfect partners** *Viburnum tinus, Daphne mezereum*.

M

Malus

Crab apples

Deciduous, mostly vigorous, small trees that are ideal as specimens for smaller gardens.

■ **Seasonal highlights** In spring they bear masses of blossom ranging from white to pink and purplish reds.

■ **Value at other times** In autumn, they bear crab apples in colours ranging from yellow to red; the leaves turn yellow and orange too.

■ **Cultivation** Grow in any fertile, well-drained soil in sun; they tolerate light shade, but purple-leaved variants are best in sun. Prune in winter to remove misplaced shoots or dead or damaged wood.

Malus x *hartwigii* **'Katherine'** ♀ has small, red-flushed, yellow fruit. H & S 6m (20ft)

Malus **'Royalty'** has flowers of crimson-purple. H & S 8m (25ft)

Malus **'John Downie'** ♀ has white flowers. H 10m (30ft), 6m (20ft)

Malus pumila **'Cowichan'** has rose-pink flowers. H & S 8m (25ft)

Malus x *zumi* **'Professor Sprenger'** has white flowers. H & S 7m (22ft)

Malus x *moerlandsii* **'Liset'** has purple-red fruit. H & S 6m (20ft)

Matthiola Brompton Group

Brompton stocks

Vigorous, bushy, woody-based perennials grown as annuals or biennials. H 45cm (18in), S 30cm (12in)

■ **Seasonal highlights** From late spring to summer, they bear densely packed spikes of scented, single or double flowers in pink, red, purple, yellow, and white. They are excellent cut flowers.

■ **Value at other times** No real value at other times.

■ **Ideal site** Cottage gardens, cutting borders, and mixed borders.

■ **Cultivation** Grow in full sun in fertile, well-drained soil. Sow seeds in warmth in spring and set out when the risk of frost has passed. For larger, earlier flowers sow in autumn and overwinter in a cold frame.

■ **Also recommended** *Matthiola* 'Giant Excelsior Column' has tall spires of double flowers.

■ **Perfect partners** China asters, border carnations.

Miscanthus sinensis 'Silberfeder' ♀

Miscanthus

Vigorous, upright, deciduous perennial grass. H 2.5m (8ft), S 1.2m (4ft)

■ **Seasonal highlights** It has silvery, pinkish-brown flowerheads in early to mid-autumn; these and the dry leaves persist through winter.

■ **Value at other times** Has arching blue-green leaves.

■ **Ideal site** Mixed or herbaceous borders.

■ **Cultivation** Grow in any fertile, moist but well-drained soil in full sun; it tolerates light shade. Cut old growth to the ground in spring. Divide congested clumps in spring.

■ **Also recommended** *Miscanthus sinensis* 'Zebrinus' ♀ has green leaves horizontally banded with yellow. There are many other cultivars.

■ **Perfect partners** *Stipa gigantea* ♀, *Glyceria maxima* 'Variegata'.

Monarda
'Mahogany'
Bergamot, Bee balm

A vigorous, clump-forming, herbaceous perennial.
H 90cm (36in), S 45cm (18in)
■ **Seasonal highlights**
From midsummer until autumn, it bears whorls of wine-red flowers at the stem tips. The flowers attract bees.
■ **Value at other times**
Has aromatic, red-veined, dark-green leaves.
■ **Ideal site** A mixed or herbaceous border, or herb garden.
■ **Cultivation** Best in sun, but will tolerate light, dappled shade. Grow in any fertile, well-drained soil that doesn't dry out in summer. Divide overcrowded clumps in spring.
■ **Also recommended**
Monarda 'Cambridge Scarlet' ♥ has scarlet-red flowers.
■ **Perfect partners**
Achilleas, border phlox, sunflowers (Helianthus).

Muscari
armeniacum ♥
Grape hyacinth

A vigorous, bulbous perennial.
H 20cm (8in), S 5cm (2in)
■ **Seasonal highlights**
In spring, it produces spikes of tubular, bright-blue flowers with white mouths.
■ **Value at other times**
Of no value at other times.
■ **Ideal site** A rock garden, the front of a mixed or herbaceous border, in containers.
■ **Cultivation** Grow in full sun in any well-drained, moderately fertile soil. Plant bulbs, 10cm (4in) deep, in autumn. Lift to divide congested clumps as the leaves fade in summer.
■ **Also recommended**
Muscari botryoides f. album has fragrant, white flowers.
■ **Perfect partners**
Erythroniums, crocus.

N

Narcissus
'Cheerfulness' ♥
Double narcissus

Robust, bulbous perennial.
H 40cm (16in), S 8cm (3in)
■ **Seasonal highlights**
In mid-spring, each stem produces several sweetly scented, double, white flowers with clustered, creamy-white segments at the centre.
■ **Value at other times**
Of no value at other times.
■ **Ideal site** Borders, and containers indoors and outside.
■ **Cultivation** Grow in sun or light, dappled shade. Plant the bulbs in autumn at twice their own depth, in any fertile, well-drained soil. If flowering declines and bulbs are congested, allow the foliage to die down naturally and lift and divide the clumps.
■ **Also recommended**
Narcissus 'Yellow Cheerfulness' ♥ has golden-yellow flowers. There are many other cultivars.
■ **Perfect partners**
Forsythia, doronicums, crocus.

Narcissus
cyclamineus ♥
Wild narcissus

A vigorous, perennial bulb.
H 15–20cm (6–8in), S 2.5cm (1in)
■ **Seasonal highlights**
In early spring, it bears nodding, golden-yellow flowers with backswept petals.
■ **Value at other times**
Of no value at other times.
■ **Ideal site** Naturalized in turf or in rock or woodland gardens.
■ **Cultivation** Grow in sun or dappled shade in any moderately fertile, well-drained soil. Plant bulbs in autumn at twice their own depth. If grown in turf, allow foliage to fade naturally before mowing.
■ **Also recommended**
Narcissus 'Jumblie' ♥ has similar but larger flowers with golden-orange cups. There are many cultivars.
■ **Perfect partners** Crocus, chionodoxas.

Narcissus
'Dutch Master' ♥
Trumpet daffodil

A vigorous perennial bulb.
H 35cm (14in), S 8cm (3in)
■ **Seasonal highlights**
In mid-spring it bears large golden-yellow flowers, with short, slightly frilled trumpets.
■ **Value at other times** Can be grown in pots to flower earlier indoors.
■ **Ideal site** Naturalized in grass, in borders, or containers.
■ **Cultivation** Grow in sun or dappled shade in fertile, well-drained soil. Plant bulbs in autumn at twice their own depth. For forcing, plant in pots and plunge in a cold frame for about eight weeks or until shoots appear. Bring into a cool greenhouse, and take indoors as flower buds begin to open.
■ **Also recommended**
Narcissus 'Little Beauty' ♥ is shorter with creamy-white, yellow-cupped flowers.
■ **Perfect partners**
Crocus, chionodoxas.

N

Nemesia caerulea
Perennial nemesia

A vigorous, bushy, woody-based perennial. H 60cm (24in), S 30cm (12in)

■ **Seasonal highlights**
Clusters of yellow-throated, pink, pale-blue, lavender-blue or white flowers appear from early summer to autumn.

■ **Value at other times**
It has dark-green leaves.

■ **Ideal site** Borders, raised beds, and decorative containers.

■ **Cultivation** Grow in a sheltered site in full sun in moderately fertile, well-drained soil. It may not survive very cold winters. If pot-grown it can be brought into a greenhouse in autumn. Otherwise, take stem cuttings in summer and overwinter young plants under glass.

■ **Also recommended**
Nemesia caerulea 'Innocence' ♀ has white flowers.

■ **Perfect partners**
Argyranthemums, osteospermums.

Nemesia strumosa 'KLM'
Annual nemesia

Bushy, free-flowering annual. H 18–30cm (7–12in), S 10–15cm (4–6in)

■ **Seasonal highlights**
Bears bicoloured, blue and white flowers with pink throats and yellow beards, from mid- to late summer.

■ **Value at other times**
Can be grown as an early spring-flowering house plant.

■ **Ideal site** Bedding, hanging baskets, and other containers.

■ **Cultivation** Grow in full sun or light, dappled shade in any moderately fertile, well-drained soil. Sow seeds in warmth in spring and plant out when the risk of frost has passed. Or sow in autumn and overwinter under glass for early flowers indoors.

■ **Also recommended**
Nemesia strumosa 'Prince of Orange' has orange flowers.

■ **Perfect partners** Clarkias and petunias.

Nepeta x faassenii ♀
Catmint, catnip

A vigorous, clump-forming, herbaceous perennial. H & S 45cm (18in)

■ **Seasonal highlights**
From early summer to early autumn, it bears fragrant, pale lavender-blue flowers with darker purple spots. Attracts bees, moths, and butterflies.

■ **Value at other times**
It also has wrinkled, hairy, aromatic, grey-green leaves.

■ **Ideal site** Mixed or herbaceous borders, cottage and wildlife gardens.

■ **Cultivation** Grow in any fertile, well-drained soil. Trim hard after the first flush of flowers to keep plants tidy and encourage more flowers. Rejuvenate old plants by dividing in spring or autumn.

■ **Also recommended**
Nepeta sibirica is taller with blue to lavender-blue flowers.

■ **Perfect partners**
Alchemillas, lavenders, roses.

Nerine bowdenii ♀
Nerine

A moderately vigorous, perennial bulb. H 45cm (18in), S 8cm (3in)

■ **Seasonal highlights** In autumn it bears rounded heads of funnel-shaped, faintly scented pink flowers. The strap-shaped leaves emerge after flowering.

■ **Value at other times**
Of no value at other times.

■ **Ideal site** At the base of a warm, sunny wall, or in raised beds.

■ **Cultivation** Grow in full sun in sharply drained soil in a warm, sheltered site. Provide a dry winter mulch in cold areas. Plant in summer with the nose (tip) of the bulb just at soil level.

■ **Also recommended**
Nerine bowdenii 'Alba' has white, often pink-flushed flowers.

■ **Perfect partners**
Schizostylis, Scilla scilloides.

Nicotiana x sanderae Starship Series
Tobacco plant

Upright, bushy, moderately vigorous, half-hardy annuals. H 30cm (12in), S 10cm (4in)

■ **Seasonal highlights**
From summer until autumn, bears a profusion of pink, red, rose-pink, white, or lime-green flowers.

■ **Value at other times**
Of no value at other times.

■ **Ideal site** Annual and mixed borders, decorative containers.

■ **Cultivation** Grow in full sun or light, dappled shade in any fertile, well-drained soil. Sow seeds under glass in early spring and plant out when the danger of frost has passed.

■ **Also recommended**
Nicotiana Domino Series 'Salmon Pink' is compact with upturned salmon-pink flowers.

■ **Perfect partners**
Pelargoniums, petunias, asters.

Nicotiana sylvestris ♀
Tobacco plant

A vigorous biennial or short-lived perennial. H 1.5m (5ft), S 60cm (2ft)
■ **Seasonal highlights**
It bears loose heads of white, trumpet-shaped flowers that are very fragrant when they open in the evening.
■ **Value at other times**
It has a basal rosette of large, dark-green leaves.
■ **Ideal site** Mixed or herbaceous borders, or woodland gardens.
■ **Cultivation** Grow in light, dappled shade in any fertile, moist but well-drained soil. Tolerates full sun in reliably moist soils. Sow seeds under glass in early spring. Plant out when the threat of frost has passed. Provide a deep winter mulch in cold areas.
■ **Also recommended**
Nicotiana 'Lime Green' ♀ is annual with lime-green flowers.
■ **Perfect partners**
Eremurus, roses.

Nigella damascena 'Miss Jekyll' ♀ ♀
Love-in-a-mist

A vigorous annual. H 50cm (20in), S 23cm (9in)
■ **Seasonal highlights**
During summer, it produces sky-blue flowers, surrounded by a ruff of slender leaves.
■ **Value at other times**
It has finely divided, feathery foliage. The seed pods can be dried for indoor arrangements.
■ **Ideal site** Annual borders, cutting borders, cottage gardens.
■ **Cultivation** Grow in full sun in any moderately fertile, well-drained soil. Sow seeds in the flowering site in spring and thin seedlings to 23cm (9in) apart. May also be sown in autumn for earlier flowers. Protect with cloches in areas with very cold wet winters.
■ **Also recommended**
Nigella hispanica 'Curiosity' has scented, dark-eyed, bright-blue flowers.
■ **Perfect partners**
Clarkias and calendulas.

Nymphaea
Waterlilies

These submerged aquatic perennials mostly have a spread of 0.9–2.2m (3–7ft); *Nymphaea tetragona* 'Helvola', only 25–40cm (10–16in) across, can be grown in very small pools.
■ **Seasonal highlights** In summer they bear large single or double flowers in white and shades of pink, red, or yellow. There are frost-tender species, like *Nymphaea capensis*, with fragrant, pale-blue flowers, which are grown in indoor pools in cold areas.
■ **Value at other times** The large, flat leaves float on the water's surface, providing shelter for fish and helping shade out algal growth. Most are glossy dark green, but several, like 'Marliacea Chromatella' ♀, have attractive bronze or purple markings.
■ **Ideal site** Pools with still water.
■ **Cultivation** Grow in full sun. Plant in aquatic planting baskets of loamy soil and cover the surface with pea gravel to prevent the soil muddying the water. Remove yellowing leaves through the summer. Lift and divide when leaves become crowded.
■ **Perfect partners** *Mimulus, Typha latifolia*.

Nymphaea 'Fire Crest'

Nymphaea 'Marliacea Chromatella' ♀

Nymphaea tetragona 'Helvola'

Nymphaea capensis

Nymphaea alba

Nymphaea 'Rose Arey'

O

Oenothera fruticosa 'Fyrverkeri' ♀
Evening primrose

Also known as sundrops. An upright, vigorous, herbaceous perennial. H 30–90cm (12–36in), S 30cm (12in)
■ **Seasonal highlights** From late spring until late summer, cupped yellow flowers open from red buds.
■ **Value at other times** It has red-tinted stems and maroon-flushed leaves.
■ **Ideal site** Mixed or herbaceous borders.
■ **Cultivation** Easily grown in moderately fertile, moist but well-drained soil in full sun.
■ **Also recommended** *Oenothera macrocarpa* ♀ is trailing with golden-yellow flowers.
■ **Perfect partners** *Coreopsis verticillata*, border phlox, *Lychnis chalcedonica* ♀.

Osteospermum jucundum
Osteospermum

A vigorous, clump-forming, evergreen perennial. H 10–50cm (4–20in), S 50–90cm (20–36in)
■ **Seasonal highlights** From late spring to autumn, it bears mauve-pink to magenta, daisy-like flowerheads.
■ **Value at other times** The dense mat of grey-green leaves are good ground cover.
■ **Ideal site** Beds and borders, especially in hot, dry sites.
■ **Cultivation** Grow in sun in any well-drained soil. Deadhead regularly to prolong flowering. May not survive cold wet winters, so take stem cuttings in late summer; overwinter young plants under glass.
■ **Also recommended** *Osteospermum* 'Buttermilk' ♀ bears primrose-yellow flowers with a bronze reverse.
■ **Perfect partners** Argyranthemums, pyrethrums, chrysanthemums.

P

Paeonia
Herbaceous peonies

Vigorous, long-lived, herbaceous perennials.
■ **Seasonal highlights** From early to midsummer, they bear very showy, bowl-shaped, single or double flowers in white and shades of red and pink.
■ **Value at other times** The dark or greyish-green leaves often colour well in autumn.
■ **Ideal site** Mixed or herbaceous borders, especially in cottage gardens.
■ **Cultivation** Best in full sun, but tolerant of dappled shade for part of the day. Grow in deep, fertile, moist but well-drained soil that is enriched with plentiful organic matter. The large-flowered sorts may need unobtrusive, grow-through supports in exposed gardens.
■ **Perfect partners** Hostas, Oriental poppies (*Papaver orientalis*), roses.

Paeonia lactiflora **'Laura Dessert'** ♀ has double flowers with pale-pink outer petals. H & S 70–75cm (30–32in)

Paeonia lactiflora **'Ballerina'** has large, double pink flowers. H & S 90–100cm (36–39in)

Paeonia lactiflora **'Kelway's Supreme'** bears fragrant, semi-double pale-pink flowers. H & S 90–100cm (36–39in)

Paeonia lactiflora **'Bowl of Beauty'** ♀ has carmine-red and creamy-white petals. H & S 80–100cm (32–39in)

Paeonia lactiflora **'Sarah Bernhardt'** produces large, double rose-pink flowers with a silvery sheen. H & S 90–100cm (36–39in)

Paeonia officinalis **'Rubra Plena'** ♀ bears large, double, satin-textured, rich-crimson flowers. H & S 70–75cm (30–32in)

Paeonia mlokosewitschii ♀
Caucasian peony

A vigorous, clump-forming herbaceous perennial. H & S 65–90cm (26–36in)
■ **Seasonal highlights** In late spring and early summer, it bears single, bowl-shaped, lemon-yellow flowers.
■ **Value at other times** The bluish-green leaves are heavily suffused with red-purple as they emerge.
■ **Ideal site** Mixed or herbaceous borders.
■ **Cultivation** Grow in full sun or part-day shade in deep, fertile, moist but well-drained soil enriched with organic matter. Shelter from strong winds.
■ **Also recommended** *Paeonia emodi* has nodding, pure-white flowers in late spring.
■ **Perfect partners** *Aquilegia alpina*, *Polemonium carneum*.

Paeonia officinalis 'Rubra Plena' ♀
Common peony

A vigorous, clump-forming herbaceous perennial. H & S 70–75cm (30–32in)
■ **Seasonal highlights** In early and midsummer it bears large, double, satin-textured, rich-crimson flowers.
■ **Value at other times** Deep-green, divided, leaves.
■ **Ideal site** Herbaceous or mixed borders, especially in cottage gardens.
■ **Cultivation** Grow in full sun or part-day shade in deep, fertile, moist but well-drained soil enriched with organic matter. Provide a grow-through support in exposed gardens.
■ **Also recommended** *Paeonia officinalis* 'Rosea Superba Plena' has large, double rose-pink flowers.
■ **Perfect partners** Lavenders, roses, campanulas.

Papaver orientale 'Cedric Morris' ♀
Oriental poppy

A vigorous, clump-forming, herbaceous perennial. H 45–90cm (18–36in), S 60–90cm (24–36in)
■ **Seasonal highlights** From late spring to midsummer, it bears bowl-shaped, satiny, soft-pink flowers with frilled petals, each with a black basal mark.
■ **Value at other times** The bristly, jagged leaves die back soon after flowering.
■ **Ideal site** Herbaceous or mixed borders, especially in cottage gardens.
■ **Cultivation** Grow in full sun, in deep, fertile, well-drained soil. Cut back hard after flowering, to produce fresh foliage and a few later flowers.
■ **Also recommended** *Papaver orientalis* 'Beauty of Livermere' ♀ has large, glossy, scarlet-crimson flowers.
■ **Perfect partners** Lupins, hemerocallis.

Papaver rhoeas Shirley Series
Shirley poppy

Vigorous, free-flowering hardy annuals. H 90cm (36in), S 30cm (12in)
■ **Seasonal highlights** During summer, bears bowl-shaped, single or semi-double flowers in white and shades of yellow, orange, pink, and red.
■ **Value at other times** They have hairy stems with downy, light-green leaves.
■ **Ideal site** Annual and mixed borders, especially in cottage gardens.
■ **Cultivation** Grow in sun in any poor to moderately fertile, well-drained soil. Sow seeds in spring in the flowering site. Self-seeds freely, but seedlings are variable.
■ **Also recommended** *Papaver somniferum* 'Paeony Flowered' has large, double, frilly flowers in white and shades of red, pink, and purple.
■ **Perfect partners** Clarkias, eschscholzias, nigellas.

Parthenocissus tricuspidata ♀
Boston ivy

A very vigorous, deciduous, self-clinging climber. H & S to 20m (70ft)
■ **Seasonal highlights** The leaves turn brilliant red and deep purple in autumn.
■ **Value at other times** Has lobed, bright-green leaves from spring onwards.
■ **Ideal site** Large walls, fences, or growing through large trees.
■ **Cultivation** Grow in any fertile, well-drained soil in sun or shade. Guide young plants into the support until they cling for themselves. Prune in late winter, if necessary, to confine to bounds.
■ **Also recommended** *Parthenocissus henryana* ♀ has dark-green, often pink-flushed, leaves with silver veins; they turn bright red in autumn.
■ **Perfect partners** *Jasminum nudiflorum* ♀, late-flowering clematis.

P

Pelargonium 'Apple Blossom Rosebud' ♀

Zonal pelargonium

Frost-tender, evergreen, fleshy-stemmed perennial. H 40cm (16in), S 25cm (10in)

■ **Seasonal highlights** From summer to autumn, it bears large clusters of white flowers with pink margins.

■ **Value at other times** Rounded, pale-green leaves.

■ **Ideal site** Containers on a patio, or in the home or conservatory.

■ **Cultivation** Grow in fertile, well-drained soil or compost in full sun. Set out when risk of frost has passed. Give a high-potash fertilizer weekly. Deadhead regularly. Take stem cuttings during spring or summer and overwinter under glass.

■ **Also recommended** *Pelargonium* Horizon Series are seed-raised and good for bedding; they have flowers in white and shades of pink and red. There are many cultivars.

■ **Perfect partners** Annual lobelias, fuchsias.

Pennisetum alopecuroides 'Hameln'

Also known as fountain grass. A vigorous, clump-forming evergreen grass. H & S 1.2m (4ft)

■ **Seasonal highlights** In summer and autumn it bears cylindrical, feathery, greenish-white flowerheads that mature to pale grey.

■ **Value at other times** The dark-green leaves turn golden yellow in autumn. The flowerheads can be dried for indoor flower arrangements.

■ **Ideal site** Mixed or herbaceous borders.

■ **Cultivation** Grow in light, well-drained soil in full sun. Cut back dead top growth in spring. Plant and divide overcrowded clumps in late spring.

■ **Also recommended** *Pennisetum villosum* ♀ is shorter and deciduous, with feathery, pale-green then purple flowerheads.

■ **Perfect partners** *Lagurus ovatus* ♀, *Stipa gigantea* ♀.

Penstemon

Penstemons

Vigorous, frost-hardy, evergreen or semi-evergreen perennials of upright growth.

■ **Seasonal highlights** From summer to late autumn, they bear bell-shaped, foxglove-like flowers in white and shades of red, pink, lilac, and maroon.

■ **Value at other times** Form dense clumps of fresh, green leaves.

■ **Ideal site** Mixed or herbaceous borders.

■ **Cultivation** Best in sun, but tolerant of dappled, part-day shade. Grow in fertile, well-drained soil. Incorporate grit into heavy clay soil. Deadhead regularly. May not survive cold wet winters, so take stem cuttings in late summer and overwinter under glass.

■ **Perfect partners** Achilleas, border phlox, hardy geraniums, *Phygelius*.

Penstemon 'Alice Hindley' ♀ has lilac-blue flowers. H 90cm (3ft), S 45cm (18in)

Penstemon 'Apple Blossom' ♀ has white-throated, pink flowers. H & S 45–60cm (18–24in)

Penstemon 'Burgundy' has wine-red flowers. H 90cm (3ft), S 45cm (18in)

Penstemon 'Chester Scarlet' ♀ has large scarlet flowers. H 60cm (2ft), S 45cm (18in)

Penstemon 'Maurice Gibbs' ♀ bears white-throated, cerise-pink blooms. H 75cm (30in), S 45cm (18in)

Penstemon 'Stapleford Gem' ♀ has large, lilac-purple flowers suffused with pink and white within. H 60cm (2ft), S 45cm (18in)

Perovskia 'Blue Spire' ♀
Russian sage

A moderately vigorous, deciduous subshrub. H 1.2m (4ft), S 1m (3ft)

■ **Seasonal highlights**
In late summer and early autumn, it bears tall spires of violet-blue flowers.

■ **Value at other times** It has grey-white stems and silver-grey leaves.

■ **Ideal site** Sunny borders, especially in hot, dry sites, chalky soils, or seaside gardens.

■ **Cultivation** Grow in poor to moderately fertile, well-drained soil in full sun. In early spring, cut back all shoots to within 30cm (12in) of the ground.

■ **Also recommended** *Perovskia* 'Hybrida' has dark lavender-blue flowers.

■ **Perfect partners** Roses, hardy fuchsias, lavenders.

Petunia Million Bells Pink
Petunia

Vigorous, half-hardy perennials grown as annuals. H & S to 30cm (12in)

■ **Seasonal highlights**
From early summer until late autumn, bears masses of small, trumpet-shaped, bright magenta-pink flowers.

■ **Value at other times**
Cuttings can be taken and plants grown inside to flower in winter and early spring.

■ **Ideal site** Bedding and containers, including hanging baskets.

■ **Cultivation** Grow in full sun in light, well-drained soil. Shelter from strong winds. This cultivar is usually sold as "plugs" or young plants.

■ **Also recommended** *Petunia* Surfinia Series are vigorous with large, white, pink, red, magenta, or violet-blue flowers. There are many cultivars.

■ **Perfect partners** Pelargoniums, fuchsias, annual lobelias, and nasturtiums (*Tropaeolum majus*).

Philadelphus microphyllus
Mock orange

A vigorous, deciduous shrub. H & S to 1m (3ft).

■ **Seasonal highlights**
In early and midsummer, it bears single, very fragrant, pure-white flowers.

■ **Value at other times** It has peeling, dark chestnut-brown bark and glossy leaves.

■ **Ideal site** A mixed or shrub border.

■ **Cultivation** Grow in full sun or light, dappled shade, in any moderately fertile, well-drained soil. After flowering, shorten flowered shoots to strong buds. When mature, cut back one in five of the oldest stems at the base.

■ **Also recommended** *Philadelphus* 'Buckley's Quill' is taller, with scented, very double, white flowers packed with quill-like petals.

■ **Perfect partners** *Jasminum humile*, shrubby potentillas, roses.

Phlox paniculata 'Eva Cullum'
Border phlox

A vigorous, strongly upright herbaceous perennial. H 1.2m (4ft), S to 1m (3ft)

■ **Seasonal highlights**
From summer to mid-autumn, it bears bright, deep-pink flowers with darker-pink centres and a heady scent. Excellent for cutting.

■ **Value at other times**
Fresh green leaves from spring onwards.

■ **Ideal site** Mixed or herbaceous borders.

■ **Cultivation** Grow in fertile, moist soil in sun or light dappled shade. Divide every 3–4 years in autumn or spring to maintain vigour. Take basal cuttings in spring or root cuttings in autumn or winter.

■ **Also recommended** *Phlox paniculata* 'Windsor' ♀ has purple-eyed, red-pink flowers.

■ **Perfect partners** Roses, penstemons, hardy geraniums.

Phygelius x rectus 'Salmon Leap' ♀
Phygelius

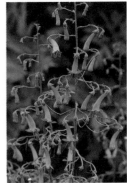

A vigorous, suckering, upright, evergreen shrub. H 1.2m (4ft), S 1.5m (5ft)

■ **Seasonal highlights**
Throughout summer and into autumn it produces curving, tubular, orange flowers that hang from slender stalks.

■ **Value at other times**
Glossy dark-green leaves look good for most of the year.

■ **Ideal site** A shrub or mixed border or against a sunny wall.

■ **Cultivation** Grow in sun in fertile, moist but well-drained soil. Deadhead regularly. Give a deep winter mulch in cold areas. Needs little pruning; cut back frost-damaged growth to strong buds in spring, to the base if necessary.

■ **Also recommended** *Phygelius aequalis* 'Yellow Trumpet' ♀ has creamy-yellow flowers.

■ **Perfect partners** Hardy geraniums, hemerocallis, penstemons.

P

Physalis alkekengi ♀
Chinese lanterns

A vigorous, rhizomatous, herbaceous perennial. H 60–75cm (2–2½ft), S 90cm (3ft)

■ **Seasonal highlights** Nodding, bell-shaped, creamy-white flowers in midsummer.

■ **Value at other times** In late summer and autumn, inflated, papery, red lanterns enclose orange-red fruits. They can be used in dried-flower arrangements.

■ **Ideal site** Mixed or herbaceous borders.

■ **Cultivation** Grow in full sun in any well-drained soil. Cut stems for drying just as the lanterns begin to colour.

■ **Also recommended** *Physalis alkekengi* var. *franchetii* is similar, with smaller flowers.

■ **Perfect partners** *Lychnis chalcedonica* ♀.

Pieris 'Flamingo'
Pieris

A dense, bushy, moderately vigorous evergreen shrub. H to 4m (12ft), S 3m (10ft)

■ **Seasonal highlights** In late winter and spring, it bears hanging clusters of urn-shaped, dark flamingo-pink flowers that open from dark-red buds.

■ **Value at other times** The glossy green leaves are attractive all year round.

■ **Ideal site** Shrub borders, as specimens, in woodland gardens.

■ **Cultivation** Grow in leafy, moist but well-drained, acid (lime-free) soil in sun or dappled shade. Shelter from cold, dry winds. Keep pruning to a minimum.

■ **Also recommended** *Pieris japonica* 'White Cascade' bears long clusters of white flowers over long periods.

■ **Perfect partners** Winter heaths (*Erica carnea* cultivars), rhododendrons, and azaleas.

Plumbago auriculata ♀
Cape leadwort

A frost-tender, scrambling, or climbing evergreen shrub. H 3–6m (10–20ft), S 1–3m (3-10ft)

■ **Seasonal highlights** From summer until late autumn, it bears long-tubed, sky-blue flowers in dense clusters at the stem tips.

■ **Value at other times** The smooth, often bluish-green-tinged leaves look good for most of the year.

■ **Ideal site** Greenhouse or conservatory.

■ **Cultivation** Grow in fertile free-draining potting compost in full sun. Tie stems in to a support as growth proceeds. Prune all sideshoots to within 3–4 buds of the main stems in spring.

■ **Also recommended** *Plumbago indica* ♀ is shrubby with rose-pink flowers in winter.

■ **Perfect partners** *Jasminum mesnyi* ♀, *J. polyanthum* ♀.

Polemonium carneum
Jacob's ladder

A moderately vigorous, bushy herbaceous perennial. H 10–40cm (4–16in), S 20cm (8in)

■ **Seasonal highlights** In early summer it bears loose clusters of shallowly bell-shaped, pale-pink, yellow, occasionally dark-purple or lavender flowers.

■ **Value at other times** It has attractive divided leaves.

■ **Ideal site** Herbaceous or mixed borders and rock gardens.

■ **Cultivation** Grow in full sun or light, dappled shade in any fertile, well-drained soil. Add grit to heavy clay soils to improve drainage. Deadhead regularly to encourage more flowers.

■ **Also recommended** *Polemonium caeruleum* is taller with lavender-blue flowers.

■ **Perfect partners** *Tradescantia* 'Purple Dome', *Erigeron* 'Serenity', *Potentilla atrosanguinea*.

Potentilla fruticosa
PRINCESS ('Blink')
Shrubby potentilla

A compact but vigorous, deciduous shrub. H 60cm (2ft), S to 1m (3ft).

■ **Seasonal highlights** From late spring until mid-autumn, it produces saucer-shaped, pale-pink flowers that fade to white.

■ **Value at other times** It has dense, dark-green leaves that make good ground cover.

■ **Ideal site** Mixed or shrub borders, containers, as low hedging.

■ **Cultivation** Prefers full sun, but tolerates light, dappled shade. Grow in poor to moderately fertile, well-drained soil. In early spring, cut back all stems to within 2.5cm (1in) of the old growth. The easiest way is to use a pair of shears.

■ **Also recommended** *Potentilla fruticosa* 'Elizabeth' has bright-yellow flowers. There are many cultivars.

■ **Perfect partners** *Philadelphus microphyllus*, hypericums.

Primula denticulata ♛
Drumstick primula

A vigorous, rosette-forming herbaceous perennial.
H & S to 45cm (18in)
■ **Seasonal highlights**
In mid-spring and early summer, stout stems bear dense, spherical clusters of purple, yellow-eyed flowers.
■ **Value at other times** It has handsome rosettes of mid-green leaves that are white-mealy beneath.
■ **Ideal site** Rock gardens, at the front of beds, and borders.
■ **Cultivation** Grow in sun or dappled shade in moist, fertile soil. Divide every three to four years in autumn or spring.
■ **Also recommended** *Primula florindae* ♛ is taller, with clusters of fragrant, bell-shaped, sulphur-yellow flowers.
■ **Perfect partners** *Euphorbia polychroma*, Welsh poppy (*Meconopsis cambrica*).

Primula Gold-laced Group
Polyanthus primula

A rosette-forming evergreen or semi-evergreen perennial.
H 25cm (10in), S 30cm (11 in)
■ **Seasonal highlights**
In mid- to late spring, it produces clusters of velvety mahogany-red flowers, each petal having a gold margin.
■ **Value at other times**
The rosettes of mid-green leaves are tinged with red.
■ **Ideal site** Borders, bedding, containers, rock garden, or alpine house.
■ **Cultivation** Grow in moist, fertile, humus-rich, neutral to acid soil. Under glass, grow in pots of loam-based potting compost (e.g. John Innes No 2).
■ **Also recommended** *Primula* 'Blossom' has gold-centred, crimson flowers.
■ **Perfect partners** Sweet violets (*Viola odorata*) and violas.

Primula 'Miss Indigo'
Primula

Vigorous, evergreen, or semi-evergreen perennial.
H 20cm (8in), S 35cm (14in)
■ **Seasonal highlights** From late winter to late spring it produces clusters of double, indigo-purple flowers with creamy-white tips.
■ **Value at other times**
Has rosettes of wrinkled, bright-green leaves for most of the year.
■ **Ideal site** Shady borders, bedding, containers.
■ **Cultivation** Grow in dappled shade in damp, fertile, humus-rich soil. Divide after flowering to maintain vigour.
■ **Also recommended** *Primula vulgaris* 'Marie Crousse' has double violet flowers.
■ **Perfect partners** Sweet violets (*Viola odorata*), and violas, pulmonarias.

Prunus avium 'Plena' ♛
Gean, Wild cherry

A vigorous, deciduous tree with a wide-spreading crown.
H & S 12m (40ft)
■ **Seasonal highlights**
In mid-spring it bears hanging clusters of double white flowers.
■ **Value at other times**
The leaves are bronze when they emerge and turn red, yellow, and orange in autumn.
■ **Ideal site** Perfect as a specimen tree.
■ **Cultivation** Grow in any moist, but well-drained soil. Prune in summer because of the risk of silver leaf infection.
■ **Also recommended** *Prunus avium* ♛ has single flowers.
■ **Perfect partners** Crab apples (*Malus*), laburnums.

Prunus padus 'Watereri' ♛
Bird cherry

A vigorous, deciduous tree with a spreading crown.
H 15m (50ft), S 10m (30ft)
■ **Seasonal highlights**
In late spring, it bears long, slender spires of many small, fragrant, white flowers.
■ **Value at other times**
The dark-green leaves turn red and yellow in autumn. In mid- to late summer it bears small, black cherries that attract birds into the garden.
■ **Ideal site** As a specimen, or in woodland gardens.
■ **Cultivation** Grow in any moist but well-drained soil. Needs minimal pruning; remove badly placed or crossing branches in winter, or in midsummer if silverleaf disease is a problem in your area.
■ **Also recommended** *Prunus padus* 'Colorata' ♛ has red-purple leaves and pink flowers.
■ **Perfect partners** Crab apples (*Malus*).

P

Prunus
Japanese cherries

Vigorous, free-flowering deciduous trees. H 10–12m (30–40ft), S 8–10m (25–30ft)
- **Seasonal highlights** They bear a profusion of fragrant blossom in spring.
- **Value at other times** Most have fine autumn colour.
- **Ideal site** All of the recommended cultivars are beautiful specimen trees.
- **Cultivation** Grow in any moist, but well-drained soil. Need minimal pruning; remove badly placed or crossing branches in winter, or in midsummer if silverleaf disease is a problem in your area.
- **Perfect partners** Crab apples (*Malus*), laburnum, amelanchier.

Prunus **'Amanogawa'** ♀ is narrowly upright with semi-double, pale-pink flowers.

Prunus **'Kiku-shidare-zakura' (syn. 'Cheal's Weeping')** ♀ is weeping, with double, bright-pink flowers.

Prunus **'Kanzan'** ♀ is vase-shaped with double, deep-pink flowers.

Prunus **'Shirotae' (syn. 'Mount Fuji')** ♀ is arching and spreading with single or semi-double white flowers.

Prunus **'Spire'** ♀ is vase-shaped with single, pale-pink flowers.

Prunus **'Ukon'** ♀ is vigorous and spreading with pink-flushed, creamy-white flowers.

Prunus sargentii ♀
Sargent's cherry

A vigorous, deciduous tree with a wide-spreading crown. H to 20m (60ft), S 15m (50ft)
- **Seasonal highlights** In early to mid-spring it bears hanging clusters of large, single, pale-pink flowers.
- **Value at other times** The bark is a shining, dark-chestnut brown. The elliptical leaves have long, tapering tips and are bronzed-red as they emerge with the flowers. Cherries follow the flowers and attract birds.
- **Ideal site** A beautiful specimen tree, it also thrives in woodland gardens.
- **Cultivation** Grow in moist, well-drained soil. It needs minimal pruning; remove crossing branches in winter, or in midsummer if silverleaf disease is a problem.
- **Also recommended** *Prunus sargentii* 'Columnaris' is a narrowly upright form that reaches 3m (10ft) tall.
- **Perfect partners** Crab apples (*Malus*), laburnum and amelanchier, with underplantings of crocus, narcissi, and daffodils.

Prunus serrula ♀
Tibetan cherry

A moderately vigorous, rounded, deciduous tree. H & S 10m (30ft)
- **Seasonal highlights** In late spring, it bears small, single, bowl-shaped, white flowers.
- **Value at other times** The polished mahogany bark is beautiful throughout the year. The leaves turn yellow in autumn.
- **Ideal site** A perfect specimen tree for small gardens.
- **Cultivation** Grow in fertile, moist but well-drained soil in sun or light, dappled shade. It needs minimal pruning (in late summer); when young, remove sideshoots from the trunk when very small, to display the bark at its best.
- **Also recommended** *Prunus maackii* has coppery bark.
- **Perfect partners** *Betula papyrifera*, crocus, and colchicums.

Prunus x subhirtella 'Autumnalis Rosea' ♥
Higan cherry, Rosebud

Also known as cherry. A moderately vigorous, spreading, deciduous tree. H & S 8m (25ft)
■ **Seasonal highlights** From late autumn to spring, it bears small, semi-double, pale-pink flowers.
■ **Value at other times** Leaves are bronzed when young and yellow in autumn.
■ **Ideal site** A perfect specimen tree for small gardens.
■ **Cultivation** Grow in fertile, moist but well-drained soil in sun or light, dappled shade. It needs minimal pruning, in late summer, to remove damaged or badly placed shoots.
■ **Also recommended** *Prunus autumnalis* 'Pendula Rosea' ♥ has weeping branches and rose-pink flowers.
■ **Perfect partners** Underplant with crocus (for spring) and colchicums (for autumn).

Pulmonaria angustifolia 'Azurea' ♥
Blue cowslip, lungwort

A vigorous, spreading, herbaceous perennial. H 25cm (10in), S 45cm (18in)
■ **Seasonal highlights** From early to late spring, it bears funnel-shaped, bright-blue flowers, tinted red in bud.
■ **Value at other times** It has smooth, unspotted, glistening dark-green leaves that make good ground cover.
■ **Ideal site** Shady borders and wild or woodland gardens.
■ **Cultivation** Grow in deep or dappled shade, in damp, humus-rich soil. Cut back after flowering for a fresh crop of new leaves. Divide every three to four years to maintain vigour.
■ **Also recommended** *Pulmonaria rubra* 'Redstart' has coral-red flowers from midwinter to spring. 'Opal' is a lovely cultivar.
■ **Perfect partners** Narcissus, crocus, doronicums, and primroses.

Pulsatilla vulgaris ♥
Pasque flower

A clump-forming, moderately vigorous herbaceous perennial. H 10–20cm (4–8in), S 20cm (8in)
■ **Seasonal highlights** Nodding, bell-shaped, silky-hairy flowers in shades of purple, or occasionally white, appear in spring.
■ **Value at other times** The finely divided, hairy leaves grow taller after flowering. Silky, silvery seedheads follow the flowers.
■ **Ideal site** A rock garden or raised bed.
■ **Cultivation** Grow in fertile, gritty, sharply drained soil in sun. It thrives on shallow chalky soils. Protect from excessive winter wet. Pulsatillas dislike being disturbed, so choose the site with care.
■ **Also recommended** *Pulsatilla alpina* has white flowers.
■ **Perfect partners** Dwarf tulips, *Aubrieta*, scillas.

Pyracantha 'Golden Charmer' ♥
Firethorn

A vigorous, bushy, spiny evergreen shrub. H & S to 3m (10ft)
■ **Seasonal highlights** Has bright-orange berries from autumn through winter.
■ **Value at other times** Clusters of small, white flowers in early summer; glossy, bright-green leaves all year.
■ **Ideal site** Sunny or shady walls; as a specimen or as hedging.
■ **Cultivation** Grow in any fertile, well-drained soil. Trim hedging in summer. On wall-trained plants, shorten outward- and inward-growing shoots in mid-spring. Trim sideshoots to two to three leaves after flowering to expose the berries.
■ **Also recommended** *Pyracantha* 'Orange Glow' ♥ has dark orange-red berries. There are many cultivars.
■ **Perfect partners** *Jasminum nudiflorum* ♥, *Garrya elliptica*.

Pyrus salicifolia 'Pendula' ♥
Weeping pear

A vigorous, weeping, deciduous tree. H 5m (15ft), S 4m (12ft)
■ **Seasonal highlights** Creamy-white flowers in spring, followed by small, hard, unpalatable green pears.
■ **Value at other times** The stiffly weeping branches bear willow-like, grey-hairy leaves from spring to autumn.
■ **Ideal site** A fine specimen tree for small gardens.
■ **Cultivation** Grow in sun in any fertile soil. It needs little pruning other than routine removal of any dead, damaged, or crossing growth in winter.
■ **Also recommended** *Pyrus ussuriensis* is taller with large clusters of white flowers in spring and green leaves that turn red-bronze in autumn.
■ **Perfect partners** *Betula pendula* 'Youngii', crab apples (*Malus*) or rowans (*Sorbus*).

R

Rhodochiton atrosanguineus ♀
Rhodochiton

A frost-tender, herbaceous perennial climber. H 3m (10ft), S 75cm (30in)
■ **Seasonal highlights** From summer to autumn, it bears hanging, tubular, deep red-purple flowers with a "skirt" of rose-pink calyces.
■ **Value at other times** It has attractive, heart-shaped, rich-green leaves.
■ **Ideal site** A warm wall, conservatory, containers, hanging baskets.
■ **Cultivation** Grow in sun or light shade, in humus-rich, moist but well-drained soil or potting compost. Trim in summer, if necessary, to keep it within bounds. Bring under glass for the winter.
■ **Also recommended** This is the only species in common cultivation.
■ **Perfect partners** Annual lobelias (in hanging baskets); twining through sweet peas (*Lathyrus odoratus*).

Rhododendron
Evergreen rhododendrons and azaleas

With over 500 species and thousands of cultivars, rhododendrons are extremely variable, ranging from tiny alpine shrubs to huge, tree-like species. Not all azaleas are deciduous.
■ **Seasonal highlights** Most bear flowers between early spring and early summer.
■ **Value at other times** Lustrous, usually dark-green leaves persist all year.
■ **Ideal site** Shrub borders and woodland gardens. If you garden on limy soil, grow them in large containers filled with lime-free (ericaceous) compost.
■ **Cultivation** All rhododendrons and azaleas must have an acid, moist but well-drained, leafy, humus-rich soil. Grow in light, dappled shade with shelter from cold, dry winds. Plant with the top of the root ball no deeper than it was in the pot. Keep pruning to a minimum; shorten any overlong shoots that spoil the shape after flowering.

Rhododendron **'Hydon Dawn'** Large clusters of pale-pink flowers with dark-pink centres in spring. H and S 1.5m (5ft)

Rhododendron cinnabarinum **subsp. xanthocodon** has yellow flowers mid-spring, early summer. H 6m (20ft), S 2m (6ft)

Rhododendron **'Beauty of Littleworth'** has huge trusses of fragrant, white flowers in late spring. H & S 4m (12ft)

Rhododendron **'Golden Torch'** ♀ has trusses of soft-yellow flowers late spring and early summer. H & S 1.5m (5ft)

Rhododendron **'Halfdan Lem'** has rounded trusses of dark-spotted red flowers in mid- to late spring. H & S 2.5m (8ft)

Rhododendron **'Polar Bear'** Beautiful clusters of white flowers in late spring. H 5m (15ft) S 4m (12ft).

Rhododendron 'Inga'
Indica azalea

A compact, frost-tender, evergreen shrub. H & S 50cm (20in)
■ **Seasonal highlights** In winter, it bears funnel-shaped, pink flowers with white margins to the slightly frilled petals.
■ **Value at other times** Small, glossy, dark-green leaves throughout the year.
■ **Ideal site** Use as a house plant.
■ **Cultivation** Grow in pots of lime-free (ericaceous) compost in bright light, but shaded from direct sun. Keep just moist and mist daily until the flower buds show colour. Keep the temperature no higher than 13–16°C (55–61°F). Re-pot after flowering. Plunge them in a shaded cold frame for the summer and keep them cool and moist. Bring back indoors in early winter.

Rhododendron 'Vuyk's Scarlet' ♀
Evergreen azalea

A hardy evergreen shrub.
H 75cm (30in), S 1.2m (4ft)
■ **Seasonal highlights**
In mid-spring is covered in funnel-shaped, scarlet flowers with frilled petals. Plants in pots flower earlier if brought into a cool greenhouse at the end of autumn.
■ **Value at other times**
Glossy, dark leaves all year.
■ **Ideal site** Shrub borders, rock gardens and woodland gardens, pots.
■ **Cultivation** Grow in acid, moist but well-drained, humus-rich soil, or in large pots in ericaceous compost, in dappled shade or full sun. Shelter from cold, dry winds. Trim shoots that spoil the form after flowering.
■ **Also recommended**
Rhododendron 'Vuyk's Rosyred' has deep rose-pink flowers.
■ **Perfect partners**
Japanese maples; smoke bush.

Rhododendron yakushimanum
Rhododendron

A very hardy, vigorous, evergreen shrub.
H to 2m (6ft)
■ **Seasonal highlights**
In mid-spring, it bears trusses of funnel-shaped flowers that open from deep-pink buds and fade gradually to white.
■ **Value at other times**
The glossy, dark-green leaves are clothed in dense tawny down when young.
■ **Ideal site** Shrub borders, woodland gardens.
■ **Cultivation** Grow in acid (lime-free), moist but well-drained, leafy, humus-rich soil in dappled shade or full sun. Shelter from cold, dry winds. Trim any shoots that spoil the shape and deadhead after flowering.
■ **Also recommended**
Rhododendron yakushimanum 'Ken Janeck' has white flowers, lined with pink-purple and green spots.
■ **Perfect partners**
Conifers, heathers, and birch.

Rhododendron 'Freya'
Azalea

Azaleas are a sub-section of the genus *Rhododendron* that have smaller leaves and bear profuse trusses of small, often vividly coloured flowers in spring or early summer. Many of the deciduous azaleas also have brilliant autumn colour.
■ **Ideal site** Rock and woodland gardens, shrub borders and containers.
■ **Cultivation** Grow in acid (lime-free), moist but well-drained, leafy, humus-rich soil in dappled shade or sun. Deciduous azaleas are more tolerant of open sites in sun than evergreen rhododendrons, but are best sited so that they do not receive early-morning sun, as this will exacerbate damage to the flowers in frosty weather. Plant with the top of the root ball no deeper than it was in the pot; they will not tolerate

Rhododendron 'Strawberry Ice' ♀
Azalea

deep planting. Keep pruning to a minimum; just shorten any overlong shoots that spoil the shape, after flowering. Deadhead carefully, if practical.
■ **Recommended**
Rhododendron 'Freya' is a compact shrub with small leaves bearing dense trusses of small, funnel-shaped "hose-in-hose" flowers (one flower within another) in late spring and early summer. They are fragrant, pink-flushed salmon-orange. It enjoys full sun. H & S 1.5m (5ft) *Rhododendron* 'Strawberry Ice' is bushy and compact with rounded trusses of widely funnel-shaped flowers in late spring. They are a soft flesh-pink with darker veins and deeper pink at the petal margins. H & S 2m (6ft)
■ **Perfect partners**
Conifers and heathers.

Rhus typhina ♀
Stag's horn sumach

A vigorous, suckering, deciduous shrub or small tree. H 5m (15ft), S 6m (20ft)
■ **Seasonal highlights**
In summer, it bears spires of yellow-green flowers that give rise, on female plants, to dense clusters of hairy, deep crimson-red fruits.
■ **Value at other times**
In autumn, the divided leaves turn brilliant orange-red.
■ **Ideal site** Mixed and shrub borders, or as a specimen.
■ **Cultivation** Gives the best autumn colour in sun, but tolerates light shade. Grow in any moist but well-drained soil. Can be pruned hard in spring to within two or three buds of the base for larger, lusher leaves.
■ **Also recommended**
Rhus glabra has smooth shoots and glossy blue-green leaves.
■ **Perfect partners**
Cotoneaster frigidus 'Cornubia' ♀, *Cotinus* 'Grace'.

R

Ribes sanguineum
Flowering currant

A vigorous, deciduous shrub. H & S to 2m (6ft)
■ **Seasonal highlights**
In spring, it bears hanging clusters of tiny, deep pinkish-red flowers.
■ **Value at other times**
It has dense, aromatic, dark-green foliage from spring to autumn. Flowers are followed by small, blue-black fruits.
■ **Ideal site** A mixed or shrub border, or as informal hedging.
■ **Cultivation** Grow in full sun or light, dappled shade in any fertile soil. Prune flowered shoots back to strong buds, or shoots lower down the shrub, after flowering, to keep compact and bushy. Trim hedging after flowering.
■ **Also recommended**
Ribes odoratum has fragrant yellow flowers.
■ **Perfect partners**
Forsythias, *Chaenomeles* x *superba* 'Rowallane' ♥.

Rosa
Hybrid tea and floribunda roses

The hybrid tea or large-flowered roses are upright, freely branching bushes.
■ **Value at other times** All have attractive dark-green leaves from spring to autumn.
■ **Ideal site** Rose beds, mixed and shrub borders, or as informal hedges.
■ **Cultivation** Grow in full sun in deep, fertile, moist but well-drained soil. They thrive in heavy clay soils. Apply a balanced fertilizer and mulch in late winter or early spring. Prune large-flowered roses in late winter or early spring, cutting the main stems back to strong, outward-facing buds, 20–25cm (8–10in) above the ground. Reduce sideshoots to 2–3 buds. For cluster-flowered roses, prune back main stems to 25–45cm (10–18in) above ground and shorten sideshoots to 2–3 buds. Deadhead to encourage more flowers.

Rosa AMBER QUEEN ('Harroony') ♥ has fragrant, cupped, double, amber-yellow flowers. H 50cm (20in), S 60cm (24in)

Rosa 'Crimson Glory' A classic hybrid tea rose with brilliant-scarlet flowers. H and S 60cm (24in)

Rosa 'Elizabeth Harkness' A hybrid tea rose with white flushed-pink flowers from early to late summer. H 80cm (32in), S 60cm (24in)

Rosa HANNAH GORDON ('Korweiso') bears double pale-pink blooms with darker pink petal margins. H 80cm (32in), S 65cm (26in)

Rosa FRAGRANT CLOUD ('Tanellis') Classic hybrid tea rose with deliciously scented red flowers. H 75cm (30in), S 60cm (24in)

Rosa BLUE MOON ('Tannacht') has large, high-centred, double flowers of soft lilac-mauve. H 1m (3ft), S 70cm (28in)

Rosa ANNA FORD
('Harpiccolo') ♥
Patio rose

These dwarf, cluster-flowered roses make compact, deciduous shrubs. From summer to autumn, they bear clusters of rounded, single to fully double flowers. They have abundant, glossy, dark-green leaves. ANNA FORD has urn-shaped, semi-double, orange-red flowers. H 45cm (18in), S 40cm (16in)
■ **Ideal site**
In containers, in mixed borders, as border edging.
■ **Cultivation**
Grow in fertile, well-drained soil in full sun. Prune in the dormant season, as for floribunda roses. Cut back the main stems and sideshoots by no more than a third to a half of their length.
■ **Also recommended**
QUEEN MOTHER ('Korquemu') has semi-double, clear-pink flowers.
■ **Perfect partners**
Lavenders and pinks.

Rosa 'Chinatown' ♀
Modern shrub rose

Diverse in size, habit, and flower form, modern shrub roses are vigorous, deciduous, and flower freely from summer to autumn. They bear single to fully double flowers in few- to many-flowered clusters and are often beautifully scented. 'Chinatown' has double, pink-flushed yellow flowers. H 1.2m (4ft), S 1m (3ft)
■ **Ideal site**
Shrub and mixed borders, as hedges, or as specimen plants.
■ **Cultivation**
Grow as for bush roses. Prune only for health and to reduce overcrowding. Every three or four years, cut an older stem or two to the base of the plant.
■ **Also recommended** 'Buff Beauty' has fragrant, double, apricot-buff flowers.
■ **Perfect partners** Lavenders, cistus, *Anemone* x *hybrida*.

Rosa
English roses

A group of modern shrub roses that have been bred to combine the shapes, colours, and scents of the Old garden roses with the vigour, disease-resistance, and repeat-flowering virtues of the modern shrubs. They are graceful, deciduous, or semi-evergreen shrubs and flower almost continuously from early summer to autumn. Many are exquisitely scented.
■ **Ideal site** Mixed and shrub borders, and as specimens.
■ **Cultivation** Grow as for bush roses. Prune as for floribunda bush roses, but much more lightly, to maintain the shrub's stature.
■ **Perfect partners** Lavenders, pinks, and border phlox go well with most roses.

Rosa **BROTHER CADFAEL ('Ausglobe')** Clear-pink peony-like flowers with a strong fragrance. H 1.2m (4ft), S 1m (3ft)

Rosa **DARCEY BUSSELL ('Ausdecorum')** The rich, crimson flowers produced in summer have a fruity fragrance. H 1m (3ft), S 60cm (24in)

Rosa **EGLANTYNE ('Ausmark')** Eglantyne has strongly scented, cupped, fully double flowers of clear pale pink. H 1.2m (4ft), S 1.5m (5ft)

Rosa **GRAHAM THOMAS ('Ausmas')** ♀ has cupped, fully double, yellow flowers with a fruity scent. H 1.2m (4ft), S 1.5m (5ft)

Rosa **GERTRUDE JEKYLL ('Ausbord')** Large rosette-shaped flowers of rich pink with old rose fragrance. H 1.2m (4ft), S 1.1m (3½ft).

Rosa **WILL SHAKESPEARE 2000 ('Ausromeo')** has fully double, fragrant flowers of velvety crimson. H 1.2m (4ft), S 1.5m (5ft)

Rosa gallica var. officinalis 'Versicolor' ♀

Also known as old garden rose (gallica), rosa mundi. Dense, vigorous, thorny, free-branching shrub. H 80cm (32in), S to 1m (3ft)
■ **Seasonal highlights**
In midsummer, bears scented, semi-double, pale-pink flowers striped with darker pink in small clusters.
■ **Ideal site** Beds, borders, and as hedging.
■ **Cultivation** Grow as for bush roses. To encourage bushy growth, after flowering, cut back any overlong shoots by up to one third and sideshoots by two-thirds.
■ **Also recommended**
Rosa 'Charles de Mills' ♀ has very fragrant, fully double, deep mulberry-pink flowers.
■ **Perfect partners**
Lavenders, cistus, *Anemone* x *hybrida*.

R

Rosa
Climbing and rambling roses

■ **Seasonal highlights** Deciduous, thorny, stiff-stemmed climbing shrubs bear single to fully double, often fragrant flowers, singly or in clusters, from summer to autumn. Rambling roses have very vigorous, deciduous, or semi-evergreen climbers with long, flexible, thorny stems. Unlike climbers, they bloom only once in summer, bearing single to fully double, often scented flowers, usually in many-flowered clusters. They have more or less glossy, pale to dark-green leaves with small leaflets.

■ **Value at other times** Deciduous, thorny, stiff-stemmed climbing shrubs grow best on pillars, walls, or fences, while rambling roses favour pergolas, arbours, and arches, and growing through large, old trees.

Rosa **'Golden Showers'** ♀ has large, fragrant, double, yellow blooms. H 3m (10ft), S 2.5m (8ft)

Rosa HANDEL ('Macha') has double white flowers with pink petal margins. H 3m (10ft), S 2.2m (7ft)

Rosa **'New Dawn'** A vigorous, hardy climbing rose with fragrant, cupped, double, pale pearl-pink flowers. H 3m (10ft), S 2.5m (8ft)

Rosa **'Albertine'** ♀ has double, soft, salmon-pink flowers. H 5m (15ft), S 4m (12ft)

Rosa **'American Pillar'** bears single, white-eyed, carmine-red flowers. H 5m (15ft), S 4m (12ft)

Rosa **'Bobbie James'** ♀ has sprays of semi-double, scented, creamy-white flowers. H 10m (30ft), S 6m (20ft)

Rosa 'Königin von Dänemark' ♀
Old garden rose (Alba)

Vigorous shrub of arching growth with grey-green leaves. H 1.5m (5ft), S 1.2m (4ft)

■ **Seasonal highlights** Flowers profusely over long periods in midsummer, bearing fully double, intensely fragrant, pink flowers with a green eye.

■ **Ideal site** In mixed or shrub borders or as specimens.

■ **Cultivation** Grow as for bush roses. Albas tolerate shade better than most roses. To encourage bushy growth, after flowering, reduce main stems by a third of their height and sideshoots by two-thirds.

■ **Also recommended** *Rosa* 'Alba Semiplena' ♀ has flat, semi-double white flowers.

■ **Perfect partners** Lavenders, cistus, *Anemone x hybrida*.

Rosa moyesii
Wild or species rose

A vigorous, upright, open deciduous shrub with long, arching branches. H to 4m (12ft), S 3m (10ft)

■ **Seasonal highlights** Single, cupped, sealing-wax red flowers in summer, very attractive to honey bees.

■ **Value at other times** In autumn, it produces large, crimson, flask-shaped hips.

■ **Ideal site** Grow as a specimen.

■ **Cultivation** Grow in any fertile, moist but well-drained soil in sun or light, dappled shade. Every three or four years, in winter, cut one or two old shoots to the ground. Overlong, wayward shoots can be shortened at any time.

■ **Also recommended** *Rosa moyesii* 'Geranium' ♀ is more compact with brighter, cherry-red flowers.

■ **Perfect partners** *Clematis florida* 'Sieboldii', *Tropaeolum speciosum* ♀.

Rosa 'Noisette Carnée'
Noisette rose

Also known as old climbing garden rose (noisette). A moderately vigorous climber, with smooth stems. H 2–4m (6–12ft), S 2–2.5m (6–8ft)
■ **Seasonal highlights**
From summer until autumn, it bears sprays of cupped, double, pale-pink flowers with a spicy fragrance.
■ **Ideal site** A warm, sheltered wall.
■ **Cultivation** The noisettes need more warmth and shelter than most climbers to flower and repeat well, otherwise grow as for bush roses and prune as for climbers.
■ **Also recommended** *Rosa* 'Madame Alfred Carrière' ♛, with tea-scented, fully double creamy-white flowers. *Rosa* 'Gloire de Dijon' with fully double, quartered, fragrant, creamy-buff flowers.
■ **Perfect partners**
Clematis 'Etoile Violette' and C. 'Lasurstern'.

Rosa rugosa
Hedgehog rose

A vigorous, deciduous shrub of dense, prickly growth. H & S 1–2.5m (3–8ft)
■ **Seasonal highlights**
In summer, it bears single, spicily fragrant, magenta to carmine-red or white flowers with a boss of yellow stamens.
■ **Value at other times**
Each flower produces a large, round, bright tomato-red hip and flowers and hips are present at the same time.
■ **Ideal site** In a border, or as an informal hedge; thrives in coastal sites.
■ **Cultivation** Grow in any fertile, moist but well-drained soil in sun or light-dappled shade. Every three or four years, in winter, cut out one or two old shoots to the ground. Shorten wayward shoots at any time.
■ **Also recommended**
Rosa rugosa var. *alba* ♛ has clove-scented, white flowers.
■ **Perfect partners**
Tropaeolum speciosum ♛.

Rosa 'William Lobb' ♛
Old garden rose (moss)

Vigorous, upright, or arching shrub with dark-green leaves. H & S 2m (6ft)
■ **Seasonal highlights**
In midsummer, bears fully double, intensely fragrant red-purple flowers that fade with lavender-grey tints, on thorny shoots with dense, mossy growth on the stem tips.
■ **Ideal site** Beds and borders.
■ **Cultivation** Grow as for bush roses. To encourage bushy growth, after flowering, reduce main stems by one-third of their height and sideshoots by two-thirds.
■ **Also recommended**
Rosa 'Nuits de Young' ♛, shorter, with dense brown-green moss and deep-maroon flowers.
■ **Perfect partners**
Lavenders, cistus, *Anemone* x *hybrida*.

Rudbeckia laciniata 'Herbstsonne' ♛
Coneflower

Vigorous, clump-forming, herbaceous perennial. H to 2m (6ft), S 90cm (36in)
■ **Seasonal highlights**
From midsummer until early autumn, it bears daisy-like, bright-yellow flowerheads with cone-shaped centres.
■ **Value at other times**
It has attractive, prominently veined, glossy, green leaves.
■ **Ideal site** Mixed or herbaceous borders, or naturalized in woodland.
■ **Cultivation** Best in full sun, but tolerates light, dappled shade. Grow in a fertile, preferably heavy, soil. After three or four years, lift and divide in spring or autumn to rejuvenate.
■ **Also recommended**
Rudbeckia laciniata 'Goldquelle' ♛ is shorter, with double, lemon-yellow flowers.
■ **Perfect partners**
Sedum spectabile ♛, *Aster novi-belgii* (Michaelmas daisies).

S

Salix caprea 'Kilmarnock' ♛
Kilmarnock willow

A top-grafted, stiffly weeping, deciduous tree. H 1.5–2m (5–6ft), S 2m (6ft)
■ **Seasonal highlights**
In mid- and late spring, it produces grey male catkins, studded with yellow anthers, on bare shoots.
■ **Value at other times**
Forms a dense umbrella of stout, yellow-brown stems and narrow dark-green leaves that are grey-green beneath.
■ **Ideal site** As a specimen, or in large containers.
■ **Cultivation** Grow in full sun or light shade, in any moist but well-drained soil. Prune annually between late autumn and early spring to thin out congested shoots.
■ **Also recommended**
Salix exigua is taller and upright with narrow, silvery leaves. There are many cultivars.
■ **Perfect partners**
Betula pendula 'Youngii', *Corylopsis glabrescens*.

S

Salix x *rubens* 'Basfordiana'
Willow

Vigorous, upright, deciduous tree; pruned regularly, it makes a twiggy shrub. H 15m (50ft), S 10m (30ft)
■ **Seasonal highlights**
It has bright orange-yellow young shoots in winter.
■ **Value at other times**
In spring it bears slender, yellow catkins with the emerging, narrow, grey-green leaves that become glossy, bright green in summer.
■ **Ideal site** In a shrub border or by the water's edge.
■ **Cultivation** Grow in any moist but well-drained soil. Cut all stems back hard each or, for catkins, every other year in early spring, to the ground or to a short trunk. Young shoots have the best colour.
■ **Also recommended**
Salix daphnoides 'Aglaia' has glossy mahogany-red shoots.
■ **Perfect partners**
Corylopsis, dogwoods.

Salvia coccinea 'Lady in Red' ♀
Salvia

An upright, bushy, half-hardy perennial, often grown as an annual. H 40cm (16in), S 30cm (12in)
■ **Seasonal highlights**
From summer to autumn, it bears slender open spikes of luminous-red flowers.
■ **Value at other times**
It has heart-shaped, toothed and veined, dark-green leaves.
■ **Ideal site** Bedding, borders, and containers.
■ **Cultivation** Grow in full sun in any moderately fertile, well-drained soil. May not survive cold, wet winters, so take softwood cuttings in spring or summer and overwinter young plants under glass.
■ **Also recommended**
Salvia patens 'Cambridge Blue' ♀ has pale-blue flowers.
■ **Perfect partners**
Osteospermums and argyranthemums.

Santolina chamaecyparissus 'Lemon Queen'

Also known as cotton lavender. Vigorous, evergreen shrub. H & S 60cm (2ft)
■ **Seasonal highlights**
From mid- to late summer, it bears pompon-like, lemon-yellow flowerheads.
■ **Value at other times**
It has white, woolly young shoots that carry slender, finely divided leaves with a wonderful sharp fragrance.
■ **Ideal site** Mixed or herbaceous borders.
■ **Cultivation** Best in full sun, but will tolerate light, part-day shade. Grow in any moderately fertile, well-drained soil. On heavy clay soils, dig in coarse grit to improve drainage. In early spring, trim over plants with shears to keep them bushy and compact.
■ **Also recommended**
Santolina pinnata subsp. *neapolitana* 'Sulphurea' is slightly taller.
■ **Perfect partners** *Salvia officinalis* 'Tricolor'.

Sarcococca hookeriana var. *humilis*

Also known as Christmas box and sweet box. A moderately vigorous, suckering evergreen shrub. H 60cm (2ft), S to 1m (3ft)
■ **Seasonal highlights**
In winter, it bears clusters of tiny, honey-scented, pink-tinted white flowers, followed by round, dark-blue fruits.
■ **Value at other times**
The glossy, dark-green leaves make good ground cover.
■ **Ideal site** In a woodland garden or shrub border, or as low, informal hedging.
■ **Cultivation** Grow in fertile, moist but well-drained soil in deep or partial shade, or in sun if soils remain moist. Needs little pruning. Dig out suckers at the margins of the clump if it encroaches on other plants.
■ **Also recommended**
Sarcococca confusa ♀ is taller but similar.
■ **Perfect partners**
Helleborus niger ♀, *Viburnum* x *bodnantense* 'Dawn' ♀, *V. tinus*.

Scabiosa 'Butterfly Blue'
Scabious

Also known as pincushion flower. A clump-forming, spreading herbaceous perennial. H & S 40cm (16in)
■ **Seasonal highlights**
From mid- to late summer, it bears wiry-stemmed, lavender-blue flowers that attract butterflies and bees.
■ **Value at other times**
It has divided, grey-green basal leaves.
■ **Ideal site** A mixed or herbaceous border, especially in cottage gardens; wildlife gardens.
■ **Cultivation** Grow in any moderately fertile, well-drained soil in full sun, or light part-day shade.
■ **Also recommended**
Scabiosa caucasica 'Miss Willmott' ♀ has white flowerheads.
■ **Perfect partners**
Lavenders, pinks (*Dianthus*) and herbaceous potentillas, such as 'Yellow Queen'.

Scaevola aemula
Fairy fan-flower

A tufted, frost-tender, evergreen perennial, grown as an annual in cold areas. H & S to 50cm (20in)

■ **Seasonal highlights**
Throughout summer, it bears leafy, trailing spikes of small, fan-shaped, purple-blue or blue flowers.

■ **Value at other times**
Is discarded after flowering.

■ **Ideal site** Containers, hanging baskets.

■ **Cultivation** Grow in full sun or light, dappled shade, in any moist but well-drained, fairly fertile soil or potting compost. Take stem cuttings in spring or summer and overwinter under glass, or sow seed in warmth in spring. Set out when risk of frost has passed.

■ **Also recommended**
Scaevola 'Mauve Clusters' has lilac-mauve flowers.

■ **Perfect partners**
Fuchsias, pelargoniums, French marigolds (*Tagetes*).

Schizostylis coccinea 'Sunrise' ♀
Kaffir lily

A vigorous, evergreen, rhizomatous perennial, also known as *Hesperantha*. H 60cm (24in), S 30cm (12in)

■ **Seasonal highlights**
From late summer to early winter, it bears spikes of glossy, salmon-pink flowers. They are good for cutting.

■ **Value at other times**
The narrowly sword-shaped, bright-green leaves persist for most of the year.

■ **Ideal site** Mixed or herbaceous borders, or in containers.

■ **Cultivation** Grow in a fertile, moist but well-drained soil. Shelter from cold winds. It benefits from an organic mulch in winter, especially in very cold areas.

■ **Also recommended**
Schizostylis coccinea 'Major' ♀ has glossy, scarlet flowers.

■ **Perfect partners**
Asters (Michaelmas daisies), *Sedum spectabile* ♀, rudbeckias.

Scilla siberica 'Spring Beauty'
Squill

A slender, perennial bulb. H 20cm (8in), S 5cm (2in)

■ **Seasonal highlights** In spring it bears loose spikes of small, nodding, deep-blue flowers amid narrow, strap-shaped, shining, green leaves.

■ **Value at other times**
Of no value at other times.

■ **Ideal site** A rock garden, at the front of a mixed border; in containers.

■ **Cultivation** Grow in full sun or light, dappled shade, in any fertile, humus-rich soil. Plant the bulbs in autumn at twice their own depth.

■ **Also recommended**
Scilla peruviana 'Alba' is taller with white flowers.

■ **Perfect partners**
Grow with chionodoxas and *Anemone blanda* ♀ cultivars beneath forsythias.

Sedum spectabile 'Brilliant' ♀
Ice plant

A vigorous, clump-forming, herbaceous perennial. H & S 45cm (18in)

■ **Seasonal highlights**
From late summer until late autumn, it bears large, flat heads of many tiny, star-shaped, bright-pink flowers. It's an excellent plant for attracting butterflies.

■ **Value at other times**
The fleshy, slightly scalloped, grey-green leaves are handsome throughout spring and summer.

■ **Ideal site** Mixed or herbaceous borders; is good in hot, dry sites.

■ **Cultivation** Grow in fertile, well-drained, preferably neutral to slightly alkaline, soil in sun. Divide in spring, every three or four years to maintain vigour.

■ **Also recommended**
Sedum spectabile 'Iceberg' has pale-green leaves and white flowers.

■ **Perfect partners** Asters, rudbeckias, *Schizostylis*.

Skimmia japonica
Skimmia

A vigorous, dome-shaped, evergreen shrub. H to 5m (15ft), S 1.5m (5ft)

■ **Seasonal highlights**
It produces dense clusters of pink buds that open in mid- to late winter to reveal scented white flowers.

■ **Value at other times**
It has slightly aromatic, glossy dark-green leaves all year. Female plants bear red berries, if male and female plants are grown together.

■ **Ideal site** A shrub or mixed border.

■ **Cultivation** Grow in dappled or deep shade, in any fertile, humus-rich soil. It needs little, if any, pruning other than to shape, if necessary, after flowering.

■ **Also recommended**
Skimmia japonica 'Bronze Knight' is shorter, male, and has dark, bronze-red buds in winter.

■ **Perfect partners**
Gaultherias, winter heaths (*Erica carnea*).

S

Solanum crispum 'Glasnevin' ♀
Chilean potato tree

A very vigorous, evergreen or semi-evergreen, scrambling shrub or climber.
H & S to 6m (20ft)
■ **Seasonal highlights**
Throughout summer, it bears fragrant, deep purple-blue flowers at the stem tips, followed by pale-yellow fruit.
■ **Value at other times**
It has handsome dark-green leaves for most of the year.
■ **Ideal site** On a warm, sunny wall.
■ **Cultivation** Grow in full sun, or light, part-day shade, in neutral to slightly alkaline, fertile, well-drained soil. After flowering, shorten sideshoots to three or four buds.
■ **Also recommended**
Solanum jasminoides 'Album' ♀ has white flowers.
■ **Perfect partners** *Clematis* 'Pagoda'; climbing or rambling roses.

Solenostemon 'Brightness'
Coleus

A bushy, fast-growing, frost-tender perennial, often grown as a foliage annual.
H 45cm (18in), S 30cm (12in)
■ **Seasonal highlights**
All year it has rust-red leaves, edged with pale green.
■ **Ideal site** As a house plant, or outdoors as bedding or in containers.
■ **Cultivation** Grow in a sheltered, sunny site, in fertile, moist but well-drained soil or potting mix. Sow seed in warmth in early spring and plant out when the risk of frost has passed. Pinch out shoot tips to promote bushiness and also any flowers to preserve good leaf colour and condition. Take stem cuttings in summer.
■ **Also recommended**
Solenostemon scutellarioides Wizard Series has leaves patterned in green, red, cream, yellow, and purple.
■ **Perfect partners** French marigolds (*Tagetes*), pelargoniums.

Solidago 'Goldenmosa' ♀
Goldenrod

A vigorous, bushy, herbaceous perennial.
H 75cm (30in), S 45cm (18in)
■ **Seasonal highlights**
In late summer and early autumn, it bears feathery, conical plumes of yellow-stalked, bright-yellow flowers.
■ **Value at other times**
It has wrinkled, mid-green leaves. The flowers are good for cutting.
■ **Ideal site** An herbaceous border or wild garden.
■ **Cultivation** Grow in full sun in any poor to moderately fertile soil. Every three or four years, lift and divide in spring or autumn to maintain vigour. Cut off the flowers as they fade to prevent them seeding.
■ **Also recommended**
Solidago 'Golden Wings' is taller, with horizontally spreading plumes of golden yellow.
■ **Perfect partners** Rudbeckias, *Sedum spectabile* ♀.

Sorbus commixta
Rowan

A vigorous, broadly conical, deciduous tree. H 10m (30ft), S 7m (22ft)
■ **Seasonal highlights**
In late spring, it bears broad heads of tiny white flowers.
■ **Value at other times**
In autumn, clusters of orange-red berries festoon the branches and the divided leaves turn yellow to red and purple. The berries attract birds into the garden.
■ **Ideal site** A beautiful specimen tree.
■ **Cultivation** Grow in any fertile, moist, but well-drained, neutral to acid soil. Little pruning is necessary except to remove any crossing or damaged branches in winter.
■ **Also recommended**
Sorbus sargentiana ♀ is similar, with many small, bright-red berries.
■ **Perfect partners** Maples (*Acers*) and birches (*Betula*).

Spiraea 'Arguta' ♀
Bridal wreath

A vigorous, deciduous shrub with arching branches.
H & S 2.5m (8ft)
■ **Seasonal highlights**
In spring, clusters of tiny, bright-white flowers wreathe the branches.
■ **Value at other times**
It has attractive leaves of fresh, bright green.
■ **Ideal site** A mixed or shrub border.
■ **Cultivation** Best in full sun, but tolerates light, part-day shade. Grow in any fertile, moist but well-drained soil. After flowering cut back the flowered shoots to strong buds. Every three or four years, cut out one in three of the oldest flowered stems to the base to encourage strong, new growth.
■ **Also recommended**
Spiraea japonica 'Little Princess' is compact with pink flowers.
■ **Perfect partners**
Chaenomeles x *superba* 'Nicoline' ♀, *Cytisus* x *praecox*.

Stipa gigantea ♔

Golden oats, giant feather grass

A vigorous, evergreen, or semi-evergreen perennial grass. H 2.5m (8ft), S 1.2m (4ft)

■ **Seasonal highlights** In summer, tall, arching stems bear open flowerheads of silvery, purple-green spikelets that turn gold as they ripen.

■ **Value at other times** It forms arching clumps of narrow green leaves.

■ **Ideal site** A fabulous specimen, border, or container plant.

■ **Cultivation** Grow in full sun in any moderately fertile soil. It tolerates light shade and heavy clay soils. Cut down the old growth in spring.

■ **Also recommended** *Stipa tenuissima* is shorter with filament-like leaves and feather-fine flowerheads.

■ **Perfect partners** *Hakonechloa macra* 'Aureola' ♔, *Carex pendula*.

Syringa vulgaris

Lilacs

Vigorous, deciduous shrubs or small trees. H & S 7m (22ft)

■ **Seasonal highlights** In late spring and early summer they bear dense, conical clusters of intensely fragrant flowers.

■ **Value at other times** They have heart-shaped, dark-green leaves from spring to late autumn.

■ **Ideal site** In a shrub border or as specimens.

■ **Cultivation** Grow in any fertile, neutral to alkaline soil. Deadhead young plants, cutting back to strong buds lower down on the shrub. If necessary, prune to shape after flowering.

■ **Perfect partners** Hawthorn (*Crataegus*) and laburnums.

Syringa vulgaris 'Charles Joly' ♔ has double, dark-purple flowers.

Syringa vulgaris 'Charles X' has single, purple-red flowers.

Syringa vulgaris 'Katherine Havemeyer' ♔ has double, lavender-blue flowers, which are purple in bud.

Syringa vulgaris 'Madame Lemoine' ♔ has double white blooms.

Syringa vulgaris 'Président Grévy' has large spires of double, lilac-blue flowers with red-violet buds.

Syringa vulgaris 'Primrose' has soft, primrose-yellow flowers.

T

Tagetes 'Naughty Marietta'

French marigold

A compact, bushy, vigorous, half-hardy annual. H & S 30–40cm (12–16in)

■ **Seasonal highlights** From early to late summer, deep-yellow flowerheads with maroon-red marks emerge above the dark-green leaves.

■ **Value at other times** They are consigned to the compost heap after flowering.

■ **Ideal site** Bedding, border edging, and containers.

■ **Cultivation** Grow in sun in moderately fertile, well-drained soil. Sow seeds in warmth under glass in spring and set out when risk of frost has passed; or sow in the flowering site in late spring. Deadhead regularly to prolong the flowering period.

■ **Also recommended** *Tagetes* 'Tangerine Gem' has deep-orange flowers.

■ **Perfect partners** Pelargoniums, annual lobelias, fuchsias.

T

Tamarix tetrandra ♀
Tamarisk

A vigorous, open, deciduous shrub or small tree.
H & S 3m (10ft)

■ **Seasonal highlights**
In mid- to late spring, it bears short spikes of many tiny, pale dusky-pink flowers all along the arching branches.

■ **Value at other times**
It has purple-brown shoots and small, needle- or scale-like green leaves.

■ **Ideal site** In a shrub border, or as a specimen; it does especially well in coastal gardens.

■ **Cultivation** Grow in full sun, in moist but well-drained soil. Shelter from cold, dry winds. It is resistant to strong winds in coastal areas. After flowering, shorten flowered shoots to strong buds lower down the shoots.

■ **Also recommended**
Tamarix ramosissima 'Pink Cascade' has pink flowers in late summer.

■ **Perfect partners** *Syringa*, *Spiraea* 'Arguta' ♀.

Thunbergia alata
Black-eyed Susan

A frost-tender, evergreen perennial climber, grown as an annual in cold areas.
H 2.5m (8ft), S 45cm (18in)

■ **Seasonal highlights**
From summer to autumn, the twining stems bear single, orange or yellow, occasionally creamy-white flowers; some have chocolate-purple centres.

■ **Value at other times**
It has pretty, heart-shaped, toothed, mid-green leaves.

■ **Ideal site** In containers, on supporting wigwams, or poles.

■ **Cultivation** Grow in sun in any moist but well-drained soil. Sow the seeds in spring in heat; plant in containers and grow on in warmth. Set out when the weather is warm and settled. Take stem cuttings in summer and overwinter under glass.

■ **Also recommended**
Thunbergia gregorii ♀ has orange flowers.

■ **Perfect partners**
Ipomoea tricolor.

Trollius x *cultorum* 'Earliest of All'
Globeflower

A moderately vigorous, clump-forming herbaceous perennial. H 50cm (20in), S 40cm (16in)

■ **Seasonal highlights**
The bowl-shaped, shining, clear-yellow flowers arise on strong stems from mid-spring to midsummer.

■ **Value at other times**
It has basal mounds of lobed, toothed, glossy, green leaves.

■ **Ideal site** Bog gardens and stream- or poolsides, damp borders, or meadow gardens.

■ **Cultivation** Best in full sun, but tolerant of partial shade. Grow in reliably moist, deep, fertile soil. Lift and divide the plants every three or four years to rejuvenate them.

■ **Also recommended**
Trollius x *cultorum* 'Alabaster' has pale creamy-yellow flowers.

■ **Perfect partners**
Caltha palustris ♀, *Lysichiton americanus* ♀, *Darmera peltata* ♀.

Tropaeolum speciosum ♀
Flame creeper

A moderately vigorous, herbaceous perennial climber.
H & S to 3m (10ft) or more.

■ **Seasonal highlights**
From summer to autumn, the slender stems form swags of long-spurred, vermilion flowers.

■ **Value at other times**
It has very attractive, lobed, bright-green leaves.

■ **Ideal site** Grow through dark-leaved shrubs or hedges, like yew, or with creamy-flowered roses.

■ **Cultivation** Grow in moist, reasonably fertile, preferably slightly acid soil, with its roots in cool shade and head in sun. It can be difficult to establish, as the long, fleshy white roots are fragile; plant carefully.

■ **Also recommended**
Tropaeolum tuberosum is a frost-tender, tuberous perennial with orange and yellow flowers.

■ **Perfect partners**
Tropaeolum peregrinum, a yellow-flowered annual.

Tulipa 'Spring Green' ♀
Viridiflora tulip

A moderately vigorous, bulbous perennial.
H 40cm (16in), S 8cm (3in)

■ **Seasonal highlights**
In late spring it produces very elegant, green-feathered, ivory-white flowers.

■ **Value at other times**
Of little value at other times.

■ **Ideal site** Bedding, borders, and decorative containers.

■ **Cultivation** Grow in full sun, in any moderately fertile, well-drained soil. Add coarse grit to heavy clay soils. Plant bulbs 10–15cm (4–6in) deep in late autumn. Lift bulbs once the leaves fade and ripen in a cool greenhouse.

■ **Also recommended**
Tulipa 'Queen of Night' has glossy, dark, maroon-purple flowers in late spring.

■ **Perfect partners**
Viola x *wittrockiana* Floral Dance Series, wallflowers (*Erysimum*), polyanthus primulas, winter-flowering pansies.

Tulipa tarda ♀
Species tulip

A vigorous, perennial bulb.
H to 15cm (6in), S 5cm (2in)
■ **Seasonal highlights**
In early and mid-spring it
produces open, starry,
greenish-white flowers that
are yellow inside.
■ **Value at other times**
Of no value at other times.
■ **Ideal site** Rock gardens,
borders, and containers.
■ **Cultivation** Best in full
sun, but it will tolerate light,
part-day shade. Grow in any
poor to moderately fertile,
well-drained soil. Add coarse
grit to heavy clay soils. Plant
the bulbs at twice their own
depth in late autumn.
■ **Also recommended**
Tulipa turkestanica ♀
has starry, white flowers.
■ **Perfect partners**
Scillas and chionodoxas.

V

Verbascum 'Cotswold Queen'
Mullein

An upright, moderately
vigorous perennial. H 1.2m
(4ft), S 30cm (12in)
■ **Seasonal highlights**
From early until late summer,
erect spires bear saucer-
shaped yellow flowers with
red-purple centres.
■ **Value at other times** It
has striking basal rosettes of
wrinkled, grey-green leaves.
■ **Ideal site** Sunny banks and
borders.
■ **Cultivation** Best in full
sun in poor, well-drained,
preferably slightly alkaline,
soil. Too rich a soil produces
soft, floppy stems that
then need staking. May
be short-lived, so divide in
spring or autumn, or take
root cuttings in winter.
■ **Also recommended**
Verbascum chaixii f. *album*
has white flowers with
mauve centres.
■ **Perfect partners**
Delphiniums, monkshood,
border phlox.

Verbena 'Showtime'
Bedding verbena

Bushy, half-hardy perennial
grown as an annual.
H & S 25cm (10in)
■ **Seasonal highlights**
From summer until autumn,
it produces masses of flowers
in shades of rose-pink to
magenta, scarlet, or white,
some with white centres. The
toothed, dark-green leaves
form dense, neat mounds.
■ **Value at other times**
Discard after flowering.
■ **Ideal site** Annual borders,
edging, containers, or
hanging baskets.
■ **Cultivation** Grow in sun, in
well-drained, not-too-fertile
soil or potting compost. Sow
seeds in early spring in
warmth. Plant out when
the risk of frost is past.
■ **Also recommended**
Verbena 'Peaches 'n'
Cream' ♀, with pale
orange-pink to apricot-
yellow flowers.
■ **Perfect partners**
Clarkias, busy Lizzies
(*Impatiens*), pelargoniums.

Verbena bonariensis ♀
Verbena

A vigorous, frost-hardy,
clump-forming perennial.
H to 2m (6ft), S 45cm (18in)
■ **Seasonal highlights**
From midsummer to autumn,
wiry, branching stems bear
heads of lilac-purple flowers.
■ **Value at other times**
It has attractive, toothed,
dark-green, basal leaves.
■ **Ideal site** Mixed or
herbaceous borders, gravel
gardens, especially in hot,
dry sites.
■ **Cultivation** Grow in any
moderately fertile soil in full
sun. It may not survive cold,
wet winters, so provide a dry
winter mulch. Take stem-tip
cuttings in late summer.
Overwinter young plants
under glass.
■ **Also recommended**
Verbena corymbosa is more
densely clump-forming, with
red-purple flowers.
■ **Perfect partners**
Verbascums, *Cynara
cardunculus* ♀, *Ferula
communis*.

Veronica gentianoides ♀
Speedwell

A moderately vigorous,
mat-forming herbaceous
perennial.
H & S to 45cm (18in)
■ **Seasonal highlights**
In early summer it produces
upright stems of shallowly
cupped, pale-blue flowers.
■ **Value at other times**
It has attractive basal
rosettes of slightly scalloped,
glossy, dark-green leaves.
■ **Ideal site** At the front of
a border or in a rock garden.
■ **Cultivation** Best in full sun,
but tolerates light, part-day
shade. Grow in moderately
fertile, well-drained soil.
Plants begin to lose vigour
after two or three years, so
divide in autumn or spring
to rejuvenate.
■ **Also recommended**
Veronica longifolia is much
taller, with lilac-blue flowers.
■ **Perfect partners**
Lavenders, hardy geraniums.

V

Viburnum x bodnantense 'Dawn' ♀
Viburnum

A sturdy, upright, vigorous deciduous shrub. H 3m (10ft), S to 2m (6ft)

■ **Seasonal highlights** From late autumn to early spring, it bears small, rounded clusters of fragrant, pink flowers, on bare branches.

■ **Value at other times** It has deeply pleated, bright-green leaves that are bronze when young.

■ **Ideal site** Shrub borders, woodland gardens, or informal hedging.

■ **Cultivation** It thrives in any reasonably fertile, well-drained soil in sun or dappled shade. It needs little pruning other than to shorten any shoots that spoil the shape and to thin out congested shoots on mature plants. Prune after flowering.

■ **Also recommended** *Viburnum farreri* ♀ has white, often pink-flushed winter flowers.

■ **Perfect partners** Mahonias, sarcococcas.

Viburnum x juddii ♀
Viburnum

A rounded, deciduous shrub. H & S 1.2m (4ft)

■ **Seasonal highlights** In mid- to late spring, it bears rounded clusters of fragrant, pink-tinted, white flowers that open from pink buds.

■ **Value at other times** In autumn, the dark-green leaves turn dark red.

■ **Ideal site** A mixed or shrub border.

■ **Cultivation** Grow in full sun. It will tolerate partial shade. Grow in any reasonably fertile, well-drained soil. After flowering, shorten any shoots that spoil the outline.

■ **Also recommended** *Viburnum carlesii* is similar but taller and has red fruits in autumn.

■ **Perfect partners** *Daphne retusa, Prunus tenella.*

Viburnum opulus 'Compactum' ♀
Guelder rose

A sturdy but slow-growing deciduous shrub. H & S to 1.5m (5ft)

■ **Seasonal highlights** In late spring and early summer, it produces showy, flat, "lacecap" clusters of white flowers at the stem tips.

■ **Value at other times** In autumn, the glossy, bright-red fruits nestle among the bright-red autumn leaves.

■ **Ideal site** Shrub borders, woodland gardens, or informal hedging.

■ **Cultivation** It thrives in any reasonably fertile, well-drained soil in sun or dappled shade. It needs little pruning other than to shorten any shoots that spoil the shape after flowering.

■ **Also recommended** *Viburnum opulus* 'Xanthocarpum' ♀ has yellow fruits.

■ **Perfect partners** *Ceratostigma willmottianum* ♀, *Lonicera x purpusii.*

Viburnum plicatum 'Mariesii' ♀
Japanese snowball tree

A vigorous, spreading, deciduous shrub with distinctively tiered branches. H & S to 4m (12ft)

■ **Seasonal highlights** In late spring it produces flat "lacecap" white flowerheads.

■ **Value at other times** It has heart-shaped leaves that turn red-purple in autumn.

■ **Ideal site** Shrub and mixed borders, woodland gardens.

■ **Cultivation** Grow in any reasonably fertile, well-drained soil in sun or partial shade. After flowering, lightly prune any shoots that spoil the outline of the shrub.

■ **Also recommended** *Viburnum plicatum*; both the shrub and the flowerheads are more rounded in shape.

■ **Perfect partners** *Osmanthus delavayi* ♀.

Viburnum sargentii 'Onondaga' ♀
Viburnum

A bushy, moderately vigorous, deciduous shrub. H 3m (10ft), S 2m (6ft)

■ **Seasonal highlights** In late spring, it bears flat "lacecap" heads of pink-flushed, white flowers.

■ **Value at other times** The maple-like leaves are purple-bronze in spring, green in summer and dark red-purple in autumn.

■ **Ideal site** Shrub and mixed borders, woodland gardens.

■ **Cultivation** Grow in any reasonably fertile, well-drained soil in sun or partial shade. After flowering, lightly prune any shoots that spoil the outline of the shrub.

■ **Also recommended** *Viburnum sieboldii* is taller, with open clusters of small white flowers in late spring and pink fruit.

■ **Perfect partners** Mahonias, *Daphne mezereum*, sarcococcas.

Viburnum tinus
Laurustinus

A dense, moderately vigorous, evergreen shrub. H & S to 3m (10ft)
■ **Seasonal highlights** Over long periods in winter and spring, it bears flattened clusters of white flowers.
■ **Value at other times** The glossy, dark-green leaves are attractive all year.
■ **Ideal site** In shrub borders or as informal hedging.
■ **Cultivation** Grow in sun or partial shade in any fertile, moist but well-drained soil. Trim hedging after flowering and, on free-standing specimens, shorten any overlong shoots that spoil the outline.
■ **Also recommended** *Viburnum rhytidophyllum* is very tall, with deeply veined, leathery, dark-green leaves.
■ **Perfect partners** Forsythias, mahonias, *Rubus thibetanus* ♀.

Vinca minor
Lesser periwinkle

A dense, vigorous, trailing evergreen shrub. H to 20cm (8in), S indefinite
■ **Seasonal highlights** From spring until autumn it bears blue-violet, occasionally pale blue, red-purple, or white flowers.
■ **Value at other times** The attractive lance-shaped, glossy, dark-green leaves make excellent ground cover.
■ **Ideal site** Shady or sunny banks and borders or woodland gardens.
■ **Cultivation** Grow in any but the driest soil in partial or deep shade. In sun, the soil needs to be reliably moist. Prune as hard as necessary to keep it within bounds.
■ **Also recommended** *Vinca major* 'Variegata' ♀ spreads rampantly and has larger, cream-variegated leaves.
■ **Perfect partners** *Euonymus fortunei* 'Emerald 'n' Gold' ♀.

Vitis coignetiae ♀
Ornamental vine

A vigorous, deciduous climber. H 15m (50ft), S indefinite
■ **Seasonal highlights** Undoubtedly at its best in the autumn when the large, heart-shaped leaves turn gold then brilliant red and purple.
■ **Value at other times** The deep-green, spring and summer leaves are wrinkled and deeply veined with thick brown felt beneath.
■ **Ideal site** On large walls, through tall trees, to disguise unsightly garden structures.
■ **Cultivation** Grow in sun or partial shade in well-drained, preferably neutral to slightly alkaline, soil. Prune in winter and again in summer, as needed, to confine to allotted space.
■ **Also recommended** *Vitis vinifera* 'Purpurea' ♀ has purple leaves (red in autumn).
■ **Perfect partners** *Parthenocissus thompsonii, Tropaeolum tuberosum.*

W
Wisteria floribunda 'Multijuga' ♀
Japanese wisteria

A very vigorous, deciduous twining climber. H & S 9m (28ft) or more
■ **Seasonal highlights** In early summer it bears hanging chains of fragrant, pea-like, lilac-blue flowers.
■ **Value at other times** It has attractive, fresh-green leaves from spring to autumn.
■ **Ideal site** Walls, arbours, pergolas, trees.
■ **Cultivation** Grow in sun in any fertile, well-drained soil. Avoid east-facing walls; early sun will exacerbate damage to frosted flower buds. Train main stems on to supporting wires. In summer, cut back the leafy sideshoots to five or six buds from the main stems, and again in winter, shortening them to two or three buds.
■ **Also recommended** *W. sinensis* 'Alba' ♀ has chains of white flowers.
■ **Perfect partners** Late-flowering clematis.

Z
Zinnia elegans 'Dasher Scarlet'
Zinnia

Bushy, half-hardy annual. H & S 30cm (12in)
■ **Seasonal highlights** From early summer to autumn, it bears semi-double heads of scarlet, weatherproof flowers above dense mounds of pale- to mid-green leaves.
■ **Value at other times** Is discarded after flowering.
■ **Ideal site** Bedding and edging, containers, windowboxes.
■ **Cultivation** Grow in sun, in any moderately fertile, well-drained soil. Sow seeds in warmth in early spring. For a longer succession of blooms, sow some in the flowering site in late spring. Deadhead regularly to keep more flowers coming.
■ **Also recommended** *Zinnia haageana* 'Orange Star' has orange flowerheads.
■ **Perfect partners** French marigolds, tuberous begonias, nemesias.

INDEX

Page numbers in *italics* indicate an illustration or boxed text. Page numbers in **bold** indicate a main topic. Species are listed before cultivation entries.

ACKNOWLEDGMENTS

Author's acknowledgments
I wish to express my heartfelt thanks to all of the people involved with this book project, for without their help and encouragement I would never have finished it. Firstly I must thank the publisher, Dorling Kindersley, and the Royal Horticultural Society for having faith in me and allowing the project to go ahead. Individually I must thank David Lamb, Louise Abbott, Alison Donovan, Anna Kruger, Lee Griffiths and Viv Watton. They have all been very professional, excellent company and I have learned a lot from all of them. Thanks to all the team at the RHS too for their editorial input. And to anyone not mentioned my apologies and special thanks.

I would also like to thank Lin Hawthorne for editing the Plant Directory. Other people to thank include Mr Chris Ayton for information on Yoder chrysanthemums from Littlehampton in West Sussex and The Met Office in Bracknell, Berkshire for the meteorological facts and figures used to help compile the Weather Watch for each month.

I also wish to express special thanks to Lynda Hamilton for the use of her garden as a setting for photography. Also my thanks to Steve Hamilton who photographed the monthly projects. For this latest edition of the book my sincere thanks to Amy Slack, Tessa Bindloss, and Jane Simmonds, and Stephanie Farrow.

Publisher's acknowledgments
DK would like to thank Susanne Mitchell, Karen Wilson, Barbara Haynes, Andrew Halstead and Chris Prior of the Royal Horticultural Society; Annelise Evans and Lin Hawthorne for editorial assistance, Stephen Josland for design assistance, and Murdo Culver for technical assistance.

For their work on the 2009 edition, DK would like to thank Jo Godfrey Wood, Sarah Ruddick, Peggy Sadler, Helen Fewster, Vicky Read, Esther Ripley, Alison Donovan, Liz Wheeler, Joanna Byrne, Mandy Inness, Jonathan Metcalf, Bryn Walls, Fiona Wild, Michèle Clarke, and Karen Gavin.

For her assistance on the 2018 edition, DK would like to thank Poppy Blakiston-Houston.

Publisher acknowledgments

DK would like to thank Devangana Ojha and Rishi Bryan for editorial assistance.

Picture credits

The publisher would like to thank the following for their kind permission to reproduce their photographs:
(Key: a-above; b-below/bottom; c-centre; f-far; l-left; r-right; t-top)

John Amand and Winchester Growers Ltd: John Amand 67tl, 311ftr;
David Austin Roses www.davidaustinroses.com: 325br, 325clb, 325tr, 326tr, 327tc; **Gillian Beckett:** 227cr, 320fcla; **Corbis:** AgStock Images 84; Michelle Garrett 124tl; Patrick Johns 81tl, 277ftl; Dency Kane/Beateworks 4cc, 132; moodboard 185t; Robert Pickett 52br; **DK Images:** Airedale Publishing 104, 160t, 234, 235 (all), 255; Airedale Publishing/Sarah Cuttle 114, 174; Alpine Garden Society/Mark Winwood 14tr; RHS Wisley/Mark Winwood 11bl, 11br, 15bl; Unwins/John Glover 9br; **Eric Crichton Photos:** 12cr, 139cr, 140br, 167cr, 226cl, 285ftl, 290tr, 320tr (sargentii), 332ftl, 333tr; **GAP Photos:** Richard Bloom 4tc, 4br, 6bl, 22bl, 35bl, 40, 62, 238; Christina Bollen 242, 243; Elke Borkowski 22br, 103; Jonathan Buckley - Design: John Massey Location: Ashwood Nurseries 25b; Jonathan Buckley - Design: Sarah Raven, Perch Hill 64t; Carole Drake - Location: The Sir Harold Hillier Gardens/Hampshire County Council 5b, 256; Victoria Firmston 233; John Glover 9bl, 244tr, 270b, 284tc, 308ftl; Jerry Harpur 182; Neil Holmes 13cr, 155t, 190cl, 317ftl; Geoff Kidd 250bl; Jenny Lilly - Location: David Austin Roses 325cra; Brian North 75bl; Rice / Buckland 173bl; S & O 18tl, 26br, 88-89, 186tl, 289tr (Chocolate cosmos), 308ftr; Jason Smalley 42bl; Friedrich Strauss 101br, 124br, 167bl, 308tl; Graham Strong - Design: Sue Jollans 65; Visions Premium 2, 4cr, 156; Jo Whitworth 16tr, 262cl; **Garden Picture Library:** Mark Bolton 204; Mark Boulton 288br; Ron Evans 186bl, 279ftr; John Glover 275ftl; Neil Holmes 47cl, 283ftl; Lamontagne 322bl; Zara McCalmont 288fclb; Howard Rice 45, 66cr, 327ftr; Friedrich Strauss 317tl; Paul Windsor 137; **The Garden Collection:** Liz Eddison 159; **Getty Images:** Chris Everard 5cr, 180; GAP Photos/Victoria Firmston 99br, 249b; GAP Photos 152; GAP Photos/Neil Holmes 4tr, 60; Image Source 158, 170; GAP Photos/Zara Napier 258; Martin Page 263tr ; GAP Photos/Juliette Wade 201, 271br; **Marianne Majerus Garden Images:** Andrew Lawson 260-261; **Clive Nichols:** 4tl, 20; Bassibones Farm, Bucks 4cl, 110; Design: Rupert Golby - Chelsea 107, 160b; Leeds City Council, Chelsea 110, 161; Clive Nichols/ Lady Farm, Somerset 272-273; **Photolibrary:** 303tc; Michele Lamontagne 237; Mark Turner 165br, 285cr; Francesca Yorke 185b; **Photos Horticultural:** 8cl, 9tl, 12br, 17br, 18cl, 46br, 66tl, 69br, 69tl, 86, 115, 117br, 119tr, 141br, 188br, 189cl, 191br, 207, 208bl, 226br, 245cr, 262tl, 274br, 276tr ('Orange Glory'), 277ftr, 281tc, 283tl, 283tr, 285crb ('Nelly Moser'), 286cla (viticella), 288fcla, 290ftl, 293ftr, 295ftl, 285tc, 303c, 306ftr, 306tr, 309ftr, 323ftl, 326ftr, 333ftl, 334ftr, 334tl, 335ftr; **Science Photo Library:** Leslie J. Borg 245br, 304ftl; Ron Chapman 319ftl; Anthony Cooper 13br, 24, 263cr, 328ftl; Ian Gowland 47tl, 286tr('Freckles'); R. Greenwood 279tr ('Variegata'); Ray Lacey 140cl, 276ftl; Jiri Loun 190tl, 316tl; Adrian Thomas 16cr, 292tr; H. Thomson 69cl, 297tl; **Wildlife Matters:** 116tl, 141cl, 164cl, 227br, 244cl, 245cl, 263br, 284ftl, 285tl, 287tl ('Golden Tiara'), 305ftr, 307tc, 324tl, 327tl, 330ftl, 334ftl; Debi Wagner Stock Pics 248; Nancy Rothwell 304ftr; Steffie Shields 68bl, 332ftr

Cover image: *Front:* **123RF.com:** Kaspri; *Back:* **123RF.com:** Kaspri
Colour tabs: **123RF.com:** Kaspri

All other images © Dorling Kindersley.
For further information see: **www.dkimages.com**

For Mum and Dad, in loving memory

LONDON, NEW YORK, MELBOURNE, MUNICH, DELHI

REVISED EDITION 2018
Editors Jane Simmonds, Amy Slack
Designer Tessa Bindloss
Senior Producer, Pre-production Tony Phipps
Producer Luca Bazzoli
Jacket Designer Nicola Powling
Jacket Co-ordinator Lucy Philpott
Managing Editor Stephanie Farrow
Managing Art Editor Christine Kielty

DK INDIA
Editors Charvi Arora, Madhurika Bhardwaj
Managing Editor Soma B. Chowdhury
DTP Designer Manish Chandra Upreti
Pre-production Manager Sunil Sharma

RHS Editors Simon Maughan, Rae Spencer-Jones

FIRST EDITION 2001
Project Editor Louise Abbott
Art Editor Alison Donovan
Managing Editor Anna Kruger
Managing Art Editor Lee Griffiths
DTP Designer Louise Waller
Media Resources Charlotte Oster, Romaine Werblow
Picture Research Sharon Southren

This edition published in 2018
First published in Great Britain in 2001 in association
with the Royal Horticultural Society by
Dorling Kindersley Limited
80 Strand, London, WC2R 0RL

10 9 8 7 6 5 4 3 2 1
001–307777–Sept/2018

Copyright © 2001, 2005, 2009, 2018
Dorling Kindersley Limited
A Penguin Random House Company

A CIP catalogue record for this book is available from the
British Library

ISBN 978-0-2413-1561-3
Printed and bound in China

see our complete catalogue at
www.dk.com